EVOLUTION AND THE
CAPACITY FOR COMMITMENT

EVOLUTION AND THE
CAPACITY FOR COMMITMENT

RANDOLPH M. NESSE

EDITOR

VOLUME III IN THE RUSSELL SAGE FOUNDATION SERIES ON TRUST

Russell Sage Foundation • New York

The Russell Sage Foundation

The Russell Sage Foundation, one of the oldest of America's general purpose foundations, was established in 1907 by Mrs. Margaret Olivia Sage for "the improvement of social and living conditions in the United States." The Foundation seeks to fulfill this mandate by fostering the development and dissemination of knowledge about the country's political, social, and economic problems. While the Foundation endeavors to assure the accuracy and objectivity of each book it publishes, the conclusions and interpretations in Russell Sage Foundation publications are those of the authors and not of the Foundation, its Trustees, or its staff. Publication by Russell Sage, therefore, does not imply Foundation endorsement.

Library of Congress Cataloging-in-Publication Data

Evolution and the capacity for commitment / Randolph M. Nesse, editor
p.   cm.
Includes bibliographical references and index.
ISBN 0-87154-622-1
1. Genetic   psychology.   2. Commitment   (Psychology).   3. Psychology, Comparative.   I. Nesse, Randolph M.

BF701 .E955   2001
155.7—dc21   2001041781

The paper used in this publication meets the minimum requirements of American National Standard for Information Sciences—Permanence of Paper for Printed Library Materials. ANSI Z39.48-1992.

Text design by Suzanne Nichols

RUSSELL SAGE FOUNDATION
112 East 64th Street, New York, New York 10021
10 9 8 7 6 5 4 3 2 1

The Russell Sage Foundation Series on Trust

T HE RUSSELL SAGE Foundation Series on Trust examines the conceptual structure and the empirical basis of claims concerning the role of trust and trustworthiness in establishing and maintaining cooperative behavior in a wide variety of social, economic, and political contexts. The focus is on concepts, methods, and findings that will enrich social science and inform public policy.

The books in the series raise questions about how trust can be distinguished from other means of promoting cooperation and explore those analytic and empirical issues that advance our comprehension of the roles and limits of trust in social, political, and economic life. Because trust is at the core of understandings of social order from varied disciplinary perspectives, the series offers the best work of scholars from diverse backgrounds and, through the edited volumes, encourages engagement across disciplines and orientations. The goal of the series is to improve the current state of trust research by providing a clear theoretical account of the causal role of trust within given institutional, organizational, and interpersonal situations, developing sound measures of trust to test theoretical claims within relevant settings, and establishing some common ground among concerned scholars and policymakers.

Karen S. Cook
Margaret Levi
Russell Hardin

SERIES EDITORS

Previous Volumes in the Series

Contents

Contributors

Randolph M. Nesse is professor of psychiatry, professor of psychology, and research associate in the ISR Research Center for Group Dynamics at the University of Michigan, where he directs the Evolution and Human Adaptation Program.

Eldridge S. Adams is associate professor of ecology and evolutionary biology at the University of Connecticut, Storrs.

Robert Boyd is professor of anthropology at the University of California, Los Angeles.

Dov Cohen is associate professor of psychology at the University of Waterloo, Ontario.

Lee Alan Dugatkin is associate professor of biology and Distinguished University Scholar at the University of Louisville.

Robert H. Frank is Goldwin Smith Professor of Economics, Ethics, and Public Policy at Cornell University.

Herbert Gintis is professor of economics at the University of Massachusetts.

Oliver R. Goodenough is professor of law at Vermont Law School and chair of the Planning and Programming Committee of the Gruter Institute for Law and Behavioral Research in Portola Valley, California.

Jack Hirshleifer is professor emeritus of economics at UCLA.

William Irons is professor of anthropology at Northwestern University.

Peter J. Richerson is professor of environmental science and policy at the University of California, Davis.

Michael Ruse is Lucyle T. Werkmeister Professor of Philosophy at Florida State University.

Thomas C. Schelling is Distinguished University Professor at the University of Maryland, and Lucius N. Littauer Professor of Political Economy, emeritus, at Harvard University.

Joan B. Silk is professor of anthropology at the University of California, Los Angeles

Joseph Vandello is post-doctoral research associate at the Woodrow Wilson School of Public and International Affairs at Princeton University.

Acknowledgments

The papers in this volume are adaptations of invited presentations to a Symposium organized by the Evolution and Human Adaptation Program at the Institute for Social Research at the University of Michigan, April 9–10, 1999: *The Biology of Belief and Trust: Has Natural Selection Shaped a Capacity for Subjective Commitment?* The Symposium was made possible by generous funding from The John Templeton Foundation, The Russell Sage Foundation, and The Ann and Gordon Getty Foundation. The Evolution and Human Adaptation Program is made possible by support from the Office of the Provost, The Institute for Social Research, Research Center for Group Dynamics, and the Departments of Psychology and Psychiatry at the University of Michigan.

Foreword

Beyond Selfishness in Modeling Human Behavior

HERBERT GINTIS

E ARLY THIS morning, while the coffee was brewing and I was mulling over this preface that I was about to write, I glanced at the Springfield *Union News*. Here are just a few of the stories for this perfectly typical day.

Front page center: Buckland, Massachusetts, USA. A picture of a nineteen-year-old boy, graduated from high school the previous night, nattily dressed with dictionaries and encyclopedias under his arm, smiling and giving the thumbs-up. He has Down syndrome. Last October he played his first varsity soccer game. "His teammates thought so much of the occasion," the story reads, "they carried him off the field on their shoulders."

Front page left: Katmandu, Nepal. Crown prince Dipendra entered the royal palace yesterday and killed eight people, including the king, the queen, and a royal princess (his mother, father, and sister). He then turned the gun on himself. He was angered by his parents' disapproval of his prospective bride. We learn in the body of the article that the king of Nepal has been a figurehead since 1990, when a national liberation movement succeeded in instituting democratic government in Nepal. The turning point in the struggle for democracy was April 6, 1990, when the police fired on a crowd of 200,000 demonstrators, killing 300.

Page three, left: Portland, Oregon, USA. The Earth Liberation Front, a shadowy group blamed for costly arson attacks across the country, claimed responsibility for a fire at a tree farm in Oregon last month.

Page three, center: Washington, D.C. The Justice Department has agreed not to seek the death penalty against a fugitive wanted for the slaying of an abortion doctor, in an effort to clear the way for his extradition to the United States from France.

Page five, left: Johannesburg, South Africa. Twelve-year-old AIDS victim and activist Nkosi Johnson succumbs to his illness. The young boy made the headlines last July, when he spoke at the International AIDS Conference in Durban. "We are all human beings," he said. "We have needs just like everyone else. Don't be afraid of us. We are the same."

Each of these stories portrays individuals concerned with the well-being of other, unrelated people, and these individuals are willing to sacrifice in some material manner to help or hurt the objects of their attention.

This book begins to lay the foundation for understanding the stories I read in the newspaper this morning. In doing so, it flies in the face of what economists have been saying for two centuries, and it adds important dimension to what biologists concerned with human behavior have been saying for thirty-five years.

People have been trying to explain human nature—without much success—at least since the time of Socrates. No satisfactory explanation was forthcoming before Darwin, because human nature is the product of evolution. The human mind and body are adaptations to the challenges we faced as members of the small hunter-gatherer bands that uniquely defined human existence until some 10,000 years ago—which is practically yesterday on an evolutionary timescale.

We now know that, by the principle of natural selection, living creatures have fitness-maximizing, genetically based behavioral repertoires. In particular we recognize that human beings are designed to make choices that maximize their biological fitness, not under contemporary conditions, but under the hunter-gatherer conditions in which we evolved. The researchers who developed this insight initially believed such choices entailed narrowly self-interested or genetically interested behavior—not only acts of personal gain, but also acts in support of one's kin (Hamilton 1964) or in support of someone who will "return the favor" (Trivers 1971).

The analysis of *commitment* in this exciting book shows that much more complex types of behavior can be explained in the same sociobiological framework. Agents make commitments when they give up options in order to influence others. Most commitments depend on some incentive that is necessary to ensure that the action is in the agent's interest and thus will be carried out. In many cases the agent voluntarily imposes the incentive on him- or herself, as when someone signs a contract, a general burns his bridges behind him, or an individual constructs a reputation that must be upheld. In other cases the incentive is built into the agent, in the form of such prosocial emotions as shame, guilt, empathy, desire to cooperate, and impulse to punish those who have inflicted hurt.

Different aspects of this concept of commitment have been proposed over the past two decades by Thomas Schelling, Jack Hirshleifer, Robert Frank, and other contributors to this book, but it is the creative vision of Randolph Nesse to bring these contributions together and to reveal both their communality and their deep links to several other areas of science. The concept of commitment, I believe, serves as a bridge between biology and social science. Economists since Adam Smith have understood voluntarily imposed commitment, although the notion has achieved some subtlety only since game theory has become a central tool of economic theory. Emotional commitment, however, is a quite distinct phenomenon. Emotions are evolutionary adaptations. Darwin began the comparative study of emotions in his brilliant *The Expression of Emotions in Man and Animals* (1872). Biology is relevant here because human emotions only can be understood when placed in the context of animal emotions and their evolutionary functions.

The great insight of the present volume is that self-interest is not so simple when you look into it through the lens of commitments. People do not always act on calculated advantage, and many actions appear irreducibly costly to the actors themselves. The pioneers of sociobiology taught us that human culture and mind are themselves products of evolutionary forces. They tended to infer from this that human behavior could be explained in terms of these evolutionary forces, and so relegated culture and human psychology to a non-causal, epiphenomenal status.

Yet, as this book suggests, such an inference is faulty, and much is gained by directly studying how the interplay of genes, culture, and psychology shape social behavior. Genes and evolutionary history *condition*, but culture and human psychology *cause*. Love and hate, war and peace, cooperation and punishment, obedience and revolt, all begin to come into focus when we recognize the uniquely human nature of emotional commitments and their reverberations in the sphere of human culture.

In light of these remarks it may be curious that human sociobiology historically has held a rather more narrow version of self-interested behavior than is presented by the contributors herein. The rest of my remarks will be directed toward understanding where we have come from, and what has forced the development of the broader vision presented in this book.

Perhaps the first principle of human behavior is that the human phenotype is an interaction of nature and nurture—genes and culture. This principle could not even be stated coherently prior to the modern synthesis of Darwinian evolution and Mendelian genetics in the mid-1930s. The idea that genes affect behavior required another few decades to achieve any scientific rigor, which it did in the immensely insightful and influential works of William Hamilton (1964), George Williams (1966), Robert Trivers (1971), and John Maynard Smith and G. R. Price (1973).

Modern sociobiology, as it came to be called, was brought to the public through two less technical but equally insightful books, Edward O. Wilson's *Sociobiology* (1975) and Richard Dawkins's *The Selfish Gene* (1976). Like their theoretical predecessors, both Wilson and Dawkins neglect both emotions and culture as causal agents in explaining behavior. Many important models of human behavior have been developed in this relatively impoverished environment, but it is now clear in hindsight that we must go beyond the methodology erected by these pioneers of behavioral theory.

In his justly famous book, *The Biology of Moral Systems* (1987), R. D. Alexander says, for instance, "ethics, morality, human conduct, and the human psyche are to be understood only if societies are seen as collections of individuals seeking their own self-interest . . ." (3). Somewhat later he notes, "That people are in general following what they perceive to be their own interests is, I believe, the most general principle of human behavior" (35). Alexander depicts humans as a selfish core with a veneer of generosity that in fact serves to strengthen the core in an indirect but nonetheless powerful manner. Yet if our evolved emotions *commit* us to experiencing the emotions of shame, guilt, empathy, and vindictiveness, then perhaps the core-veneer analogy must be replaced by a vision of a more balanced interpenetration of self-interest and irreducibly prosocial behaviors.

In Richard Dawkins's equally highly regarded manifesto for the gene-centered approach to evolutionary biology, *The Selfish Gene* (1976), we read in the course of the first four pages, "We are survival machines—robot vehicles blindly programmed to preserve the selfish molecules known as genes . . . a predominant quality to be expected in a successful gene is ruthless selfishness. This gene selfishness will usually give rise to selfishness in individual behavior. . . . Let us try to *teach* generosity and altruism, because we are born selfish . . . anything that has evolved by natural selection should be selfish." Dawkins certainly recognizes the possibility of altruism. "However," he notes, "as we shall see, there are special circumstances in which a gene can achieve its own selfish goals best by fostering a limited form of altruism at the level of individual animals." He describes altruism toward kin (inclusive fitness) and examples of reciprocal altruism, but does not consider the possibility of other routes to stronger kinds of altruism.

We can try to reconcile Dawkins's doctrine with the daily newspaper by arguing that organisms often pursue reproductive success in a rather indirect manner. Being nice to a handicapped boy may bring social approval that is actually fitness enhancing. Killing abortion doctors, demonstrating for freedom, and torching tree farms may conceivably be ways to exhibit personal fitness and may lead to increased offspring. Funding for AIDS patients may not have increased in the wake of the young boy's pleading. The crown prince of Nepal may have been an evolutionary dead end. Alternatively, we can argue that the newspaper reports *extraordinary* events, not the 99.9 percent of the time people behave selfishly.

We can try, but I do not think we can succeed. I believe we can better understand human events in the newspaper and elsewhere by simply admitting that people have emotions that lead them to make commitments that move them from selfish to prosocial (and at times antisocial) behavior. We do not yet understand the evolutionary mechanisms responsible for the prosocial emotions so uniquely characteristic of *Homo sapiens*, but several plausible models may be relevant (Gintis 2000b; Gintis, Smith, and Bowles 2000; Bowles and Gintis 1998). That genes are selfish simply does not imply that self-interest lies at the core of the human psyche; it does not.

To my mind the strongest arguments against a simple notion of self-interest come from the experimental laboratory. As Randolph Nesse reports in the opening chapter, we now have a vast array of behavioral evidence in favor of the existence of non–self-interested behaviors, some of it cooperative, some of it nasty and vindictive. The most salient of these is what I call *strong reciprocity*, which is a predilection for cooperation in a social effort with a taste for punishing noncooperators, even when no plausible long-term personal benefit from cooperating or punishing exists (Fehr and Gächter 2000; Gintis 2000a, 2000b). This process can be modeled, and many experiments now demonstrate a close match between its predictions and much actual human behavior. Ideas about strong reciprocity developed independently from ideas about commitment, but both call attention to strikingly similar phenomena.

The leading problem in sociobiology today is explaining why we have prosocial emotions. Clearly it must be in our "genetic interest" to have such a repertoire of emotions, or as Dawkins makes clear, they would necessarily disappear. Without the emotions of shame, guilt, empathy, and revenge seeking that enrich our lives, we would all be sociopaths, and human society would not exist, however strong the institutions of contract, exchange, and reputation. Democracy, civil rights, and representative government—to name a few of the key institutions that foster human dignity and wealth—were brought about by people involved in spontaneous collective action, fighting not for their selfish ends but for a vision for all of humanity. Our freedom is based on the emotional commitments of generations past.

I would like to thank the John D. and Catherine T. MacArthur Foundation for financial support.

References

Alexander, R. D. 1987. *The Biology of Moral Systems*. New York: Aldine.

Bowles, S., and H. Gintis. 1998. "The Evolution of Strong Reciprocity." Santa Fe Institute Working Paper 98-08-073E.

Darwin, Charles. 1998 [1872]. *The Expression of Emotions in Man and Animals*, edited by Paul Eckman. Oxford: Oxford University Press.

Dawkins, Richard. 1976. *The Selfish Gene*. Oxford: Oxford University Press.

Fehr, E., and S. Gächter. 2000. "Cooperation and Punishment." *American Economic Review* 90.

Gintis, Herbert. 2000a. *Game Theory Evolving*. Princeton, N.J.: Princeton University Press.

———. 2000b. "Strong Reciprocity and Human Sociality." *Journal of Theoretical Biology* 206: 169–79.

Gintis, Herbert, E. A. Smith, and S. Bowles. 2000. "Costly Signaling and Cooperation." Typescript.

Hamilton, W. D. 1964. "The Genetical Evolution of Social Behavior." *Journal of Theoretical Biology* 37: 1–16, 17–52.

Maynard Smith, J., and G. R. Price. 1973. "The Logic of Animal Conflict." *Nature* 246: 15–18.

Trivers, R. L. 1971. "The Evolution of Reciprocal Altruism." *Quarterly Review of Biology* 46: 35–57.

Williams, G. C. 1966. *Adaptation and Natural Selection: A Critique of Some Current Evolutionary Thought*. Princeton, N.J.: Princeton University Press.

Wilson, E. O. 1975. *Sociobiology: The New Synthesis*. Cambridge, Mass.: Harvard University Press.

Chapter 1

Natural Selection and the Capacity for Subjective Commitment

RANDOLPH M. NESSE

O NCE YOU recognize them, commitments are everywhere. The commitment we all know is marriage. By giving up the option to leave for someone else, spouses gain security and an opportunity for a much deeper (and more efficient!) relationship than would otherwise be possible.Yet many commitments are not at all nice. When John F. Kennedy committed the United States to eliminating missiles from Cuba, millions of human lives were put at risk. When a thuggish-looking man offers unrequested fire insurance to a small retail shop, the implied threat of arson may well influence the owner's behavior. In a more banal vein, nearly everyone has waited for a repairman who never arrives. From the personal to the political to the mundane, commitments are everywhere. Threats and promises change people's beliefs and, therefore, their actions.

In a world without commitments social exchanges arise mainly from helping relatives and trading favors. In such a world individuals can reliably be expected to act straightforwardly in their own interests. The advent of commitment changes everything. As soon as one individual finds a way to convince another that he or she will act other than in simple self-interest, social life is transformed. Now, individuals must consider the possibility that others may fulfill promises and threats. Sometimes the situation itself makes fulfillment worthwhile, but apparently irrational commitments also may influence others profoundly. A whole new category of social influence emerges.

Reputations become important predictors of behavior, and people begin spending vast amounts of effort to convince others that they will fulfill their promises and threats.

One way to convince others of one's credibility in a commitment is to give up options in order to change the incentives in a situation. Others observe that compliance is now in the person's interests, and change their expectations and behavior accordingly. By signing a lease, for instance, a person gives up the option to leave on short notice, and induces the landlord to give up the option of raising the rent in the middle of winter. Not all commitments, however, are backed by such tangible incentives. As Frank and Hirshleifer argue (Hirshleifer 1987; Frank 1988), people also can convince others that they will keep their promises by emotional displays that testify to their irrationality. Such commitments give rise to profound paradoxes. In order to influence others an individual must convince people that he or she will act in ways that are not in his or her interests. Sometimes it is possible to reap the benefits of this influence without having to fulfill the commitment. Kennedy did not want a fight, he simply wanted the missiles out of Cuba; because the Russians believed he would follow through on his threat, he didn't have to. More often, however, convincing others requires fulfilling the commitment to some degree. If your fiancée gets sick on the day you have tickets for the big game, too bad, you have to stay home. Also, once commitment strategies are widespread, reputation becomes so valuable that maintaining it requires fulfilling some commitments irrespective of the effects. The gang leader who rules by ruthlessness cannot show mercy for fear of losing his power. Before you know it, commitments lead people to do all kinds of things they would rather not do, whether this means carrying out spiteful threats or helping others who will never be able to reciprocate. Social life becomes rich and complex. Foresight and empathy become essential tools for social survival. In a world where commitments influence behavior a workable theory of mind becomes more useful than a sharp stone axe.

The capacity for using commitment strategies effectively is so important that natural selection may have shaped specialized capacities to make this possible. These capacities may help to explain the human tendency to emotionally extreme behaviors that often seem senseless. Such explanations may help to bridge the gap between the social sciences and evolutionary approaches to behavior. Even more important, they may help us find ways to cope with the great moral and intellectual crisis precipitated by the discovery that natural selection works mainly at the level of the gene, and its corollary, that natural selection cannot shape a capacity for altruism that gives a selective advantage to genes different from one's own This is turning out to be a major psychic trauma to humankind, one that may be even more disturbing than the previous two: while the Copernican revolution shook religious cosmology off its foundations, it did little to challenge people's belief that human life has special meaning as the culmination of a divine plan; the second trauma—the discovery of natural selection and our evolutionary origins—was more personal (Richards 1987; Cronin 1991). Finding out we are only one species among many, all shaped by the mindless force of natural selection, fundamentally threatens our sense of the significance of human life (Ruse 1989; Dennett 1995). Resistance to this fact remains passionate, and creates an emotional fissure that still ruptures the political and social landscape.

Even as we struggle to accept the facts about our evolutionary origins, however, we confront a third trauma, this one a more direct threat to our individual moral identities. For decades biologists complacently had thought that selection shapes traits that benefit groups and species (Wynne-Edwards 1962). This assumption made it easy to view self-sacrifice for the sake of the group as entirely natural and expected. With simple but ruthless logic, Williams showed in 1966 that selection at the group level is feeble compared to selection at the individual level (Williams 1966). Natural selection, it turns out, acts mainly to benefit genes and individuals, not groups or species (Maynard Smith 1964). Many implications follow from this, but the most profound is the transformation of altruism from a natural tendency into an evolutionary mystery (Dawkins 1976; Badcock 1986; Barash 1977; Krebs 1970). E. O. Wilson called altruism "the central theoretical problem of sociobiology" (Wilson 1975, 3). Previously, animals were thought to help each other because natural selection shaped behavioral tendencies to sacrifice for the good of the group. It is now clear, however, that genes that lead to sacrifice for the group tend to become less and less frequent, except in very special circumstances. Any natural tendency to help others now must be explained in terms of how it benefits the actor's genes. If no such explanation can be found, the tendency becomes an anomaly in need of special explanation. Notice that the object of explanation here is a tendency, not a behavior. Individuals may decide to behave in ways that are not in their reproductive interests, and social structures may foster many such behaviors. Yet all tendencies shaped by natural selection must provide an inclusive fitness benefit in the long run, otherwise they will be eliminated.

Most people think of altruism as a costly effort that helps others. Many people also identify with their genes. Learning that organisms are shaped to act in ways that benefit their genes can make people feel that helping their relatives is somehow helping themselves and, therefore, not generous in the same way that helping a nonrelative would be. From this viewpoint, genuine altruism can appear impossible, or at least contrary to nature (Richards 1993). Furthermore, many people, on grasping that all organisms are necessarily designed to act in the interests of their selfish genes, instantly (and incorrectly) conclude that individuals must be selfish by nature. Some take this a step further, concluding that our moral passions are mere pretensions or, worse, self-deceptive strategies for manipulating others (Ghiselin 1969).

Of course, individuals do help each other. To explain this, Williams's insight was quickly complemented by the recognition of two specific ways in which helping others can benefit the helper's genes. The first is kin selection. As Hamilton pointed out, because related individuals share a proportion of genes that are identical by descent, natural selection can shape tendencies to act in ways harmful to the self if there is enough benefit to kin (Hamilton 1964). Thus, natural selection can increase the frequency of a genetic tendency that makes a mother blue jay risk her life to defend her eggs because of the benefits to identical copies of the same genes that exist in other individuals (who are not yet hatched). The second way in which altruistic acts can offer benefits is by reciprocal exchange. As Trivers made clear, trading favors can yield a net reproductive benefit to both parties (Trivers 1971). In the long run mutual helping gives a net payoff, so long as one avoids being exploited. On these two pillars, a new theory of sociality is being constructed (Trivers 1985). Every social tendency has been attributed to benefits from some combination of kin selection and reciprocity. Those that cannot be explained in these terms have become anomalies that require interpretation as abnormal behavior, or products of manipulation or socialization in our novel modern environment.

The scientific impact of these developments has been enormous. They have transformed social ethology from a descriptive science to a predictive one based firmly on evolutionary theory (Trivers 1985; Alcock 1997). Hundreds of studies now investigate the role of kin selection in behaviors ranging from mating strategies to food sharing and defense (Alcock 1997). Tom turkeys court females in cooperative groups; it turns out that the groups are almost always composed of brothers. The sentinel prairie dog that warns the group about approaching coyotes is especially likely to have many relatives in the group. Human infants are eighty times more likely to die from child abuse if they are in a family with a stepparent (Daly and Wilson 1987). Kin selection is one of the great discoveries in our time.

The principle of reciprocity is an equally powerful advance for explaining social behaviors among unrelated individuals (Trivers 1985; Cronin 1991). Examples range from mating alliances between male chimpanzees to blood sharing in vampire bats (Dugatkin 1997). Individuals who trade favors judiciously do better than those who go it alone. Often, of course, individuals trade favors with relatives, thus getting benefits via both mechanisms. Together, kin selection and reciprocity are widely thought to fully explain social behavior. They are certainly hugely important, but are they sufficient? Or, as many have suggested (Boehm 1999; Hirshleifer 1999; Humphrey 1999), might there be other routes to social behavior that have been neglected? Certainly there are. The tendency to use reciprocity to stand for all cooperative relationships is itself a vast oversimplification. Among other possibilities, cooperation also can arise from mutualism, coercion, and social organizations that control incentives. Mutualism, in particular, has been neglected. A great proportion of social cooperation is mutualistic; individuals get benefits only if they contribute, so cheating is not possible. (For more on this discussion see Adams in chapter 5.) Much additional cooperation is coerced; an individual with control over resources can impose punishments that make cheating of no value. These are among several routes to cooperation that are often neglected. Here we are concerned in particular with one additional means of social influence—commitment. Our goal is to examine how commitment strategies work, how they are used in practice, and the core question of whether the ability to make and assess commitments gives selective advantages that have shaped our minds. The importance of this core question, and its place in the explanation of social behavior, will be clear only after outlining the full magnitude of the current crisis and the responses it has provoked.

The sketch described here uses intentionally bold brushstrokes to illustrate the crisis at the intersection of science and morality created by the demise of group selection and its replacement by kin selection and reciprocity. Subtleties and caveats abound, but here they are set aside intentionally to highlight the dark simplicity of the problem, summarized best in Dawkins's phrase "the selfish gene." He knows perfectly well that genes have no motives, but his metaphor of genes as self-serving agents has enabled thousands of readers to view life from this dramatically new perspective (Dawkins 1989). We are jerked to attention by picturing ourselves as lumbering robots acting at the behest of our genes. Given how natural selection works, we know that the genes that influence behavior in any species are those that have given rise to actions that tend to increase the numbers of copies of those genes in future generations. All evolved tendencies, including those motivating generosity and morality, somehow must have increased the frequency of the genes that give rise to them. The extrapolation that individuals must therefore be selfish, however, is incorrect. Indeed the very existence of sympathy and moral passions suggests that they likely give a selective advantage; yet how do such traits advance the interests of an individual's genes? One possibility is by improving the individual's capacity to benefit from commitment.

Is this issue really so dramatic? Is all this talk about psychic traumas and moral crises just the latest attempt by academics to inflate the importance of their arcane arguments about human nature? I think not. What we believe about ourselves and human nature is important because it influences how we act (Beck 1976). Those actions shape our societies that in turn shape our beliefs, thus setting long-running cultural cycles in motion (Fukuyama 1995). Evidence that much is at stake can be seen in the intensity of reactions to these ideas (Caplan 1978; Ruse 1982; Rose and Rose 2000). Many people find it repugnant to think that humans are inherently selfish, and despicable to think of altruism as just another way to serve one's interests. They assume that people who advocate such ideas must themselves be selfish and lacking in respect for society's rules. Attacking such apparently immoral nonconformists is sanctioned and even required by many social groups. Thus, criticisms of evolutionary approaches to human behavior often segue, without notice, qualms, or apologies, into ad hominem attacks against individuals and moral condemnations of whole groups. If the tone of recent letters in the *New York Review of Books* provides insufficient evidence, consider the subtitle of a new book: *Arguments Against Evolutionary Psychology*. (Rose and Rose 2000). The acrimony in this debate has created a dust storm of rhetoric and anger that obscures many legitimate issues. The battle has engaged the general public, whose insights often are considerable, thanks to the availability of accessible yet meaningful treatments of the main issues (Wright 1994; Ridley 1997; Wilson 1993). For professional audiences, the number of books and articles exceeds anyone's ability to keep up (Campbell 1975; Schwartz 1986; Ruse 1986; Alexander 1987; Oyama 1989; Maxwell 1990; Frank 1992; Nitecki and Nitecki 1993; Wilson 1993; Bradie 1994; Midgley 1994; Petrinovich 1995; Hurd 1996; Katz 2000).

Reactions to the Trauma

Responses to this psychic trauma take a variety of forms. A brief treatment cannot catalog all of them, nor can it adequately explain and justify any of them in full detail; it can, however, map the landscape of these controversies. Moreover, the intensity and diversity of reactions are testimony to the central role of the problem of altruism. A review of twelve kinds of reactions to this crisis will set the stage for further consideration of the role of commitment as a possible, albeit partial, solution.

- Many people take one look at this controversy and dismiss the idea that all motivational systems must benefit the actor's genes. The theory seems to be contradicted by too many examples. Soldiers dive on grenades to save their buddies. Enraged spouses murder their partners, knowing that this will mean decades spent in prison. Suicide bombers destroy themselves to advance their causes. Heroes dive into icy rivers. Ascetics meditate for years. Some people decide not to have children. Some even decide not to have sex. Others quit jobs to care for their disabled children or demented spouses. Anonymous benefactors give money to charity. Saints sacrifice their lives for their beliefs. Do such examples suffice to demonstrate that an evolutionary view is simply wrong? It is possible that we may attend to such examples precisely because they are so anomalous, but they still offer a challenge. They suggest that models based only on kin selection and reciprocity are inadequate; some other principle is needed.

- The crudest form of opposition is also the most prevalent—to deny the very phenomenon of evolution, or at least its application to humans. Fundamentalist Christian theology fosters pride in such denial. According to a 1999 Gallup poll, 47 percent of Americans believe "God created human beings pretty much in their present form at one time within the last 10,000 years or so" (Moore 1999). Scientific evidence has little impact on such beliefs, except to spawn more subtle and apparently scientific versions of creationism (Behe 1996; Dembski 1998) that are so insidiously confusing that they befuddle not only school boards but even some otherwise clear-thinking scientists. Conversations with creationists often reveal high motives, however; many sincerely believe that natural selection is incompatible with the possibility of human goodness and meaning in life.

- Others challenge the fundamental genetic perspective of evolutionary thinking. Oyama, in particular, views organisms as systems that sustain themselves by passing along various characteristics by diverse means, genetic material being only one source of information among many (Oyama 2000). Her developmental systems theory interprets individuals as products of overlapping cycles of gene-environment interaction far more complex than those usually considered. She wants to challenge what she calls the "central dogma" that phenotypes are genetically programmed, and to replace the nature-nurture dichotomy with "a radical reformulation of both." Interestingly, these views become the basis for an attack on the notion that individuals are naturally selfish (Caporael et al. 1989; Oyama 1989, 48). Whether these ideas simply lend themselves to such arguments or helped to motivate their development is hard to determine.

• Scientists do not have the option of denying the fact of natural selection, and most seek to understand nature through descriptions that increase simplicity, not complexity. Those who object can, however, try to blunt the impact of this new knowledge in other ways. One is to emphasize the limits of natural selection—its stochastic nature, its inability to create perfection, and the difficulties of studying adaptations (Gould and Lewontin 1979; Kitcher 1985). Such criticisms are certainly justified when applied to silly just-so stories and the uncritical and naïve view of adaptation that gives rise to them. Some critiques, however, tend to damn the whole enterprise of using evolutionary theory to understand adaptations in general, behavior in particular, and human behavior especially. As Wright points out, they also may give fuel to creationists (Wright 2000, chapters 18 and 19). Daunting challenges remain, however, including finding better criteria for determining what is an adaptation and what is not, and better understanding how natural selection shapes maladaptations as well as adaptations. These tasks are difficult, but by no means impossible (Williams 1992; Rose and Lauder 1996). Criticism of specific proposals is valuable, but even more valuable are well worked-out tests of adaptationist hypotheses.

• This brings us to objections based on admittedly political aims that sometimes come with the trappings of science (Caplan 1978; Segerstråle 2000). For instance, in critiques of so-called genetic reductionism, otherwise careful scientists create confusion by confounding questions about evolution and adaptation with quite different questions about genes and mechanisms (Gould and Lewontin 1979; Lewontin, Rose, and Kamin 1984). Closely related is the tendency to fail to distinguish evolutionary studies about the functions of behavior from fundamentally different behavioral genetic studies that seek to explain individual differences as a result of genetic differences. Such conflation fosters overtly political attempts to associate modern evolutionary approaches to understand human behavior with eugenics and the horrors of the Third Reich (Lewontin, Rose, and Kamin 1984). As the political motivations of these gambits are better recognized, they are having less and less effect, at least in the natural sciences (Segerstråle 2000). Furthermore, any association of evolutionary biology with conservative causes is dissolving because most in the field today lean toward the political left. Some even argue that evolutionary principles give direct support to such liberal goals as combating inequality, sexism, and racism (Konner 1999; Singer 2000). The general debate over the utility of evolutionary approaches to behavior is coming to a close. Sociobiology has demonstrated its utility and has developed into a strong new branch of science (Alcock 2001), even if sometimes called by other names, even if proponents sometimes advocate unsupportable theories, and despite the difficulty of finding the best ways to formulate and test some specific hypotheses.

- Another way to attempt to escape the controversy is to try to go back, to resurrect the principle of group selection. One tireless, outgoing scientist, David Sloan Wilson, has made this his mission. In a series of articles, books, interviews, and lectures he has succeeded in making it appear that a mistake was made, that group selection is important after all (D. Wilson 1975; Wilson and Sober 1994). In fact, his model of trait group selection is considerably different from the original naïve models of group selection. Trait group selection for genes is certainly theoretically possible, and Wilson describes a few examples from nature, although others contest their significance (Wilson and Sober 1994). What is clear, however, are his motives. He and his colleagues want to find a mechanism by which natural selection can shape motivations for moral behavior (Sober and Wilson 1998; Smuts 1999). I share that motive and agree that some behaviors and emotions cannot be explained by kin selection and reciprocity alone; however, group selection is not the only possible alternative. I also agree that emergent properties of social groups are powerful forces of selection that are likely to explain important aspects of human nature, including our moral capacities. Along with most other scientists (Dawkins 1982; Williams 1992; Smuts 1999; Maynard Smith 1998), however, I remain unconvinced that differential success of human social groups is a viable potential explanation for the genetic tendencies that shape brain mechanisms that give us moral capacities. Furthermore, if group selection indeed were powerful, it would account equally well not only for cooperation within the group, but also for competition between groups— including tendencies to dehumanize, exploit, and kill members of out-groups, hardly typical examples of moral behavior. While attention to different levels at which selection acts is essential (Maynard Smith and Szathmáry 1995; Williams 1992), trying to resurrect the phrase *group selection* creates unnecessary confusion that distracts attention from trying to understand exactly how the emergent properties of social groups may have shaped the moral passions.

- A related explanation is better supported. In two decades of work Richerson and Boyd have developed models that show how cultural group selection can account for many complex traits, including cooperation (Boyd and Richerson 1985; Richerson and Boyd 1999; see also chapter 9). In their model these traits, not genes, give benefits to groups and therefore spread. The benefits these traits bestow on the group can themselves influence the course of natural selection. Boyd and Richerson do not challenge the predominance of selection's power at the level of the individual; they instead show how cultural selection of socially transmitted traits can help to explain the rise and fall of groups and the nature of culture, and how emergent properties of social groups can become forces of genetic selection for at least two instincts, ethnocentrism and moralistic aggression (Richerson and Boyd 1999).

- Others present culture as if it were an alternative to evolutionary explanations. When pressed, they usually describe examples of people fulfilling the expectations of cultural roles, even when that seems to do little for their reproductive success. Or, they describe the vast variety of human behaviors in different cultures in order to show that human nature is profoundly malleable, that our behavior is not susceptible to explanation as a product of a few drives and fixed action patterns (Lewontin 1982). There is no disputing that humans live in grandly diverse ways, and that our capacity for learning allows us to adapt to vastly different environments. It remains an elementary mistake, however, to posit culture as an alternative to evolutionary explanations (Tooby and Cosmides 1989; Barkow 1989a). In fact, our capacity for culture has almost certainly been shaped by natural selection, and it seems likely that emergent properties of cultures are powerful forces of natural selection (Durham 1982; Tooby and Cosmides 1989; Cosmides and Tooby 1989; Tooby and Cosmides 1992; Flinn and Alexander 1982). Understanding culture is important, even essential, if we are to understand how cooperation is possible, as is well known by those who have developed models of gene-culture coevolution (Cavalli-Sforza and Feldman 1981; Lumsden and Wilson 1981; Durham 1991; Wilson 1998).

- Then there is human will. People can decide to do things that harm their reproductive success. They can decide to inhibit deep impulses. They can decide not to eat, not to sleep, to sacrifice their firstborn, or to be generous even when they are being exploited. This profoundly human capacity—a property of mental mechanisms shaped by natural selection—is an observable reality. It is admirable when it motivates helping, terrifying when it motivates enduring attempts to harm an enemy at all costs. Whether such a capacity offers the best explanation for altruistic behavior is far less certain. After providing extensive reviews of the distressing discoveries described here, several books on evolution and human behavior conclude with the hope that we can use this sad and frightening new knowledge about ourselves to make willful decisions to hold back our primal tendencies in ways that can improve our societies and ourselves (Wilson 1978; Dawkins 1989; Wright 1994; Ridley 1997). This may be correct, yet there is a canyon of ignorance between this hope and realizing the dream of a more peaceful world.

- The distress aroused by these discoveries does not always result in opposition. Some, especially those whom William James would characterize as "hardheaded," look at the facts with an unwavering gaze and proclaim that genuine morality cannot emerge from nature, and we should get used to it. Barash, in particular, seems to have been deeply affected by the recognition that what had seemed selfless turns out to help one's genes (Barash 1979; Barash 1982). Williams, who was perhaps the first to confront these issues (Williams and Williams 1957), has even gone so far as to call Mother Nature a "wicked old witch," because all organisms are inherently selfish in the sense that natural selection has shaped them inexorably to do whatever maximally benefits their genes (Williams 1993). His position follows that of Julian Huxley (Huxley and Huxley 1989 [1893]), which in turn follows Thomas Henry Huxley's in his 1894 Romanes lecture (Huxley 1897). From this point of view, moral action is inherently in opposition to natural tendencies. While such views seem bleak, they often arise, it seems to me, from the same deep dismay that arouses others to oppose an evolutionary view.

- Others react by embracing and extolling the brutality of nature. The initial political offspring of Darwinian theory was, after all, Social Darwinism, with its grand leap from the facts of nature to advocacy of ethical principles that now are widely recognized as promoting vast social harm. The distinction between what is and what should be was trampled. Social Darwinism remains a signal example of powerful people using their resources to spread an ideology that benefits their interests. More recently, some with a cynical bent seem almost gleeful in their attempts to explain every apparently altruistic act as somehow deviously selfish. As Ghiselin puts it, "Scratch an altruist and watch a hypocrite bleed" (Ghiselin 1969, 247). Kohn cites Santayana as going even further: "Generous impulses are self-deceptive hypocrisies. Dig a little beneath the surface and you will find a ferocious, persistent, profoundly selfish man" (Kohn 1990, 205). Such statements make it clear that these issues are deep and emotionally charged. It should be no surprise that people's reactions are intense and markedly varied.

- Finally, one can respond to the difficulties by carrying out a careful analysis of exactly what we mean by altruism and whether it indeed follows that selfish genes necessarily make selfish individuals. Radcliffe-Richards has done just this, examining the flawed reasoning that concludes that a behavior is in the individual's self-interest just because it is in the interests of that person's gene (Radcliffe-Richards 2000). She goes further, still in a strictly gene-selectionist paradigm, to consider the philosophical problem of whether the altruism that is shaped by natural selection can be "*real* altruism." She notes that while natural selection cannot shape a completely altruistic organism, "*genuine* and *limited* concern are not opposed. . . . Coming to show how altruism comes to exist no more shows that it is not real altruism than explaining how a cake was made shows it is not a real cake" (170, 175). This analysis focuses attention where it belongs, on the question of whether natural selection could have shaped capacities that induce people to fulfill their commitments even when they would rather not. Even if such actions advance a person's genetic interests in the long run, they are examples of genuine altruism.

This concludes our summary of twelve responses to the debate concerning altruism precipitated by recognition that selection acts at the level of the gene. Their extraordinary range and intensity 'are as important as their content. These reactions demonstrate the remarkable impact and continuing controversy arising from the discovery that innate tendencies to altruism can exist only if they have somehow increased the frequency of genes that shape them. While there is no hole in this logic, it leaves many observations unexplained. People often follow rules, do their duty, remain loyal, keep their promises and fulfill their threats, even when such actions are clearly not in their interests. How can this be possible? Wouldn't it be better to decide what is in one's best interests at each stage of the game? Why keep a promise if it requires a big sacrifice with no payoff? Why follow a rule if violating it will bring no punishment? Something seems to be missing.

Commitment

Signing an apartment lease, threatening nuclear retaliation, taking religious vows, burning bridges behind you, changing lanes without looking, caring for a spouse with Alzheimer's, threatening arson to enforce an extortion scheme, and waiting for a tardy deliveryman—these all have something in common. All are social strategies carried out not because they bring benefits via kin selection or reciprocity, but because they influence others via commitment. A credible commitment changes other people's expectations, and thus their behavior. For the dictator of a small country, launching nuclear missiles would be suicidal. Nonetheless, if he can convince others that he will really do it, they will be extraordinarily cautious about violating his borders. A renter who signs a lease gives up the option to move out on a whim, but gains a secure place to live at a stable rent. An army that has burned its bridges motivates itself and intimidates its foe. Taking religious vows of celibacy certainly is usually not in one's reproductive or personal interests, but priests do it, and we therefore treat them differently. The taxi driver who changes lanes without looking will certainly cause an accident if others do not yield. So they do. It is one thing to promise to care for each other in sickness and in health, but when one spouse succumbs to Alzheimer's, what can be the sense of keeping a commitment to someone who does not even recognize you? Yet some do. As for the mob, it has to convince business owners that their businesses will burn if they do not pay protection money. To make the threat believable, the mob must, on occasion, commit arson.

Note that the initial focus has shifted. The discussion began with the challenge of explaining altruism but moves now to commitment, which covers not only altruistic promises to help, but also terrible threats of harm. That threats and promises influence by different means is an argument for treating them separately, yet commitment binds them together as two ways of influencing people by changing their expectations.

In a series of books and articles starting in the 1960s Thomas Schelling laid out the framework for understanding commitments (Schelling 1960, 1978a, 1978b, forthcoming). He was preoccupied with cold war strategy, but he extended his analysis to personal relationships and problems of social life in general. This work has influenced many, not only economists but also philosophers who see that it can help to solve some long-standing puzzles involving morality (Parfit 1984; McClennen 1990).

Commitment is fundamentally different from kin selection and reciprocity. Kin selection changes behavior toward relatives owing to the benefits of helping those who share genes identical by descent. More a phenomenon than a social strategy, kin selection explains why organisms help kin even when an action is costly and gives no direct payoff. Reciprocity is based on the expectation of a net benefit from the actions of exchange partners who also act in their own calculated best interests. Commitment, however, is different—it changes behavior by giving up options and thereby changing people's beliefs.

A commitment is an act or signal that gives up options in order to influence someone's behavior by changing incentives or expectations. Some commitments change the objective situation so that fulfilling them becomes in a person's interests. Other commitments are pledges to act in ways that will be contrary to obvious self-interest; they are not enforced by external incentives, but by some combination of reputation and emotion.

Examples are everywhere. If you believe your spouse will care for you in sickness, you will be much more likely to make and keep the same promise. If you believe your spouse will kill you if you try to divorce, you will be much more reluctant to leave. If either unfortunate circumstance arises, it will be disadvantageous to make good on these commitments. Caring for a sick spouse can sap life's energies; murder is likely to result in a long prison term (to say nothing of guilt). Yet people do make such commitments, and others believe them and are influenced because people often fulfill commitments even when doing so is costly. In the long run, however, a capacity for making commitments brings net benefits. These benefits may explain how natural selection shaped tendencies to follow rules and fulfill promises and threats even when that is not in a person's interests. In short, commitment may offer some of what has been missing from an evolutionary understanding of social behavior—a potential means by which natural selection could shape mental faculties for genuinely moral (and immoral) action.

This use of the word *commitment* follows its technical meaning in economics and game theory; other uses need to be distinguished. Sometimes people say they are committed to having dinner tonight or to going to a movie. These are only announcements of plans, not commitments in the sense used here. As Hirshleifer puts it, "A promise or a threat must be to do something that the individual would not otherwise be motivated to do. That is what distinguishes these pledges from mere forecasts" (Hirshleifer 1987, 309). Similarly, people sometimes say they have a commitment at two o'clock. Such obligations that a person cannot easily abrogate are related to the technical sense of commitment in that options are foreclosed, and many such commitments are intended to influence the behavior of others. If you make a commitment to meet others for lunch, they will likely be there.

In psychology commitment often refers to the strength of a person's determination to pursue a goal (Brickman and Coates 1987; Klinger 2000). The goal may be a specific task or a desire to change relationships, religion, or employment. This concept of psychological commitment is also similar to the meaning considered here; both indicate that a person will follow through to reach a difficult goal. The game theory sense of strategic commitment, however, emphasizes the influence on others, while commitment as studied in psychology more often refers to personal commitments individuals make to control their own future behavior—a commitment to lose weight, for instance, or to write for three hours each morning. One strategy for controlling one's behavior is to change the incentive structure by giving up options so that short-term pleasures are set aside to achieve long-term gains. Some people keep their cigarettes in their car, where they cannot easily reach them; others mail their own computer cables to themselves to enjoy a weekend free from Internet addiction (Burnham and Phelan 2000). Gibbard sees such examples as evidence for a system "peculiar to human beings" of normative motivation that can conflict with what he calls the "animal control system" (Gibbard 1990, 57). Such internal mental conflicts, usually between short- versus long-term benefits, have long been recognized by psychoanalysts, although they tend to emphasize the mental conflict and neglect the real strategic dilemmas that give rise to them (Nesse 1990b). Brickman and colleagues have conducted a provocative early exploration of the interfaces between these several aspects of commitment (Brickman and Coates 1987), with particular attention to the utility of irrationality: "Behavior that is not rational, behavior that is chosen on logically inadequate grounds or carried out with utter disregard for costs, can still be functional and effective for the actor. . . . The apparent blindness that follows commitment may be irrational and still a precondition for effective action" (35).

Within the game theory concept of commitment addressed here, several distinctions can help to separate different subtypes. Some commitments are promises to help, others are threats to harm; the difference is whether others perceive a new potential benefit or a new danger. Threats and promises are treated here as two faces of commitment, although an argument could be made that they should be considered as independent phenomena. Commitments can be conditional or unconditional. Threats are usually conditional attempts to prevent another person's potential action; promises are more likely to be unconditional, though often they are conditional on the other fulfilling a matching promise. Commitment can be intentional or unintentional; some commitments are entered into specifically to influence people, others are not. Schelling's chapter describes these varieties in vivid detail.

Perhaps the most profound distinction between different kinds of commitments arises from how they are enforced—that is, why others believe the commitment will be fulfilled. Sometimes the commitment itself makes some options impossible (for example, burning bridges or being bound to the mast). In other situations the options remain available but are no longer advantageous after a third party is given control over tangible incentives (a lease, for instance). A pledge of reputation, such as a public oath, is another way to convince people that a commitment is valid. Finally, commitments can be enforced by emotions such as pride and guilt. Observing such emotions may increase confidence in a commitment.

The first two kinds of commitments—those enforced by the situation itself or by third parties—can be thought of as "secured" because once such a commitment is made, its fulfillment becomes in the actor's interests. Many commitments are, however, unsecured by such tangible enforcers—their fulfillment depends on emotions and concerns about reputation; we will call these subjective commitments. While reputational commitments put real social resources at risk, they also are strongly enforced by emotions such as pride and guilt, so it seems appropriate to include them under subjective commitments. The fulfillment of externally enforced commitments also involves emotions, yet the emotions involved are not these special moral passions but rather the usual emotions that regulate goal pursuit (Nesse 1999). Many actual situations incorporate several of these mechanisms simultaneously. Marriage, for instance, is enforced by a mix that includes legal contracts, reputational pledges, and emotional bonds. Thomas Schelling has distinguished the subtleties of various kinds of commitments. He points out, for example, that belief in a deity who will reward goodness and punish evil transforms many situations from subjective to secured, at least in the believer's mind (Schelling, personal communication, 2000).

Subjective commitments are of special interest because they influence others only by convincing them that an individual will, in some specified future situation, act in ways not in his or her interests. The possibility that natural selection has shaped emotions to help to guarantee subjective commitments was brought to wide attention by Robert Frank's book *Passions Within Reason* (Frank 1988) and by Jack Hirshleifer's chapter "Emotions as Guarantors of Threats and Promises" (Hirshleifer 1987). Each recognized that the utility of commitment strategies could have provided a selection force that shaped emotions such as anger, trust, pride, and guilt, and that the very existence of these emotions might be evidence for this hypothesis. Hirshleifer and Frank summarize their positions in very similar terms:

It is possible to analyze, in terms of effects upon rationally calculated self-interest, the consequences of non-self-interested motivations and of limitations upon the ability to calculate. The economist must go beyond the assumption of "economic man" precisely because of the economic advantage of not behaving like economic man—an advantage that presumably explains why the world is not populated solely by economic men. (Hirshleifer 1987, 322)

> The commitment model is a tentative first step in the construction of a theory of unopportunistic behavior. It challenges the self-interest model's portrayal of human nature in its own terms by accepting the fundamental premise that material incentives ultimately govern behavior. Its point of departure is the observation that persons *directly* motivated to pursue self-interest are often for that reason doomed to fail. They fail because they cannot solve commitment problems. These problems can often be solved by persons known to have abandoned the quest for maximum material advantage. The emotions that lead people to behave in seemingly irrational ways can thus indirectly lead to greater material well-being (Frank 1988, 258).

This insight is profound. It means that the rational pursuit of self-interest is sometimes an inferior strategy. People influence others by convincing them that they will do things that would not otherwise be in their interests. This is the essence of intimate social life. The social fabric has a warp of promises and a weft of threats. We spend our lives making and assessing commitments. We are constantly preoccupied with assessing other people's reputations and protecting our own. We are enraged when others do not fulfill deep commitments. Most of us are a bundle of anxieties when tempted to renege on a pledge. Elster (who remains unconvinced) points out that Frank and Hirshliefer have turned the usual idea of emotions on its head (Elster 2000). Instead of interfering with rational strategy they claim that emotional behaviors can be strategically superior to those based on rational calculation. If it turns out to be correct that natural selection has shaped emotional mechanisms for mediating strategic commitments, this will be of enormous importance. This book is devoted to further developing this idea and trying to determine where it does and does not apply.

To summarize, there are four main reasons to believe that a commitment will be fulfilled:

1. a commitment can be *self-enforcing* if it is secured by incentives intrinsic to the situation;

2. a commitment can be secured by *external incentives* controlled by third parties;

3. a commitment can be backed by a pledge of *reputation*; and

4. a commitment can be enforced by *internal emotional motives*.

In a sense these are four different kinds of commitments: *self-enforcing*, *contractual*, *reputational*, and *emotional*. As already noted, all four factors may influence a single commitment, so it is probably better to think of them as factors rather than distinct kinds. Note that the first two types of commitment are secured, in much the same way that a loan is secured by collateral. Making the commitment changes the situation so that fulfillment becomes in the individual's interests. Such commitments give up options in ways that change the objective nature of the situation. The latter two types of commitment are quite different: they do not change the objective contingencies, only what a person says he or she will do; they are subjective commitments in that they involve a continuing option for reneging. This may be why there is a special need for emotions to maintain motivation to fulfill such commitments, and to try to convince others that the commitment will be fulfilled.

The Significance of Commitment

The importance of commitment is no doubt becoming clear, but a few points deserve emphasis. Benefits that come from an ability to make and assess commitments could shape mental mechanisms that induce individuals to follow rules, even when that is not in their interests. This requires the peculiarly human ability to inhibit short-term self-interested action, offers a potential explanation for the origins of motives for moral behavior, and suggests that the apparently irrational excesses of both love and hatred may emerge from the same source. Commitment offers a framework that engages much of the richness and complexity of human relationships, and it gives genuine moral capacities a place in human nature. This gives it the potential for decreasing the stigma associated with pursuing evolutionary studies of human behavior,thus allowing those studies to proceed with new understanding and support.

Commitment even offers a potential link with much recent social science based on postmodern theories. Criticism of the excesses of such thinking has obscured the value of recognizing how we create our own social environments. Our commitments change other people's expectations about what we will do. Although there is usually nothing coldly calculating about them, our commitments can be seen as strategies for creating beliefs in others. Taken together, these beliefs are the fabric of culture. If our capacity for inducing and assessing such subjective beliefs has been shaped to some degree by natural selection, this may offer a much-needed bridge between fields that otherwise seem determined to ignore or misunderstand each other. While much progress has been made in understanding culture in an evolutionary context (Barkow 1989a, 1989b; Boyd and Richerson 1985; Atran 1990; Sperber 1996; Diamond 1997), much remains to be done to find the mechanisms that make culture possible (Flinn and Alexander 1982; Dunbar, Knight, and Power 1999) and the extent to which these mechanisms have been shaped by natural selection.

Similarly, commitment can offer insights into the origins and functions of religious beliefs. One main function of religious groups is to systematically cultivate and reinforce beliefs that make commitment more accessible and less risky. Many religions insist vehemently that their beliefs are not intended to bring gain, but to foster goodness, at least toward members of the church. Such explicitly subjective ideologies that disavow any motive for individual gain may provide stronger foundations for deep commitments than any appeal to rationality or self-interest (Irons 1996). When a religious group is difficult to enter, and involves most of a person's relationship partners, all of whom monitor one another's behavior, the cost of defecting can become so high that what began as subjective commitments become strongly secured. Religious communities, even more than other groups, provide members with protections that allow commitments to flourish (Dennett 1995; Wilson and Sober 1994). This may help to explain why so many religious groups oppose an evolutionary approach to human behavior, and perhaps why some Islamic cultures take such desperate measures to inhibit the importation of Western influences.

The major Western religions, according to Rue, offer commitment on a grand scale (Rue 1989). Worshipers enter into a covenant with God, agreeing to submit and obey unconditionally in return for a better life and, often, eternal life. The deepest blessings of such systems are, Rue says, in the mental changes that come from living in a world imbued with meaning and order, and the social benefits of living among other people who follow the rules. He contrasts this sharply with the alienated and meaningless worlds inhabited by so many nonreligious people in modern industrial economies (Klinger 1998; Emmons 1999). As noted earlier, if entering a religious group has high opportunity costs and requires major continuing investments of time, effort, and money, then the cost of leaving the group will be so substantial that the threat of expulsion is a potent enforcer of group norms. This is a classic example of commitment—giving up options in order to influence others in a way that changes their behavior and yields net benefits. Almost any emotional or mystical justification for the rules will do, but as soon as calculated self-interest comes to the fore, subjective commitment is fatally undermined.

Finally, as becomes especially clear from practicing psychiatry, our individual social worlds are much of our own making. Individuals who believe that everyone is out for himself or herself are incapable of making subjective commitments; their social worlds are populated only by exchange partners whose motives are always suspect. By contrast, individuals who can believe in other's subjective commitments reap the benefits of relationships that go beyond mere reciprocity. They also run the risk of major betrayal. Frank has conducted a series of studies to show that learning economic theory decreases contributions to public goods, although how widely the findings can be replicated and generalized remains unclear (Frank, Gilovich, and Regan 1993). One presumes that the same would be true for teaching about social evolution, but the study has not been done insofar as I know. The novelist A. S. Byatt recently looked at the conflict between social science and evolutionary science and concluded that it arouses such intense passions because we care so much about our fundamental human nature (Byatt 2000). We intuitively know that what we believe about human nature profoundly shapes how we conduct our lives and the structure of our societies. The belief that all behavior is fundamentally selfish itself changes behavior. As Oyama puts it, "Assuming cooperation to be, at best, a competitive strategy can make it conceptually unstable" (Oyama 2000, 207). It seems possible that the spread of simplistic notions about the evolutionary origins of social relationships could make individual relationships more conflicted and society even more brutal. One antidote may be an evolutionary approach to behavior that incorporates a capacity for commitment.

Background

The concept of commitment, as developed by Frank and Hirshleifer following the lead of Schelling, emerges from a long line of related thinking. Actually the precursors are better described as several lines, since many of them seem to be unaware of each other. This section outlines some of these ideas, starting with those from economics and game theory, and moving to those from philosophy and ethics.

The initial application of game theory to animal behavior by John Maynard Smith (1982) developed in parallel with the application of game theory in economics (Von Neumann and Morgenstern 1944). The possibilities for synergy seem substantial, especially since economists have long restricted their studies to a species well-suited to such explanations, *Homo economicus*. As Kohn puts it, "Egoism is not *an* assumption but *the* assumption underlying neoclassical economics" (Kohn 1990, 185). Such individual utility maximizers are little different from the animals studied by evolutionary ethologists. There is no room for genuine altruism, spiteful threats, or other such irrationality here. People are expected to do whatever best advances their own interests. This grand assumption generally works very well indeed. Economists claim to be able to predict not only what specimens of *Homo economicus* will buy, but also which ones will join a labor

Table 1.1   Social Emotions and the Prisoner's Dilemma

	Other Cooperates	Other Defects
You cooperate	Trust or friendship	Suspicion or anger
You defect	Anxiety or guilt	Rejection

Source: Nesse 1990a.

union, when they will choose to retire, and even whom they will marry (Becker 1991).

Studies of reciprocity relationships have prospered in this framework. The usual model is the prisoner's dilemma, a game in which two players each choose, on every move of the game, to either cooperate or defect. Mutual cooperation brings the greatest net benefit (say, three points each, for a total of six), but an individual who chooses defection gets a greater reward (say, five points) if the other chooses cooperation (and gets zero). This creates a continuing tension between a wish to get steady maximal mutual rewards, the temptation to defect, and the suspicion that the other might defect. Hundreds of experiments have confirmed that this is quite a good model for much cooperation. The strategy of doing whatever the other person did on the past move (tit for tat) has proved a robust strategy (Axelrod and Hamilton 1981; Axelrod 1984) that allows individuals to avoid exploitation while taking advantage of cooperation when that is available. Much work now compares tit for tat to other strategies, some of which are superior in some circumstances. Playing this game well is essential for members of a species where fitness depends on reciprocal exchange. As seen in table 1.1, the four situations defined by the four boxes in the prisoner's dilemma have arisen so often in the course of evolution that they seem to have shaped emotions specific to each situation (Trivers 1971, 1981; Gibbard 1990; Nesse 1990, 1999).

People do not, however, always do what is predicted by rational choice theory (Gintis 2000a, ch. 11). They do not always pursue straight self-interest, and their decisions are not always Bayesian rational. In the prisoner's dilemma, for instance, the game theory optimum for any limited sequence of plays against a game theory–rational opponent is to defect right from the start. This is because defection is the optimal last move of any finite game, and cooperation unravels backward from this endpoint. Yet that is not what people do. Most cooperate early on in the game, and stop cooperating only if the other defects or a specific endpoint is near (Axelrod 1984). Likewise, in public goods games, people cooperate vastly more than expected. According to game theory, an individual's best strategy is to accept the advantages while letting others contribute money to public radio, blood to the blood bank, and land to preservation trusts. Actual human behavior is different. Gintis provides a comprehensive review, emphasizing, *"In neither the everyday nor the narrower economic sense of the term does rationality imply self-interest"* (Gintis 2000a, 243). Even in the laboratory people don't act according to the dictates of rational choice theory. When each subject contributes anonymously to a pot that is then sweetened by a percentage and then divided equally among all players in the game, the average contribution is about half of an individual's reserves in the early moves of the game. The individual variation is huge, however, from large contributions to none. When it becomes obvious that some individuals are not cooperating, contributions taper off and usually end. When individuals can find out who is not contributing, some will spend their resources to punish such individuals, even though they get no individual benefit from such actions (Fehr and Gächter 2000). The suggestion has even been made that complex human organizations became possible only when the ability to throw projectiles precipitously reduced the "cost of punishment" for coalitions trying to enforce their rules (Bingham 1999).

In the ultimatum game one person proposes how to divide a resource (say, ten dollars), and a second person decides either to accept that split or turn all the money back to the experimenter. The Subgame-Perfect Equilibrium is for the proposer to offer the smallest possible amount and for the responder to accept anything offered. A penny is better than nothing, after all. The corresponding game theory–rational strategy for the individual who proposes the split is to offer one penny to the other player. Yet this is not what most university student subjects do. Instead they tend to offer something close to an even split. And the recipients of a low offer often choose to forgo all benefits, thus getting spiteful revenge (Roth et al. 1991; Fehr and Falk 1999). Interestingly, there are wide cultural variations in patterns of response, with most individuals in some groups accepting low offers (Henrich 2000). Recent work has shown that men with low testosterone are more willing to accept an unfair split, while those with high testosterone are likely to turn down anything but a nearly fair division (Burnham, forthcoming.). Such tendencies seem closely related to the norms in honor-based societies, where even the slightest insult may lead to threats of violence (Nisbett and Cohen 1996; see also Cohen and Vandello, chapter 8 herein). Such threats signal an intention to defend resources from others who try to take them, even if that means accepting a huge cost. The alternative—fighting only when it is rational to do so—yields ridicule and impoverishment. Males who are not "demonic" may do poorly (Wrangham and Peterson 1996).

Most attempts to explain the anomalies in behavioral economics are basically within the framework of rational choice theory (RCT) and its two assumptions: that people ultimately pursue self-interest exclusively, and that self-interest is maximized by acting on the basis of rational calculation. Binmore, for instance, emphasizes how difficult it is to escape the implications of RCT. He observes that people only rarely base their behavior on predictions that others will act in ways that are not in their self-interest (Binmore 1994), and he will have none of Gauthier's concept of constrained maximization (Binmore 1993). Likewise, Skyrms at first seems to have little sympathy for attempts to transcend RCT, saying, "A strategy that is not modular rational in these terms is just one that in certain circumstances would require such a rational agent to choose what she would not choose. . . . If expected utility theory is kept in mind, the idea of modifying the normative theory by somehow building in commitment appears quixotic" (Skyrms 1996, 41). He avoids contradiction by incorporating emotional outcomes as a part of utility, citing Frank and Hirshleifer. He proceeds to demonstrate how "Fairman" strategies can persist in equilibrium with other strategies, even when they might not survive otherwise, and concludes, "Evolution may—if the conditions are right—favor commitment over modular rationality strategy. Mixed populations that include individuals using strategies that are not modular rational in Darwinian fitness can evolve according to the replicator dynamics" (42).

Such models assume rational self-interested agents and pose the problem in terms of finding situations in which tendencies to cooperate can survive. Much depends on the details of the model. Axelrod has shown how the initial proportion of cooperators and defectors are powerful determinants of whether a group goes to increasing cooperation or devolves into constant defection (Axelrod 1986, 1997). Yet even here there is a stochastic element to the outcome, which is stable once it tips in one direction or the other. In actual human groups, as managers know all too well, organizational cultures have enduring power far beyond that of any individual.

Another line of work has emphasized the role of reputation. Alexander was one of the first to elaborate this in an evolutionary framework (Alexander 1982, 1985, 1987). He noted how hard it is to explain generalized cooperation and concluded that it may arise mostly from indirect reciprocity. This works because people observe whether or not others are cooperators and seek to create relationships with those who appear generous. In his framework, the optimal strategy is to appear very generous while actually contributing as little as possible. This leads to substantial emphasis on deception and self-deception, including the idea that our experiences of ourselves as moral agents is a self-deception that allows us to better deceive others (Alexander

1974; Trivers 1976; Alexander 1987; de Waal 1984; Mitchell and Thompson 1986; Lockard and Paulhus 1988; Nesse and Lloyd 1992).

Akerlof challenges the "core assumption of economic behavior . . . that all persons are totally selfish. . . . [T]his assumption is made for reasons of convenience, not because economists empirically assume that all persons act only out of selfishness" (Akerlof 1983, 54). He presents a model showing "that honest and cooperative behavior pays off; the honest person is not just a systematic 'sucker'" (55). As an example he cites the rewards of being a "bonded" courier. While the need for such bonding demonstrates the need for external enforcers to motivate honesty, Akerlof claims the system can lead to genuine honesty because "the *appearance* of honesty and class loyalty are beneficial; the easiest way to achieve these appearances is to *be* honest and loyal, even though honesty and loyalty themselves involve sacrifices" (61). Thus his model is parallel to Alexander's but emphasizes the benefits of integrity despite its costs, instead of the benefits of deception despite its risks. Note the central role that reputation plays in this argument.

Kitcher takes a very similar position, arguing that morality can persist in the face of cheaters because individuals can choose those with whom they play prisoner's dilemma games. "Discriminating altruists" eschew contact with defectors, to the substantial cost of those known to be defectors. His mathematical model demonstrates the viability of this strategy, and thus, presumably, how it could have been favored by natural selection (Kitcher 1993). These selective associations are the same engine that allows moral tendencies to prosper in Wilson's trait groups.

More recently, Nowak and Sigmund have developed a computer simulation that demonstrates how tendencies to provide benefits via indirect reciprocity can evolve even when the players meet each other only once (Nowak and Sigmund 2000). This is possible when information about an individual's cooperative "image" is public and when a reputation as a cooperator brings increased benefits via indirect reciprocity. They note, parenthetically and profoundly, "The evolution of human language as a means of such information transfer has certainly helped in the emergence of cooperation based on indirect reciprocity" (576). This work has been replicated and extended with experiments on humans (Wedekind and Milinski 2000; Nowak and Sigmund 2000). Reputation proves crucial to making indirect reciprocity viable. A capacity for commitment allows individuals to act in ways that reap the benefits of image scoring, and to avoid the costs of being recognized as an exploiter. In this and similar models individual agents generally are assumed to pursue one strategy. The strategy may take account of the reputations of other individuals, but it has trouble coping with social groups in which individuals act differently toward each other based on a long history of prior interactions.

Clearly, reputation is a major mediator for the benefits of indirect reciprocity. So long as each player's reputation is revealed sufficiently, cooperation can grow. The optimal cost to spend on monitoring others depends on the ratio of cooperators to defectors in the population. In intermediate proportions monitoring allows cooperators to exclude defectors and to benefit from exchanges with one another. If either type is too rare, the costs will not be worth it. On a grand scale this has been used as the foundation for a theory of sociopathy as a frequency-dependent strategy that succeeds when it is rare in comparison to the proportion of cooperators who, when prevalent, let down their guard (Mealey 1995).

Elster emphasizes that rationality often requires taking steps to make precommitments in anticipation of temptations that will yield a short-term gain and a long-term cost (Elster 1979). By "depositing one's will" one gains global maximization. While he emphasizes the limitations of the human ability to resist temptation, and the workaround of making temptations inaccessible or ultimately more painful than the reward, he also describes strategies of building up one's character that make this much more feasible and yield moral behavior (Elster 2000). He sees perfect rationality as supporting something like Gauthier's constrained maximization, but he doubts that many humans have sufficient willpower to use such strategies.

Gintis defines *strong reciprocity* as a tendency to follow norms that promote cooperation with cooperators, and punishment of cheaters even when those acts are costly. He contrasts this with *weak reciprocity*, which is reciprocal altruism (Gintis 2000b). Strong reciprocity produces fewer replicas in the next generation, but the strategy can still invade and persist because those who violate the norms are recognized and excluded from the benefits of being in groups with strong reciprocators. This is not exactly group selection, because it does not depend on the relative success of different groups. It is, however, social selection, because emergent properties of groups become forces of natural selection that change the prevalence of genotypes, and thus individual behavior. He summarizes many laboratory experiments demonstrating otherwise unaccountable cooperation and presents a formal model demonstrating the viability of strong reciprocity. The key is that "defectors are excluded from participation in the community for a number of periods just sufficient to make defecting a suboptimal strategy, at zero cost to the community" (Gintis 2000a, 273). Many examples in the ethnographic literature also support the thesis that tendencies to strong reciprocity evolved via this route. His position is summarized by his preference for viewing humans as *Homo reciprocans* rather than *Homo economicus*.

Strong reciprocity is very nearly the same as subjective commitment. The main difference is that strong reciprocity models place less emphasis on individual communications of threats and promises and the associated complexities of relationships and signaling, and instead focus on groups that monitor deviations from norms and exclude nonconformists. Strong reciprocity may be possible because individuals have capacities for subjective commitments to enforce group norms, even when that is costly. One could equally well explain the evolution of the capacity for commitment as a result of the costs of being excluded from a group of cooperators, especially if you consider groups with only two members. As Gintis notes, his position is presaged by Campbell, who said in 1983, "mutual monitoring forc[es] altruism on group members who cannot survive without cooperative group membership" (Campbell 1983, 37). On the macro scale, the proportion of strong reciprocators may vary from society to society, perhaps with major economic consequences, such as lack of economic growth (Knack and Keever 1997). For instance, in low-trust environments levels of investment are low, possibly explaining the poverty trap in which some groups and countries find themselves mired (Zak and Knack 2001).

Ideas closely related to commitment are found throughout the development of evolutionary and game theory perspectives on relationships. Even in *The Origin of Species* Darwin was aware of a "special difficulty" with respect to sterile castes of insects, "which at first appeared to me insuperable, and actually fatal to the whole theory" (Darwin 1859). Hamilton, after answering Darwin's quandary, explored the psychological mechanisms that mediate cooperation (Hamilton 1975). Even earlier, Alexander had worked out the dynamics of evolved sociality and some implications for morality (Alexander 1974). Trivers, in the original paper on the evolution of reciprocity, said, "People who are altruistically motivated will make more reliable partners than those motivated by self-interest" (Trivers 1971, 157). He also recognized that "The tendency to like others, not necessarily closely related, to form friendships and to act altruistically towards friends and towards those one likes will be selected for. . . . In other words, selection will favor liking those who are themselves altruistic" (Trivers 1971, 48). He saw the possibilities for gross and subtle cheating in friendships and said that this would shape moralistic aggression, although it has turned out to be difficult to see exactly how benefits come to those who bear the costs of moralistic aggression. He further went on to show how emotions such as gratitude and guilt could be shaped by natural selection, and crucial roles of trust and suspicion in regulating relationships (Trivers 1981).

McClennen (1990) notes that in the publication that established game theory, Von Neumann and Morgenstern anticipate commitment strategies in their distinction between "dead" variables and those that "reflect another person's will or intention." He goes on to say,

> What Von Neumann and Morgenstern proceed to do, however, and what others have done since, is build a theory denying, in the end, that the behavior of each other player could be parameterized. . . . In effect what they do is reduce the problem for each participant to that of a standard maximization problem. . . . The assumption that rational players are bound by the principle of maximization of expected utility proves to be quite paradoxical . . . it ensures that rational players . . . will have to settle for outcomes that are mutually disadvantageous . . . why, if the possibility of gain drives them to enforcement devices, does it not also drive them *beyond*, to an even more efficient form of coordination? (McClennen 1990, 258–60)

The usual solution—to create precommitments and constraints—is suboptimal and fails to explain the existence of moral constraints that cannot be set aside when they become disadvantageous. Justifications for following such rules have been divided, he says, between those, such as Hobbes and Hume, who emphasize the tangible benefits of acting according to moral principles, as compared to others "like Kant [who] postulate that they must be grounded in some radically different fashion" (264). Neither, he says, is satisfactory because both are stuck in a limited view of rationality. Building on Gauthier (Gauthier 1986), his solution, *resolute choice*, "might, one would hope, provide a way to bridge the gap between moral choice and rational interested choice" (McClennen 1990, 260). As important, resolute choice also postulates a force of selection that could shape the moral passions that make commitment possible. "Whereas the sophisticated self acts under a constraint on choice imposed by the logic of belief, the resolute self acts under a constraint of a different sort altogether, a constraint of *commitment*" (160).

Gauthier provides a rationalist foundation for Rawls's contractarian ethics (Rawls 1971; Gauthier 1986). Gauthier's notion of rationality transcends the usual standard of modular rationality, which expects only "straightforward maximization" and instead says there are advantages to having a disposition to practice "constrained maximization," by which he means fulfilling promises even when that will not be advantageous (Gauthier 1986). These advantages are the key to his thesis that it can be rational to follow rules even when that means sometimes acting in ways that are not in a person's self-interest (Sugden 1993). Gibbard takes this further in his suggestion that natural selection has shaped emotional dispositions supporting a "normative control system" to facilitate constrained maximization and thereby give a selective advantage (Gibbard 1990). In Frank's terms, the emotions are "self-control devices" (Frank 1988, 81) that allow people to protect themselves and their reputations from their impulses to act in their short-term interests.

All of this harks back to Hume and Adam Smith with their emphasis on the importance of sympathy. Hume made it the foundation of his moral theory. We cannot, he said, derive oughts from our observations of the world or from any theory. They come instead from our intuitions, from our emotions. Mill, for all his utilitarianism, also emphasized the emotional origins of social cooperation, especially "the fear of exposure" (Mill 1848, 135). This theme continues to the present with work by psychologists showing that our moral choices emerge more from emotion than reason (Kagen 1984) and philosophical treatments of morality based on the natural origins of "apt feelings" for making normative judgments (Gibbard 1990).

Adam Smith, subtle psychologist that he was, emphasized the role of natural emotions in human affairs, especially empathy.

> However selfish soever man may be supposed, there are evidently some principles in his nature, which interest him in the fortunes of others, and render their happiness necessary to him, though he derives nothing from it except the pleasures of seeing it. Of this kind is pity or compassion, the emotion which we feel for the misery of others. . . . That we often derive sorrow from the sorrows of others, is a matter of fact too obvious to require any instances to prove it. . . . Nature, when she formed man for society, endowed him with an original desire to please, and an original aversion to offend his brethren. She taught him to feel pleasure in their favourable and pain in their unfavourable regard. (Smith 1984 [1759], 91, 116)

His outrage at a cynical view of commitments makes it clear that at least one aspect of the so-called sociobiology controversy has been going on for centuries:

> There is, however, another system which seems to take away altogether the distinction between vice and virtue, and of which the tendency is, upon that account, wholly pernicious: I mean the system of Dr. Mandeville . . . Dr. Mandeville considers whatever is done from a sense of propriety, from a regard to what is commendable and praiseworthy, as being done from a love of praise and commendation, or as he calls it from vanity . . . I shall endeavour to show that the desire of doing what is honourable and noble, of rendering ourselves the proper objects of

esteem and approbation, cannot with any propriety be called vanity. (Smith 1984 [1759], 308–9)

Hobbes, in 1651, said it best of all in his Third Law of Nature: *"That men performe their Covenants made.* . . . In this law of Nature, consisteth the Fountain and Originall of JUSTICE . . . the definition of INJUSTICE is no other than the not Performance of Covenant."* He notes that "there must be some coërcive Power to compel men equally to the performance of their Covenants, by their terror of some punishment greater than the benefit they expect by the breach of their Covenant" (Hobbes, 1996 [1651] no. 2693, 100). But then he goes on, in the parable of the Foole, to ask why people should keep their promises if the violation will not be punished.

> The Foole hath sayd in his heart, there is no such thing as Justice; and sometimes also with his tongue; seriously alleaging that every mans conservation and contenement, being committed to his own care, there could be no reason why every man might not do what he thought conduced thereunto: and therefore also make or not make, keep or not keep Covenants, was not against reason, when it conduced to ones benefit. . . . From such reasoning as this, Successful wickedenesse hath obtained the name of Vertue. . . . Where there is no Civill Power erected over the parties promising . . . there is the question whether it be against reason, that is against the benefit of the other, to performe, or not. And I say it is not against reason. . . . He therefore that breaketh his Covenant, and consequently declareth that he thinks he may with reason do so, cannot be received into any Society that unite themselves for Peace and Defense, but by the errour of them that receive him . . . if he be left, or cast out of Society, he perisheth." (Hobbes, 1996 [1651], 100–102)

This Foole will be recognized, of course, as *Homo economicus*. Centuries ago Hobbes understood why commitment persists. Those who announce that they do not need to keep their promises are cast out from society, where they perish. What could be a more fitting description of how natural selection shapes motives for keeping commitments? Moreover, what explanation could better explain why people are so hostile toward economists and evolutionists who seem to portray human behavior as self-interested and cynically deceptive?

Natural Selection

The core question remains: What does natural selection have to do with the capacity for commitment? In one sense, it may not matter that much. There are wide cultural variations in patterns of commitment, and much of this variation seems to arise from different beliefs about human nature. It should be possible to understand how commitment functions in relationships and societies without knowing whether natural selection shaped tendencies specifically to make commitments possible. Yet, as noted by Byatt, we care deeply about our biological nature. Perhaps this should not influence us, but it does. Perhaps we should realize that what is natural is no guide to what is good, but when we discover (or start to believe in the absence of any evidence) that a tendency is a part of our nature, in fact we behave differently. As Hume pointed out, it is logically incorrect to try to get oughts from what is in nature; emotionally, though, the leap from is to ought seems easy and natural. This tendency fuels the fire about debates on human nature (Ruse 1982; Rose and Rose 2000; Segerstråle 2000).

This enormous range of cultural variation indicates that tendencies to use commitment strategies are by no means as hardwired as the preference for sweets. This variation does not, however, mean that natural selection is unimportant, any more than the wide variation in the foods people eat means that food preferences are not shaped by natural selection. Is it possible that the capacity for commitment in fact has not been shaped by natural selection? Yes, but this seems unlikely. If selection has not shaped special faculties for making and assessing commitments, some other explanation must be found for our moral passions, our preoccupations with reputation and honor, and our irrational wishes to fulfill commitments to help loved ones and harm enemies. Furthermore, despite wide variation in specific patterns, the emotional capacity for commitment seems to be a human universal, one that is complex, costly, and peculiar, and therefore difficult to explain unless it somehow increases reproductive success.

Psychological studies of mechanisms that could mediate commitment are just beginning; increasingly these studies have used an evolutionary context. Cosmides and Tooby have pursued an extensive program of research designed to show that our minds have a built-in system for conducting social relationships, especially a "cheater detection module" (Cosmides and Tooby 1992). They find support in their extensive data showing that people make fewer mistakes on the Wason selection task when the content is related to social obligations as compared to nonsocial information (Tooby and Cosmides 1989). This cheater detection module presumably has evolved not just to calculate the odds that another player will cooperate on the next move, but whether the partner is pretending to be a friend when he is actually just a "banker" who is willing to invest only when a payoff can be guaranteed (Tooby and Cosmides 1984, 1996). This model is closely related to the notion of commitment developed here.

Theories of social relationships on a large scale likewise nearly always identify some relationships as intimate or based on "communal sharing" in which the boundaries of the individuals merge (Fiske 1991). People take great pains to differentiate these relationships from those based on mere exchange. Psychological studies have found that friendship satisfaction is highly predicted by self-disclosure and trust, and is *decreased* by an exchange orientation (Jones 1991). Most people experience friendships as communal relationships (Mills and Clark 1982) as distinct from exchange relationships, with a "deep structure" that is distinct from the "superficial structure" of exchange (Hartup and Stevens 1999).

Perhaps the strongest evidence that friendships are based on commitment and not reciprocity is the revulsion people feel on discovering that an apparent friend is calculating the benefits of acting in one way or another. People intuitively recognize that such calculators are not friends at all, but exchangers of favors at best, and devious exploiters at worst. Abundant evidence confirms this observation. Mills has shown that when friends engage in prompt reciprocation, this does not strengthen but rather weakens the relationship (Mills and Clark 1982). Similarly, favors between friends do not create obligations for reciprocation because friends are expected to help each other for emotional, not instrumental reasons (Mills and Clark 1994). Other researchers have found that people comply more with a request from a friend than from a stranger, but doing a favor prior to the request increases cooperation more in a stranger than a friend (Boster et al. 1995). Owing to the important differences between friendship and acquaintanceship, people seem to take care with new potential friends to communicate whether they do or do not intend for the relationship to become a friendship. Communications that blur this distinction make people distinctly uncomfortable (Lydon, Jamieson, and Holmes 1997).

The importance of commitment is also a likely explanation for why people care so much about not only what others do, but why they do it. The meaning of an act differs dramatically depending on whether it is motivated by desire to influence or by emotional concern for a person's well-being. This is consistent with the emphasis philosophers have long placed on motives in determining the moral status of an act (Darwall, Gibbard, and Railton 1997). The significance of the difference between calculated versus real altruism has been long recognized (Krebs 1970). The capacity for making and keeping commitments allows people to engage in relationships that are impossible for those who just exchange favors. The more negative side of this same capacity is seen in studies of honor cultures (Nisbett and Cohen 1996). Individuals who give a calculated response to aggression can be exploited easily. Those who are taken over by rage are far more formidable opponents. This is expanded at length in the chapter by Cohen and Vandello herein.

Finally, contemporary studies of moral psychology are compatible with evolutionary perspectives on commitment. As Krebs notes:

> From an evolutionary perspective Kohlberg's stages represent cognitive structures that were selected in ancestral environments because they upheld adaptive systems of social interaction. For example, Stage 1 structures upheld social systems based on obedience to authority; Stage 2 judgments upheld cooperative systems based on instrumental, individual exchanges (e.g., tit-for-tat reciprocity) and Stage 3 judgments upheld cooperative systems based on harmonious in-group relations. The cognitive structures that uphold Stage 4 judgments may have evolved relatively recently to uphold the maintenance of social structures, such as legal systems, within more complex societies. . . . Put another way, the original function of moral judgment was to constrain others from advancing their interests at the expense of those with whom they formed cooperative relations. (Krebs, Denton, and Wark 1997, 131)

Demonstrating how such psychological traits give a fitness advantage is only one half of an evolutionary explanation; the other is discovering their precursors and how they were shaped to their present forms. This brings us to the precursors of capacities for commitment. While commitment itself is a strategy, not a trait, it offers benefits that may well have shaped various psychological mechanisms. Certainly capacities for commitment may have precursors in tendencies shaped by kin selection and reciprocity. As many have pointed out, we evolved in small kin groups where helping others often helps the actor's genes (Alexander 1985; Irons 1998; Richerson and Boyd 1999). In such a circumstance it may be more efficient to just help rather than to calculate. Likewise, while the reciprocity literature emphasizes sequential favor trading, many social relationships seem to be based on metacommitments that people make to keep cooperating despite occasional difficulties. Our relationships, even those based on commitment, depend on some balance between what is offered and what is received. Yet success in social life depends on the ability to maintain relationships during dry periods without being exploited. Likewise, conflicts are inevitable, and it appears that humans, like primates, have a built-in motivation to reconcile differences (de Waal 1989). Such motivations may be crucial precursors to capacities for commitment.

A closely related second possibility is that the capacity for commitment may have emerged from the benefits of political alliances. Chimpanzees spend their lives making alliances. Subdominant males routinely make coalitions to compete against the alpha male who, in turn, must maintain alliances with others to keep his position (de Waal 1982, Goodall 1986; Runciman, Maynard Smith, and Dunbar 1996). Human hierarchies are different from those of other primates, with strong tendencies toward egalitarianism (Boehm 1999) and are based as much on prestige as they are on dominance (Henrich and Gil-White 2000). Nonetheless, political alliances are central to human competition, and modeling them as reciprocal exchanges misses much of how they work (Masters 1983; Trivers 1981). Instead of monitoring each move to anticipate patterns of cooperation and defection, political partners support each other in general, over multiple situations during long periods of time. This is exactly the kind of situation in which selection might well shape tendencies for emotional loyalty and commitment. Such relationships are, of course, continually threatened by third parties. Social life is composed of triangles (Kerr and Bowen 1988). An individual cannot always fulfill the wishes of both other parties, especially when each seeks an ally in a conflict with a fourth party. Furthermore, humans routinely use the strategy of *splitting*—flattering one member of a partnership while denigrating the other in order to disrupt the alliance and get a new ally. Ending all relationships at the first such difficulty is not an option; that would end participation in social life. Finding ways to overlook these deviations in order to continue can be of great value. Tact—the ability to suppress just the right information while talking with someone—may be deception of a sort, but it is the glue that makes social life possible (Nesse 1990b).

One further consideration may turn out to be enormously important. When potential mates are assessing each other, one of their top priorities is to find someone who is kind and honest. (This is the central but neglected finding of the cross-cultural study of mate choice by Buss [1989].) Otherwise, when bad times come, all the good genes and resources in the world will not be of much use. Miller (2000) has suggested, in the course of his work on selection for traits that display quality, that sexual selection may have augmented the capacity for altruism in a runaway escalation. If men and women each have a genetic tendency to seek mates who are kind and honest, this will select strongly for acting kind and honest, and the best way to accomplish this is to actually be kind and honest. In short, in addition to all the other selective advantages of a capacity for commitment, it may have been subject to sexual selection.

Social selection may be crucial to the capacity for commitment. If groups routinely give rise to emergent forces of natural selection, this can shape otherwise unaccountable individual behavior tendencies. For instance, if individuals simply avoid those who have betrayed them, the net effect on an individual prone to defection is, as Hobbes said, exclusion from the group and probable death. It is as if the group had decided to shape its future membership, but no foresight is needed. The effect emerges from the uncoordinated actions of many individual agents. Groups, of course, often do make decisions about who is welcome and who is not, and they sometimes act in unison to punish a deviant. Once commitments are established, such actions are especially easy to explain. Such sequences readily give rise to coevolution, in which social structures shape individual traits that in turn create slightly different social structures (Cavalli-Sforza and Feldman 1981; Lumsden and Wilson 1981; Boyd and Richerson 1985; Durham 1991; Dunbar, Knight, and Power 1999). Many psychological traits seem to exist to make culture possible, such as the tendency to conformity and identification with the group leader, and the susceptibility of children to indoctrination (Boyd and Richerson 1985; Barkow 1989a). Simon has suggested that the benefits of conforming to cultural expectations have shaped a tendency to "docility," a tendency to learn and follow social norms that can result in genuine altruism (Simon 1990). His argument depends on bounded rationality and the assumption that individuals cannot accurately distinguish what is good for them from what is good for their group, but it has the virtue of explaining prosocial traits as a result of social selection (West-Eberhard 1987; Simon 1990; Jason, Brodie, and Moore 1999).

The benefits of using commitment strategies effectively are themselves likely to be potent selection forces that emerge from the structure of a complex social environment. Furthermore, the functions of the newest part of our brain, the frontal lobes, closely match the abilities needed to use commitment strategies. The frontal lobes seem crucial in calculating the tradeoffs between the short-term costs of giving up options and long-term benefits that may or may not be obtained. Many of these calculations involve social capital, with resulting inordinate complexity (Alexander 1975; Humphrey 1976). The frontal lobes also are essential to inhibiting the pursuit of short-term goals in order to fulfill commitments in pursuit of long-term goals. They are deeply involved in the social calculations needed to decide whether another person will fulfill a commitment. This decision is made best by an empathic identification with the other in order to anticipate what he or she is likely to do. To use commitment successfully requires not only higher cognition, but also a theory of mind (Baron-Cohen 1995), intuitive empathy, and a capacity for "mind reading" (Krebs and Dawkins 1984).

Our ability to read fiction, indeed perhaps our tendency to crave and enjoy stories, may well arise because of the huge advantages of getting into the mind of another in order to anticipate whether he or she is likely to follow through on commitments (Carroll 1995; Turner 1996). We watch Sophocles' play with understanding and horror as Antigone reveals her determination to bury the body of Polynices, despite the king's edict. As she keeps her commitment, and the king keeps his, tragedy unfolds. As we watch, we consider the importance and the risks of keeping our commitments. Likewise, Odysseus overcomes giant obstacles and forgoes the pleasures of various isles to make his way home to his wife. Penelope, the very model of faithfulness, has been using her wiles to stave off the rapacious suitors. When Odysseus finally arrives home, we understand his state of mind perfectly as he takes his bloody revenge. One wonders if the rise of commitment was a key to the growth and power of Greek civilization.

To be explicit about this line of speculation, it seems possible that capacities for commitment have given such substantial fitness advantages that they could have shaped high intelligence, language ability, empathy, a theory of mind, an ability to inhibit impulses, and our fascination with fiction. Furthermore, once commitments become established in a group, they create emergent forces of selection that further speed development of these capacities in a runaway race for social intelligence. Expulsion of those who do not keep commitments will quickly shape tendencies to honesty and loyalty, even if that results in tendencies to act in ways that are genuinely altruistic, or self-destructively spiteful.

Such a scenario could address many long-standing problems. Most important, it offers a possible explanation for how natural selection could shape a moral capacity for acting according to rules instead of calculated self-interest. The parallel benefits of threats and promises offer a deep link between the origins of good and evil. Commitment also offers a possible explanation for why we humans are such extraordinarily emotional and apparently irrational creatures. Many commitments work only if they are based on emotion or beliefs that are outside the range of reason. This offers a way to understand our human fascination with mythology, religion, and ideology, why we spend so much effort constructing social realities, and how those social realities cycle back into tangible costs and benefits that further shape human minds by means of natural selection.

While plausible and consistent with much evidence, these speculations are nowhere near being facts. Taken together they make an intriguing story, but we do not yet even know how important the capacity for commitment really is, nor do we know how people use commitment strategies differently within and among cultures. That capacities for commitment have been shaped by natural selection seems likely, but this needs much more exploration. This book reviews prior work and summarizes the state of the field from diverse perspectives in order to call attention to the importance of commitment and pose clear questions that will advance our understanding.

This chapter was greatly improved by comments and suggestions from Stephanie Brown, Terry Burnham, Dov Cohen, Lee Dugatkin, Alexander Field, Alan Gibbard, Lillian Gleiberman, Martin Gold, Jack Hirshleifer, Matt Keller, Philip Kulkulski, Peter Railton, Thomas Schelling, Natalie Smith, two anonymous reviewers, and members of the University of Michigan Evolution and Human Adaptation Program Weekly Seminar.

References

Akerlof, George A. 1983. "Loyalty Filters." *American Economic Review* 73: 54–63.

Alcock, John. 1997. *Animal Behavior: An Evolutionary Approach*, 6th ed. Sunderland, Mass.: Sinauer.

———. 2001. *The Triumph of Sociobiology*. New York: Oxford University Press.

Alexander, Richard D. 1974. "The Evolution of Social Behavior." *Annual Review of Systematics* 5: 325–83.

———. 1975. "The Search for a General Theory of Behavior." *Behavioral Science* 20: 77–100.

———. 1982. "Biology and the Moral Paradoxes." *Journal of Social and Biological Structures* 5: 389–95.

———. 1985. "A Biological Interpretation of Moral Systems." *Zygon* 20(1): 3–20.

———. 1987. *The Biology of Moral Systems*. New York: Aldine de Gruyter.

Atran, Scott. 1990. *Cognitive Foundations of Natural History: Towards an Anthropology of Science*. New York: Cambridge University Press.

Axelrod, Robert. 1984. *The Evolution of Cooperation*. New York: Basic Books.

———. 1986. "An Evolutionary Approach to Norms." *American Political Science Review* 80: 1095–1111.

———. 1997. *The Complexity of Cooperation: Agent-Based Models of Competition and Collaboration*. Princeton Studies in Complexity. Princeton, N.J.: Princeton University Press.

Axelrod, Robert, and William D. Hamilton. 1981. "The Evolution of Cooperation." *Science* 211: 1390–96.

Badcock, Christopher R. 1986. *The Problem of Altruism*. Oxford: Blackwell.

Barash, David 1977. *The Biology of Altruism, Sociobiology and Behavior*. New York: Elsevier.

———. 1979. *Sociobiology: The Whisperings Within*. New York: Harper and Row.

———. 1982. *Sociobiology and Behavior*, 2d ed. New York: Elsevier.

Barkow, Jerome H. 1989a. *Darwin, Sex, and Status: Biological Approaches to Mind and Culture*. Toronto: University of Toronto Press.

———. 1989b. "The Elastic Between Genes and Culture." *Ethology and Sociobiology* 10: 111–29.

Baron-Cohen, Simon. 1995. "Mindblindness: An Essay on Autism and the Theory of Mind." Cambridge, Mass.: MIT Press.

Beck, Aaron T. 1976. *Cognitive Therapy and the Emotional Disorders*. New York: International Universities Press.

Becker, Gary. 1991. *A Treatise on the Family*. Cambridge, Mass.: Harvard University Press.

Behe, Michael J. 1996. *Darwin's Black Box: The Biochemical Challenge to Evolution*. New York: Free Press.

Bingham, Paul M. 1999. "Human Uniqueness: A General Theory." Quarterly Review of Biology 74(2): 133–69.

Binmore, Ken. 1993. "Bargaining and Morality." In *Rationality, Justice and the Social Contract: Themes from Morals by Agreement*, edited by D. Gauthier and R. Sugden. Ann Arbor, Mich.: University of Michigan Press.

———. 1994. *Game Theory and the Social Contract*. Cambridge, Mass.: MIT Press.

Boehm, Christopher. 1999. "The Natural Selection of Altruistic Traits." *Human Nature* 10(3): 205–52.

Boster, Franklin J., Jose I. Rodriguez, Michael G. Cruz, and Linda Marshall. 1995. "The Relative Effectiveness of a Direct Request Message and a Pregiving Message on Friends and Strangers." *Communication Research* (Special Issue), *Communication and Social Influence* 22(4): 475–84.

Boyd, Robert, and Peter J. Richerson. 1985. *Culture and the Evolutionary Process*. Chicago: University of Chicago Press.

Bradie, Michael. 1994. *The Secret Chain: Evolution and Ethics*. Suny Series in Philosophy and Biology. Albany: State University of New York Press.

Brickman, Philip, and Dan Coates. 1987. "Commitment and Mental Health." In *Commitment, Conflict, and Caring*, edited by C. B. Wortman and R. Sorrentino. Englewood Cliffs, N.J.: Prentice-Hall.

Burnham, Terry. Forthcoming. "Testosterone and Negotiations: An Investigation into the Role of Biology in Economic Behavior." Unpublished paper. Harvard University, Cambridge, Mass.

Burnham, Terry, and Jay Phelan. 2000. *Mean Genes: From Sex to Money to Food, Taming Our Primal Instincts*. Cambridge, Mass.: Perseus Publishing.

Buss, David M. 1989. "Sex Differences in Human Mate Preferences: Evolutionary Hyotheses Tested in 37 Cultures." *Behavioral and Brain Sciences* 12: 1–49.

Byatt, Antonia Susan. 2000. "The Darwin Wars." *Prospect* (November).

Campbell, Donald T. 1975. "On the Conflict Between Biological and Social Evolution and Between Psychology and the Moral Tradition." *American Psychologist* 30: 1115–22.

———. 1983. "Two Distinct Routes Beyond Kin Selection to Ultrasociality: Implications for the Humanities and the Social Sciences." In *The Nature of Prosocial Development*, edited by D. L. Bridgeman. New York: Academic Press.

Caplan, Arthur L. 1978. *The Sociobiology Debate: Readings on the Ethical and Scientific Issues Concerning Sociobiology*. New York: Harper and Row.

Caporael, Linda R., Richard M. Dawes, John M. Orbell, and Alphons J. C. Van de Kragt. 1989. "Selfishness Examined: Cooperation in the Absence of Egoistic Incentives." *Behavior and Brain Sciences* 12(4): 683–739.

Carroll, Joseph. 1995. *Evolution and Literary Theory*. Columbia, Mo.: University of Missouri Press.

Cavalli-Sforza, Luca L., and Marcus W. Feldman. 1981. *Cultural Transmission and Evolution: A Quantitative Approach*. Monographs in Population Biology, 16. Princeton, N.J.: Princeton University Press.

Cosmides, Leda, and John Tooby. 1989. "Evolutionary Psychology and the Generation of Culture, Part II. Case Study: A Computational Theory of Social Exchange." *Ethology and Sociobiology* 10(1–3): 51–98.

———. 1992. "Cognitive Adaptations for Social Exchange." In *The Adapted Mind: Evolutionary Psychology and the Generation of Culture*, edited by J. H. Barkow, L. Cosmides, and J. Tooby. New York: Oxford University Press.

Cronin, Helena. 1991. *The Ant and the Peacock: Altruism and Sexual Selection from Darwin to Today*. New York: Cambridge University Press.

Daly, Martin, and Margo Wilson. 1987. "Children as Homicide Victims." In *Child Abuse and Neglect: Biosocial Dimensions*, edited by R. J. Gelles and J. B. Lancaster. New York: Aldine de Gruyter.

Darwall, Stephen L., Allan Gibbard, and Peter Albert Railton. 1997. *Moral Discourse and Practice: Some Philosophical Approaches*. New York: Oxford University Press.

Darwin, Charles. 1859. *On the Origin of Species by Means of Natural Selection*. London: John Murray.

Dawkins, Richard. 1976. *The Selfish Gene*. Oxford: Oxford University Press.

———. 1982. *The Extended Phenotype: The Gene as the Unit of Selection*. San Francisco: W. H. Freeman.

———. 1989. *The Selfish Gene*, new ed. Oxford and New York: Oxford University Press.

de Waal, Frans B. M. 1982. *Chimpanzee Politics: Power and Sex Among Apes*. New York: Harper and Row.

———. 1984. "Deception in the Natural Communication of Chimpanzees." In *Deception: Perspectives on Human and Nonhuman Deceit*, edited by R. W. Mitchell and N. S. Thompson. New York: SUNY Press.

———. 1989. *Peacemaking Among Primates*. Cambridge, Mass.: Harvard University Press.

Dembski, William A. 1998. *Mere Creation: Science, Faith & Intelligent Design*. Downers Grove, Ill.: InterVarsity Press.

Dennett, Daniel. 1995. *Darwin's Dangerous Idea*. New York: Simon & Schuster.

Diamond, Jared M. 1997. *Guns, Germs, and Steel: The Fates of Human Societies*. New York: Norton.

Dugatkin, Lee Alan. 1997. *Cooperation Among Animals: An Evolutionary Perspective*. Oxford Series in Ecology and Evolution. New York: Oxford University Press.

Dunbar, Robin I. M., Chris Knight, and Camilla Power. 1999. *The Evolution of Culture: An Interdisciplinary View*. New Brunswick, N.J.: Rutgers University Press.

Durham, William H. 1982. "Interactions of Genetic and Cultural Evolution: Models and Examples." *Human Ecology* 10(3): 289–323.

———. 1991. *Coevolution: Genes, Culture, and Human Diversity*. Stanford, Calif.: Stanford University Press.

Elster, Jon. 1979. *Ulysses and the Sirens: Studies in Rationality and Irrationality*. London: Cambridge University Press.

———. 2000. *Ulysses Unbound*. London: Cambridge University Press.

Emmons, Robert A. 1999. *The Psychology of Ultimate Concerns: Motivation and Spirituality in Personality*. New York: Guilford Press.

Fehr, Ernst, and Armin Falk. 1999. *Homo Reciprocans and Homo Cooperation*. Zurich: University of Zurich Press.

Fehr, Ernst, and Simon Gächter. 2000. "Cooperation and Punishment in Public Goods Experiments." *American Economic Review* 90(4): 980–94.

Fiske, Alan Page. 1991. *Structures of Social Life*. New York: Free Press.

Flinn, Mark V., and Richard D. Alexander. 1982. "Culture Theory: The Developing Synthesis from Biology." *Human Ecology* 10(3): 383–400.

Frank, Robert H. 1988. *Passions Within Reason: The Strategic Role of the Emotions*. New York: Norton.

———. 1992. "The Role of Moral Sentiments in the Theory of Intertemporal Choice." In *Choice over Time*, edited by G. Loewenstein. New York: Russell Sage Foundation.

Frank, Robert H., Thomas Gilovich, and Dennis Regan. 1993. "Does Studying Economics Inhibit Cooperation?" *Journal of Economic Perspectives* 7(Spring): 159–71.

Fukuyama, Francis. 1995. *Trust : Social Virtues and the Creation of Prosperity*. New York: Free Press.

Gauthier, David. 1986. *Morals by Agreement*. New York: Oxford University Press.

Ghiselin, Michael T. 1969. *The Economy of Nature and the Evolution of Sex*. Berkeley: University of California Press.

Gibbard, Allan. 1990. *Wise Choices, Apt Feelings: A Theory of Normative Judgment*. Oxford: Oxford University Press.

Gintis, Herbert. 2000a. *Game Theory Evolving*. Princeton, N.J.: Princeton University Press.

———. 2000b. "Strong Reciprocity and Human Sociality." *Journal of Theoretical Biology* 206: 169–79 (Available at Gintis's personal web site).

Goodall, Jane. 1986. *The Chimpanzees of Gombe: Patterns and Behavior*. Cambridge, Mass.: Belknap Press.

Gould, Steven J., and Richard C. Lewontin. 1979. "The Spandrels of San Marco and the Panglossian Paradigm: A Critique of the Adaptationist Programme." *Proceedings of the Royal Society of London* 205: 581–98.

Hamilton, William D. 1964. "The Genetical Evolution of Social Behavior I and II." *Journal of Theoretical Biology* 7: 1–52.

———. 1975. "Innate Social Aptitudes of Man: An Approach from Evolutionary Genetics." In *Biosocial Anthropology*, edited by R. Fox. New York: Wiley.

Hartup, Willard W., and Nan Stevens. 1999. "Friendships and Adaptation Across the Life Span." *Current Directions in Psychological Science* 8(3): 76–79.

Henrich, Joseph. 2000. "Does Culture Matter in Economic Behavior? Ultimatum Game Bargaining Among the Machiguenga." *American Economic Review* 90(4): 973–79.

Henrich, Joseph, and Francisco Gil-White. 2000. "The Evolution of Prestige: Freely Conferred Status as a Mechanism for Enhancing the Benefits of Cultural Transmission." *Evolution and Human Behavior* 22: 1–32.

Hirshleifer, Jack. 1987. "On the Emotions as Guarantors of Threats and Promises." In *The Latest on the Best: Essays on Evolution and Optimality*, edited by J. Depré. Cambridge, Mass.: MIT Press.

———. 1999. "There Are Many Evolutionary Pathways to Cooperation." *Journal of Bioeconomics* 1: 73–93.

Hobbes, Thomas. 1996 [1651]. *Leviathan*. Cambridge: Cambridge University Press.

Humphrey, Nicholas K. 1976. "The Social Function of Intellect." In *Growing Points in Ethology*, edited by P. G. Bateson and R. A. Hinde. London: Cambridge University Press.

———. 1999. "Varieties of Altruism." *Social Research* 64: 199–209.

Hurd, James P. 1996. "Investigating the Biological Foundations of Human Morality." *Symposium Series*, vol. 37. Lewiston, N.Y.: E. Mellen Press.

Huxley, Thomas Henry. 1897. *Evolution and Ethics and Other Essays*. 6 vols. *The Works of Thomas Henry Huxley*, vol. 1. New York: D. Appleton.

Huxley, Thomas Henry, and Julian Huxley. 1989 [1893]. *Evolution and Ethics*. Princeton, N.J.: Princeton University Press.

Irons, William. 1996. "Morality, Religion and Human Evolution." In *Religion and Science: History, Methods, Dialogue*, edited by W. M. Richardson and W. J. Wildman. New York: Routledge.

———. 1998. "Adaptively Relevant Environments Versus the Environment of Evolutionary Adaptedness." *Evolutionary Anthropology* 6(6): 194–204.

Jason, B. Wolf, Edmund D. Brodie III, and Allen J. Moore. 1999. "Interacting Phenotypes and the Evolutionary Process II. Selection Resulting from Social Interactions." *American Naturalist* 153: 254–66.

Jones, Diane Carlson. 1991. "Friendship Satisfaction and Gender: An Examination of Differences in Contributors to Friendship Satisfaction." *Journal of Social and Personal Relationships* 8: 167–85.

Kagen, Jerome. 1984. *The Nature of the Child*. New York: Basic Books.

Katz, Leonard. 2000. *Evolutionary Origins of Morality: Cross Disciplinary Perspectives*. Devon: Imprint Academic.

Kerr, Michael E., and Murray Bowen. 1988. *Family Evaluation: An Approach Based on Bowen Theory*. New York: Norton.

Kitcher, Philip. 1985. *Vaulting Ambition: Sociobiology and the Quest for Human Nature*. Cambridge, Mass.: MIT Press.

———. 1993. "The Evolution of Human Altruism." *Journal of Philosophy* 90(10): 497–516.

Klinger, Eric. 1998. "The Search for Meaning in Evolutionary Perspective and Its Clinical Implications." In *Handbook of Personal Meaning: Theory, Research & Application*, edited by P. T. P. Wong and S. F. Prem. Mahwah, N.J.: Lawrence Erlbaum.

———. 2000. "Commitment." In *Encyclopedia of Psychology*. New York: American Psychological Association and Oxford University Press.

Knack, Stephen, and Philip Keever. 1997. "Does Social Capital Have an Economic Payoff? A Cross-Country Investigation." *Quarterly Journal of Economics* 112(4): 1252–88.

Kohn, Alfie. 1990. *The Brighter Side of Human Nature: Altruism and Empathy in Everyday Life*. New York: Basic Books.

Konner, Melvin. 1999. "Darwin's Truth, Jefferson's Vision: Sociobiology and the Politics of Human Nature." *American Prospect* (45): 30–38.

Krebs, Dennis. 1970. "Altruism: An Examination of the Concept and a Review of the Literature." *Psychological Bulletin* 73: 258–303.

Krebs, Dennis, Kathy Denton, and Gillian Wark. 1997. "The Forms and Functions of Real-Life Moral Decision-Making." *Journal of Moral Education* 26(2): 131–46.

Krebs, John, and Richard Dawkins. 1984. "Animal Signals: Mind-Reading and Manipulation." In *Behavioral Ecology: An Evolutionary Approach*, edited by J. R. Krebs and N. B. Davies. Sunderland, Mass.: Sinauer.

Lewontin, Richard C. 1982. *Human Diversity*. New York: Scientific American Library.

Lewontin, Richard C., Steven Rose, and Leon J. Kamin. 1984. *Not in Our Genes: Biology, Ideology, and Human Nature*. New York: Pantheon Books.

Lockard, Joan S., and Delroy L. Paulhus, eds. 1988. *Self-Deception: An Adaptive Mechanism?* Englewood Cliffs, N.J.: Prentice Hall.

Lumsden, Charles J., and Edward O. Wilson. 1981. *Genes, Mind, and Culture*. Cambridge, Mass.: Harvard University Press.

Lydon, John E., David W. Jamieson, and John G. Holmes. 1997. "The Meaning of Social Interactions in the Transition from Acquaintanceship to Friendship." *Journal of Personality & Social Psychology* 73(3): 536–48.

Masters, Roger D. 1983. "The Biological Nature of the State." *World Politics* 35(2): 161–93.

Maxwell, Mary. 1990. *Morality Among Nations: An Evolutionary View*. Suny Series in Biopolitics. Albany: State University of New York Press.

Maynard Smith, John. 1964. "Group Selection and Kin Selection." *Nature* 201: 1145–47.

———. 1982. *Evolution and the Theory of Games*. London: Cambridge University Press.

———. 1998. "Too Good to Be True." *Nature* 400(6741): 223.

Maynard Smith, John, and Eörs Szathmáry. 1995. *The Major Transitions in Evolution*. Oxford: W. H. Freeman Spektrum.

McClennen, Edward F. 1990. *Rationality and Dynamic Choice: Foundational Explorations*. New York: Cambridge University Press.

Mealey, Linda. 1995. "Sociopathy." *Behavioral and Brain Sciences* 18(3): 523–99.

Midgley, Mary. 1994. *The Ethical Primate: Humans, Freedom, and Morality*. London: Routledge.

Mill, John Stuart. 1848. *Principles of Political Economy*. London: John W. Parker.

Miller, Geoffrey F. 2000. *The Mating Mind: How Sexual Choice Shaped the Evolution of Human Nature*. New York: Doubleday.

Mills, Judson R., and Margaret S. Clark. 1982. "Communal and Exchange Relationships." In *Annual Review of Personality and Social Psychology*, edited by L. Wheeler. Beverly Hills, Calif.: Sage.

———. 1994. "Communal and Exchange Relationships: Controversies and Research." In *Theoretical Frameworks for Personal Relationships*, edited by Ralph Erber and Robin Gilmour. Hillsdale, N.J.: Lawrence Erlbaum.

Mitchell, Robert W., and Nicholas S. Thompson. 1986. *Deception: Perspectives on Human and Nonhuman Deceit*. New York: State University of New York Press.

Moore, David W. 1999. *Divided on Origins of Human Species*. Gallup Organization Reports.

Nesse, Randolph M. 1990a. "Evolutionary Explanations of Emotions." *Human Nature* 1(3): 261–89.

———. 1990b. "The Evolutionary Functions of Repression and the Ego Defenses." *Journal of the American Academy of Psychoanalysis* 18(2): 260–85.

———. 1999. "The Evolution of Hope and Despair." *Journal of Social Issues* 66(2): 429–69.

Nesse, Randolph M., and Allen T. Lloyd. 1992. "The Evolution of Psychodynamic Mechanisms." In *The Adapted Mind: Evolutionary Psychology and the Generation of Culture*, edited by J. H. Barkow, L. Cosmides, and J. Tooby. New York: Oxford University Press.

Nisbett, Richard E., and Dov Cohen. 1996. *Culture of Honor: The Psychology of Violence in the South, New Directions in Social Psychology*. Boulder, Colo.: Westview Press.

Nitecki, Matthew H., and Doris V. Nitecki. 1993. *Evolutionary Ethics*. Suny Series in Philosophy and Biology. Albany: State University of New York Press.

Nowak, Martin A., and Karl Sigmund. 2000. "Evolution of Indirect Reciprocity by Image Scoring." *Nature* 393: 573–77.

———. 1998. "Shrewd Investments." *Science* 288(5467): 819.

Oyama, Susan. 1989. "Innate Selfishness, Innate Sociality." *Behavioral and Brain Sciences* 12(4): 717–18.

———. 2000. *Evolution's Eye*. Durham, N.C.: Duke University Press.

Parfit, Derek. 1984. *Reasons and Persons*. Oxford: Clarendon.

Petrinovich, Lewis F. 1995. *Human Evolution, Reproduction, and Morality*. New York: Plenum Press.

Radcliffe-Richards, Janet. 2000. *Human Nature After Darwin: A Philosophical Introduction*. New York: Routledge.

Rawls, John. 1971. *A Theory of Justice*, vol. HP 27, a Harvard Paperback. Cambridge, Mass.: Belknap Press of Harvard University Press.

Richards, Robert John. 1987. *Darwin and the Emergence of Evolutionary Theories of Mind and Behavior*. Chicago: University of Chicago Press.

———. 1993. "Birth, Death and Resurrection of Evolutionary Ethics." In *Evolutionary Ethics*, edited by M. H. Nitecki and D. V. Nitecki. Albany, N.Y.: State University of New York Press.

Richerson, Peter J., and Robert Boyd. 1999. "Complex Societies: The Evolutionary Origins of a Crude Superorganism." *Human Nature* 10(3): 253–89.

Ridley, Matt. 1997. *The Origins of Virtue: Human Instincts and the Evolution of Cooperation*. New York: Viking.

Rose, Hilary, and Steven Rose, eds. 2000. *Alas, Poor Darwin: Arguments Against Evolutionary Psychology*. New York: Harmony Books.

Rose, Michael R., and George V. Lauder, eds. 1996. *Adaptation*. San Diego: Academic Press.

Roth, Alvin E., Vesna Prasnikar, M. Okuno-Fujiwara, and S. Zamir. 1991. "Bargaining and Market Behavior in Jerusalem, Ljubljana, Pittsburgh and Tokyo: An Experimental Study." *American Economic Review* 81(5): 1068–95.

Rue, Loyal D. 1989. *Amythia: Crisis in the Natural History of Western Culture*. Tuscaloosa: University of Alabama Press.

Runciman, W. G., John Maynard Smith, and Robin I. M. Dunbar, eds. 1996.

Evolution of Social Behaviour Patterns in Primates and Man. New York: British Academy/Oxford University Press.

Ruse, Michael. 1982. *Darwinism Defended: A Guide to the Evolution Controversies*. Reading, Mass.: Addison-Wesley.

———. 1986. *Taking Darwin Seriously: A Naturalistic Approach to Philosophy*. New York: Blackwell.

———. 1989. *The Darwinian Paradigm*. London: Routledge.

Schelling, Thomas C. 1960. *The Strategy of Conflict*. Cambridge, Mass.: Harvard University Press.

———. 1978a. "Altruism, Meanness, and Other Potentially Strategic Behaviors." In *Choice over Time*, edited by G. Loewenstein and J. Elster. New York: Russell Sage Foundation.

———. 1978b. "Egonomics, or the Art of Self-Management." *American Economic Review: Papers and Proceedings* 68: 290–94.

———. In press. "Commitment." In *New Palgrave Dictionary of Economics and the Law*, edited by P. Newman. New York: Macmillan.

Schwartz, Barry. 1986. *The Battle for Human Nature: Science, Morality and Modern Life*. New York: Norton.

Segerstråle, Ullica C. O. 2000. *Defenders of the Truth*. New York: Oxford University Press.

Simon, Herbert A. 1990. "A Mechanism for Social Selection and Successful Altruism." *Science* 250: 1665–68.

Singer, Peter. 2000. *A Darwinian Left: Politics, Evolution, and Cooperation*. New Haven: Yale University Press.

Skyrms, Brian. 1996. *Evolution of the Social Contract*. New York: Cambridge University Press.

Smith, Adam. *The Theory of the Moral Sentiments*. 1984 [1759]. Edited by D. D. Raphael and A. L. Macfie. Indianapolis: Liberty Classics.

Smuts, Barbara B. 1999. "Multilevel Selection, Cooperation, and Altruism: Reflection on Unto Others." *Human Nature* 10(3): 311–27.

Sober, Elliott, and David Sloan Wilson. 1998. *Unto Others: The Evolution and Psychology of Unselfish Behavior*. Cambridge, Mass.: Harvard University Press.

Sperber, Dan. 1996. *Explaining Culture: A Naturalistic Approach*. Oxford: Blackwell.

Sugden, Robert. 1993. "The Contractarian Enterprise." In *Rationality, Justice and the Social Contract: Themes from Morals by Agreement*, edited by D. P. Gauthier and R. Sugden. Ann Arbor, Mich.: University of Michigan Press.

Tooby, John, and Leda Cosmides. 1984. *Friendship, Reciprocity and the Banker's Paradox*. Institute for Technical Studies Report 1.

———. 1989. "Evolutionary Psychology and the Generation of Culture, Part I: Theoretical Considerations." *Ethology and Sociobiology* 10(1–3): 29–50.

———. 1992. "The Psychological Foundations of Culture." In *The Adapted Mind: Evolutionary Psychology and the Generation of Culture*, edited by J. H. Barkow, L. Cosmides, and J. Tooby. New York: Oxford University Press.

———. 1996. "Friendship and the Banker's Paradox: Other Pathways to the Evolution of Adaptations for Altruism." In *Evolution of Social Behaviour Patterns in Primates and Man*, edited by J. M. Smith, W. G. Runciman, and R. I. M. Dunbar. London: British Academy/Oxford University Press.

Trivers, Robert L. 1971. "The Evolution of Reciprocal Altruism." *Quarterly Review of Biology* 46: 35–57.

———. 1976. Foreword. In *The Selfish Gene*, by Richard Dawkins. New York: Oxford University Press.

———. 1981. "Sociobiology and Politics." In *Sociobiology and Human Politics*, edited by E. White. Lexington, Mass.: Lexington.

———. 1985. *Social Evolution*. Menlo Park, Calif.: Benjamin/Cummings.

Turner, Mark. 1996. *The Literary Mind*. New York: Oxford University Press.

Von Neumann, John, and Oskar Morgenstern. 1944. *Theory of Games and Economic Behavior*. Princeton, N.J.: Princeton University Press.

Wedekind, Claus, and Manfred Milinski. 2000. "Cooperation Through Image Scoring in Humans." *Science* 288: 850–52.

West-Eberhard, Mary Jane. 1987. "Sexual Selection, Social Competition, and Speciation." *Quarterly Review of Biology* 58: 155–83.

Williams, George C. 1966. *Adaptation and Natural Selection: A Critique of Some Current Evolutionary Thought*. Princeton, N. J.: Princeton University Press.

———. 1992. *Natural Selection: Domains, Levels, and Challenges*. New York: Oxford University Press.

———. 1993. "Mother Nature Is a Wicked Old Witch." In *Evolutionary Ethics*, edited by M. H. Nitecki and D. V. Nitecki. Albany: State University of New York Press.

Williams, George C., and Doris C. Williams. 1957. "Natural Selection and Individually Harmful Social Adaptations Among Sibs with Special Reference to Social Insects." *Evolution* 17: 249–53.

Wilson, David Sloan. 1975. "A General Theory of Group Selection." *Proceedings of the National Academy of Sciences* 72: 143–46.

Wilson, David Sloan, and Elliott Sober. 1994. "Reintroducing Group Selection to the Human Behavioral Sciences." *Behavioral and Brain Sciences* 17(4): 585–607.

Wilson, Edward O. 1975. *Sociobiology*. Cambridge, Mass.: Harvard University Press.

———. 1978. *On Human Nature*. Cambridge, Mass.: Harvard University Press.

———. 1998. *Consilience: The Unity of Knowledge*. New York: Knopf.

Wilson, James Q. 1993. *The Moral Sense*. New York: Free Press.

Wrangham, Richard W., and Dale Peterson. 1996. *Demonic Males: Apes and the Origins of Human Violence*. Boston: Houghton Mifflin.

Wright, Robert. 1994. *The Moral Animal: The New Science of Evolutionary Psychology*. New York: Pantheon Books.

———. 2000. *Non-Zero: The Logic of Human Destiny*. New York: Pantheon Books.

Wynne-Edwards, Vero Copner. 1962. *Animal Dispersion in Relation to Social Behavior*. Edinburgh: Oliver and Boyd.

Zak, Paul J., and Stephen Knack. 2001. "Trust and Growth." *Economic Journal* (April).

PART I

CORE IDEAS FROM ECONOMICS

T HE FIRST challenge is to define the object of inquiry. The three chapters in this section provide definitions and examples of commitment from the best possible sources: Thomas Schelling, Robert Frank, and Jack Hirshleifer, the three economists who have done the most to develop the theory. Their chapters establish a common ground for the generic idea of commitment, and reveal interesting variations in perspectives.

All of them emphasize that commitments are strategies that work by changing what others believe, and that commitments are interesting mainly when they are for actions that would not otherwise be expected. Thus, intrinsic to the idea of commitments is some uncertainty as to whether they will be fulfilled. Each of these authors agrees that a core question is why people would believe that someone would act in ways that will not be in their self-interest. They differ somewhat in emphasizing commitments based on the situation and reputation (Schelling), the role of emotions in communicating commitments (Frank), and the importance of move order effects in a variety of formal games (Hirshleifer).

Schelling notes that there are many ways to commit to a threat. His elegant prose describes nearly the same factors that make up my list, in the first chapter, of core reasons why people would believe commitments: the situation is self-enforcing; a third party; reputation; and emotions. His emphasis is on the power of a credible threat. He attends carefully to the effectiveness of probabilistic threats, an avenue that seems likely to be very productive in helping to explain the paradox that people often believe other's commitments to act in irrational ways. He also nicely distinguishes the differences between getting committed, being committed, and being the kind of person whose commitments are worthy of respect.

Following directly from the importance of credibility, reputation occupies the core of the argument for all three authors. Commitments enforced by situations or by contracts are useful and interesting, but not paradoxical; I have called them *secured*; Hirshleifer calls them *rational*. Commitments get really interesting when they are based on reputation or emotions: Hirshleifer calls them *emotional*, but I prefer to call them *subjective* commitments because they may not involve any experienced emotion. If people believe that you will keep your promises and fulfill your threats, you are a formidable social player. If they think your commitments may be mere bluffing, you will have a very limited ability to inspire the most potent emotions, love and fear. I predict that studies of commitment will advance rapidly as they begin to intersect with other studies of reputation. Reputation is the key to understanding social complexity. A reputation for certain kinds of irrationality may offer advantages beyond any ability to calculate rational strategy.

The flip side of credibility is deception. In the best tradition of economists and evolutionists all three authors consider the costs and benefits of fulfilling versus abandoning commitments, and the challenge of assessing whether others will keep theirs. This seemingly cynical perspective may put some readers off, but it should not. The authors are not saying that people should not keep their word, they are asking why people so often do, given the frequent benefits of breaking it. Traditional economists view humans as specimens of *Homo economicus*, a rational strategizer who does whatever maximizes individual utility. These three chapters agree that promises and threats somehow in the long run must confer benefit. Yet they take issue with the core assumption of most economics by suggesting that people often behave according to principles and promises even when that is not in their obvious self-interest. This is a very serious challenge indeed, and the time seems to be ripe for it. As each author notes, mounting data, especially from behavioral economics, demonstrates that people in fact do not behave according to the predictions of game theory. They cooperate too early and too much, and when crossed, they spend excessive resources to punish the offender. This data poses problems for economics that commitment may help to explain. If people are designed to pursue relationships based on commitment, not calculation, then many of these results make perfect sense.

These chapters, for all their clarity, also reveal that the concept of commitment is not as simple as it may seem. There is room yet for efforts to agree on a common definition. Schelling emphasizes situations in which circumstances make it worthwhile to fulfill a commitment, while also noting the power of reputation, including a reputation for apparently irrational actions. Frank agrees, but slants his presentation more toward the role of emotions as communication signals that can help others assess the genuineness of a commitment, rational or irrational. He also makes careful note of research that demonstrates that a society's beliefs about whether others will fulfill commitments is a potent factor that influences how actual social relationships transpire. This makes questions about commitments of great practical and moral significance. Hirshleifer presents his argument in the context of a formal model, which is perhaps the only way the concept will be nailed down sufficiently to support extensive research. While those who do not know some economics or game theory will find it challenging, those who do will appreciate the rigor. This approach allows Hirshleifer to distinguish two rather different concepts of commitment. *Preemptive* commitment consists of being the first to make an irrevocable action move, thus facing the opposing party with a fait accompli (for example, burning your bridges behind you). Hirshleifer distinguishes this from *reactive* commitment, which is a promise to respond in a specified way to the opponent's prior action move. Thus, promises and threats (and combinations thereof) are reactive commitments. For either type of commitment, the key is giving up options, or what is the same thing, leaving the opponent with (as Schelling describes it) "the last clear chance to decide the outcome." This framework allows clear definitions of threats versus promises, and allows calculation of the effects of varying degrees of credibility.

The reader should not expect complete congruence among these chapters. Having all three somewhat different perspectives gives a realistic view of the breadth of the concept of commitment, and the work that remains to be done to understand it. Likewise, while the chapters taken together are quite convincing about the importance of commitment, it is essential to recognize the depth of the challenge they offer to simpler views of human action that are often cited by economists and evolutionists. If their arguments are valid, the implications are substantial.

Chapter 2

Commitment:
Deliberate Versus Involuntary

Thomas C. Schelling

ORTY-ONE years ago I wrote about commitment (Schelling 1960a), and some colleagues have conjectured that I originated the concept. While this pleases me, I must decline. I was scooped by at least 2,400 years. When the Greek, Xenophon, pursued by Persians, halted against an almost impassable ravine, one of his generals expressed alarm that they would have no escape. Xenophon reassured him.

> As for the argument that . . . we are putting a difficult ravine in our rear just when we are going to fight, is not this really something that we ought to jump at? I should like the enemy to think it easy going in every direction for him to retreat; but we ought to learn from the very position in which we are placed that there is no safety for us except in victory. (Xenophon 1957)

Elsewhere in similar circumstances Xenophon notes that when retreat is impossible, no soldier need fear that while he is preoccupied with the enemy his companions in arms will desert him; the commitment is thus to each other, as well as toward the enemy.

I use *commitment* to mean becoming committed, bound, or obligated to some course of action or inaction or to some constraint on future action. To commit is to relinquish some options, eliminate some choices, surrender some control over one's future behavior—and doing so with a purpose. The purpose is to influence someone else's choices. Commitment does so by affecting that other person's expectations of one's behavior.

Commitment is pertinent to promises and threats, both overt and implicit, and to many bargaining tactics. A take it or leave it offer, for example, requires some commitment to be credible, and commitment may not be easy to arrange. A threat to take someone expensively to court to recover modest damages may not be credible, hence not persuasive, unless the person or organization making the threat can show a believable commitment.

Creating Commitment

Xenophon's device was simple: get yourself in a position where it is physically impossible, and manifestly so to your adversary, to do other than what you want your adversary to believe you must do.

The ways to commit to a threat, like the ways to commit to a promise, are many. Legally, one files suit. Reputationally, one takes a public position. Physically, one gathers speed before an intersection. Emotionally, one becomes obsessed. Locationally, one occupies a position from which retreat is impossible ("burns bridges"). One can rely on a third party: "I'll be punished (divorced, fired, foreclosed, exposed, liquidated) if I don't." In the film *Dr. Strangelove* the doomsday machine was set to cover the world automatically with lethal radioactivity if its sensors detected some number of atomic bomb detonations in Soviet territory. In Europe NATO forces were positioned where (it appeared) they could not avoid triggering nuclear war if attacked from the east. Such a commitment, of course, works only if the intended recipient knows of it and believes it. The *Strangelove* device was a faulty stratagem: it was kept secret, but couldn't deter an American attack unless it was known about (and known to be impossible to disconnect in the event of an attack).

Probabilistic Commitment

Usually a commitment is credible only if firm and inflexible: "If you lend me the money I will probably pay you back" doesn't sound quite like commitment. "If you come one step closer I may shoot" leaves too easy a way out. Still, there can be commitments of a probabilistic sort.

One familiar example is tailgating. Nobody is intimidated by a tailgater until he is close enough to be dangerous. An eighteen-inch distance is okay as long as nothing goes wrong; but at seventy miles an hour on a crowded beltway something can always go wrong—and if something goes wrong, lives are at stake. The tailgater has no more interest in a fatal crash than I do; he will use all of his driving skills, if something goes wrong, to save us both. Yet we both know that all of his driving skills may not suffice: we both might end up dead. By coming close the other driver puts me on notice. If I don't wish to accommodate, I have to consider how long it will take to make the driver back off and whether that is longer than I want to risk it; I may sense that the tailgater believes I'll eventually change lanes and can hold out longer than I. "Buzzing" an airplane to make it change course or land invokes the same principle: flying close enough for collision to be a genuine possibility is the commitment.

The Cuban Missile Crisis offers a perfect example. The president's decision to impose a naval blockade against Soviet vessels approaching Cuba was recognized to threaten the risk of nuclear war. Evidently nuclear war was the last thing either side wanted; evidently no outcome of the crisis could have been worse than nuclear war; evidently the president and his executive committee believed the blockade to carry the possibility of a nuclear war that neither side would ever deliberately undertake; evidently they believed that things could get beyond control once the blockade was under way. They considered the risk tolerable for what was at stake; they hoped the Soviets would find it intolerable for what was at stake. The blockade itself was the (probabilistic) commitment. (In 1959 I coined the phrase "the threat that leaves something to chance," which occasionally shows up in the literature of diplomacy and defense [Schelling 1960b, 187–203].)

This tactic is even older than Xenophon's. The modern version is called "Chicken": two drivers head for each other to see who will swerve aside first; the one who does is called chicken. The earliest account I have come across, in a race with horse-drawn chariots, antedates the auto by some time:

> The road here led through a gully, and in one part the winter flood had broken down part of the road and made a hollow. Menelaos was driving in the middle of the road, hoping that no one would try to pass too close to his wheel, but Antilochos turned his horses out of the track and followed him a little to one side. This frightened Menelaos, and he shouted at him: "What reckless driving Antilochos! Hold in your horses. This place is narrow, soon you will have more room to pass. You will foul my car and destroy us both!"
>
> But Antilochos only plied the whip and drove faster than ever, as if he did not hear. They raced about as far as the cast of a quoit . . . and then [Menelaos] fell behind: he let the horses go slow himself, for he was afraid that they might all collide in that narrow space and overturn the cars and fall in a struggling heap. (Homer 1950, 273)

This game of Chicken took place outside the gates of Troy three thousand years ago. Antilochos won, though Homer says—somewhat ungenerously—"by trick, not by merit" (Homer 1950, 273).

Promises

Promises, like threats, usually require some commitment, especially if the promise is conditional on some reciprocal performance by the recipient (beneficiary) of the promise. Some people feel honor bound to certain promises; some can swear by a god; some can put their reputations on the line. It helps if the party promised can believe in the honor, the religious fealty, or the value of the reputation of the person promising.

In extreme cases—in Alfred Hitchcock, anyway—a witness to a crime may volunteer to be blinded as a promise not to be able to testify, or may reveal a horrid secret with which he can be blackmailed, or commit a crime in the presence of those to whom he wants to promise silence, leaving evidence they can use against him. In a John Collier story televised by Hitchcock, an inadvertent eavesdropper on a murder is offered the choice between joining the body down the well or grasping the murder weapon firmly, thereby leaving his fingerprints. Eunuchs, another example of a certain promise, often were favored with the best jobs because of what they were committed not to do.

Promises also include acts that are not primarily verbal and that can be appreciated by a second party. The pawnshop pledge is an example. Taking hostages is another. Until that term lost its traditional definition in the last couple of decades—coming to mean any prisoner or victim of kidnaping—a hostage was "a person held as security for the fulfillment of certain terms," and by another definition, "a person held by one party in a conflict as a pledge that promises will be kept or terms met by the other party." Hostages are sometimes freely given as pledges, sometimes taken to enforce a pledge. When Caesar's soldiers conquered unruly tribes in Gaul, they took children as hostages to enforce the good behavior of the remaining villagers. That hostages should be taken was in the villagers' interest; the alternative, to ensure tranquility, would have been to kill the men. During the half century before 1989, Soviet visitors to the west, even on extended visits, went without family to guarantee good behavior and return.

Threats

Here threat is used to mean a commitment, or intended commitment, to a conditional act—conditioned on the performance or behavior of the object of the threat—that one would not ordinarily be motivated to carry out. If I have every reason to sue for damages in the event you do me harm, saying so is not a threat: it is merely a communication, what I call a warning. Arranging incentives so that I must sue whether I want to or not and communicating that I must do so is the threat; if I am an insurance company, I need my reputation for suing, which I may lose if on any occasion I neglect to follow through. That my threat be believed therefore is always in my interest. Not to be actually committed would, however, usually be in my interest: if despite the threat you misbehave (not knowing of the threat or not believing it, or for some reason being incapable of what I thought you were capable of), carrying out the threat likely serves no purpose and is costly. Consequently, any threat may be suspected of being a bluff; and so with many promises: I want my promises believed, especially when their purpose is to elicit some reciprocal performance. Usually the promise entails some cost or sacrifice on my part that I'd prefer not to incur, except in consideration of the reciprocity; so there can be suspicion that my promise is not truly committed. I may be faking, making an insincere promise, one I actually cannot carry out or, able to carry out, do not intend to.

Personal Credibility

Credibility is the issue here. Commitments, deliberately incurred to influence the behavior of others, must be believed in order to have influence. Institutions such as the law of contracts help make performance credible: coercion, incurred voluntarily (perhaps via contract), is at one end of the scale, while friendship and personal loyalty, love and devotion, honor, or the love or fear of God are at the other end. Just as people may consciously and deliberately commit themselves with a gamut of techniques and arrangements to influence others' behavior—whether for personal benefit or the common good—so too does a spectrum of personal traits, qualities, abilities, and techniques (including constraints as well as capabilities) allow them to become credibly committed through *who and what they are* rather than through *what they deliberately do* for the sake of commitment.

To illustrate, in Joseph Conrad's (1923) *The Secret Agent*, anarchists plot to destroy Greenwich Observatory. They get their nitroglycerin from "the professor," a stunted little chemist. The authorities know who provides the stuff, but this chemist walks the London streets with immunity. A young man tied in with the Greenwich job is in wonderment: Why, he asks, don't the police apprehend him? The professor answers that the police may not shoot him from a safe distance, for that would be a denial of the "bourgeois morality" that the anarchists want to discredit—and they dare not try to capture him, since he always keeps some of the "stuff" on his person. He keeps his right hand in his trouser pocket, holding a hollow ball at the end of a tube that reaches a container of nitroglycerin in his jacket. All he has to do is press that little ball and anybody near will be blown to bits. The young man wonders why the police would ever believe anything so preposterous as the professor's threat to blow himself up. The stunted chemist's explanation is calm. "In the last instance it is character alone that makes for one's safety. . . . I have the means to make myself deadly, but that by itself, you understand, is absolutely nothing in the way of protection. What is effective is the belief those people have in my will to use the means. That's their impression. It is absolute. Therefore I am deadly" (65–68).

Conrad intended that we believe the professor truly would destroy himself. We can deduce that he's never been tested: if the police had laid hands on him and he hadn't immolated himself, they wouldn't be avoiding him now, and if they had laid hands on him and he had detonated the nitroglycerin, they would have new respect for his spirit but he wouldn't be around for the Greenwich escapade. He could be bluffing, but he doesn't sound like it. To me it is plausible that there are people with the "character" he claims, and "the belief those people have in my will to use the means" is crucial. Rigging the nitroglycerin in his clothing is deliberate; being the kind of person who would actually detonate the nitroglycerin is not.

In the language of this book the chemist is certainly committed. Yet he didn't commit himself. He simply *is* committed. In "The Art of Commitment" (Schelling 1966, 35–91) I wrote about *getting* committed, which is different from *being* committed. We doubt that the professor got himself committed—incurred his commitment, arranged his commitment, negotiated his commitment. He didn't make himself the kind of person who would blow himself up rather than surrender; he just is that kind of person. We might diagnose pride, honor, obstinacy, destiny, identity; he himself might not know why he's that kind of person.

Sources of Commitment

We cannot tell—I cannot, anyway—whether the chemist is "hard wired" biologically to be so obstinately determined or has been conditioned by experience and surrounding culture. An interesting contrast, at the level of group rather than individual, is the "character" of the sixteenth-century Swiss, who acquired similar respect by the way they lost battles as well as the way they sometimes won them.

> The [Swiss] Confederates were able to reckon their reputation for obstinate and invincible courage as one of the chief causes which gave them

political importance. . . . It was no light matter to engage with an enemy who would not retire before any superiority in numbers, who was always ready for a fight, who would neither give nor take quarter. (Oman 1953, 96)

The Swiss evidently recognized the value of reputation—costly to acquire but invaluable once acquired. It is also evident that a propensity for such behavior could become embedded in their culture and cease to be only strategically instrumental. The professor may have been uniquely genetically different from the rest of us, the sixteenth-century Swiss probably not.

The subject of this book is whether for human beings the value of being recognized as the kind of person who keeps his commitments purely on the basis of his own character and emotional make-up, not by rearranging incentives or external constraints, could be so great in interpersonal relations that those with a slight genetic proclivity to be that kind of person, and to communicate that proclivity, would enjoy enhanced reproductive success, and the genetic propensity would proliferate and become embedded in the species.

Being Versus Becoming

I distinguish between being committed and becoming committed. Some people simply *are* trustworthy, trusting, vengeful, charitable, faithful, grudge bearing, forgiving, vindictive, hot-tempered, stubborn, easygoing, brave, persevering; imbued with pride, honor, hatred, cruelty, or kindliness; passionately identified with tribe, race, language, gender, class; devoted to a deity, fearful of God, believing in a consequential afterlife, capable of calling on God as a witness ("cross my heart"); and often they are so recognized, at least by some. The hypothesis of this book is that many of these recognizable traits are advantageous on balance, although some may make a person vulnerable.

Becoming is the ability to adopt for the occasion the capacity for recognizable commitment. One who by nature turns the other cheek may be able to swear resistance and retaliation when it seems crucial; one who abhors violence may be able to threaten punishment; one who is known to be devious and selfish may be able to commit convincingly to loyalty or honesty when it most matters; one who is normally hard to arouse may become incensed when presented with certain challenges. *Becoming* committed probably is more strategic—that is, less a matter of abiding character than rising to the occasion.

Becoming apparently is more optional than *being*. A proclivity to lose my temper may be an occasional advantage, perhaps more often a disadvantage, in interpersonal relations. Being able to lose it when this serves my purpose (to make threats credible, even unspoken threats, whether dealing with mischievous children or adults—especially if I can keep my temper when losing it would not be advantageous) can have genuine instrumental value.

Becoming and being overlap. If I am devoted to a deity or belong to a culture of honor that obliges fealty to any sworn obligation, I *become* committed only if I swear, but I *am* the kind of person who can swear credibly.

A Genetic Basis?

The evidence is overwhelming that some people truly are committed, and are recognized as committed, to certain performances. Less obvious is that genetic inheritance is a significant contributor. People can behave strategically, knowing, for example, the value of maintaining a reputation for good behavior. People can be dedicated to a deity that issues commandments. People can be reared in a culture that gives them little choice about some behaviors, whether truthful, vengeful, or self-sacrificing. And people can be biologically predisposed, in a visible way, to behave in ways that are advantageous if anticipated. Just as people wisely avoid disturbing a mother bear with cubs, they can wisely avoid antagonizing a large man known to be easily enraged.

Bluffing

Evolutionary theory suggests that if the human race acquired a capacity for persuasive commitment, it may also have acquired a capacity for faking. And if faking becomes a significant phenomenon, the race may have developed at least some capacity to detect falsity. The rest of the essays in this book no doubt will pursue some of these fascinating issues.

I conclude with the advice Daniel Schorr received upon succeeding Edward R. Murrow, dean of television commentators: "The secret to success in television broadcasting is sincerity. If you can fake that, you've got it made."

References

Conrad, Joseph. 1923. *The Secret Agent*. New York: Doubleday.
Homer. 1950. *The Iliad*, translated by W. H. D. Rouse. London: Mentor Books.
Oman, C. W. C. 1953. *The Art of War in the Middle Ages*. Ithaca, N.Y.: Cornell University Press.

Schelling, T. C. 1960a. *The Strategy of Conflict*. Cambridge, Mass.: Harvard University Press.

———. 1960b. *The Strategy of Conflict*. Cambridge, Mass.: Harvard University Press.

———. 1966. *Arms and Influence*. New Haven: Yale University Press.

Xenophon. 1957. *The Persian Expedition*, translated by Rex Warner. New York: Penguin Books.

Chapter 3

Cooperation Through Emotional Commitment

ROBERT H. FRANK

T HE IDEA that people can improve their lot by making commitments that restrict their options has received considerable attention from economists and philosophers (Schelling 1960, 1978; Akerlof 1983; Parfit 1984; Gauthier 1985; Sen 1985; Frank 1987, 1988; Hirshleifer 1987; McClennan 1990; Gibbard 1990). The most vivid illustration remains an early example offered by Schelling (1960), who described a kidnapper who suddenly gets cold feet. He wants to set his victim free but is afraid the victim will go to the police. In return for his freedom the victim gladly promises not to do so. The problem, however, is that both realize it will no longer be in the victim's interest to keep this promise once he is free. So the kidnapper reluctantly concludes that he must kill the victim.

The kidnapper and his victim confront a commitment problem, and to solve it they need a commitment device, something that gives the victim an incentive to keep his promise. Schelling (1960, 43, 44) suggests the following way out: "If the victim has committed an act whose disclosure could lead to blackmail, he may confess it; if not, he might commit one in the presence of his captor, to create a bond that will ensure his silence." Keeping his promise will still be unpleasant for the victim once he is freed, but clearly less so than not being able to make a credible promise in the first place.

In Schelling's example the blackmailable offense is an effective commitment device because it changes the victim's material incentives in the desired way. Is it also possible to solve commitment problems by means of less tangible changes in incentives? Can moral emotions, for example, function as commitment devices? And if so, what evidence might persuade a skeptic that natural selection had favored such emotions at least in part for that reason? These questions are my focus in this discussion. A first step in trying to answer them will be to adopt a common language. In what follows the term *contractual commitments* describes commitments facilitated by contracts (formal or informal) that alter material incentives. Schelling's parable is an example of contractual commitment. The term *emotional commitments* describes commitments facilitated by emotions.

Two Examples

What kinds of problems are contractual commitments and emotional commitments meant to solve? I will discuss two illustrative examples. The first is a commitment problem typically solved by legal contracts, while the second is one for which such contracts are not quite up to the task.

Consider first the problem of searching for an apartment. You have just moved to a new city, and you need a place to live. If you are in Los Angeles or some other metropolis, you cannot possibly inspect each of the thousands of vacant apartments, so you check the listings and visit a few to get a rough idea of what is available—the range of prices, amenities, locations, and other features you care about. As your search proceeds, you find a unit that seems unusually attractive on the basis of your impressions of the relevant distributions. You want to close the deal. At that point, you *know* there is a better apartment out there somewhere, but your time is too valuable to justify looking further. You want to get on with your life.

Having made that decision, the next important step is to make a commitment with the owner of the apartment. You do not want to move in and then a month later be told to leave. After all, by then you will have bought some curtains, hung your art on the walls, installed phone and cable service, and so on. If you are forced to leave, not only will those investments be for naught, but you also will have to begin searching anew for a place to live.

The landlord too has an interest in seeing you stay for an extended period, since he went to a lot of trouble and expense to rent the apartment. He advertised it and showed it to dozens of other prospective tenants, none of whom seemed quite as stable and trustworthy as you.

The upshot is that even though you know there is a better apartment out there, and even though your landlord knows that a better tenant will eventually come along, you both have a strong interest in committing yourselves to ignore such opportunities. The standard so-lution is to sign a formal lease—a contractual commitment that pre-vents each of you from accepting other offers that might later prove attractive. If you move out, you still must pay your rent for the dura-tion of the lease. If your landlord asks you to leave, the lease em-powers you to refuse.

The ability to commit by signing a lease raises the amount a tenant would be willing to pay for any given apartment, and reduces the amount that its owner would be willing to accept. Without the secu-rity provided by this contractual commitment, many valuable ex-changes would not occur. Leases foreclose valuable options, to be sure; but that is exactly what the signatories want them to do.

The person searching for a mate confronts an essentially similar commitment problem. You want a mate, but not just any old mate. In the hope of meeting that special someone you accept additional social invitations, and make other efforts to expand your circle of friends. After dating for a while, you feel you know a fair amount about what kinds of people are out there—what sorts of dispositions they have, their ethical values, their cultural and recreational interests, their so-cial and professional skills, and so on. Among the people you meet, you are drawn to one in particular. Your luck holds, and that person feels the same way about you. You both want to move forward and start investing in your relationship. You want to get married, buy a house, have children. Few of these investments make sense, however, unless you both expect your relationship to continue for an extended period.

Yet what if something goes wrong? No matter what your mate's vision of the ideal partner may be, you know there's someone out there who comes closer to that ideal than you. What if that someone suddenly shows up? Or what if one of you falls ill? Just as landlords and tenants can gain by committing themselves, partners in marriage have a similar interest in foreclosing future options.

The marriage contract is one way of attempting to achieve the de-sired commitment. On reflection, however, we see that a legal con-tract is not particularly well-suited for creating the kind of commit-ment both parties want in this situation. Even fiercely draconian legal sanctions can at most force people to remain with spouses they would prefer to leave; but marriage on such terms hardly serves the goals each partner had originally hoped to achieve.

A far more secure commitment results if the legal contract is rein-forced by emotional bonds of affection. The plain fact is that many relationships are not threatened when a new potential partner who is kinder, wealthier, more charming, and better looking comes along.

Someone who has become deeply emotionally attached to his or her spouse does not *want* to pursue new opportunities, even ones that, in purely objective terms, might seem more promising.

That is not to say that emotional commitments are failsafe. Who among us would not experience at least mild concern on hearing that his wife was having dinner with Ralph Fiennes this evening, or that her husband was having a drink with Gwyneth Paltrow? Yet even imperfect emotional commitments free most couples from such concerns most of the time.

Again, the important point is that even though emotional commitments foreclose potentially valuable opportunities, they also confer important benefits. An emotional commitment to one's spouse is valuable in the coldly rational Darwinian cost-benefit calculus because it promotes fitness-enhancing investments. Note, however, the ironic twist. These commitments work best when they deflect people from thinking explicitly about their spousal relationships in cost-benefit terms. People who consciously approach those relationships in score-keeping terms are much less satisfied with their marriages than others; and when therapists try to get people to think in cost-benefit terms about their relationships, it often seems to backfire (Murstein, Cerreto, and MacDonald 1977). This just may not be the way we're *meant* to think about close personal relationships.

Sustainable Cooperation

Solving commitment problems is important not only for successful pair bonding but also for achieving a variety of other forms of cooperation. Indeed the prisoner's dilemma—the ubiquitous metaphor for the difficulty of achieving cooperation among rational, self-interested individuals—is in essence a simple commitment problem. Both players in a prisoner's dilemma get higher payoffs when they both cooperate than when they both defect, yet no matter which choice one player makes, the other can get a still higher payoff by defecting. When each player defects, however, each receives a lower payoff than if both had cooperated, hence the dilemma. Each player would be happy to join a mutual commitment to cooperate if he could. But when such commitments cannot be made, the dominant strategy is to defect.

The metaphor is a powerful one: it helps to explain the generally pessimistic tone of evolutionary biologists who have written on the subject of altruism and cooperation. Consider a population consisting of two distinct types of people, cooperators and defectors, who earn their living by interacting with one another in a game whose payoffs take the form of a prisoner's dilemma. When interacting with others, cooperators always cooperate and defectors always defect. Both types do best when they interact with cooperators. If the two types looked exactly the same, though, they would interact with other individuals at random. And since defection is the dominant strategy in the prisoner's dilemma, defectors always would receive a higher expected payoff than cooperators in these random interactions. By virtue of their higher payoffs, defectors would eventually drive cooperators to extinction—hence the standard result in behavioral biology that genuine cooperation or altruism cannot survive in competitive environments.

If the same individuals face a prisoner's dilemma repeatedly, cooperation often can be sustained, because individuals will have future opportunities to retaliate against those who defect in the current round (Rapoport and Chammah 1965; Trivers 1971; Axelrod and Hamilton 1981; Axelrod 1984). But although cooperation motivated by threat of punishment is surely better than none at all, such behavior does not really capture what we mean by genuine cooperation. When cooperative play is favored by ordinary material incentives, as when interactions are repeated, it is more aptly called prudence than cooperation.

Writers in the standard tradition seem to agree that universal defection is the expected outcome in prisoner's dilemmas that are not repeated. Yet examples abound in which people cooperate in one-shot prisoner's dilemmas. Waiters usually provide good service in restaurants located on interstate highways, and diners in those restaurants usually leave the expected tip at meal's end, even though both realize they are unlikely ever to see each other again. People return wallets they find on street corners, often anonymously, and usually with the cash intact. Millions of people brave long lines and unpleasant November weather to vote in presidential elections, even though they know their individual votes will not be decisive, even in a contest as close as the one for Florida's twenty-five electoral votes in 2000.

The pessimistic conclusion that genuine cooperation is impossible would be reversed completely if cooperators and defectors could somehow be distinguished from one another at a glance. Suppose, for example, that cooperators had a birthmark on their foreheads in the form of a red C, and that defectors had a birthmark in the shape of a red D (or no birthmark at all). Then those with a C on their foreheads could pair off together and reap the higher payoff from mutual cooperation. The defectors would be left to interact with one another. In this situation the defectors are the ones who would be driven to extinction.

If experience is any guide, however, this optimistic conclusion is also flawed. Although millions of public radio listeners make generous contributions to support the programming they enjoy, substantially larger numbers free ride; and at least some people keep the cash in the wallets they find on sidewalks.

To describe the mixture of motives and behavior we actually observe, we need an intermediate model, one in which cooperators and defectors are observably different in some way, but not transparently so. We may have some idea of whether a specific individual is likely to cooperate in the prisoner's dilemma, but we cannot be sure.

As Adam Smith and David Hume realized, the emotion of sympathy is a good candidate for the moral sentiment that motivates cooperation in social dilemmas. Your goal as an individual is to interact with someone who feels sympathy for your interests, in the hope that such a person will be internally motivated to cooperate, even though he could earn more by defecting.

Yet how do you know whether someone feels sympathy for your interests? Darwin (1965 [1872]) wrote of the hardwired link between emotional states in the brain and various details of involuntary facial expression and body language. Consider this crude drawing:

The drawing shows only a few details of a facial expression, yet people in every culture recognize even this simple abstraction as an expression of sadness, distress, sympathy, or some other closely related emotion. Most people cannot produce this expression on command (Ekman 1985); sit in front of a mirror and try it. Yet the muscles of the human face create the expression automatically when the relevant emotion is experienced (Darwin 1965 [1872]). Suppose you stub your toe painfully in front of someone, leading that person to manifest the expression in sympathy. Such a person is more likely to be a trustworthy trading partner than someone who reacts to your injury without expression.

Simple facial expressions, of course, are not the only clues on which we rely, or even the most important ones. In ways I will describe, we construct character judgments over extended periods on the basis of a host of other subtle signals, many of which enter only subconscious awareness. On the basis of these impressions, we choose among potential trading partners those we feel are most likely to weigh not just their own interests when making a decision but our own interests as well.

As Schelling and others have pointed out, defectors have an obvious incentive to mimic whatever signs we use for identifying reliable trading partners. Selection pressure should strongly favor capacities for effective deception, and examples of such capacities clearly abound in human affairs. If signals of emotional commitment could be mimicked perfectly and without cost, these signals eventually would cease to be useful. Over time, natural selection would mold false signals into perfect replicas of real ones, driving the capacity for signaling genuine commitment to extinction.

Whether such a capacity has been able to stay a step ahead of attempts to mimic it is an issue that is difficult to settle on a priori grounds. Granted, natural selection ought to be good at building a copy of a useful signal; but it also ought to be good at modifying an existing signal to evade mimicry. Which of these opposing tendencies wins out in the end is an empirical question, one to which I devoted considerable attention in my 1988 book. There I also argued that even if we grant the existence of reliable signals of emotional commitment, the resulting equilibrium must entail a mixed population of cooperators and defectors. In any population consisting only of co-operators no one would be vigilant, and opportunities thus would abound for defectors. In a mixed population cooperators can survive only by being sufficiently vigilant and skilled in their efforts to avoid good mimics.

Can we in fact identify people who are emotionally predisposed to cooperate? Frank, Gilovich, and Regan (1993b) present evidence from an experimental study that appears to support this possibility. In that study we found that subjects of only brief acquaintance were able to identify defectors with better than twice chance accuracy in a one-shot prisoner's dilemma game. And as the following thought experiment suggests, substantially higher accuracy rates may be possible among people who know one another well:

Imagine yourself just having returned from a crowded sporting event to discover that you have lost an envelope containing $5000 in cash from your coat pocket. (You had just cashed a check for that amount to pay for a used car you planned to pick up the next morning.) Your name

and address were written on the front of the envelope. Can you think of
anyone, not related to you by blood or marriage, who you feel certain
would return your cash if he or she found it?

Most people answer this question affirmatively. Typically the persons they name are friends of long duration, choices that seem natural for two reasons. First, the more time one spends with someone
else, the more opportunities there are to observe clues to that person's
emotional makeup. Second, the more time people spend with a friend,
the deeper their emotional bonds are likely to be. Sympathy, affection,
and other emotions that motivate trustworthy behavior are likely to
be more strongly summoned by interactions with close friends than
with perfect strangers.

Notice that although the people named are usually those with
whom we engage in repeated interactions, the particular episode involving the cash is not a repeated game: keeping the cash would not
lead to retaliation in the future, because there would be no way of
knowing that your friend had found and kept the cash. You are also
unlikely to have direct evidence regarding your friend's behavior in
similar situations in the past. When pressed, most people respond
that they chose the friends they did because they felt they knew these
people well enough to be able to say that they would want to return
the cash. The prospect of keeping a friend's cash would make them
feel so bad that it just wouldn't be worth it.

If you chose the people you named for roughly similar reasons,
then you accept the central premise of the signaling argument: that
we can identify behavioral tendencies such as trustworthiness in at
least some other people. This doesn't prove the premise is correct, but
it constitutes a hurdle for those who would persuade us otherwise.

Toward a More Realistic Model

The foregoing is a description of the simple stick-figure model laid
out in *Passions Within Reason* (Frank 1988, ch. 3). If I were writing the
book today, I would take greater care to emphasize that this model
simply cannot pretend to capture the most interesting details of the
forces that motivate cooperation in social dilemmas. For example, although the model assumes that some people are pure cooperators
and others pure defectors, most of us are in fact more complex creatures. All but the most extreme sociopaths have within them the capacity to experience sympathy for others and to weigh others' interests when deciding what to do. And although almost all of us have
cooperated in situations in which it would have paid to defect, most
of us have also let people down on occasion.

The search for a reliable trading partner is not a quest to identify an indiscriminately trustworthy individual, but rather a process of creating conditions that make us more likely to elicit cooperative tendencies in one another. In a remarkably insightful paper, Sally (2000) has summarized a large literature that bears precisely on this process. This literature also speaks to Nesse's question of how one might test the claim that moral emotions had been forged by natural selection.

The Emergence of Sympathy

Beginning with the writings of David Hume and Adam Smith, Sally traces the intellectual history of the concept of sympathy and reports on some extremely fascinating results on the mechanics of how it develops in human interactions. I use the term *mechanics* advisedly, for an important thread in the studies he reviews is that we often are remarkably mechanical in the ways we respond to stimuli.

Many of these studies remind me of a behavior that I have puzzled over for a long time, which is that I usually set my watch five minutes ahead. Not everyone does this, of course, but I know many who do. We do it because it seems to help us get to appointments on time, but *why*? When someone asks me what time it is, I always report the correct time by simply subtracting five minutes from whatever my watch says. So I am not really fooling myself by setting it ahead. Yet if I have an appointment across campus at 11:00, merely seeing a dial reading 10:55 apparently triggers an emotional reaction, which in turn gets me going a little more quickly than if I had relied only on my knowledge that the correct time was 10:50. Whatever the details of how the actual mechanism works, clearly it does work, as I know from experiments in which I have set my watch to the correct time for extended periods.

Other studies confirm the importance of seemingly mindless physical motions. For example, if you are pulling a lever toward you when an experimenter shows you a Chinese ideograph, you are much more likely to give the image a positive evaluation when you are queried about it later. If you are pushing a lever away from you when you are shown the ideograph, however, you are much more likely to give it a negative evaluation later (Cacioppo, Priester, and Berntson 1993). If you put a pen between a person's teeth—forcing him to smile, as it were—then show him a cartoon, he is much more likely to find it funny than if he does not have a pen between his teeth (Strack, Martin, and Stepper 1988).

Similar mechanical stimulus-response patterns are also strongly implicated in the processes by which sympathetic bonds form between people. An important factor in these processes is the concept of valence—an evaluation that is either positive or negative. Psychologists have identified a universal human tendency to assign an initial valence in response to virtually every category of stimulus—even words that may seem neutral, or photographs, or visual scenes of any kind (Lewin 1935; Bargh 1997).

So too with persons. When you meet another person, you make an initial up-down categorization very quickly, probably before you are even consciously aware of it (if indeed you ever become aware of it). Likeness seems to play a role in these judgments (Lazarsfeld and Merton 1954). You are more apt to assign positive valence to someone who is like you in some way—say, in dress, speech patterns, or ethnic background. Reputation matters, as does the character of your initial exchange. Distressingly, attractiveness also seems important. Physically attractive persons are far more likely than others to receive a positive initial evaluation (Eagly et al. 1991; Sally 2000).

Once the initial valence has been assigned, a biased cognitive filter appears to become activated. You still evaluate further aspects of your experience with a new acquaintance, but with a slant. If the initial evaluation is positive, you are much more likely to treat ambiguous signals in a positive light. If your initial impression is negative, though, you are more likely to assign negative interpretations to those same signals. Such positive feedback effects often make first impressions far more important than we might like them to be on ethical grounds.

A colleague once described a vivid example of how an initial negative assessment had distorted several subsequent judgments made by his three-year-old son. He had taken his son to visit Will Rogers's ancestral home, a dark, forbidding gothic structure. The boy did not want to go in, but finally gave in to his father's urgings. As they toured the house, a tape of Will Rogers reading from one of his works was playing in the background. To passages in Rogers's narrative that had an ambiguous sound or meaning, the boy seemed to assign the darkest possible interpretations. For example, when Rogers said at one point, "Well, I tried," the boy asked his father, "Why'd he die?" Time and again, the boy's interpretations were slanted to the negative.

Given the importance of such cognitive and emotional feedback effects, the development of successful personal relationships hinges powerfully on getting off to a good start. If your first experience in a relationship is positive, you engage further. But if you begin with a negative experience, things are likely to get worse.

Psychologists report that an important component of normal sympathetic responses in relationships is a subconscious impulse to mimic what your conversation partner is doing. If she smiles, you smile. If she yawns, you yawn. If she leans to one side, you lean the same way (Bavelas et al. 1986; Hatfield, Cacioppo, and Rapson 1994).

Although such mimicry turns out to be critically important, most people are not consciously aware of it. In one study, for example, a group of confederates had separate conversations with two groups of subjects—a control group in which the confederates interacted without special inhibition, and a treatment group in which the confederates made an effort not to mimic the postures and other movements and expressions of their conversation partners (Chartrand and Bargh 1998). Subjects in the treatment group reported generally negative feelings toward the experimenter's confederates, while those in the control group found the same confederates generally likable. Apart from the suppression of physical acts of mimicry in the treatment group, no other observable details of the interactions differed between groups. This finding clearly is consistent with the view that people subconsciously interpret failure to mimic as signifying a deficit of sympathy.

Studies of how the appearance of married couples evolves over time also suggest that physical mimicry is an important aspect of social interaction. In one study subjects were shown individual wedding-year photos of a large sample of men and women, and then asked to guess which men had married which women. The accuracy of their guesses was no better than chance. Yet when other subjects were given the same matching task on the basis of individual photos taken after twenty-five years of marriage, the accuracy of their guesses was far better than chance (Zajonc et al. 1987). Over the course of a quarter-century of married life, apparently, the furrow of the brow, the cast of the lip, and other subtle details of facial geography seem to converge perceptibly. I have two friends, a married couple, who have been professional storytellers for several decades. As is common among storytellers, they employ exaggerated facial expressions to highlight the emotional ebb and flow of their tales. I don't know how much they resembled one another in their youth, but people often remark on how strikingly similar they look today.

The process of bonding with another person influences and is influenced by physical proximity and orientation. Being too close invites a negative response, but so does being too far away, where too close and too far depend partly on cultural norms (Hall 1982). The gaze is also important (Sally 2000). Frequency and intensity of eye contact correlates strongly with the duration and intimacy of personal relationships (Patterson 1973). Among recent acquaintances, both extremely high levels of eye contact and extremely low levels often prove aversive. If experimenters seat subjects too close together, they will look at one another less frequently than if they are seated at a more comfortable distance (Argyle and Dean 1965).

The intensity of the initial interaction—even if purely the result of chance—has important consequences for long-term bonding. For example, combat troops under heavy shelling in the same unit corresponded with one another for many more years and much more frequently than combat troops not shelled heavily in the same engagement (Elder and Clipp 1988). The heavyweight fighters Gene Tunney and Jack Dempsey wrote to one another for years after their legendary title bouts, and did many favors for one another. They were not friends. They never even particularly liked one another, but they were thrown together in very intense circumstances that seemed to forge a bond (Heimer 1969).

Laughter also seems to be important in the development of relationships. Why do we have such a pronounced capacity to experience mirth in our interactions with one another? Most other animal species seem to lack this capacity; and even our closest relatives among primates do not have it to anything like the same degree. One possibility is that laughter not only promotes the development of social bonds, it may also be an unusually effective test of shared sympathy and understanding. People who find the same things funny often find they have many other attitudes and perceptions in common.

In short, the emergence of sympathetic bonds among people is a complex physical, cognitive, and emotional dance. People feel one another out, respond to one another, choose to develop closer bonds with some, and abandon further contact with others.

This brief account describes only a small sample of the literature surveyed in Sally's paper. Suffice to say, this literature suggests a far more complex phenomenon than the one sketched in *Passions Within Reason*. My simple stick-figure model gave the impression that some people feel sympathy toward others and some people do not, suggesting that the challenge is to interact selectively with those in the first group. Sally's insight is that it would be far more descriptive to say that most people have the capacity to experience sympathy for the interests of others *under the right circumstances*. The challenge is to forge relationships in which mutual sympathy will develop sufficiently to support cooperation.

Does Sympathy Predict Cooperation?

Substantial evidence suggests that the same factors that promote the development of sympathetic bonds between individuals also predict an increased likelihood of cooperation. A large literature, for example, documents the importance of physical proximity and communication as predictors of the likelihood of cooperation in prisoner's dilemmas (Sally 1995 offers a review). If you are sitting next to your partner and there's a screen between you so you can't see one another, you are more likely to cooperate than if you are sitting across the table with a screen between you. You are closer, physically, in the first condition, even though you can't see one another in either case; but take the screens away and the people sitting side by side are less likely to cooperate than the people who are sitting opposite one another (Gardin et al. 1973). Apparently the side-by-side pairs are sitting too close together to feel comfortable with extended eye contact, while those seated opposite one another do not suffer from this inhibition.

Many experiments have found that friends are much more likely to cooperate in social dilemmas with one another than are others of lesser acquaintance (Sally 2000 reviews several studies that confirm this finding). All else constant, the longer you have known a person, the stronger your mutual bond, and the greater your assurance of cooperation. Written exchanges among participants stimulate cooperation in prisoner's dilemma experiments, but not by nearly as much as face-to-face exchanges, even if the content of the exchanges is essentially the same (Sally 1995; Valley, Moag, and Bazerman 1998).

Considered as a whole, the evidence is consistent with an affirmative answer to our question of whether moral emotions such as sympathy facilitate commitment. This evidence does not rule out alternative interpretations conclusively, but in my view it places a substantial burden of proof on those who argue that moral emotions do not facilitate commitment.

Was the Capacity for Sympathy Forged by Natural Selection?

What about our second question: Does available evidence provide any reason to believe that natural selection favored the evolution of sympathy at least in part *because* of its ability to solve commitment problems? A moral emotion won't be favored by natural selection merely because it motivates cooperation; it must motivate cooperation in such a way that cooperation *pays*. Does sympathy meet that test? Here, too, existing studies suggest an affirmative answer.

Consider again the two conditions that must be satisfied for a moral emotion such as sympathy to facilitate mutual cooperation in one-shot prisoner's dilemmas.[1] First, the emotion must motivate players to cooperate, even though they would receive higher payoffs by defecting. Second, players must have statistically reliable means of predicting which potential trading partners will be trustworthy. Available evidence provides support for both conditions—that is, the conditions that have been shown experimentally to foster the development of sympathy also have been shown to promote cooperation in one-shot prisoner's dilemmas. Many studies also show that people are aware—sometimes unconsciously, but in ways that influence observable behavior—of the degree of sympathetic bonding that exists between themselves and others. And, as noted earlier, subjects were able to predict cooperation and defection by individual players at far better than chance accuracy in at least one experimental study (Frank, Gilovich, and Regan 1993b).

As we have seen, the development of sympathetic bonds is a process involving multiple perceptual, cognitive, and emotional capacities. These are extremely complex capacities. No one in the scientific community questions that these capacities exist in most humans; nor does anyone question that these capacities involve specialized components of the inborn neural circuitry of humans. To my knowledge, no one has offered a plausible theory other than natural selection that could account for the presence of such components.

Of course, the claim that moral emotions help solve commitment problems could be valid, even if the relevant capacities through which these emotions act were selected for altogether different purposes—just as, for example, the human capacity to produce and enjoy music could have emerged as an accidental by-product of capabilities selected for other purposes.

Indeed theoretical considerations from the animal-signaling literature suggest that moral sentiments almost certainly could not have *originated* purely because of their capacity to solve one-shot dilemmas. The basic problem is that natural selection cannot be forward-looking: it cannot recognize, for example, that a series of mutations might eventually produce an individual with the capacity to solve one-shot prisoner's dilemmas, then favor the first costly step to that end, even though it yields no immediate benefit. As I will explain, this first step presents the difficulty, because the initial appearance of a signal would have no meaning to external observers. Thus it would entail costs but no benefits—and the Darwinian rule is that a mutation must offer an immediate surplus of benefits over costs, or else be consigned to the evolutionary scrap heap.

Then how do signals ever originate? Essentially by accident, according to the derivation principle developed by Tinbergen (1952). The constraint imposed by this principle is clearly illustrated by the example of the dung beetle. The insect gets its name from the fact that it escapes predators by virtue of its resemblance to a fragment of dung. Biologists argue that this advantage cannot explain how this beetle came to resemble dung in the first place. The problem is that if we start with a species whose individuals bear not the slightest resemblance to a dung fragment, a minor mutation in the direction of a dunglike appearance would not have been of any use, since, as Gould (1977, 104) asks, ". . . can there be any edge in looking 5 percent like a turd?" A mutation toward dunglike appearance will enhance fitness only if the individual's appearance *already* happened to be similar enough to a dung fragment for the mutation to have fooled the most myopic potential predator. Thus the initial path toward near-resemblance must have been essentially a matter of chance—the result of mutations that were favored for other reasons and just happened to produce a dunglike appearance in the process. Once the resemblance crosses the recognition threshold by chance, however, natural selection can be expected to fine-tune the resemblance in the same ruthlessly effective way it fine-tunes other useful traits.

The same logic should apply to the emergence of an observable signal of a moral emotion such as sympathy. If the *only* behavioral effect of having sympathy were to motivate cooperation in one-shot prisoner's dilemmas, the first mutants with a small measure of this emotion would have enjoyed no advantage, even if their mutation happened to be accompanied by an observable signal. By virtue of its novelty, no one would have known what the signal meant, so it could not have facilitated selective interaction among sympathetic individuals. Since an undiscriminating tendency to cooperate entails costs, natural selection should have worked against sympathy, for reasons described earlier.

If sympathy and other moral emotions were favored by natural selection in their earliest stages, they must therefore have conferred some other benefit. For example, perhaps a mutant with the capacity for sympathy was a more effective parent, a fitness enhancement that might have compensated for the initial costs of an indiscriminately sympathetic posture toward unrelated individuals.

A second possibility that I explore in more depth here is that moral sentiments may function as self-control devices. In a world of perfectly rational, self-interested individuals, self-control problems would not exist. Such individuals would discount future costs and benefits at a constant exponential rate, which means that any choice that would seem best right now also would seem best in hindsight. Extensive evidence summarized by Ainslie (1992), however, suggests that all creatures, animal and human, tend to discount future rewards not exponentially but hyperbolically. As Ainslie explains, hyperbolic discounting implies a temporary preference for "the poorer but earlier of two goals, when the earlier goal is close at hand." Seated before a bowl of salted cashews, for example, people often eat too many, and then later express sincere regret at having spoiled their dinners.

A similar time-inconsistency problem confronts people who inter-act in a sequence of repeated prisoner's dilemmas. In such situations Rapoport and Chammah (1965), Axelrod (1984), and others have demonstrated the remarkable effectiveness of the tit-for-tat strategy— in which you cooperate in the first interaction, then in each successive interaction mimic whatever your partner did in the immediately pre-ceding one. Note, however, that implementation of tit-for-tat entails an inherent self-control problem. By cooperating in the current round, the tit-for-tat player must incur a small present cost to receive a po-tentially much larger future benefit. In contrast, a player who defects in the current round receives an immediate benefit, whereas the costs of that action are both delayed and uncertain. Thus someone might realize he would come out ahead in the long run if he cooperated in the current interaction, yet find himself unable to resist the tempta-tion to reap the immediate gains from defecting.

A person who is sympathetic toward potential trading partners is, by virtue of that concern, less likely than others to yield to temptation in the current interaction. Such a person would still find the gains from defecting attractive, but their allure would be mitigated by the prospect of the immediate aversive psychological reaction that would be triggered by defecting. For this reason, persons with sympathy for their trading partners would find it easier than others to implement the tit-for-tat strategy in repeated prisoner's dilemmas. To the extent that the ability to execute tit-for-tat enhances fitness, people who ex-perienced sympathy would have fared better than those who did not, even if no observable signal of sympathy were generally recognized.

Similar reasoning applies in the case of commitment problems that entail deterrence. It often will be prudent to exact revenge against an aggressor, even at considerable personal cost, when doing so would help create a reputation that will deter future aggression. Self-interested rational persons with perfect self-control would always seek revenge whenever the future reputational gains outweighed the current costs of taking action. As before, however, the gains from a tough reputation come only in the future, while the costs of ven-geance-seeking come now. A person may know full well that it pays to be tough, yet still be tempted to avoid the current costs of a tough response. Thus an angry person may be more likely to behave pru-dently than a merely prudent person who feels no anger.

The empirical literature described earlier documents the existence of reliable markers of sympathy and other moral emotions that influ-ence human interaction. The animal-signaling literature provides compelling theoretical reasons for believing that both the emotions themselves and their observable signals are unlikely to have origi-nated because of their capacity to resolve one-shot dilemmas. But given that these emotions and their markers exist, for whatever reasons, there is every reason to expect natural selection to have refined them for that purpose. We know, for example, that individual differences in emotional responsiveness are at least weakly heritable (Bruell 1970). If selective trustworthiness is advantageous and observable, natural selection should favor individual variants who are both more trustworthy and better able to communicate that fact to others.

An Optimistic Note

If, as available evidence suggests, moral emotions such as sympathy help to solve commitment problems, we are no longer compelled to accept the traditional view that universal opportunism is the only stable equilibrium. That is good news if, as Frank, Gilovich, and Regan have argued (1993b), the traditional view has had negative social consequences. We found, for example, that economics training—both its duration and content—affects the likelihood that students will defect in prisoner's dilemma games. In one version of our experiments economics majors were almost twice as likely to defect than noneconomics majors (Marwell and Ames 1981, and Carter and Irons 1991, report similar findings).

This finding should come as no surprise. We know, for example, that when an experimental subject is told that his partner already has defected in a prisoner's dilemma, defection is the almost universal response. The standard behavioral model to which economics students are repeatedly exposed assumes pure self-interest in the narrow sense. That model predicts everyone will defect in one-shot prisoner's dilemmas, and it would be strange indeed if the model had no impact on practitioners' expectations of other people's behavior. The decision to cooperate is the culmination of a long chain of contingent events in which people are constantly revising their assessments of one another, even if only unconsciously. In such processes, predictions based on a theoretical model that insists cooperation cannot be sustained are inevitably self-fulfilling.

In any event, the fact that many people cooperate in one-shot prisoner's dilemmas is well-documented and of long standing. If moral sentiments such as sympathy eliminate or reduce the fitness penalty from such behavior, society would benefit if more people knew about that. Of course, the mere fact that the traditional self-interest theory causes social harm does not constitute scientific grounds for rejecting it; and as Kuhn (1996) has stressed, an entrenched theory is seldom rejected in any event until a plausible alternative theory stands ready to displace it. The ideas and evidence advanced by the authors in this volume lay the groundwork for just such a theory.

I want to thank Randy Nesse for his generous encouragement over the years, and for his efforts to develop and call attention to the ideas discussed in *Passions Within Reason*.

Note

1. By one-shot prisoner's dilemmas I do not mean only games that are played once between perfect strangers. Such dilemmas also include interactions among friends of long standing, as in situations in which partners are unable to discover who is responsible for the bad outcome they experience.

References

Ainslie, George. 1992. *Picoeconomics*. New York: Cambridge University Press.

Akerlof, George. 1983. "Loyalty Filters." *American Economic Review* 73 (March): 54–63.

Argyle, Scott T., and Janet Dean. 1965. "Eye Contact, Distance, and Affiliation." *Sociometry* 28: 289–304.

Axelrod, Robert. 1984. *The Evolution of Cooperation*. New York: Basic Books.

Axelrod, Robert, and William Hamilton. 1981. "The Evolution of Cooperation." *Science* 211: 1390–96.

Bargh, John A. 1997. "The Automaticity of Everyday Life." *Advances in Social Cognition* 10: 1–61.

Bavelas, J. B., A. Black, C. R. Lemery, and J. Mullett. 1986. "I Show How You Feel: Motor Mimicry as a Communicative Act." *Journal of Personality and Social Psychology* 50: 322–29.

Bruell, Jan. 1970. "Heritability of Emotional Behavior." In *Physiological Correlates of Emotion*, edited by Perry Black. New York: Academic Press.

Cacioppo, John T., Joseph R. Priester, and Gary G. Berntson. 1993. "Rudimentary Determinants of Attitudes, II: Arm Flexion and Extension Have Differential Effects on Attitudes." *Journal of Personality and Social Psychology* 65: 5–17.

Carter, John, and Michael Irons. 1991. "Are Economists Different, and if So, Why?" *Journal of Economic Perspective* 5(2) 171–78.

Chartrand, Tanya L., and John A. Bargh. 1998. "The Chameleon Effect: How the Perception-Behavior Link Facilitates Social Interaction." New York University mimeo.

Darwin, Charles. 1872. *The Expression of Emotions in Man and Animals*. Reprint, Chicago: University of Chicago Press, 1965.

Eagly, A. H., R. D. Ashmore, M. G. Makhijani, and L. C. Longo. 1991. "What Is Beautiful Is Good, But . . . : A Meta-Analytic Review of Research on the Physical Attractiveness Stereotype." *Psychological Bulletin* 110: 109–28.

Ekman, Paul. 1985. *Telling Lies*. New York: Norton.

Elder, G. H., and E. C. Clipp. 1988. "Wartime Losses and Social Bonding: Influence Across 40 Years in Men's Lives." *Psychiatry* 51: 177–98.

Frank, Robert H. 1987. "If *Homo Economicus* Could Choose His Own Utility Function, Would He Want One with a Conscience?" *American Economic Review* 77(September): 593–604.

———. 1988. *Passions Within Reason: The Strategic Role of the Emotions*. New York: Norton.

Frank, Robert H., Thomas Gilovich, and Dennis Regan. 1993a. "Does Studying Economics Inhibit Cooperation?" *Journal of Economic Perspectives* 7(Spring): 159–71.

———. 1993b. "The Evolution of One-Shot Cooperation." *Ethology and Sociobiology* 14(July): 247–56.

Gardin, Hershel, Kalman J. Kaplan, Ira J. Firestone, and Gloria A. Cowan. 1973. "Proxemic Effects on Cooperation, Attitude, and Approach-Avoidance in a Prisoner's Dilemma Game." *Journal of Personality and Social Psychology* 27: 13–18.

Gauthier, David. 1985. *Morals by Agreement*. Oxford: Clarendon.

Gibbard, Alan. 1990. *Wise Choices, Apt Feelings: A Theory of Normative Judgment*. Cambridge, Mass.: Harvard University Press, and Oxford: Oxford University Press.

Gould, Stephen Jay. 1977. *Ever Since Darwin*. New York: Norton.

Hall, Edward T. 1982. *The Hidden Dimension*. New York: Anchor Books.

Hatfield, Elaine, John T. Cacioppo, and Richard Rapson. 1994. *Emotional Contagion*. Paris: Cambridge University Press.

Heimer, Mel. 1969. *The Long Count*. New York: Atheneum.

Hirshleifer, Jack. 1987. "On the Emotions as Guarantors of Threats and Promises." In *The Latest on the Best: Essays in Evolution and Optimality*, edited by John Dupre (307–26). Cambridge, Mass.: MIT Press.

Kuhn, Thomas. 1996. *The Structure of Scientific Revolutions*. 3d. ed. Chicago: University of Chicago Press.

Lazarsfeld, Paul F., and Robert K. Merton. 1954. "Friendship as a Social Process." In *Freedom and Control in Modern Society*, edited by M. Berger (18–66). Princeton, N.J.: Van Nostrand.

Lewin, K. 1935. *A Dynamic Theory of Personality*. New York: McGraw-Hill.

Marwell, Gerald, and Ruth Ames. 1981. "Economists Free Ride, Does Anyone Else?" *Journal of Public Economics* 15: 295–310.

McClennen, Edward F. 1990. *Rationality and Dynamic Choice: Foundational Explorations*. New York: Cambridge University Press.

Murstein, B. I., M. Cerreto, and M. MacDonald. 1977. "A Theory and Investigation of the Effect of Exchange-Orientation on Marriage and Friendship." *Journal of Marriage and the Family* 39: 543–48.

Parfit, Derek. 1984. *Reasons and Persons*. Oxford: Clarendon.

Patterson, Miles L. 1973. "Compensation in Nonverbal Immediacy Behaviors: A Review." *Sociometry* 36: 237–52.

Rapoport, Anatol, and A. Chammah. 1965. *Prisoner's Dilemma*. Ann Arbor, Mich.: University of Michigan Press.

Sally, David. 1995. "Conversation and Cooperation in Social Dilemmas: A

Meta-Analysis of Experiments from 1958 to 1972." *Rationality and Society* 7: 58–92.

————. 2000. "A General Theory of Sympathy, Mind-Reading, and Social Interaction, with an Application to the Prisoner's Dilemma." *Social Science Information* 39(4): 567–634.

Schelling, Thomas. 1960. *The Strategy of Conflict*. Cambridge, Mass.: Harvard University Press.

————. 1978. "Altruism, Meanness, and Other Potentially Strategic Behaviors." *American Economic Review* 68: 229–30.

Sen, Amartya. 1985. "Goals, Commitment, and Identity." *Journal of Law, Economics, and Organization* 1: 341–55.

Smith, Adam. 1759. *The Theory of Moral Sentiments*. Reprint, New York: Kelley, 1966.

Strack, Fritz, L. L. Martin, and S. Stepper. 1988. "Inhibiting and Facilitating Conditions of the Human Smile: A Nonobtrusive Test of the Facial Feedback Hypothesis." *Journal of Personality and Social Psychology* 54: 768–76.

Tinbergen, Niko. 1952. "Derived Activities: Their Causation, Biological Significance, and Emancipation During Evolution." *Quarterly Review of Biology* 27: 1–32.

Trivers, Robert. 1971. "The Evolution of Reciprocal Altruism." *Quarterly Review of Biology* 46: 35–57.

Valley, Kathleen L., Joseph Moag, and Max H. Bazerman. 1998. "A Matter of Trust: Effects of Communication on the Efficiency and Distribution of Outcomes." *Journal of Economic Behavior and Organization* 34: 211–38.

Zajonc, Robert B., Pamela K. Adelmann, Sheila T. Murphy, and Paula M. Niedenthal. 1987. "Convergence in the Physical Appearance of Spouses." *Motivation and Emotion* 11: 335–46.

Chapter 4

Game-Theoretic Interpretations of Commitment

JACK HIRSHLEIFER

I N HIS contribution to this volume, Thomas C. Schelling disclaims having originated the concept of commitment. Even if that disclaimer is accepted, a strong case remains for recognizing him as inventor at least of the game-theoretic approach to the commitment problem (Schelling 1960). This chapter follows Schelling's lead, employing the tools of game theory in the hope of providing more precision and rigor to a concept often discussed rather too loosely.

More specifically, I will address the following topics:

How does the concept of commitment relate to the categories of game theory: strategies, payoffs, moves, information sets, and so forth?

Is commitment one single thing, or have two or more concepts been conflated that game theory can help us distinguish?

In what environments and under what rules of the game is commitment *possible*? Where commitment is possible, when is it *profitable* as well—to the committing party, to the targeted party, or possibly to both at once?

Finally, although this topic has considerable overlap with discussions elsewhere in the volume, I will be going beyond pure theory to say something about the mechanisms whereby a party's commitment can be effectuated and communicated.

The title of this book refers to the *evolution* of commitment. It is plausible, though not certain, that when commitment is profitable it also will be favored by selection—natural or cultural. However, I will not attempt to model the evolutionary process whereby commitment actions might or might not become part of the behavioral repertoire of a population.

Payoff Environment Versus Protocol of Play

The discussion that follows presumes familiarity with basic concepts of game theory such as payoffs, strategies, moves, and the like. I will expand on one point not usually brought out in textbook presentations: the distinction between *the payoff environment* and *the protocol of play* (or rules of the game).[1]

Most readers will be acquainted with payoff matrices such as those illustrated in table 4.1 and table 4.3. The names of several such matrices, among them prisoner's dilemma, Chicken, and Battle of the

Table 4.1   2 × 2 Matrices, by Decreasing Opposition of Interests

Matrix 1: Land or Sea

	C1	C2
R1	2, 1	1, 2
R2	1, 2	2, 1

Matrix 2: Chicken

	C1	C2
R1	3, 3	2, 4
R2	4, 2	1, 1

Matrix 3: Battle of the Sexes

	C1	C2
R1	1, 1	3, 2
R2	2, 3	1, 1

Matrix 4: Coordination Game

	C1	C2
R1	3, 3	1, 1
R2	1, 1	2, 2

Source: Author.

Sexes, have in some cases entered the common lingo of academic discourse. Each of these patterns can be regarded as a distinct ecological environment within which social interactions take place. The protocol of play is a somewhat less familiar concept. The idea is that, within any given environment, in order to have a properly structured game the players must be constrained to follow a definite set of procedures—the rules of the game. The rules might provide, for example, only for a one-time encounter after which play is terminated and the contenders go their separate ways. Or alternatively, perhaps the players will be interacting with one another two or more times in succession. In the latter case the choice options becoming available in later rounds might well influence decisions in round one. However, only single-round interactions will be dealt with in this discussion.

Essential for the analysis here is a different aspect of the protocol of play: the sequence of moves. Do the rules require the players to make their choices simultaneously, or do they take turns? And if they take turns, who moves first? (Note that in game theory, simultaneity refers not to clock or calendar time but to the state of information. So long as neither side, when making its own move, is aware of the opponent's choice, their two actions are regarded as simultaneous.)

What Is Commitment?

"[C]ommitment is a device to leave the last clear chance to decide the outcome with the other party" (Schelling 1960, 37). So the concept of commitment turns quite centrally upon the protocol of play, and in particular upon the sequence of moves. There are at least two distinct ways, however, in which the "last clear chance" can be left to the opponent. Schelling distinguishes between commitment pure and simple, and commitment that takes the form of a threat:

> The threat differs from the ordinary commitment, however, in that it makes one's course of action *conditional* on what the other player does. . . . The commitment is a means of gaining *first move* in a game in which first move carries an advantage; the threat is a commitment to a strategy for *second move*. (Schelling 1960, 124)

What Schelling calls "ordinary" commitment corresponds to taking the opening move in sequential play (seizing the high ground, in military usage), or, equivalently, forcing the opponent to take the final move. I will call this *preemptive* commitment. To constitute preemption, a player's opening action must be irrevocable: as long as he keeps his options open, he is not committed. (In fact, in game-theory terms he has not yet moved at all.) Preemptive commitment—taking the first move—is not necessarily profitable. One topic to be taken up here concerns the conditions under which a player might prefer not to move first, but to "have the last word" instead.

Schelling is too limiting, however, in referring to the other type of commitment as a "threat." Not only threats but also promises, and perhaps certain other types of conditional engagements as well, fall into the general category of *reactive* commitment. Reactive commitment occurs when the decision maker with the last move convincingly pledges to respond, in a specified contingent way, to the opponent's earlier choice.

To avoid possible confusion it is helpful to distinguish between *execution moves* and *pre-play moves*. Consistent with Schelling's usage, the terms *first move* and *last move* here always refer exclusively to execution moves—the choices that actually generate the payoffs. In contrast, commitments come even earlier: they are pre-play moves. A *preemptive* commitment is a pre-play move that allows one to take the first execution move. In contrast, a *reactive* commitment, although also a pre-play move, can be made only by the player who has the last execution move. In either case, by giving up his or her freedom of choice the committing player leaves the opponent with (in Schelling's words) "the last clear chance to decide the outcome."

In table 4.1 consider the matrix associated with the game of Chicken.[2] In each cell of the matrix the first number is the payoff to the Row player, the second the payoff to the Column player. (These are to be interpreted as *ranked* rather than quantitatively scaled payoffs.) Row's highest payoff 4 is in the lower left cell; Column's 4 is at the upper right. Chicken takes its name from a hypothetical test of nerve. Two teenagers are steering their jalopies toward one another at full speed; the first to swerve aside must suffer the scorn of being the chicken. Maintaining the ornithological metaphor, the alternative strategy options are often termed Hawk (the R2 and C2 strategies for Row and Column, respectively) and Dove (the R1 and C1 strategies). As the matrix shows, Row as Hawk does best if Column chooses Dove, the achieved payoff-pair being (4,2). But if both sides choose Hawk lots of feathers fly (the jalopies crash). The payoffs are (1,1)— each side suffers its worst possible outcome.

Consider labor-management negotiations. Hawk corresponds to readiness to go on strike or impose a lockout (as the case may be) if one's demands are not met. Dove represents willingness to come to a reasonable compromise. The side playing Hawk will get the better of an opponent playing Dove; a tough negotiator might win big. Yet if both sides insist on playing Hawk, the result may be a mutually undesired work stoppage.

Suppose Row can make a *preemptive* commitment—that is, he seizes the chance to make the first execution move. Then Row should logically play Hawk (the lower row in the matrix). Column must rationally respond with Dove (the left-hand column of the matrix). The strategy pair is R2,C1 with payoffs (4,2). The advantage is to Row— his preemptive commitment has paid off.

What does such a commitment entail, behaviorally speaking? The key point is that a committing player irrevocably surrenders freedom of action. So long as the teenage driver retains the option to swerve or not, he has not yet actually made his move. How can he give up the option to swerve? Schelling has suggested one possibility: demonstratively tossing the steering wheel out of the speeding vehicle! In labor-management negotiations a union leader might become committed by making himself vulnerable to being voted out of office unless the contract satisfies his publicly proclaimed demands. (These and other possible mechanisms for achieving commitment will be discussed later on.)

So much for preemptive commitment, seizing the first move. Suppose instead that, in pre-play negotiations before any execution move has been made, Column can make a *reactive* commitment. A number of different reactive commitments are possible, but let us assume Column convincingly conveys to Row that "if you choose Hawk I will respond with Hawk; if you choose Dove I will respond with Dove." Now, although Column will be making the last execution move, she has given up her freedom of action: it is Row who has the "last clear chance" to determine the outcome. So, when the time comes to take action, Row should rationally choose Dove. After Column carries out her commitment by playing Dove in response, the achieved payoffs will be (3,3). Thus Column's reactive commitment has won her equality of payoff, despite Row's being able to move first in action terms. (Is Column's commitment here a *threat* or a *promise*? As will be seen, it has elements of both.)

Preemptive Commitment: When Is It Profitable?

Preemptive commitments—ways of seizing the first move—can be profitable for the committing side in one of two ways: they may allow the committing side to gain a relative advantage over the opponent or, conceivably, both parties may benefit. Which of these outcomes eventuates, if either does, depends also upon the payoff environment.

The payoff matrices of table 4.1 are ordered in terms of *decreasing opposition of interests*. Of the patterns shown, the parties' goals are the most discordant in Land or Sea and the most harmonious in the Coordination Game.[3] More specifically:

Land or Sea (LOS). This constant-sum pattern represents total disharmony of interests. Each side's gain is the mirror-image of the other side's loss. The title recalls the Paul Revere story. A mismatch of strategies would have been best for the British. If attacking by sea they would prefer the Americans to defend by land; if attacking by land they would like to have the American forces lined up to defend by sea. Paul Revere's task was to ensure this did not happen. Biological predator-prey interactions represent a somewhat similar situation. The predator wants to prowl wherever the prey locates itself, the prey hopes for the reverse.[4]

Chicken (CH). This payoff environment has already been described. On the one hand, both parties want to avoid the worst-for-both (1, 1) payoffs associated with the R2,C2 strategy pair. Apart from that, each side prefers a particular discoordination outcome: best for Row is the strategy pair R2,C1 with payoffs (4,2), but this is next to worst for Column. The reverse applies to the strategy pair R1,C2 with payoffs (2,4). The Chicken payoff pattern is characteristic of bargaining in the shadow of potential conflict, as in labor-management negotiations, provided that actual conflict is regarded as the *worst* possible outcome by each side.[5] The strategy pair R1,C1 might seem like a reasonable compromise but may not be easy to achieve, because neither of the contenders wants to be perceived as a soft bargainer.

Battle of the Sexes (BOS). Here the players' interests are mainly in accord, though not perfectly so. Of the two mutually advantageous patterns, strategy pair R1,C2 slightly favors Row with payoffs (3,2), whereas R2,C1 favors Column with payoffs (2,3). The BOS pattern is typical of choices arrived at by alliances. Members of an alliance share a strong interest in defeating a common enemy, but each partner might want to jockey for advantage against its associate. In the traditional story the two allies are husband and wife going out for the evening. Although they both strongly desire togetherness, one prefers they attend the opera while the other favors a boxing match. As a military example, after breaking out of the Normandy perimeter in 1944, the British and Americans needed to concentrate logistically on a single line of attack against Germany. The Americans preferred supporting a drive by General Patton in the south, whereas the British favored supplying Field Marshal Montgomery in the north. (The latter was the action chosen, seemingly the wrong decision, as it led to an Allied disaster at Arnhem.)

Coordination Game (CG). There is perfect correspondence of interests: the players' payoff ranks are equal in each cell. Both parties do best if they can coordinate on the strategies R1,C1 with payoffs (3,3), next best coordinating upon R2,C2 with payoffs (2,2), but worst of all (1,1) if their strategies fail to match. Examples of CG situations are choice of a common language, systems of measures and weights, and

Table 4.2   Equilibria for Matrices of Table 4.1

	Land or Sea	Chicken	Battle of the Sexes	Coordination Game
Opposition of interests	Greatest	Substantial	Slight	None
Sequential-move equilibrium (Row moves first)				
Strategy-pair	R1,C2	R2,C1	R1,C2	R1,C1
Payoffs	1, 2	4, 2	3, 2	3, 3
Advantage to	Second-mover	First-mover	First-mover	Neither

Source: Author.

rules of the road. In some cases it makes no difference which particular pattern of coordination or convention is chosen, provided that one of them is. Everyone driving on the right may be just as good as everyone driving on the left. Yet in the environment postulated by the CG here, by assumption one pattern of coordination is better for both sides. For example, the agreed-on convention of changing over to daylight saving time in the spring appears to be more efficient than remaining on standard time.

In what circumstances can preemptive commitment be *profitable* to one side or, conceivably, to both? For each of the four payoff environments considered here, table 4.2 indicates: the degree of opposition of interests between the two players; the strategy pair and numerical payoffs arrived at in rational play (assuming it is Row who commits to moving first); and where the advantage lies.

In game-theoretic language each of the outcomes shown is the Subgame-Perfect Equilibrium (SGPE) for the corresponding game. This equilibrium concept is based on the hypothesis that the first mover will be making his rational (payoff-maximizing) choice on the assumption that the second mover will be doing the same when her turn comes.

Setting aside the Coordination Game, where there is no conflict of interest at all, table 4.2 suggests an inverse association between opposition of interests and first-mover advantage—or put another way, it pays to preemptively commit to the first move when the conflict of interest is only slight, but not when it is strong. Intuitively, when the opposition of interests is strong, a second mover doing best for herself automatically will be harming her opponent. Whatever the first mover's strategy choice might be, he remains vulnerable to such a countermove by the opponent. So in Land or Sea—the environment with the most extreme opposition of interests—it is vital to have not the first but the *last* move. In the Paul Revere story, for the British to proclaim a preemptive commitment to attacking by sea (or by land) would have been fatal for their chances of victory, and similarly for the Americans to commit to defending by land or defending by sea.

In contrast, if the parties' interests are highly correlated, the second mover cannot punish her opponent without injuring herself to some degree as well. Thus in Battle of the Sexes, where there is only slight opposition of interests, an ally having the first move can profitably commit to his more advantageous option: rather than letting the mutual enemy win, his confederate does better by accommodating to his choice as best she can.

Without getting into the mathematical and logical considerations making for strong or mild opposition of interests, notice that in the relatively "friendly" Battle of the Sexes environment the parties share an interest in avoiding either of the two discoordination outcomes in which both incur the worst possible payoffs (1,1). Chicken is less "friendly" an environment, but nevertheless the parties still share one strong interest: avoiding the Hawk–Hawk strategy pair with its (1,1) payoffs. So again there is a first-mover advantage. Yet in Land or Sea, there is no strategy pair they *both* want to avoid: any combination of strategies that is bad for one side must be good for the other. Hence the advantage shifts to the second mover.

Finally, in the Coordination Game there is no opposition of interests at all. Here allowing *either* party to have the first move leads both sides to the Pareto-efficient payoff pair (3,3). So if the baseline situation for purposes of comparison were the simultaneous-play protocol, either side should be happy to convert play of the game to a sequential protocol, no matter which side is empowered to make the preemptive commitment (move first).[6]

The upshot is that ability to move first tends to be of *differential* advantage in interactions with slight (BOS) or moderate (CH) opposition of interests between the players, and it is in those environments that we would expect the ability to preempt to be cultivated (or to emerge by evolutionary selection). Ability to move first is also of advantage when there is no conflict of interest at all, although the advantage redounds to the benefit of both players. With very strong conflict of interests, as in the constant-sum (LOS) game, we would expect to see contention for the position of second mover.[7]

Threats and Promises

We now turn to the second commitment concept. *Reactive commitment* typically takes the form of a threat or a promise (or combination

Table 4.3   Threats and Promises in Two Payoff Environments

Prisoner's Dilemma

	c	d
c	3, 3	1, 4
d	4, 1	2, 2

Chicken

	c	d
c	3, 3	2, 4
c	4, 2	1, 1

Source: Author.

thereof). The protocol of play goes as follows: first comes the commitment itself (a pre-play move), then the first execution move by the target player, and finally the reactive execution move by the committing player.

To illustrate the nature of threats and promises, consider the prisoner's dilemma and Chicken payoff matrices in table 4.3. In each case the first row and column represent the more cooperative action, symbolized here as *c*, and the second row and column the less cooperative action, denoted as *d*. As before, I will be using the Subgame-Perfect Equilibrium (SGPE) concept: first mover will be making a rational (own payoff-maximizing) choice, in anticipation that second mover will be doing the same in her turn. Yet under the reactive-commitment protocol it is the second mover (Column) who makes the *pre-play* threat or promise—the first actual execution move remaining with Row.

Promise

In the prisoner's dilemma context, absent any commitment possibility for Column, if Row moves first the SGPE would be the *d,d* strategy pair at lower right with payoffs (2, 2).[8] To escape this mutually unsatisfactory outcome, the committing Column player might announce a strategy in which her play is contingent upon Row's opening move, as follows:

If Row cooperates (chooses *c*), my reply will be *c*—payoffs (3,3);
If Row defects (chooses *d*), my reply will be *d*—payoffs (2,2).

Row, if he regards Column's conditional commitment as credible, will then rationally prefer the first option. This part of Column's strategy is a *promise*: it is a commitment to choose her more cooperative action c, leading to the payoff pair (3,3), even though action d leading to payoffs (1,4) would be more advantageous for her in terms of immediate profitability. But the second option is *not a threat*, properly speaking—because responding to d with d is just what Column would be doing in any case, even were there no question of commitment.

Threat

Threat commitments stand out more clearly in the Chicken environment. Given the CH matrix of table 4.3, in the absence of any reactive commitment on the part of Column the SGPE would be the d, c strategy pair at lower left with payoffs (4,2). Row, having the first action move, comes out ahead. Yet Column can reverse the advantage if she has the power to commit to a *threat*. She does so by announcing the following strategy:

If Row chooses c, my reply will be d—payoffs (2,4);

If Row chooses d, my reply will be d—payoffs (1,1).

Assuming credibility, Row of course prefers the first option. The second option is Column's *threat*: her commitment to take action d leading to payoffs (1,1) even though, in terms of immediate profitability, action c leading to payoffs (4,2) would be more advantageous for her. But the first option is *not a promise*, properly speaking—since responding to c with d in the Chicken environment is just what Column would be doing in any case, even were there no question of commitment.

Note that if a promise succeeds in eliciting the desired behavior, then—absent deception—it may require costly performance by the committing party. But a threat, if it works, does not have to be carried out. (Thus Row, if he accedes to it, would not be able to determine whether in fact the threat was real and would actually have been fulfilled.)

Threat and Promise

Finally, a reactive commitment might involve *both a threat and a promise* (stick and carrot). Still in the Chicken environment, the committing Column player announces the strategy:

If Row chooses c, my reply will be c—payoffs (3,3);

If Row chooses d, my reply will be d—payoffs (1,1).

Once again Row prefers the first option. Here the second option is the same *threat* as before: it is a commitment on Column's part to take action d leading to payoffs (1,1) even though, in terms of immediate profitability, action c leading to payoffs (4,2) would be more advantageous for her. But the first option now is indeed a *promise*: Column does not respond to c with d leading to payoffs (2,4), which would maximize her immediate profit, but instead commits to respond to c

with c leading to payoffs (3,3). Here, if the commitment was truthful and it works, only the promise but not the threat needs to be carried out.

One might wonder why Column would ever commit to a threat and promise, since it does no more for her than a simple promise and less for her than a simple threat. As a possible explanation, consider the problem of credibility.

Credibility

To be effective, a commitment not only must be made but conveyed: the targeted player must find the threat or promise to be credible (Klein and O'Flaherty 1993). But, 100 percent credibility may not be necessary.

Returning to the prisoner's dilemma matrix of table 4.3 and the associated promise commitment, recall that the purpose of Column's pre-play move was to induce Row to shift his first execution action from the less cooperative d to the more cooperative c. Let us suppose now that Row does not find the promise fully credible, and indeed only assigns the likelihood k_P to its being faithfully executed (on a scale from 0 to 1). How high does the partial credibility k_P have to be for the promise to be effective?

We can readily calculate: if Row accedes to the inducement (and chooses the upper row c of the matrix), his expected payoff will be the average of his reward over the two possible outcomes:

$$V_R(c) = 3k_P + 1(1 - k_P)$$

If Row does not respond to the promise and continues to choose the lower row d of the matrix, his payoff is simply:

$$V_R(d) = 2$$

In the latter case Column will simply pursue her own advantage on the final move, so the parties end up at the lower-right cell of the prisoner's dilemma matrix with payoffs (2,2).

Simple calculation shows that $V_R(c) > V_R(d)$ if and only if $k_P > 1/2$. Thus, given the illustrative payoff numbers of the prisoner's dilemma payoff environment in table 4.3, a credibility of only 50 percent is required for the promise to be effective.

Dealing exactly the same way with the Chicken environment, for the specific numbers employed in table 4.3, Column's pre-play threat will be effective—that is, Row will rationally accede to it rather than defy it—if and only if its level of credibility is $k_T > 2/3$.

That brings us finally to the rationale for a reactive commitment ever taking the form of a threat and promise. In general these two elements of the conditional commitment might have distinct degrees of credibility k_P and k_T. If Row chooses the c strategy (accedes to the promise and threat), Column will carry out her promise and Row's payoff will be:

$$V_R(c) = 3k_P + 2(1 - k_P)$$

If he chooses not to accede, Column will carry out her threat so that Row's expected payoff from his d strategy will be:

$$V_R(d) = k_T + 4(1 - k_T)$$

The first expression allows for the partial credibility of Column's promise; the second allows for the partial credibility of Column's threat. It follows that Row will rationally choose his c strategy if and only if:

$$k_T + k_P/3 > 2/3$$

Recall that, to be effective, the threat alone required credibility $k_T > 2/3$. *So the credibility of an associated promise may to some extent make up for a deficiency in the credibility of a threat.* The upshot is that a threat and promise may be effective in circumstances where a threat alone would not be.

Mechanisms of Commitment

What is it that makes commitments feasible and (wholly or partially) credible?

The essence of commitment is forgoing certain options, closing off a portion of one's own choice set. Just how can that be done? In dealing with these issues it will be useful to distinguish—although the terms are somewhat unsatisfactory—between *rationalistic* and *nonrationalistic* considerations. Under the former heading, patterns of payoffs or protocols of play might exist (or might perhaps be created by an appropriate pre-play move) in which rational players would be enabled to make a commitment. Under the latter heading, it may be that certain nonrational psychic patterns, notably the emotions, are capable of being exploited for this purpose—that is, to guarantee that one or more otherwise available actions would not in fact be chosen.

Rational Commitments

The supporting mechanisms are much the same for both the *preemptive* and the *reactive* forms of commitment. To begin with, consider first the Chicken game (in which, as we have seen, there is a first-mover advantage). A famous technique for achieving preemptive commitment, for gaining the first-mover advantage, is burning your bridges behind you. Suppose the options are attack (the less cooperative d move) versus retreat (the more cooperative c move). Burning your bridges behind you amounts to telling the opponent, "Since you now know I cannot retreat, you can be sure of having a costly fight on your hands unless you give way." In game-theory terms, you have drastically reduced your own payoff from choosing the c or retreat strategy—or even made it absolutely impossible. This having been visibly achieved, the opponent faces a fait accompli: preemption is effective. In contrast, there is no motivation for preemption in prisoner's dilemma, where there is neither a first-move nor a last-move advantage; and certainly no motive to do so in Land or Sea, where the advantage lies with the second mover. Similarly, effectuating *reactive* commitment requires penalizing oneself for failure to carry out the associated threat or promise.

Various techniques that might guarantee performance of a commitment have been suggested by Schelling (1960) and others. I can only briefly describe a few of them here.

As already mentioned, in labor-management negotiations (the Chicken payoff environment) a union leader might preemptively commit to a tough strategy by promising his constituency, in a pre-play move, that he will resign his position if he does not get his way. Knowing that the opposing negotiator is so constrained, management may have to accept a bad bargain as an alternative to an even worse work stoppage. As a related possibility, a negotiator might make a side bet with some third party that he will not give way—thereby reducing his own payoffs in the event of his failing to stand fast.

Also of interest are the reverse techniques, pre-play actions that commit the player *not* to make the first execution move. The U.S. Constitution provides that a treaty signed by the president becomes effective only if ratified by the Senate. At least when facing an opponent not so constrained, and provided that a *second-move advantage* exists, a ratification requirement might strengthen the president's hand in treaty negotiations. As previously indicated, a second-move advantage is associated with payoff environments characterized by strong conflict of interests, for example, the Land or Sea payoff environment. So we would expect the Senate to be insistent on retaining this power over negotiations with hostile nations—and the president ought not object. On the other hand, where the conflict of interest is not nearly so strong, as in international trade negotiations, the Senate is more likely to grant the president freedom to conclude Executive Agreements without requiring ratification.

In a pre-play contest for sequential advantage, differing time urgencies may play a role. Supposing a second-move advantage, a player may so arrange matters that he is in no great hurry to terminate the interaction by an execution move. So an opponent under time pressure may be forced to take the first move. In battle encounters where the advantage lies with the defense, a better-supplied general may be able to stand and wait until the opponent risks going on the attack.

When it comes to reactive commitments, pledging fortune or reputation as surety for one's promise or threat is very much like making a side bet that you will not default. Giving hostages or placing monetary collateral at risk also serve the same function.

Beyond Rationality

Stepping outside the bounds of rationality, there are possible psychic predispositions that may promote the ability to preemptively commit (take the first move) or the reverse. Some people are by nature impulsive, rushing in where angels fear to tread. Then there are the ditherers and procrastinators ("the native hue of resolution is sicklied o'er with the pale cast of thought"—*Hamlet*). Is it possible that without rationally thinking it through, people have evolved an ability to turn on the former psychic mode when there is a first-move advantage, and the latter when the balance of benefit tilts the other way?

Turning now to reactive commitments, it has been proposed that what are called *emotions*—or more properly *passions*, such as anger and gratitude—may have evolved to guarantee the execution of threats and promises (Hirshleifer 1987, 1993; Frank 1988). Under the influence of passion, an individual may no longer calculate profitability; he or she "loses control."

Passions are intrinsically reactive; they are triggered by the other party's prior move. Outrageous behavior, even on the part of your beloved child, may precipitate a furious response. Yet a surprising act of chivalry, even on the part of an enemy, may trigger an unwarrantedly magnanimous rejoinder. Economic experiments have shown that subjects are indeed typically willing to respond favorably to generous actions and to punish ungenerous ones, even when not "rationally" warranted in terms of benefits and costs to themselves (Fehr and Gachter 2000).

Summary

Preemptive commitment corresponds to taking the opening move in sequential play or, equivalently, forcing the opponent to take the final move. To constitute preemption, the opening action must be irrevocable: the opponent must face a fait accompli. *Reactive* commitment occurs when the decision maker who will be acting last pledges to respond, in a specified contingent way, to the opponent's earlier choice. Both types of commitment can be regarded as pre-play moves, as distinguished from the parties' actual execution moves that generate payoffs.

Having the first move is not always desirable. First move is advantageous when the parties' interests are relatively harmonious, as in intra-alliance negotiations (epitomized by the payoff environment Battle of the Sexes); but second move is advantageous when strong opposition of interests exists (as in the constant-sum environment Land or Sea).

Reactive commitments take the form of promises, threats, or combinations thereof. The possibility and potential efficacy of reactive commitments also depend on the nature of the payoff environment. In prisoner's dilemma a credible *promise* can generate a gain for the committing player (and the target player also benefits). In Chicken, a promise would be ineffective, but a credible *threat* would gain an advantage for the committing player (although the target player thereby loses).

Threats and promises are only effective when credible. In general something short of 100 percent credibility may suffice. If a threat and promise can be combined, their respective credibilities tend to reinforce one another in influencing the targeted player.

Mechanisms of commitment can be divided between rationalistic and nonrationalistic. A player might rationally preempt by foreclosing all but his desired choice option (burning one's bridges). This corresponds to unilaterally reducing one's own payoffs from the options not to be chosen. To do the same for reactive commitment, the payoffs would have to be *selectively* reduced—that is, the committing player would have to make it unprofitable for herself not to carry out the promise or threat previously made.

On the nonrationalistic level, taking the first move might be supported by a psychic predisposition toward impulsiveness, and avoiding the first move by a predisposition toward dithering and procrastination. Whether these attitudes are triggered in contexts in which the indicated behavior indeed would be profitable if rationally thought through remains to be seen. When it comes to reactive commitment, the picture is somewhat clearer. Hot anger serves to deter undesired behavior by making the threat of a punishing response credible, even if executing that punishment is not actually materially profitable. On the positive side, passionate gratitude may serve the same function by guaranteeing a reward for desired behavior.

Notes

1. See Schelling 1960, 46. An exposition appears in Hirshleifer and Hirshleifer 1998, 284–91. Although just about every work on game theory covers alternative *payoff environments*, systematic treatments of alternative *protocols of play* are relatively rare. The most thorough analysis is in the work of Steven J. Brams (1994).

2. More precisely, the matrix displays only the *payoff environment* of Chicken. A fully defined *game* requires specifying not only the payoff environment but also the protocol of play.

3. A quantitative scale for measuring divergence of interests is proposed in Axelrod 1970, chs. 2–3.

4. Note that the constant-sum patterns referred to here are defined only in terms of ranks. Even when the ranks are constant-sum, the actual *quantitative* payoffs need not be. Victory or defeat may have differing significance for the two sides. For example, if the prey escapes, the predator loses a dinner; if the predator wins, the prey loses its life (Dawkins 1982, ch. 4).

5. If a contender prefers "death with honor" to "surrender," the mutually destructive R2,C2 strategy pair is not the worst possible outcome for him or her. Should this be true for both players, the payoff environment is converted from Chicken to prisoner's dilemma.

6. Under the standard Nash equilibrium concept for the simultaneous-move protocol, there are three possibilities: convergence upon the Pareto-superior strategy pair R1,C1, upon the inferior coordination pattern R2,C2, or adoption by both sides of mixed strategies (which imply some likelihood of total coordination failure). Only the first of these three possibilities is as efficient as the outcome under sequential play.

7. Baik and Shogren (1992) analyze a somewhat different aspect of the possible contention between decision makers as to which will be the first mover.

8. Actually, in PD the noncooperative *d,d* strategy pair is the equilibrium outcome for the sequential protocol regardless of who moves first, and for the simultaneous-play protocol as well.

References

Axelrod, Robert. 1970. *Conflict of Interest*. Chicago: Markham.

Baik, Kyung H., and Jason F. Shogren. 1992. "Strategic Behavior in Contests: Comment." *American Economic Review* 82(1): 359–62.

Brams, Steven J. 1994. *Theory of Moves*. Cambridge: Cambridge University Press.

Dawkins, Richard. 1982. *The Extended Phenotype*. Oxford: Oxford University Press.

Fehr, Ernst, and Simon Gachter. 2000. "Cooperation and Punishment in Public Goods Experiments." *American Economic Review* 90(4): 980–94.

Frank, Robert H. 1988. *Passions Within Reason: The Strategic Role of the Emotions.* New York: Norton.

Hirshleifer, Jack. 1987. "On the Emotions as Guarantors of Threats and Promises." In *The Latest on the Best: Essays in Evolution and Optimality,* edited by John Dupré. Cambridge Mass.: MIT Press.

———. 1993. "The Affections and the Passions: Their Economic Logic." *Rationality and Society* 5(2): 185–202.

Hirshleifer, Jack and David Hirshleifer. 1998. *Price Theory and Applications.* 6th ed. Upper Saddle River, N.J.: Prentice Hall.

Klein, Daniel B., and Brendan O'Flaherty. 1993. "A Game-Theoretic Rendering of Promises and Threats." *Journal of Economic Behavior and Organization* 21: 295–314.

Schelling, Thomas C. 1960. *The Strategy of Conflict.* London: Oxford University Press.

PART II

COMMITMENT IN ANIMALS

T HE CHAPTERS in Part I define and describe commitment. Those in Part II address the questions of whether examples can be found in animal behavior, and whether we even should expect to find them. These apparently simple questions demand even more careful consideration of what exactly we mean by commitment: Is it simply giving up options, or is it signaling that one will, in a future situation, act in ways not directly in one's interests? The rigor of modern animal behavior research is evident as each chapter asks what criteria can distinguish a possible example of commitment from other related phenomena. All three authors quickly zero in on two of the same issues that came to the fore in Part I. The first is why other organisms would believe a signal committing an organism to a nonadaptive action. The second, closely related, is how reputations can make commitment signals credible. Adams focuses on threats, Dugatkin covers cooperation, and Silk reports on observations of primates—how they use signals of nonaggression, and why those signals are believed.

Adams systematically works his way through various possible explanations for threat displays, from the benefits of honest displays to the mechanisms of costly signaling and handicaps to the roles of reputation and subjective commitments. Displays that are inherently unfakable pose few problems because they benefit both the signaler and the receiver; for this reason they also have little to do with subjective commitment. Handicaps are more complex. Zahavi has argued for years that some costly behaviors are adaptive precisely because they are costly; only animals in excellent condition can afford to make costly signals, and this gives them credibility (Zahavi 1975). There have been few critical tests, but the search has become much more serious since models showed how such a tendency could be maintained by natural selection (Nur and Hasson 1984; Grafen 1990). Adams suggests that some costly signals entail a simple form of commitment; he notes, however, that the evolutionary theory of communication now incorporates deceptive communication and that deceptive threats have been convincingly demonstrated in nonhuman animals. Adams assesses how such costly signals are similar to and different from commitments, and offers an extended analysis of bluffing and why this kind of deception works, using his own studies on mantis shrimp as an example. His analysis carefully distinguishes deceptive threats that indicate future behavior from those that do not, and the importance of reputation as an enforcement mechanism. Adams concludes by assessing subjective commitments, observing that no example is known in which an animal fights in a way that lowers its own fitness without some external enforcement. He sees the issue of deception as a crucial obstacle that would make it hard or impossible for natural selection to maintain a capacity for using commitment strategies. To be convinced that subjective commitment is operating, a demonstration of why they are not made useless by deception is necessary. Note that Adams indeed recognizes the value of actions that have a major short-term cost if they give a long-term benefit via reputation effects, although he does not consider them subjective commitments.

Dugatkin takes on the problem of cooperation, noting the crucial advance in Maynard Smith's central concept of an evolutionarily stable strategy (Maynard Smith 1982). The chapter offers an overview of four possible mechanisms that could sustain cooperation: mutualism, kin selection, reciprocity, and trait-group selection. The focus is on reciprocity, and Dugatkin reviews data, including his own work on guppies, on the question of whether relatively simple animals can cooperate. There is no doubt that these animals recognize each other and recall other's actions. The question he focuses on is whether the kinds of cooperation they exhibit fulfill the requirements for commitment.

Silk begins by suggesting that state of musth in male elephants may signal an intent to fight that may qualify as a commitment. As she moves to primates, Silk carefully notes their very limited ability to get into the minds of other individuals in order to anticipate their actions based on presumed motives. Finally, she draws on her long experience in observing primates to ask if "quiet signals" comprise a kind of commitment not to harm. Again the question is why others would believe the signal; again the answer is that deception simply is not worth the costs of lost reputation. This is why such low-cost signals can persist.

Together, these chapters focus careful attention on the exact benefits offered by commitment strategies, how commitment signals are constantly undermined by deception, and the crucial role of reputation in making such signals believable.

Much related literature in animal behavior remains to be considered in the context of commitment. There is no way to consider this body of knowledge in any detail here, but the large amount of related work bears attention. In addition to general advances in understanding animal behavior (Alcock 1997), the functions and mechanisms of sociality in animals have been a major focus of ethological research in the past generation (Alexander 1996; Runciman, Maynard Smith, and Dunbar 1996). The publication of *Sociobiology* (Wilson 1975) and Wilson's extension of related ideas to humans have inspired much work in the field (Wilson 1978; Wilson 1984). In recent years more and more studies have addressed cooperation in animals (Alexander and Tinkle 1981; Alcock 1997; Dugatkin 1997), with extension to implications for complex and deep kinds of cooperation (Dugatkin and Reeve 1998; Pepper and Smuts 1999). Data-based fieldwork has also progressed, showing the remarkable kinds of short- and long-term relationships in primates (Harcourt 1992), especially chimpanzees (Goodall 1986) and baboons (Smuts 1985). De Waal has described the complexities of primate relationships based on his observations at the Arnhem Zoo (de Waal 1982) and has tried to understand reconciliation (de Waal 1989) and morality (de Waal 1996) from an evolutionary perspective. In just the past twenty years the study of primate cooperation has developed from the work of a few people to well-organized groups making steady progress (Hinde and Berman 1983; Rubenstein and Wrangham 1986; Smuts 1987; Cheney and Seyfarth 1990; Wrangham et al. 1994). It will be most interesting to see whether the idea of commitment proves useful in the study of animal behavior.

References

Alcock, John. 1997. *Animal Behavior: An Evolutionary Approach*. 6th ed. Sunderland, Mass.: Sinauer.

Alexander, R. D., and D. W. Tinkle. 1981. *Natural Selection and Social Behavior: Recent Research and New Theory*. New York: Chiron Press.

Alexander, R. McNeil. 1996. *Optima for Animals*. Princeton, N.J.: Princeton University Press.

Cheney, Dorothy L., and Robert M. Seyfarth. 1990. *How Monkeys See the World: Inside the Mind of Another Species*. Chicago: University of Chicago Press.

de Waal, Frans B. M. 1982. *Chimpanzee Politics: Power and Sex Among Apes.* New York: Harper and Row.

———. 1989. *Peacemaking Among Primates.* Cambridge, Mass.: Harvard University Press.

———. 1996. *Good Natured: The Origins of Right and Wrong in Humans and Other Animals.* Cambridge, Mass.: Harvard University Press.

Dugatkin, Lee Alan. 1997. *Cooperation Among Animals: An Evolutionary Perspective.* Oxford Series in Ecology and Evolution. New York: Oxford University Press.

Dugatkin, Lee Alan, and Hudson Kern Reeve, eds. 1998. *Game Theory and Animal Behavior.* Oxford: Oxford University Press.

Goodall, Jane. 1986. *The Chimpanzee of Gombe: Patterns of Behavior.* Cambridge, Mass.: Belknap Press.

Grafen, A. 1990. "Biological Signals as Handicaps." *Journal of Theoretical Biology* 144: 517–46.

Harcourt, Alexander H., and Frans B.M. De Waal, eds. 1992. *Coalitions and Alliances in Humans and Other Animals.* Oxford: Oxford University Press.

Hinde, Robert A., and Carol M. Berman. 1983. *Primate Social Relationships: An Integrated Approach.* Sunderland, Mass.: Sinauer.

Maynard Smith, John. 1982. *Evolution and the Theory of Games.* Cambridge: Cambridge University Press.

Nur, Nadav, and Oren Hasson. 1984. "Phenotypic Plasticity and the Handicap Principle." *Journal of Theoretical Biology* 110(2): 275–97.

Pepper, John W, and Barbara B. Smuts. 1999. "The Evolution of Cooperation in an Ecological Context: An Agent-Based Model." In *Dynamics of Human and Primate Societies: Agent-Based Modelling of Social and Spatial Processes,* edited by T. A. Kohler and G. J. Gumerman. New York: Oxford University Press.

Rubenstein, Daniel I., and Richard W. Wrangham. 1986. *Ecological Aspects of Social Evolution: Birds and Mammals.* Princeton, N.J.: Princeton University Press.

Runciman, W. G., John Maynard Smith, and Robin I. M. Dunbar. 1996. "Evolution of Social Behaviour Patterns in Primates and Man: A Joint Discussion Meeting of the Royal Society and the British Academy." In *Proceedings of the British Academy.* Vol. 88. New York: British Academy/Oxford University Press.

Smuts, Barbara B. 1985. *Sex and Friendship in Baboons.* New York: Aldine.

———. 1987. *Primate Societies.* Chicago: University of Chicago Press.

Wilson, Edward O. 1975. *Sociobiology.* Cambridge, Mass.: Harvard University Press.

———. 1978. *On Human Nature.* Cambridge, Mass.: Harvard University Press.

———. 1984. *Biophilia.* Cambridge, Mass.: Harvard University Press.

Wrangham, Richard W., W.C. McGrew, Frans B.M. de Waal, and Paul Heltre. 1994. *Chimpanzee Cultures.* Cambridge, Mass.: Harvard University Press, in cooperation with the Chicago Academy of Sciences.

Zahavi, Amotz. 1975. "Mate Selection—A Selection for a Handicap." *Journal of Theoretical Biology* 53: 205–14.

Chapter 5

Threat Displays in Animal Communication: Handicaps, Reputations, and Commitments

ELDRIDGE S. ADAMS

T HE STRATEGIC roles of animal threats are strikingly similar to those described for humans, despite independent origins. Threats are signals that reduce the probability or severity of aggressive behavior by opponents during conflicts. This interpretation is widely accepted by ethologists and behavioral ecologists and is well supported by experimental and observational studies. (For recent reviews of the biology of animal communication see Bradbury and Vehrencamp 1998; Hauser 1996; Johnstone 1997). Not so obvious, however, is why threats are effective, and whether the reasons why are the same in humans as in other animals. The essential problem is easily stated: if an individual can drive opponents away simply by expressing a threat, this produces a means of winning contests that is less costly than direct fighting. So long as the deterred individual is the one that would have lost the contest anyway, both animals benefit. Yet the relatively low cost of threats seems to invite their use by individuals lacking the ability or motivation to prevail in escalated fights. Widespread use of threats by weak or unmotivated animals in turn would lower or even eliminate the incentive for recipients to withdraw. Why are threats convincing? What, if anything, prevents deception? These questions have been central to much recent research on animal threat communication.

This book emphasizes how individuals can influence the behavior of others by making commitments to courses of action that would not otherwise be in their best interests. Commitments, including subjective commitment, have been suggested as the basis of threats by humans (Frank 1988; Hirshleifer 1987; Schelling 1960); these ideas subsequently will be summarized. Commitments, however, rarely have been discussed as possible determinants of animal behavior (for an exception see Maynard Smith 1982), and probably no explicit tests have been made of the commitment hypothesis with nonhuman animals. Behavioral ecologists instead have developed their own set of explanations for the efficacy of threats, some of which have been tested experimentally. This chapter will briefly review these hypotheses to evaluate whether any might include commitments, and consider what evidence would support or falsify the commitment hypothesis.

Why dwell on the multiplicity of current hypotheses, especially when the species described often are only distantly related to humans? First and most important, threat communication does not *require* commitment. In many cases simpler explanations have strong support. To demonstrate the plausibility of commitment or subjective commitment is therefore not sufficient; instead, the difficult task of eliminating feasible alternatives must be completed. The same is true for cooperation. As Dugatkin points out (ch. 6, herein), cooperation can evolve without commitment or reciprocity, even among nonrelatives. Indeed many well-documented cases of animal cooperation involve simple mutualism, in which there is no temptation to defect and hence no need for commitment.

This chapter investigates whether commitment is known to play any role in animal threat displays, and more specifically, whether subjective commitments are ever the underlying mechanism. Here I suggest that simple forms of commitment, enforced by the animal's posture or position, are likely to be found in animal threats. Indeed this hypothesis is implicit in some versions of the handicap principle, an idea that drives much of the current research on the reliability of signals. Partial confirmation has been provided by empirical studies on threat displays in several species of birds. It will be quite difficult to demonstrate convincingly, however, that subjective commitment enforces the reliability of threats in nonhuman animals. The chief problem is to explain what prevents deception. An animal that appears to be committed, but that can in fact back out when it is favorable to do so, often will fare better than one that is truly committed. What, then, could maintain the reliability of a signal enforced only by internal emotions? Since deceptive threats have been demonstrated in some animal species, this presents a serious challenge to the subjective commitment hypothesis.

Threats and Commitment

The commitment hypothesis explains why an individual animal might preclude acting in its own best interest in particular future situations. By doing so, it can influence the behavior of other individuals in ways that increase its own expected long-term gains. Most of the contributors to this volume focus on commitment to cooperation, for which the signal of intent may be called a *promise* (for example, the chapters by Nesse and Schelling herein; Hirshleifer 1987). The promise advertises that the signaler will forgo opportunities for selfish behavior so that a cooperative action may be achieved. Such a commitment can potentially be enforced either by external devices or by internal emotions.

The threat is the evil twin of the promise. Under the commitment hypothesis, an individual expressing a threat restricts itself by some mechanism to behaviors or situations that ensure severe consequences if a fight occurs (Schelling, ch. 2 herein). At first glance this might seem to be a foolish tactic, but if the commitment is advertised it may persuade an opponent to withdraw. To begin with an often cited human example, if an army "burns its bridges"—that is, if it conspicuously removes opportunities to escape—then it is forced to fight to the finish if attacked (Schelling 1960). Such an opponent should be a more daunting foe than one that has retained the ability to escape; this is precisely the point of taking such a drastic action. If a superior force attacks, however, then an army that has burned its bridges cannot flee and therefore is doomed to suffer high costs.

This example illustrates the essential features of the commitment hypothesis as it applies to threats. The commitment precludes a behavioral option (for example, escape from a stronger opponent) that otherwise would be in the signaler's best interest. This can be advantageous only if the commitment is known by opponents and if it convinces at least some of them not to attack. If the tactic fails, the individual (or the army) is worse off than had it not made the commitment. The commitment in this case is enforced by external circumstances; specifically, the loss of escape routes. Frank (1988) has suggested that the effectiveness of threats as signals also may be enforced by emotions of anger or vindictiveness: these may cause an individual to fight more persistently and more dangerously than a rational analysis would favor. One must ask, though, whether the lack of external enforcement leaves such a display open to deception.

That this meaning of the term *commitment* is much more restrictive than the many alternative meanings in everyday speech is worth emphasizing. As used here, commitment does not refer generally to all decisions that an individual is resolved to follow or to all decisions that are irreversible; instead it refers only to cases in which particular future acts have been precluded, even when they are favorable. Is this within the capabilities of nonhuman animals? While I know of no cases of animals eliminating escape routes to produce a more effective threat, there are potentially other ways that animals can commit themselves to severe fights. The essence of the tactic is that the animal seeks a higher average payoff by lowering its payoff in some situations.

Alternative Hypothesis for the Effectiveness of Threats

With these ideas in mind, we can examine the alternative explanations offered by biologists for the effectiveness of threats. Throughout this chapter the animal producing the threat is referred to as the signaler and the animal responding to the threat as the recipient. The current view of most behavioral ecologists is that animals assess one another during fights and that threats influence assessments made by opponents (for example, Bradbury and Vehrencamp 1998; Enquist and Leimar 1983; Maynard Smith 1982; Maynard Smith and Parker 1976; Parker 1974; Parker and Rubenstein 1981). If a threat shows that the signaler has a high fighting ability or places a high value on the contested resource, such a threat may convince an opponent that it will probably lose the fight and therefore should withdraw. Since we can expect selection on the recipient to distinguish reliable information from bluffs, the only stable threat communication systems are those in which bluffing is restricted. What might ensure the reliability of threats?

Displays of Size and Alertness

One of the primary functions of threat displays is to communicate the signaler's size. Size often is tightly correlated with fighting ability, and size differences are important predictors of the probable outcome of competitive encounters (for example, Adams and Caldwell 1990; Caldwell and Dingle 1979; Hack 1997; Reichert 1978; Ribowski and Franck 1993). Some threats may seem to exaggerate size and strength, as when an animal rears up to full height, erects its fur, or holds its appendages outward. Once a successful form of exaggeration has spread through a population, however, it is likely that comparisons can be made accurately by any pair of opponents. Size therefore is difficult to fake. Indeed experimental studies have shown that many animals respond to the sizes of opponents as revealed through threat displays. For example, male snapping shrimp, which use enlarged claws to threaten and fight, can be induced to display not only to live opponents but also to isolated claws presented on the end of a stiff wire. Male shrimp are most likely to threaten when facing a claw smaller than their own; they become progressively less likely to threaten as the relative size of the opposing claw increases (Hughes 1996). This and many other experiments demonstrate that fighting animals decide how to behave based on a comparison of their own fighting ability to that of the opponent, and that threats are used in making these comparisons.

Another kind of information is inherently difficult to fake: when the threat display is oriented toward a particular opponent, it indicates that the opponent has been seen and recognized as an adversary. This informs the opponent that a "sneak attack" will be unsuccessful and that the signaler will be prepared to defend against aggressive actions (Parker, Hayhurst, and Bradley 1974). These aspects of threat communication are not particularly controversial. Such displays do not involve commitments, since their efficacy does not depend on the signaler precluding particular future behaviors.

Handicaps and Costly Signals

The Importance of Signal Costs   The handicap principle proposed by Zahavi postulates that signals must be reliable to be evolutionarily stable, and that signal costs, or handicaps, are required to maintain reliability (Zahavi 1987; Zahavi and Zahavi 1997). The hypothesis is that if signals are costly, animals of low quality may not be able to afford to communicate in the same way as animals of high quality. Variation in the use of the signal therefore can provide reliable information about the quality of the signaler. Similar ideas have been developed in other fields (Frank 1988; Spence 1973, 1974). Handicaps have been invoked to explain the reliability of a wide variety of signals, including those used in mate choice, fights among members of the same species, parent-offspring interactions, and defense against predators (Grafen 1990; Nur and Hasson 1984; Zahavi and Zahavi 1997). Although few rigorous tests of the handicap principle have been made (Johnstone 1995, 1997), it has transformed the way biologists look at signals and led to heightened interest in models of signaling interactions (for example, Adams and Mesterton-Gibbons 1995; Getty 1998a; Getty 1998b; Grafen 1990; Iwasa, Pomiankowski, and Nee 1991; Johnstone 1998; Nur and Hasson 1984).

To explain the relationship of handicaps to commitments, it is helpful to distinguish between two kinds of costly signals: those that are costly to produce, and those that have costly consequences due to actions of other animals (Dawkins 1993). The term *handicap* most often is associated with signals that are costly to produce or to bear, such as large and conspicuous ornaments. These costs are paid regardless of the effect of the signal on other animals. To illustrate with a hypothetical example, large antlers may require a substantial investment of limited nutrients for their development and may impede foraging or escape from predators (Nur and Hasson 1984; Zahavi 1977). Several models have shown that costs of this kind can lead to stable and reliable communication, provided that certain conditions are met (Nur and Hasson 1984; Grafen 1990; Getty 1998a). The animal must be able to adjust the magnitude of the display according to its own condition and circumstances. Displays of greater magnitude must yield higher benefits, such as greater mate attraction or deterrence of competitors, but also incur greater costs. For a display of a given magnitude, the costs and, perhaps, the benefits depend on the animal's quality. For example, antlers of a particular size may impose a greater cost on a weak individual than on a robust animal. The net effect is that animals of high quality are favored to produce larger or more intense displays than animals of low quality (Getty 1998a; Grafen 1990; Nur and Hasson 1984).

There is a kernel of similarity between handicaps and commitments in that both are disfavored but for their effects on communication with other individuals. Yet handicaps as burdens represent past expenditures. To argue that this type of handicap produces a reliable display of commitment, one must show how costs incurred in the past enforce threats or promises about future actions, which is a difficult proposition. Furthermore, although biologists now widely agree that burdensome handicaps can evolve as reliable indicators of quality, this is based more on mathematical demonstration that the idea is logically sound (Grafen 1990) than on evidence from examples in nature (Johnstone 1995). Moreover, high production costs are neither necessary nor sufficient to guarantee the honesty of a display (Getty 1998b; Johnstone and Grafen 1993). Thus it is not at all clear that the handicap principle explains how the costs of producing a signal guarantee the reliability of commitments.

Many threat displays fall into the second category of costly signals: they are not expensive to produce, requiring only brief movements, but have costly consequences that some animals may not be able to afford. This is a more promising area in which to search for commitments. Costly consequences may result, for example, if the display puts the signaler in a vulnerable position so that if it is attacked by an able opponent, it will suffer greater costs than had it not produced the display. If strong animals can afford to take this risk while weak animals cannot, then the display provides information about the signaler's fighting ability and should cause at least some recipients to withdraw. For this kind of display, threats drive away some opponents inexpensively, but when opponents are not deterred, the signaler is worse off than had it not threatened. This fulfills the definition of a commitment: by accepting a riskier posture, an animal precludes fighting in the way that otherwise would be in its best interest. Like the army that burns its proverbial bridges, the animal tries to reduce the probability of attack by committing to higher costs when the threat fails.[1]

In Zahavi's own discussions of threats the handicaps are thought to be due to costly consequences, such as increased vulnerability or reduced preparedness to fight, rather than to the costs of producing the display (Zahavi 1977, 1982, 1987; Zahavi and Zahavi 1997). The Zahavis have argued that "for a threat to be reliable, the signal must increase the danger to the signaler—and an escalation of the threat must increase the danger even further"; also, a "reliable threat leaves the signaler open to attack" (Zahavi and Zahavi 1997, 16). Possible examples include threats that entail moving within striking distance of the opponent, relaxation of the body, exposing the flanks, or other postures that make it more difficult to defend against direct blows by the opponent. For such a display, the costs are paid only if the threat fails—an important contrast to burdensome handicaps.

A Mathematical Model of Threats with Costly Consequences   The handicap principle has become so widely accepted that there is now an unfortunate tendency to assume that the problem of signal reliability has been solved. Signals must be reliable, the argument goes, or they will be weeded out by natural selection. One might think that to confirm the application of the handicap signal in a particular instance, all that is needed is to point to a signal cost. Or, to be more rigorous, one could demonstrate that costs increase with the magnitude of the signal. Yet these beliefs no longer are supported as general statements about animal communication. Summarized here is a model of threat communication that refutes several aspects of this point of view (Adams and Mesterton-Gibbons 1995; Mesterton-Gibbons and Adams 1998). This model shows that costly consequences resulting from simple types of commitment can underlie a stable system of threat communication. They do not ensure fully "honest" or reliable communication, however; instead, weak animals are expected to bluff.

Like many analyses of animal communication, this model uses evolutionary game theory, which describes strategies that can be expected to evolve within a particular kind of interaction. Jack Hirshleifer's and Lee Dugatkin's chapters include brief introductions to this approach. Other general introductions to game theory and animal behavior are offered by Maynard Smith (1982), Dugatkin and Reeve

(1998), Sigmund (1993) and Mesterton-Gibbons and Adams (1998). The usual goal is to seek an evolutionary stable strategy (ESS), which is a strategy that cannot be improved on by rare mutations specifying alternative strategies. The ESS describes how animals should behave if they have evolved or learned the best set of responses within a particular game.

To expose the logic of the model, its structure was kept very simple, representing only a single display and a single response. Animals vary in strength and, at the beginning of an interaction, each animal knows its own strength but not that of its opponent. Upon seeing its rival, the signaler decides whether to threaten or whether to defend the resource without threatening. The recipient then decides whether to attack or to flee. If it attacks, a fight ensues and the stronger animal wins. To represent the increased vulnerability of an animal producing a threat display, it is assumed that when the threat fails and the signaler is attacked by a stronger animal, the signaler pays an additional fighting cost beyond what it would have paid had it chosen not to threaten.

The evolutionary stable strategy for this game has several interesting characteristics (Adams and Mesterton-Gibbons 1995). Threats deter attacks by some opponents and the percentage of opponents deterred rises with the degree of increased vulnerability. Not all animals can afford the increased vulnerability; as a result, the threat contains information on the fighting ability of the signaler. Yet this threat communication system is not characterized by fully reliable signaling: both the strongest and weakest members of the population threaten, while animals of intermediate strength do not. Threats by weak animals can be considered bluffs, since these weak signalers could not win fights against the stronger opponents that are driven away by threats.

The presence of bluffing might seem to contradict the expectation that stable signaling systems must be reliable. The analysis of this and other models of communication, however, shows that while signals must contain some reliable information in order for recipients to be favored to respond, they need not be completely reliable. If a recipient tries to call bluffs by opponents, often it will find that the signaler is a strong opponent that can back up its threat with punishing blows. Thus threats by very strong animals can protect weak bluffers from discovery. If weak animals can bluff successfully, then why don't all animals threaten? The reason is that weak animals have more to gain from threats than strong animals, because this is the only way a weak animal can win a fight. (For further details see Adams and Mesterton-Gibbons 1995; Mesterton-Gibbons and Adams 1998). In short, this model shows that costly consequences can stabilize threat communication but that complete reliability cannot be always expected (see also Dawkins and Krebs 1978; Dawkins and Guilford 1991; Johnstone and Grafen 1993; Számadó 2000).[2]

The prediction that weak animals should bluff is confirmed by studies on the mantis shrimp *Gonodactylus bredini*, a marine crustacean that fights for possession of cavities in coral reefs. Mantis shrimp must shed their exoskeletons to grow and are highly vulnerable for several days after molting, being unable to deliver or to withstand blows. Despite this vulnerability, newly molted mantis shrimp often threaten, and their threats are effective in deterring attack by stronger animals (Steger and Caldwell 1983; Adams and Caldwell 1990). When attacked, newly molted animals do not attempt to strike their opponents but often attempt to flee immediately, especially if their opponent is a larger animal (Adams and Caldwell 1990). So both theory and data on threat communication indicate that animal threats may be deceptive. As will be further argued, deceptive threats falsify the subjective commitment hypothesis, at least in the particular species in which they have been demonstrated.

Data on Costly Consequences   Since threats with costly consequences represent a form of commitment, the supporting data are of particular interest. Studies on several species of birds confirm a key prediction of the costly consequences hypothesis: specifically, they show that actions that are most effective as threats also lead to the highest costs if the threat fails. Effective threats in these species tend to force an all-or-none response: either the opponent flees, or it escalates to higher levels of aggression. Enquist, Plane, and Röed (1985) examined the behavior of fulmars, which are gull-like seabirds, during struggles for bits of fish tossed on the surface of the water. Costs were evaluated by scoring the probability of a dangerous response by the opponent, such as physical contact, blows with the wings, or pecks with the beak. For fighting fulmars, the actions most likely to lead to victory also were the most likely to stimulate dangerous responses when the opponent was not deterred. Similarly, in a study on little blue penguins fighting for possession of caves, Waas (1991) found that behaviors most likely to drive away opponents were the riskiest, in that they were most likely to be followed by overt aggression from the opponent. The behaviors analyzed in both studies included displays but also elements of direct fighting, such as pecking or moving toward the opponent. Popp (1987) performed similar analyses, focusing solely on displays, for encounters among American goldfinches at feeders: he found that the signal most likely to elicit retreat by opponents, a high-intensity "head forward" display accompanied by wing flapping, was also the display associated with the greatest risk of attack by the recipient. These results confirm that effective threats expose the signaler to higher costs when the threats fail.

In summary, both models and data support the hypothesis that some animal threat displays are effective because they increase the vulnerability of the signaler to attacks by opponents and therefore entail commitments to costly fights when threats fail. Yet we must be cautious. The same data have been cited as supporting an alternative model, which includes neither vulnerability nor any other form of commitment. This model proposes that threats are "conventional signals" of arbitrary form that are not expensive to produce and that do not affect the vulnerability of the signaler. Instead weak animals are disfavored from expressing threats because this causes strong animals to attack more quickly so that the signaler loses opportunities to escape (Enquist 1985; Hurd 1997; Hurd and Enquist 1998). Although this is a plausible explanation for some signals, it does not appear to apply to the bird studies described here. The threats used by these birds are not arbitrary conventional displays but are instead incomplete or modified fighting actions that can directly increase danger to the signaler. For example, in both fulmars and little blue penguins the most effective acts bring the animal closer to or in direct contact with its opponent (Enquist, Plane, and Röed 1985; Waas 1991). The most effective threats of the American goldfinch involve extending the neck and pointing the beak toward the opponent from a very short distance (Coutlee 1967; Popp 1987). In short, these actions seem to vary in how much they expose the signaler to injury, in keeping with the vulnerability model and the commitment hypothesis. Strictly speaking, however, none of these studies has cleanly distinguished between the degree to which the threat exposes the signaler to risks and that to which it stimulates more aggressive behaviors by the opponent. We therefore may conclude that simple commitments are suggested by studies on some animal threat displays, but that the field is engaged in an unfinished process of describing costs that can stabilize threat communication and defining empirical tests that can distinguish among alternative models.

Reputation

Previous models assume that the interacting animals have no prior knowledge of one another. Animals living in social groups or stable neighborhoods often can remember the past behavior of particular individuals and modify their responses accordingly. Thus an animal that consistently follows through on threats by vigorous fighting conceivably can build a reputation for aggressiveness that reinforces the effectiveness of its subsequent threats. The future advantage of such a reputation may outweigh heavy fighting costs in one or more early encounters. If so, the intensity of fighting behavior may appear maladaptive and spiteful in the short run but in fact is adaptive and selfish in the long run. (In the vocabulary of behavioral ecology *spite* refers to behaviors that lower the fitness of both the animal that performs the behavior and the recipient.) Thus the reputation hypothesis, like the commitment hypothesis, provides a reason why animals may fight in ways that appear ill-advised by short-term analysis—but there is an important difference. If a threat fails to deter a rival, an animal that is building its reputation should not be tempted to renege if it is behaving rationally. Instead an animal is favored to persist in highly escalated fighting, even at a considerable cost to itself, to enhance the efficacy of its future threats. The animal's reputation depends on pairing threats with subsequent aggressiveness. By contrast, under the commitment hypothesis, if the threat fails, the animal should prefer to back out, but is unable to do so.

A large body of evidence shows that animals learn characteristics of competitors through repeated encounters, and that this can lead to the formation of dominance relationships. Typically, initial encounters are characterized by comparatively high levels of fighting, but in later encounters the submissive animal yields to the dominant much more rapidly and without fighting (Schjelderup-Ebbe 1935; Wilson 1975). In many species dominance is influenced not only by fighting ability but also by winner or loser effects—that is, an animal's likelihood of winning a fight with an unfamiliar opponent is increased by a history of prior wins, or is decreased by a history of prior losses (for example, Bakker and Sevenster 1983; Chase et al. 1994; Francis 1987; Frey and Miller 1972). This increases the premium for victory in early contests.

Although there have been numerous studies on the variables determining dominance and their effects on social structure (for example, Mesterton-Gibbons and Dugatkin 1995), few of these focus on the particular role of threats. Van Rhijn and Vodegel (1980), drawing on extensive research showing that social animals can recognize individuals, developed simple game theoretical models of threat strategies in the context of repeated encounters. Their results show that when animals know the fighting ability of an opponent, either because it can be assessed visually or has been learned during a previous encounter, the optimal strategy may be to threaten weaker animals and then to attack if that animal does not withdraw. Thus learned aspects of fighting ability may underlie the efficacy of the display, and handicaps are not required for stable and reliable signaling. Reputations also can protect animals from attack during temporary losses of strength (Caldwell 1986). An interesting extension is that signals used during aggressive encounters may be seen not only by the direct opponent but also by other observers. For example, Oliveira, McGregor, and Latruffe (1998) allowed male Siamese fighting fish to observe interactions among other males without themselves being seen. These males subsequently were much slower to approach or to display to the winners of these interactions than the losers.

Subjective Commitments

Subjective commitments are enforced by internal mechanisms. This possibility has been described at length in Robert Frank's book on the strategic roles of human emotions (Frank 1988). Frank describes how subjective commitments can arise due to emotional states that prevent the individual from acting in its best interest in particular situations. In the case of threat communication the underlying emotion can be anger or vindictiveness that causes the individual to fight vigorously when a calm and rational analysis would discourage such high levels of aggression. A violent temper can take on a strategic value if indicators of the emotion are visible to other individuals and inform them that the actor is committed to dangerous actions if challenged. To fight so aggressively that the costs exceed the value of the contested resource is maladaptive, unless the external signs of being prepared to fight in this way deter opponents.

The language of emotion has been avoided in some behavioral disciplines, particularly behaviorist psychology, because it may refer to internal mental events that cannot be observed directly, except by introspection. Ethologists and evolutionary biologists often are more comfortable with these terms, and Darwin himself wrote about the expression of anger, fear, and other emotions in nonhuman animals (Darwin 1965 [1872]). Yet evaluation of the central claim of the subjective commitment hypothesis does not require any particular beliefs about the internal mental lives of animals, since it can be stated in terms of externally visible aspects of behavior. This hypothesis proposes that an animal can enter a motivational state in which it will fight, if attacked, so intensely and persistently that it lowers its own net fitness, and that reliable correlates of this state are detectable by opponents. I know of no instances in which a nonhuman animal has been shown to use such a strategy, so the focus here is on the possible biological roots of subjective commitment and on the difficulties of testing this hypothesis.

To begin with one possible example, Jane Goodall (1971, 1986) has described the charging display of chimpanzees, given primarily by males during disputes within and between social groups. A charging display is a series of running movements that may be accompanied by loud vocalizations, erection of the hair, stomping on the ground, rock throwing, and dragging or waving of branches (Goodall 1971, 1986). When directed toward a particular individual, this threat is more likely to lead to attack than any other display in the chimpanzee's repertoire. During charging displays, chimpanzees engage in injurious behaviors that they otherwise avoid and that may be ill-advised, but for their value as signals. "The performer seems to lose certain inhibitions. Thus a male, usually gentle and protective toward small infants, may seize, drag, or throw one during such a display; an adolescent male may charge very close to a senior male to whom he is usually deferential, and may even hit him" (Goodall 1986, 316). Goodall suggests that one function of these displays is to allow young males to ascend the first rungs of the adult dominance hierarchy.

> It may well be that the charging display is particularly adaptive in this respect. Earlier I discussed the possibility that during such a display the male chimpanzee might lose many of his social inhibitions. This could explain why a young male may actually charge toward a chimpanzee to whom during less frenzied moments he would show great respect. Even a high-ranking male may on occasions move out of the way of a vigorously displaying adolescent. If an adolescent is able to displace low-ranking adult males frequently enough, this would undoubtedly increase his self-confidence; and possibly the pattern of dominance will be permanently disrupted. Certainly it seems that the more spectacular and violent his charging display, the more likely the youngster is to break into the hierarchy of his elders. (Goodall 1971, 178)

This description of the adaptive value of the charging display is consistent with the subjective commitment hypothesis. Under this interpretation, chimpanzees induce in themselves a motivational state in which they lose their restraints against attacking other members of their social group, including high-ranking males. Since the display is an indicator of a propensity to violence, even animals with a greater fighting ability may yield to the signaler. I do not mean to suggest that this is the only possible explanation of Goodall's observations or one that she favors, but it is helpful to have a concrete and natural example in mind of the way in which emotions can underlie threat communication.

The Origin of Subjective Commitment   Consider how subjective commitments might arise mechanistically. An animal might become committed to highly escalated fighting if its aggressiveness is physiologically constrained. Preparation for a fight involves not just neuronal control of movements, which can be rapidly altered, but also slower and longer-lasting hormonal changes (Huntingford and Turner 1987). These physiological changes may affect behavioral reactions so that when an animal is better prepared to fight, it also is more likely to attack particular stimuli. This is illustrated by "priming" of aggression in fish, in which repeated exposure to an aggressive stimulus— such as a rival or dummy fish—results in heightened levels of aggressiveness to other objects. Male siamese fighting fish, for example, allowed to view a rival male for a short period subsequently are more aggressive toward their own mirror images, a thermometer, or the experimenter's finger (Hogan and Bols 1980). The effects of priming can last for hours or days (Colgan 1986); because these tendencies change slowly, an animal primed to fight may have difficulty reducing its aggressive responses even when it is favored to do so. Indeed in some territorial species, potential mates must exercise caution during courtship lest they be attacked by their partner. In black-headed gulls, for example, territorial males initially are aggressive toward both male and female intruders. A female seeking to mate with a male responds to his threats with appeasement displays, but at first she stays on the male's territory for only a few minutes at a time. To become his mate, she must visit repeatedly, over a period of days, until the intensity of his threats diminishes and a pair bond is formed (Moynihan 1955).

If indications of hormonally mediated states of heightened aggression are visible to rivals, they can acquire a signaling function in addition to physiological preparation for fighting. Aggressive tendencies may be detectable if they are linked to diverse behavioral and physiological cues, such as breathing rates, postures, facial expressions, changes in voice, arrangement of feathers and fur, skin coloring, and odors (Zahavi 1982; Frank 1988). If the deterrent effect of these cues rises with their intensity, this can select for higher levels of aggressiveness than would be favored solely by preparation for fighting. In this way the signaler may become committed to self-punishing levels of aggression.

Maintenance of Subjective Commitment: The Problem of Deception
Although it is not difficult to see how a display of subjective commitment might arise, it is not so easy to understand how such a display could be maintained. As subjective commitments spread within a population, rivals will adopt this strategy simultaneously with increasing frequency, bringing disastrous results. Either subjective commitments proliferate until they no longer yield any increase in fitness, or the strategy must be limited to particular circumstances. Moreover, an even better strategy is to *appear* to be committed to highly escalated fights, thereby gaining the signaling advantages, but to retain the possibility of withdrawing or fighting by less escalated means should this tactic fail. If animals can evolve or learn to appear com-

mitted when they are not, then the value of the signal to the recipient is severely undermined.

The stability of displays of subjective commitment therefore depends on limits to deception. The underlying requirement is that not all individuals can appear to be angry, or otherwise motivated to engage in highly punishing fights, unless they truly are angry. Yet external signs of aggressive motivation do not appear to be characteristics that are, by their nature, unfakable. Indeed deceptive threats are well documented in some species, such as the mantis shrimps described earlier. These instances provide strong evidence against subjective commitment. So why would deception be impossible? Frank (1988) suggests that emotions produce diverse and subtle cues, so that if one aspect of a display is faked, then some ancillary cue will give away the true intentions of the signaler—but if the payoff for bluffing is high, then it is hard to see why diverse aspects of communication cannot all be faked. Exceptions might occur when the signal is expensive to produce or, for example, when an animal needs to face one way when ready to fight, but another way when it needs to flee. This puts us back in the realm of costly signals, whose reliability is enforced by external factors, rather than invoking any new subjective mechanisms.

In developing his theory of moral sentiments (Frank 1988, ch. 3), Frank also suggests that cheaters may not be able to mimic reliable displays accurately and that recipients can detect the difference if they are willing invest enough effort. Similar ideas have been expressed in the animal behavior literature (for example, Wiley 1983). Yet bluffing may be a matter of triggering a display rather than mimicking one: for example, I can make myself yawn even when I'm alert without willfully having to coordinate all of the muscular actions needed to produce this complex action. If yawning served an important signaling function, it's hard to see why fakery could not be perfected. Even for threat signals such as the chimpanzee's charging display, a bluffer need not pretend to be aggressively aroused if it can induce arousal in itself while retaining the option of fleeing at any moment. In this case no amount of scrutiny could distinguish bluffs from reliable displays.

Other explanations for lack of deception invoke the benefits of reliable signaling; Frank, for example, writes, "Indeed, at first glance the largest payoff of all appears to go to shameless liars. Yet most of us reserve special contempt for such persons, and will go to great trouble to inform others when we stumble upon them" (Frank 1988, 11). In other words, deception can lower one's reputation. As previously discussed, when an individual seeks to develop a reputation for following up threats with highly escalated fights, it is not in the individual's best interest to flee when its threat fails to deter opponents. The animal is favored to pay the short-term cost to gain long-term benefits; but this situation does not require subjective commitment, for commitment is not needed when there is no benefit for deception.

Biologists might add an additional possibility: that the possible range of behaviors can be constrained by genetics or developmental systems. Indeed evolutionary biologists perennially remind behavioral ecologists that we cannot assume that genetic and developmental systems allow access to all phenotypes (see, for example, Gould and Lewontin 1979). So it is possible that humans or other animals cannot always evolve false but convincing signs of commitment, even when that would increase fitness. Yet constraints on evolution are difficult to measure (Schlicting and Pigliucci 1998), and few studies show that particular combinations of traits cannot be attained under persistent and strong selection. Even though hormonal mechanisms often link multiple aspects of behavior, which could make bluffing especially difficult, variation in the behavioral correlates of hormone production across taxa suggest that novel relationships can evolve readily when they are favored (for example, Crews and Moore 1986; Crews 1993). Moreover, while genetic correlations among behavioral characters have been well established in some species (for example, Roff 1996), selection experiments often find that the linkages among characters vary from one replicate to another and are themselves subject to selection (Scharloo 1987; Gromko 1995). So it would be a formidable task to demonstrate the impossibility of self-restraint by animals advertising propensities to high levels of aggression.

Without demonstration of such constraints, it is difficult to rule out other explanations of heightened aggression. Showing that animals don't cheat differs from showing that they can't cheat. Nor is it sufficient to show that signalers suffer when threats fail. Animals often are favored to fight vigorously, even lethally, in many natural circumstances; they may make decisions on the basis of probabilistic outcomes and then become unlucky; they make errors due to poor information or lack of experience. Fighting behavior also may be maladaptive due to historical changes in selective forces. These possibilities must be distinguished from commitments as sources of fights that seem to be irrationally escalated. More common, and perhaps equally interesting, is that emotions may underlie the capacity to do what *is* in one's self-interest: for example, although the chimpanzee charging display was offered earlier as a starting point for discussing how subjective commitments might arise, Goodall's observations suggest the alternative possibility that these prolonged displays and their underlying motivations allow young males to challenge group members when they would otherwise be fearful, and by doing so to begin to establish higher positions in the group hierarchy.

Demonstration of subjective commitment in animal threat communication will not be easy, and no solid examples can be offered at present. Understanding how such a display can be maintained is more difficult than understanding its possible origins. It must be admitted, though, that the evolution and mechanisms of threat displays are incompletely understood, and that there are numerous examples of threats among nonhuman animals that cannot convincingly be assigned to one of the explanations reviewed here. Many threats do not appear to be costly to produce, to increase vulnerability, to be reinforced by reputation, or to function only in advertising size and alertness. This field of study needs more diverse and realistic models and clever experiments to distinguish among alternative hypotheses. Much is unexplained; we must be open to new ideas and methods.

Notes

1. One important difference between these examples is that while bridge burning threatens greater losses to the attacker as well as the signaler, signals that increase vulnerability do not; they are essentially displays of confidence.

2. Two recent papers have made inaccurate claims about this model. Hurd and Enquist (1998) state that the fraction of signalers that bluff is set by factors external to the game. While this is true in some analyses of deceptive communication, in which two or more classes of individuals occurring in fixed proportions are assumed, the model of Adams and Mesterton-Gibbons (1995) makes no such assumption. Instead, the proportion of bluffers is set by frequency-dependent selection. Számadó (2000) makes the same error and also attributes to Adams and Mesterton-Gibbons (1995) the view that bluffing must be rare. Our paper instead shows that bluffs can be common and may even outnumber reliable displays in a stable signaling system.

References

Adams, Eldridge S., and Roy L. Caldwell. 1990. "Deceptive Communication in Asymmetric Fights of the Stomatopod Crustacean *Gonodactylus bredini.*" *Animal Behaviour* 39(4): 706–16.

Adams, Eldridge S., and Michael Mesterton-Gibbons. 1995. "The Cost of Threat Displays and the Stability of Deceptive Communication." *Journal of Theoretical Biology* 175(4): 405–21.

Bakker, Theo C. M., and Piet Sevenster. 1983. "Determinants of Dominance in Male Sticklebacks (*Gasterosteus aculeatus* L.)." *Behaviour* 86(1–2): 55–71.

Bradbury, Jack W., and Sandra L. Vehrencamp. 1998. *Principles of Animal Communication*. Sunderland, Mass.: Sinauer.

Caldwell, Roy L. 1986. "The Deceptive Use of Reputation by Stomatopods." In *Deception: Perspectives on Human and Nonhuman Deceit*, edited by Robert W. Mitchel and Nicholas S. Thompson. Albany: State University of New York Press.

Caldwell, Roy L., and Jeri Dingle. 1979. "The Influence of Size Differences on Agonistic Encounters in the Mantis Shrimp, *Gonodactylus viridis*." *Behaviour* 69(3–4): 255–63.

Chase, Ivan, Costanza Bartolomeo, and Lee A. Dugatkin. 1994. "Aggressive Interactions and Inter-contest Interval: How Long Do Winners Keep Winning?" *Animal Behaviour* 48(2): 393–400.

Colgan, Patrick. 1986. "The Motivational Basis of Fish Behaviour." In *Behaviour of Teleost Fishes*, edited by Tony J. Pitcher. London: Chapman and Hall.

Coutlee, Ellen L. 1967. "Agonistic Behavior in the American Goldfinch." *Wilson Bulletin* 79(1): 89–109.

Crews, David. 1993. "Diversity of Hormone-Behavior Relations in Reproductive Behavior." In *Behavioral Endocrinology*, edited by Jill B. Becker, S. Marc Breedlove, and David Crews. Cambridge, Mass.: MIT Press.

Crews, David, and Michael C. Moore. 1986. "Evolution of Mechanisms Controlling Mating Behavior." *Science* 231(4734): 121–25.

Darwin, Charles, 1965 [1872]. *The Expression of the Emotions in Man and Animals*. Reprint, Chicago: University of Chicago Press.

Dawkins, Marian S. 1993. "Are There General Principles of Signal Design?" *Philosophical Transactions of the Royal Society of London*, ser. B 340(1292): 251–55.

Dawkins, Marian S., and Tim Guilford. 1991. "The Corruption of Honest Signalling." *Animal Behaviour* 41(5): 865–73.

Dawkins, Richard, and John R. Krebs. 1978. "Animal Signals: Information or Manipulation." In *Behavioral Ecology*, edited by John R. Krebs and Nicholas B. Davies. 1st ed. Oxford: Blackwell Scientific Publications.

Dugatkin, Lee A., and Hudson K. Reeve, eds. 1998. *Game Theory and Animal Behavior*. Oxford: Oxford University Press.

Enquist, Magnus. 1985. "Communication During Aggressive Interactions with Particular Reference to Variation in Choice of Behaviour." *Animal Behaviour* 33(4): 1152–61.

Enquist, Magnus, and Olof Leimar. 1983. "Evolution of Fighting Behaviour: Decision Rules and Assessment of Relative Strength." *Journal of Theoretical Behaviour* 102(3): 387–410.

Enquist, Magnus, Elisabeth Plane, and Jan Röed. 1985. "Aggressive Behavior in Fulmars (*Fulmarus glacialis*)." *Animal Behaviour* 33(3): 1007–20.

Francis, Richard. 1987. "The Interaction of Genotype and Experience in the Dominance Success of Paradise Fish (*Macropodus opercularis*)." *Biology of Behaviour* 12(1): 1–11.

Frank, Robert H. 1988. *Passions Within Reason: The Strategic Role of the Emotions*. New York: Norton.

Frey, Dennis F., and Rudolph J. Miller. 1972. "The Establishment of Dominance Relationships in the Blue Gourami, *Trichogaster trichopterus* (Pallas)." *Behaviour* 42(1–2): 8–62.

Getty, Thomas. 1998a. "Handicap Signalling: When Fecundity and Viability Do Not Add Up." *Animal Behaviour* 56(1): 127–30.

———. 1998b. "Reliable Signalling Need Not Be a Handicap." *Animal Behaviour* 56(1): 253–55.

Goodall, Jane. 1971. *In the Shadow of Man*. Boston: Houghton Mifflin.

———. 1986. *The Chimpanzees of Gombe: Patterns of Behavior*. Cambridge, Mass.: Belknap Press.

Gould, Stephen J., and Richard C. Lewontin. 1979. "The Spandrels of San Marco and the Panglossian Paradigm: A Critique of the Adaptationist Programme." *Proceedings of the Royal Society of London*, ser. B 205(1161): 581–98.

Grafen, Alan. 1990. "Biological Signals as Handicaps." *Journal of Theoretical Biology* 144(4): 517–46.

Gromko, Mark H. 1995. "Unpredictability of Correlated Response to Selection: Pleiotropy and Sampling Interact." *Evolution* 49(4): 685–93.

Hack, Mace A. 1997. "Assessment Strategies in the Contests of Male Crickets, *Acheta domesticus* (L.)." *Animal Behaviour* 53(4): 733–47.

Hauser, Marc D. 1996. *The Evolution of Communication*. Cambridge, Mass.: MIT Press.

Hirshleifer, Jack. 1987. *Economic Behavior in Adversity*. Chicago: University of Chicago Press.

Hogan, Jerry A., and R. Jean Bols. 1980. "Priming of Aggressive Motivation in *Beta splendens*." *Animal Behaviour* 28(1): 135–42.

Hughes, Melissa. 1996. "Size Assessment Via a Visual Signal in Snapping Shrimp." *Behavioral Ecology and Sociobiology* 38(1): 51–57.

Huntingford, Felicity A., and Angela K. Turner. 1987. *Animal Conflict*. London: Chapman and Hall.

Hurd, Peter L. 1997. "Is Signalling of Fighting Ability Costlier for Weaker Individuals?" *Journal of Theoretical Biology* 184(1): 83–88.

Hurd, Peter L., and Magnus Enquist. 1998. "Conventional Signalling in Aggressive Interactions: The Importance of Temporal Structure." *Journal of Theoretical Biology* 192(2): 197–211.

Iwasa, Yoh, Andrew Pomiankowski, and Sean Nee. 1991. "The Evolution of Costly Mate Preferences, II: The 'Handicap' Principle." *Evolution* 45(6): 1431–42.

Johnstone, Rufus A. 1995. "Sexual Selection, Honest Advertisement and the Handicap Principle: Reviewing the Evidence." *Biological Reviews* 70(1): 1–65.

———. 1997. "The Evolution of Animal Signals." In *Behavioural Ecology: An Evolutionary Approach*, edited by John R. Krebs and Nicholas B. Davies. 4th ed. Oxford: Blackwell Science.

———. 1998. "Game Theory and Communication." In *Game Theory and Animal Behavior*, edited by Lee A. Dugatkin and Hudson Kern Reeve. Oxford: Oxford University Press.

Johnstone, Rufus A., and Alan Grafen. 1993. "Dishonesty and the Handicap Principle." *Animal Behaviour* 46(4): 759–64.

Maynard Smith, John. 1982. *Evolution and the Theory of Games*. Cambridge: Cambridge University Press.

Maynard Smith, John, and Geoffrey A. Parker. 1976. "The Logic of Asymmetric Contests." *Animal Behaviour* 24(1): 159–75.

Mesterton-Gibbons, Michael, and Eldridge S. Adams. 1998. "Animal Contests as Evolutionary Games." *American Scientist* 86(4): 334–41.

Mesterton-Gibbons, Michael, and Lee A. Dugatkin. 1995. "Toward a Theory of Dominance Hierarchies: Effects of Assessment, Group Size, and Variation in Fighting Ability." *Behavioral Ecology* 6(4): 416–23.

Moynihan, Martin. 1955. "Some Aspects of the Reproductive Behavior in the Black-headed Gull (*Larus ridibundus ridibundus* L.) and Related Species." *Behaviour Supplement* 4: 1–201.

Nur, Nadav, and Oren Hasson. 1984. "Phenotypic Plasticity and the Handicap Principle." *Journal of Theoretical Biology* 110(2): 275–97.

Oliveira, Rui F., Peter K. McGregor, and Claire Latruffe. 1998. "Know Thine Enemy: Fighting Fish Gather Information from Observing Conspecific Interactions." *Proceedings of the Royal Society of London*, ser. B 265(1401): 1045–49.

Parker, Geoffrey A. 1974. "Assessment Strategy and the Evolution of Fighting Behaviour." *Journal of Theoretical Biology* 47(1): 223–43.

Parker, Geoffrey A., G. R. G. Hayhurst, and J. S. Bradley. 1974. "Attack and Defense Strategies in Reproductive Interactions of *Locusta migratoria*, and Their Adaptive Significance." *Zeitschrift fur Tierpsychologie* 34(1): 1–24.

Parker, Geoffrey A., and Daniel I. Rubenstein. 1981. "Role Assessment, Reserve Strategy, and Acquisition of Information in Asymmetric Animal Conflicts." *Animal Behaviour* 29(1): 221–40.

Popp, James W. 1987. "Risk and Effectiveness in the Use of Agonistic Displays by American Goldfinches." *Behaviour* 103(1–3): 141–56.

Reichert, Susan E. 1978. "Games Spiders Play: Behavioral Variability in Territorial Disputes." *Behavioral Ecology and Sociobiology* 3(2): 135–62.

Ribowski, Alexander, and Dierk Franck. 1993. "Demonstration of Strength and Concealment of Weakness in Escalating Fights of Male Swordtails (*Xiphophorus helleri*)." *Ethology* 93(4): 265–74.

Roff, Derek A. 1996. "The Evolution of Genetic Correlations: An Analysis of Patterns." *Evolution* 50(4): 1392–1403.

Scharloo, W. 1987. "Constraints in Selection Response." In *Genetic Constraints on Adaptive Evolution*, edited by Volker Loeschcke. Berlin: Springer-Verlag.

Schelling, Thomas C. 1960. *The Strategy of Conflict*. Cambridge, Mass.: Harvard University Press.

Schjelderup-Ebbe, Thorleif. 1935. "Social Behavior of Birds." In *A Handbook of Social Psychology*, edited by Carl A. Murchison. Worcester, Mass.: Clark University Press.

Schlicting, Carl D., and Massimo Pigliucci. 1998. *Phenotypic Evolution: A Reaction Norm Perspective*. Sunderland, Mass.: Sinauer.

Sigmund, Karl. 1993. *Games of Life: Explorations in Ecology, Evolution, and Behaviour*. London: Penguin.

Spence, Andrew Michael. 1973. "Job Market Signalling." *Quarterly Journal of Economics* 87(3): 355–74.

————. 1974. *Market Signaling, Information Transfer in Hiring and Related Screening Processes.* Cambridge, Mass.: Harvard University Press.

Steger, Rick, and Roy L. Caldwell. 1983. "Intraspecific Deception by Bluffing: A Defense Strategy of Newly Molted Stomatopods (Arthropoda: Crustacea)." *Science* 221(4610): 558–60.

Számadó, Szabolcs. 2000. "Cheating as a Mixed Strategy in a Simple Model of Aggressive Communication." *Animal Behaviour* 59(1): 221–30.

van Rhijn, Johan G., and Ron Vodegel. 1980. "Being Honest About One's Intentions: An Evolutionary Stable Strategy for Animal Conflicts." *Journal of Theoretical Biology* 85(4): 623–41.

Waas, Joseph R. 1991. "The Risks and Benefits of Signalling Aggressive Motivation: A Study of Cave-dwelling Little Blue Penguins." *Behavioral Ecology and Sociobiology* 29(2): 139–46.

Wiley, R. Haven. 1983. "The Evolution of Communication: Information and Manipulation." In *Animal Behaviour*, vol. 2: *Communication*, edited by Tim R. Halliday and Peter J. B. Slater. New York: W. H. Freeman.

Wilson, Edward O. 1975. *Sociobiology: The New Synthesis.* Cambridge, Mass.: Belknap Press.

Zahavi, Amotz. 1977. "Reliability in Communication Systems and the Evolution of Altruism." In *Evolutionary Ecology*, edited by Bernard Stonehouse and Christopher M. Perrins. London: Macmillan.

————. 1982. "The Pattern of Vocal Signals and the Information They Convey." *Behaviour* 80(1–2): 1–8.

————. 1987. "The Theory of Signal Selection and Some of Its Implications." In *International Symposium of Biological Evolution*, edited by V. P. Delfino. Bari, Italy: Adriatica Editrica.

Zahavi, Amotz, and Avishag Zahavi. 1997. *The Handicap Principle.* Oxford: Oxford University Press.

Chapter 6

Subjective Commitment in Nonhumans: What Should We Be Looking for, and Where Should We Be Looking?

LEE ALAN DUGATKIN

I just don't want to belong to any club that would have me as a member.

—Groucho Marx

A s FUNNY as the Groucho quote is, it also captures a fascinating yet relatively unexplored aspect of human behavior. We often make commitments that appear not to be in our own interest, at least not in any direct, short-term sense. Yet the nature of such commitments (be they positive or negative) are only now being investigated seriously. As is evident from other contributions to this volume, human subjective commitment has now caught the attention of some of the leading thinkers in anthropology, psychology, economics, political science, evolutionary biology, and behavioral ecology. The focus of this chapter will be on the last two of these disciplines—evolutionary biology and behavioral ecology. In particular I am interested in whether work on animal social behavior can shed light on natural selection and subjective commitment in any living creatures (including *Homo sapiens*).

Any attempt to use animal social behavior as a means for studying what appears so uniquely human a trait as subjective commitment is, from the outset, bound to meet with criticism. As such, I tackle this subject with some trepidation, but at the same time, with some methodological rigor. I begin with an overview of strategic behavior in animals, and argue that work on evolutionary game theory, aggression, and cooperation is the logical starting point for examining strategic commitment in nonhumans. To begin exploring this topic, a road map detailing where to search for such commitments in nonhumans is laid out, and putative cases of subjective commitment in nonhumans will be reviewed, assessing the strengths and weaknesses of such cases (I expect very few animal cases to meet even the most lax criteria for what constitutes subjective commitment in humans). Various scenarios then will attempt to explain the dearth of such commitments in the behavioral ecology literature. This adaptationist argument concludes that, despite the lack of evidence for subjective commitment in animals, natural selection is quite capable of favoring subjective commitment in nonhumans, and indeed, lays out one general experimental protocol for how to test for this phenomena in animals.

Strategic Behavior in Nonhumans

To begin a serious investigation into subjective commitment in animals, one must recognize a very large extant database on the use of *strategic* behavior in animals. Evolutionary biologists and behavioral ecologists were formally introduced to strategic thinking with the publication of Maynard Smith and Price's (1973) paper "The Logic of Animal Conflict" and subsequently, Maynard Smith's (1982) book *Evolution and the Theory of Games*. Modeling strategic behavior in humans has been common in economics since the 1950s and falls under the mathematical rubric of game theory. The theory of games was explicitly constructed to model situations in which the payoff an individual receives depends not only on its own actions but on the actions of others as well. When placed in an evolutionary context, game theory becomes *evolutionary game theory*.

Evolutionary game theory has now become a subdiscipline of its own, the major modifications to economic models being that payoffs are explicitly linked to fitness and the games are iterated over multiple generations (to create an evolutionary dynamic). The central concept in evolutionary game theory is the evolutionary stable strategy (ESS) (Maynard Smith 1982). An ESS is a strategy that once adopted cannot be "invaded" by any other strategies. This concept, simple as it is, is quite powerful and is now commonly referred to not only in the behavioral ecology literature but in economics, political science, and mathematics as well.

Originally, most work on animal social behavior and games followed Maynard Smith and Price's lead, and focused on aggressive behavior (and specifically on the question of why animals rarely fight to the death). Evolutionary theory has grown and its scope today is much broader. In a recent edited volume on game theory and animal behavior (Dugatkin and Reeve 1998), in addition to aggressive behavior (Riechert 1998), entire chapters were devoted to game theory and the following: social foraging (Giraldeau and Livoreil 1998); cooperation (Dugatkin 1998); communication (Johnstone 1998); nepotism (Reeve 1998); sibling rivalry and parent-offspring conflict (Mock, Parker, and Schwagmeyer 1998); habitat selection (Brown 1998); predator-prey interactions (Sih 1998); and learning (Stephens 1998).

To illustrate how animals invoke strategic behavior (as a prelude to a discussion of the more complicated issue of animals and subjective commitment), consider the case of cooperation and antipredator behavior in a small fish, the guppy (*Poecilia reticulata*). In 1971 Robert Trivers suggested that one path leading to animal cooperation may involve the exchange of altruistic acts among individuals. Any small cost that one individual might pay to help another could be more than made up for if the second individual helps the first, sometime in the future. Trivers (1971) noted that this type of exchange system is subject to cheating, as the greatest payoff attainable in such scenarios goes to the recipient of a cooperative action, who then fails to reciprocate.

The question of how reciprocity might evolve in such a world is formalized in what is known as the prisoner's dilemma (PD) game (figure 6.1). In this game, if both players choose to cooperate, they each receive R (Reward). This payoff, however high, is not as great as T (the temptation-to-cheat payoff—that is, the payoff obtained by a cheater paired up with a cooperator). If both players cheat, they each receive P (Punishment), and if a cooperator is matched with a cheater, the cooperator receives S (Sucker's Payoff). The PD game is defined as the scenario in which $T > R > P > S$ (sometimes an additional stipulation, namely, $2R > T + S$, is added to the definition of this game). The dilemma is that on any single interaction, it is always better to cheat, as $T > R$ and $P > S$. Therefore, both players should opt to cheat, in which case they both receive P; but if they had opted to cooperate with one another, they each would have received R, which is greater than P.

Can cooperation in animals evolve when they are trapped in a PD? Using both mathematics and computer simulations, Axelrod and Hamilton (1981) examined the success of different strategies competing in the iterated PD game. What they found was that if the probability of meeting a given partner in the future was above some critical threshold, then a conditionally cooperative strategy called Tit for Tat

Figure 6.1   The Two-Player Prisoner's Dilemma Game

Player 2

	Cooperate	Defect
Cooperate	R	S
Defect	T	P

Player 1

Source: Author's configuration.
Payoffs are shown for the row player (player 1). T > R > P > S, 2R > T + S.

(TFT, created by Anatol Rapport) was a robust solution to the iterated PD. TFT instructs a player to cooperate on the initial encounter with a partner and to subsequently copy its partner's last move. Axelrod (1984) hypothesized that TFT's success is attributable to its three defining characteristics: *niceness* (someone employing TFT is never the first to defect); swift *retaliation* (TFT immediately defects on a defecting partner); *forgiving* (TFT remembers only one move back in time). As such, the TFT strategy forgives prior defection if a partner is currently cooperating (that is, it does not hold grudges).

TFT has been studied extensively in the context of a specific type of antipredator behavior. In many species of fish, one to a few individuals move away from their school and approach a putative predator to gain information about this potential danger. Pitcher, Green, and Magurran (1986) coined the term *predator inspection* to describe this behavior (see Pitcher 1992 for a review). Potential benefits of inspection behavior include: determining whether the potential danger is in fact a predator; announcing to an ambush predator that it has been spotted; calculating the motivational state of the predator (for example, is it hunting?); obtaining information on the distance between the school and the predator (Magurran and Pitcher, 1987). Surprisingly, Magurran and Higham (1988) have found that the information obtained by the inspector(s) is either actively or passively transmitted to the noninspectors.

Experimental work in conjunction with indirect evidence supports the notion that the payoffs to predator inspection satisfy the requirements of the PD game—that is, for inspectors, $T > R > P > S$ (see Dugatkin 1997 for more on the long-standing and vociferous debate over the payoffs of predator inspection). The best action to take is to stay back and watch your partner inspect ($T > R$), but if both fish fail to inspect (and receive P), they are likely worse off than had they both gone out toward the predator (and received R).

Given that inspection satisfies the PD, my colleagues and I have examined the behavior of pairs of inspectors to see whether they behave cooperatively, and specifically whether they use something akin to the TFT strategy, as evolutionary game theory models predict. The data gathered so far support the notion that inspectors in fact do use the TFT strategy when inspecting potential predators. As predicted by TFT, inspectors appear to be nice (each starts off inspecting at about the same point in time), retaliatory (inspectors cease inspection if their partner stops), and forgiving (if inspector A's partner has cheated on it in the past, but resumes inspection, A then resumes inspection as well [Dugatkin 1991]). In addition to this direct support for TFT, evidence exists that inspectors remember the identity and behavior of their coinspectors and prefer to associate with cooperators over defectors (Dugatkin and Alfieri 1991a, 1991b; Milinski, Kulling, and Kettler 1990a; Milinski et al. 1990b).

Although TFT can evolve without assuming sophisticated animal cognition, it is more likely to evolve if animals can remember individuals with whom they have interacted, associate past interactions with these individuals, and base future behavior on this information. As such, my colleague, Michael Alfieri, and I designed a series of experiments to test the hypothesis that guppies remember the previous behavior of their associates during predator inspection and subsequently prefer to associate with the more cooperative individual (Dugatkin and Alfieri 1991a). In our experiment three guppies were placed in an experimental apparatus with three lanes in which fish could swim. Adjacent to the experimental tank was a tank containing a predator.

Immediately following each inspection trial, fish were placed into preference tanks. First, the fish from the center lane of the inspection trial (the center fish) was put into a tank placed between two smaller side chambers. The two fish from the side lanes (the side fish) were placed into the smaller side chambers. The position of the center fish was noted every five seconds. In twenty-four of the thirty trials the center fish preferred the side fish who had the average position clos- est to the predator during the inspection trial—that is, the more coop- erative of the side fish. Furthermore, similar results were obtained when the inspection and preference parts of a trial were separated by four hours. The ability to distinguish cooperators from cheaters ap- pears, however, to break down when guppies are in larger groups for longer stretches (Dugatkin and Wilson 2000).

Cooperation during predator inspection in guppies is only one of hundreds of examples of cooperation that could be chosen to illus- trate strategic behavior in animals (Dugatkin 1997). One reason for choosing guppies as a test case is to demonstrate that strategic behav- ior is not in any way, shape, or form limited to primates or, for that matter, to what some people still anachronistically refer to as "higher" organisms. Guppies have a brain smaller than most pebbles and still are capable of quite complex social maneuvering. For our purposes, the hundreds of studies of cooperation and animal behavior are meant to illustrate one critical point: animals are capable of complex strategic behavior, and therefore we should not a priori rule out the possibility of subjective commitment in animals (and not just pri- mates, as the guppy case illustrates).

What Is Subjective Commitment and Where Should We Be Looking for It in Animals?

In the conference report leading to this book Nesse defines subjective commitment as "the capacity for believing that another individual will act according to a personal moral code or emotional commitment instead of short-term interest, and the capacity for inducing such be- liefs in others." Something very similar to this definition can be found in the introductory chapter of this volume. To me this seems a reason- able definition, and not being a philosopher or economist, I shy away from redefining subjective commitment when a diverse group of re- searchers are at last beginning to investigate it in a systematic way. New definitions perhaps may be needed as we progress, but the focus here is on evolution and animal social behavior, not on a re- definition of terms.

Accepting this interpretation of subjective commitment, the follow- ing question must be asked: Where is the best place to search for examples in the animal social literature? Other contributors to this volume, Adams and Silk, address subjective commitment in the con- text of signaling and aggression and coordination signaling in primates. Here the focus is on subjective commitment and cooperation (Frank 1988) in nonprimate animals.

Such a focus simplifies the task somewhat, but only to a degree. There are hundreds of examples of cooperation in nonprimates peppered throughout the behavioral ecology literature (Dugatkin 1997). Where shall we begin the search for subjective commitment? First we must recognize numerous evolutionary trajectories that can lead to cooperative behavior.

Mesterton-Gibbons and I have argued that there are four paths to cooperative behavior (Mesterton-Gibbons and Dugatkin 1992; Dugatkin, Mesterton-Gibbons, and Houston 1992; Dugatkin 1997). These paths are kinship, by-product mutualism, reciprocal altruism, and group selection. Kinship favors cooperation, as related individuals are more likely than unrelated individuals to carry genes that are identical by descent. This translates into clusters of cooperators and clusters of noncooperators, simply known as families. Cooperators thrive when surrounded by like-minded individuals, and cheaters do poorly when surrounded by other cheaters. As such, kinship favors the evolution of cooperation.

Much work has been done on cooperation via kinship (particularly in the social insects). While this work has revolutionized the field of evolutionary approaches to social behavior, we should not necessarily focus our search for subjective commitment on kin-selected cooperation. To begin with, kinship is a very powerful (arguably the most powerful) force shaping animal social behavior, so in one sense subjective commitment hardly would add much to the picture when kinship is driving the game to begin with. This alone, however, is not a sufficient reason for not focusing on kinship in our search for subjective commitment in animals. After all, subjective commitment among kin would likely be stronger than among nonkin, even if only modestly so.

The primary argument against using kinship as a launching point in our search is that kin-selected cooperation generally tends to be unconditional. Animals may use quite sophisticated rules for determining who is and isn't kin (Reeve 1989), and kinship may play a role in a whole series of variables that animals use to determine how to act (Reeve 1998), but the actions (per se) undertaken by kin tend not to have a large impact on an animal's behavior toward such a partner (see Reeve and Nonacs 1992, and Ratnieks and Visscher 1988 for fascinating exceptions). That is, while kinship is important and often can favor some form of strategic behavior, animals typically do not use conditional strategic rules such as "do x when someone does y, otherwise, do z" when interacting with relatives. If you are detected as a relative, you are treated one way; if not, you are treated another. Since the ability to use sophisticated conditional rules seems to go hand in hand with an ability to employ subjective commitment, kinship may not be the logical starting point for uncovering subjective commitments in nonprimates. Obviously, should it prove true that when researchers start looking harder they uncover more conditional rules in the context of kinship—and this may prove true—we would be obliged to reconsider its role in subjective commitment in animals.

The second path to cooperation is labeled *by-product mutualism* (Brown 1983; Connor 1995; West-Eberhard 1975). In many regards this is the simplest of the paths leading to cooperation. In by-product mutualism animals cooperate because it is in their immediate best interest. To act otherwise (uncooperatively) would cause an animal to incur an immediate penalty. For example, lions hunt in groups when stalking large prey that cannot be taken by a single hunter, but hunt alone when hunting smaller prey (Scheel and Packer 1991). The lions cooperate when it provides immediate benefits, but do not do so otherwise, as by-product mutualism models predict.

Although possible in principle, little evidence exists for the use of conditional strategies during cooperation via by-product mutualism. Individuals respond to the state of the environment but not to the specific action of others. As such, an argument can be made against focusing our search for subjective commitment in animals in this category of cooperation, which is a shame, because by-product mutualism indeed may be the most common path to cooperation in animals (see, for example, Clements and Stephens 1995; Dugatkin 1997).

The third category of cooperation is reciprocal altruism. The earlier guppy example captures the notion of reciprocal altruism: acts of cooperation are repaid, while acts of cheating are punished. This is one of the paths to cooperation that I shall focus on in searching for examples of subjective commitment in animals.

Given that subjective commitment has been posed as an alternative to reciprocity in terms of the glue that holds together social bonds, to suggest that we should be looking at examples of reciprocity for cases of subjective commitment in animals may seem odd. The rationale for this suggestion stems in part from my belief that reciprocity is the most strategically complicated of the paths leading to animal cooperation. Given the complex nature of subjective commitment, we should be searching where strategic complexity (for example, conditional cooperation) is already known in animals—but there is something more.

Reciprocity arguably is the best studied of the four paths to cooperation and also happens to be that which could most easily contain miscategorized cases of subjective commitment. Given that few, if any, studies in behavioral ecology specifically have searched for subjective commitment in animals, subjective commitment perhaps already has been documented in animal cooperation, and if this is so, my bet is that it has been miscategorized as reciprocity.

The final path to cooperation is via group selection. While clearly the most contentious of the four paths to cooperation (Wilson 1983; Dugatkin and Reeve 1994; Sober and Wilson 1998), group selection holds some promise with respect to subjective commitment in animals. The *trait-group selection* (also referred to as modern or group selection) path to the evolution of cooperation is quite straightforward (Sober and Wilson 1998; Wilson and Sober 1994; see Sober and Wilson 1998 for more on the distinction between these models and older models of group selection). Cooperators pay a cost relative to others in their group that they help. Cooperation can evolve even when it has a relative cost to the individual performing it if this *within-group cost* is offset by a sufficiently large *between-group benefit*, such that *cooperative groups are more productive than selfish groups* (Wilson 1977, 1980). For such group-level benefits to be manifest, groups must differ in the frequency of cooperators within them, and must be able to "export" the productivity associated with cooperation.

Consider the case of *Acromyrmex versicolor*, a desert-dwelling species of ant that nests in shady areas. Many *A. versicolor* nests are founded by multiple ant queens, no dominance hierarchy exists among queens, queens are unrelated, and all queens produce workers. A single *A. versicolor* ventures forth from the nest and brings back food for herself and all her nestmates as well. As a result of increased predation pressure and parasitization, foraging is a very dangerous activity for a queen, but once a queen takes on the role of forager, she remains in that role. Which queen eventually emerges as the group's sole forager is still not well understood. Yet this decision appears to not be a coercive one—that is, it is not forced upon a particular queen by other groupmates (Rissing et al. 1989).

Once a queen becomes the sole forager for her nest, she shares all the food brought into her nest with her cofounders. The forager, then, assumes the risks of foraging and obtains the benefits, while the other queens simply obtain the benefits without risks. Within-group cooperation on the part of the forager appears to lead to more workers per nest. This is critical, because at some point after workers are produced, all nests in a given area will fight for access to the best (usually most shaded) area. Only one group will win, and the probability of victory in this struggle (called *brood-raiding*) is proportional to the number of workers in a nest. Thus between-group selection for a cooperative specialized forager overwhelms any within-group costs associated with this behavior (Rissing et al. 1989; Seger 1989; see also Wilson 1990 for a more extended discussion).

That the group selection and cooperation literature may prove fertile in our understanding of subjective commitment stems from the notion of *group identity* and the related idea of *in-group biasing* (Sherif 1966; Tajfel 1978, 1981; see also Brewer and Schneider 1990 for more on social identity theory). These concepts seem to be integrally tied to both subjective commitment and group selection. Group identity refers to the phenomenon in which individuals act as if the group of which they are a member is an entity with needs and objectives not necessarily in line with any given member's needs and objectives. In-group biasing occurs when individuals favor members of their own group over "foreigners." In-group biasing is obvious in religious, military, and sports groups, but also may occur in more mundane situations.

Tajfel (1970) set out to study in-group biasing in English teenagers in the late 1960s and early 1970s. Children from the same school were asked to estimate the number of dots flashed on a wall. The boys in this experiment then were informed that they fell into either one of two groups: those that overestimated the number of dots in the vision experiment and those that underestimated the number of dots. Each of the teenagers then was placed in a room by himself and given a series of forms.

The forms required the subjects to tell how they would divide up monetary rewards and penalties between two other boys in the study: either two individuals from their own group, two from the other group, or one from each group (again, groups refer to the tendency to over- or underestimate dot number).

Results were striking. When asked to partition rewards and punishments between two individuals from the same group—either that to which the subject belonged or that to which he did not—then rewards and punishments were distributed equally. If, however, the choice was between someone from one's own group (for example, the dot overestimators) and an individual from the other group (the dot underestimators), subjects consistently favored members of their own group. Simply knowing that others overestimated dots as you did, even if you never met such dot overestimators, was sufficient information to cause an unequal distribution of monetary rewards and punishments.

Clearly in-group biasing starts early in humans and can revolve around groups formed for almost any reason. Similar results have been found when group identity was based on a subject's favorite artist. From an evolutionary perspective, important and noteworthy is that subjects in these experiments were more concerned that their own group received a greater payoff than the other group (that is, their group "won"); they were concerned about having their group receive the largest amount of money possible. In natural selection terms, relative, not absolute, fitness was being maximized in studies such as that of Tajfel.

Given that group selection models rely on between-group competition to favor cooperation, it is not surprising that any factor that favors such between-group selection—such as in-group biasing—will be selected in such models. When this is juxtaposed to the role of group identity and in-group biasing in entities such as religious groups, the group-selection path to cooperation seems a potentially fruitful one to explore in terms of subjective commitment examples.

Examples of Subjective Commitment in Nonhumans

With the reciprocity and group-selection paths to cooperation as guideposts, and focusing primarily on nonprimates, is there any controlled work demonstrating subjective commitment in animals? Using the aforementioned definition of subjective commitment, the answer to this appears to be no. Despite the fact that cooperation has been studied in many different contexts, I could not find a single documented case of what we are referring to as subjective commitment.

The only study that remotely touched on what might be subjective commitment did not in fact support the notion that animals employ this sophisticated tool. Recall the guppy experiment outlined earlier, in which three fish first inspected a predator and then were allowed to choose which coinspectors they preferred to associate with later on. Fish clearly preferred to spend their time near others who cooperated during the first part of a trial. In a second treatment, however, fish were given the choice between associating with cooperators or cheaters, the catch being that they had no experience with other such individuals, and hence did not know who was a cooperator and who wasn't. In this treatment focal animals displayed no preference for cooperators. When they do not have firsthand experience with cooperators and cheaters, the guppies apparently cannot use other cues to categorize conspecifics as trustworthy or untrustworthy.

Why the Lack of Evidence for Subjective Commitment in Animals?

The most obvious reason that little evidence exists that animals use some form of subjective commitment is that the entire subject of the evolution of subjective commitment is rather new, and is only now being discussed in scientific circles. This volume is the first integrative attempt to examine subjective commitment in any rigorous way, and in many ways is a statement more about what needs to be done than about what has been accomplished to date. In this regard behavioral ecologists and ethologists cannot be blamed for not examining subjective commitment in nonhumans. Yet there is another reason for the lack of behavioral ecological data that could be used to infer subjective commitment—and this reason is not so easily excused.

My general sense is that in some paradoxical way, behavioral ecologists are biased against arguing for complex, strategically based behavior in animals. Paradoxical in that hundreds, if not thousands, of game theory models fill journals in animal behavior and evolutionary theory. Furthermore, many studies of strategic behavior and cooperation have been undertaken (Dugatkin 1997). The rush to test game theory models, however, has never really occurred. For example, on closer inspection one finds that many of the studies on animal cooperation were not done in the context of *testing* game theory models, but rather were interpreted by some in the light of game theory after the fact. The truth is that twenty-five years after the birth of evolutionary game theory, everyone talks about the subject (and it has made its way into virtually all major texts in behavioral ecology), but relatively few do rigorous, controlled experiments designed to specifically test evolutionary game theory models. No doubt there are many reasons for this (fear of mathematics, confusing levels of analysis, and so forth; see Reeve and Dugatkin 1998) but that it is true is a shame.

A number of areas are, however, ripe for examination with respect to animal behavior and commitment. For example, courtship, pair-bonding, and parental care in birds appears to be one good candidate for experimental manipulations centering on commitment. In many species of birds, females appear to "test" a male's level of commitment before acquiescing to courtship and eventual joint care of offspring. Whether this turns out to be a means by which females truly measure male commitment remains to be seen, but it is an enticing possibility, as females occasionally "divorce" a male long before normal courtship bonds would disintegrate (Choudhury 1995).

Constructing Animal Experiments on Subjective Commitment in Nonhumans

It is my hope, and no doubt the hope of all the contributors to this volume, that this book will spur on a variety of ideas and experiments focusing on the evolution of subjective commitment. Based on a review of the animal literature, I am confident that subjective commitment is well worth exploring in nonhumans, even nonprimates. The strategic behavior evident in many different creatures in a wide variety of contexts suggests that subjective commitment in animals should not be ruled out a priori. Whether this behavior proves to be uniquely human remains to be seen, but the only way to know this is to combine the human work with animal experiments. In that light I would suggest at least one general procedure researchers could use when testing for subjective commitment (in the context of cooperative behavior) in animals.

The suggested procedure has its roots in both psychological work on learning and partner-choice studies in behavioral ecology (Dugatkin and Wilson 1993; Dugatkin and Sih 1995; Dugatkin and Sih 1998). In the experimental protocol outlined here we are searching for subjective commitment in the context of cooperation. That is, we are examining whether animals are capable of acting as if they think that others will not necessarily behave in their best interest in the short term or have the capacity to induce such beliefs in others, all in the context of cooperative behavior.

Experimental Protocol for Examining Subjective Commitment in Animals

Each trial in this experiment would involve three individuals, and new individuals would be used in each step of the experiment. Each individual on which we are gathering data is referred to here as the *focal* individual.

Step 1. Single Task Learning and Cooperation   We begin by studying cooperation with respect to a single task. To illustrate, imagine that we decide to look at cooperative foraging. From a large pool of potential experimental subjects, determine who cooperates and who doesn't cooperate on your foraging task. Randomly choose a single individual who will serve as the focal. Furthermore, choose one cooperator and one noncooperator from your pool (for a total of three subjects). Subsequent to this, using any one of a number of standard social learning paradigms (Zentall and Galef 1988; Heyes and Galef 1996), teach all three subjects that all other individuals are noncooperators. In so doing the focal will see an array of other individuals tested, but will never actually see the specific cooperator and noncooperator whom the focal will soon choose between. Now, allow the focal to choose between the other two subjects (one a cooperator and one a noncooperator) in a foraging context and examine whether they exhibit any preference.

Step 2. Multiple Task Learning   This stage will be similar to step 1, except now individuals will be tested for their cooperative tendencies in an array of contexts. For example, imagine that in addition to foraging, one examined cooperation in the context of territory defense and antipredator behavior. As in step 1, test a large pool of individuals on each task and determine who cooperates in *all* contexts and who cooperates in *none*. Randomly choose a single individual who will serve as the focal, and an additional cooperator and noncooperator from your pool of potential experimental subjects. Employing social learning protocols, now teach your three subjects that all other individuals they see are cheaters in the context of foraging, and cooperators in the other two contexts. Here again, the focal sees an array of other individuals tested in all contexts, but it never actually sees the specific cooperator and noncooperator that it will soon choose between. Subsequent to this, allow the focal to choose between the other two subjects in the context of foraging and examine whether the focal has any preference.

Suppose that in step 1 focals showed no preference, but in step 2 they consistently preferred the cooperative individual. If this proved to be the case, it might be a sign of commitment on the part of the cooperator (not the focal individual) in step 2. Why? In both steps 1 and 2 the focal individual has no experience with the cooperator and noncooperator and so is reliant on some sort of cue from them as to their cooperative tendencies. If such a cue is absent in step 1, but present in step 2, this suggests that the cooperator in step 2 is providing some information that it is willing to cooperate. This information is provided even though the cooperator has been trained to believe that everyone else is uncooperative in the task of foraging. It is not in the cooperator's short-term best interest to provide any information that it will forage cooperatively with someone whom it believes is a cheater. Yet from the cooperator's perspective it may be willing to sacrifice a short-term loss in order to set up an environment where cooperation is displayed in other contexts (recall that the cooperator has been trained to believe that others will act cooperatively in terms of predators and territory defense). This seems close to what we have been referring to as subjective commitment.

Should the preceding scenario prove to be the case, an alternative explanation to that of subjective commitment is possible. In any learning experiment on multiple tasks, crossover effects must be carefully detailed. Crossover simply refers to learning in one context affecting learning in a different venue. For example, it is possible that either the focal individual, the cooperator, or both simply may have treated everyone as a cooperator since they observed cooperation in two of three contexts. Cooperation as the norm in antipredator behavior and territory defense may have crossed over and affected how much weight individuals gave to their foraging observations. If crossover effects exist, the animal is not sacrificing short-term gains for a potentially long-term cooperative environment, but simply is categorizing individuals as cooperators because they display such behavior in two of three contexts.

If crossover effects were present, any claim of subjective commitment would be severely weakened. Yet there are ways to tease out the potential confounding effects of crossover. The simplest of these is to choose to work with a species in which crossover effects already are known to be weak or nonexistent. If such data is unavailable, then experiments could be devised to examine crossover effects more directly. For example, one could test whether learning to forage for food type 1 had any effect on an individual's ability to forage for food type 2, 3, and so on. If crossovers were absent within a specific behavioral scenario (such as foraging), then they would be unlikely (but certainly not impossible) between behavioral contexts (for example, foraging, antipredator behavior, territory defense).

No doubt some will feel that the protocol outlined here for examining subjective commitment is flawed. Since the whole endeavor to study subjective commitment from an evolutionary perspective is new, such a criticism may prove true as we learn more about this fascinating subject. I hope, though, that my protocol serves as a starting point for experimentation, or at the very least, the impetus for a full-fledged debate about how best to test subjective commitment in nonhumans.

For a research scientist, the most exciting ventures are those that qualify as something new under the sun. While there is much exciting experimental and theoretical work under way these days in behavioral ecology, projects that attack fundamentally new ideas are few. I believe that the work on subjective commitment falls in this category and I am delighted to be in on the ground floor. Examining subjective commitment in animals has the potential to shed new light on this phenomenon in humans, and more generally on the evolution of complex social behavior.

Multidisciplinary work on subjective commitment is in its infancy, but I have no doubt that as it matures its theoretical and empirical evidence will be strong. For the reasons stated earlier, despite not having uncovered a single crystal-clear, controlled example of subjective commitment in nonhumans, I am confident that in five to ten years work on nonhumans and subjective commitment will have contributed significantly to our understanding of this fascinating behavior. That we will find solid cases of subjective commitment may just be a matter of asking the right questions and searching hard enough. Obviously, I may be wrong about this. Who knows? Perhaps in the end the ability to employ subjective commitment strategies may well be something that separates humans from nonhumans. The only way to be certain is to continue down the path that this volume has established.

References

Axelrod, Robert. 1984. *The Evolution of Cooperation*. New York: Basic Books.

Axelrod, Robert, and William D. Hamilton. 1981. "The Evolution of Cooperation." *Science* 211: 1390–96.

Brewer, Marilyn, and Susan Schneider. 1990. "Social Identity and Social Dilemmas: A Double-Edged Sword." In *Social Identity Theory*, edited by Dominic Abrams and Michael Hogg. New York: Harvester/Wheatsheat.

Brown, Jerram. 1983. "Cooperation—A Biologist's Dilemma." In *Advances in the Study of Behavior*, edited by J. S. Rosenblatt. New York: Academic Press.

Brown, Joel. 1998. "Game Theory and Habitat Selection." In *Game Theory and Animal Behavior*, edited by L. A. Dugatkin and H. K. Reeve. New York: Oxford University Press.

Choudhury, Sharmila. 1995. "Divorce in Birds—A Review of the Hypotheses." *Animal Behaviour* 50: 413–29.

Clements, Kevin, and D. W. Stephens. 1995. "Testing Models of Non-Cooperation: Mutualism and the Prisoner's Dilemma." *Animal Behaviour* 50: 527–35.

Connor, Richard. 1995. "The Benefits of Mutualism: A Conceptual Framework." *Biological Review*: 1–31.

Dugatkin, Lee Alan. 1991. "Dynamics of the TIT FOR TAT Strategy During Predator Inspection in Guppies." *Behavioral Ecology and Sociobiology* 29: 127–32.

———. 1997. *Cooperation Among Animals: An Evolutionary Perspective*. New York: Oxford University Press.

———. 1998. "Game Theory and the Evolution of Cooperation." In *Game Theory and Animal Behavior*, edited by L. A. Dugatkin and H. K. Reeve. New York: Oxford University Press.

Dugatkin, Lee Alan, and Michael Alfieri. 1991a. "Guppies and the TIT FOR TAT Strategy: Preference Based on Past Interaction." *Behavioral Ecology and Sociobiology* 28: 243–46.

———. 1991b. "TIT FOR TAT in Guppies: The Relative Nature of Cooperation and Defection During Predator Inspection." *Evolutionary Ecology* 5: 300–309.

Dugatkin, Lee Alan, Michael Mesterton-Gibbons, and Alasdair Houston. 1992. "Beyond the Prisoner's Dilemma: Towards Models to Discriminate Among Mechanisms of Cooperation in Nature." *Trends in Ecology and Evolution* 7: 202–5.

Dugatkin, Lee Alan, and Hudson Kern Reeve. 1994. "Behavioral Ecology and 'Levels of Selection': Dissolving the Group Selection Controversy." *Advances in the Study of Behaviour* 23: 101–33.

———, eds. 1998. *Game Theory and Animal Behavior*. New York: Oxford University Press.

Dugatkin, Lee Alan, and Andrew Sih. 1995. "Behavioral Ecology and the Study of Partner Choice." *Ethology* 99: 265–77.

————. 1998. "Evolutionary Ecology of Partner Choice." In *Cognitive Ecology*, edited by Reuven Dukas. Chicago: University of Chicago Press.

Dugatkin, L. A., and D. S. Wilson. 1993. "Fish Behaviour, Partner Choice Experiments and Cognitive Ethology." *Rev. Fish. Biol. Fisheries* 3: 368–72.

————. 2000. "Assortative Interactions and the Evolution of Cooperation in Guppies." *Evolutionary Ecology* 2: 761–67.

Frank, Robert. 1988. *Passions Within Reason: The Strategic Role of the Emotions.* New York: Norton.

Giraldeau, Luc-Alain, and Barbara Livoreil. 1998. "Game Theory and Social Foraging." In *Game Theory and Animal Behavior*, edited by Lee Alan Dugatkin and Hudson Kern Reeve. New York: Oxford University Press.

Heyes, Celia, and Bennet Galef, eds. 1996. *Social Learning in Animals: The Roots of Culture.* London: Academic Press.

Johnstone, Rufus. 1998. "Game Theory and Communication." In *Game Theory and Animal Behavior*, edited by Lee Alan Dugatkin and Hudson Kern Reeve. New York: Oxford University Press.

Magurran, Anne, and Anthony Higham. 1988. "Information Transfer Across Fish Shoals Under Predator Threat." *Ethology* 78: 153–58.

Magurran, Anne, and Anthony Pitcher. 1987. "Provenance, Shoal Size and the Sociobiology of Predator-Evasion in Minnow Shoals." *Proceedings of the Royal Society of London B* 229: 439–65.

Maynard Smith, John. 1982. *Evolution and the Theory of Games.* Cambridge: Cambridge University Press.

Maynard Smith, John, and George Price. 1973. "The Logic of Animal Conflict." *Nature* 246: 15–18.

Mesterton-Gibbons, Michael, and Lee Alan Dugatkin. 1992. "Cooperation Among Unrelated Individuals: Evolutionary Factors." *Quarterly Review of Biology* 67: 267–81.

Milinski, Manfred, David Kulling, and Rolf Kettler. 1990a. "Tit for Tat: Sticklebacks 'Trusting' a Cooperating Partner." *Behavioral Ecology* 1: 7–12.

Milinski, Manfred, David Pfluger, David Kulling, and Rolf Kettler. 1990b. "Do Sticklebacks Cooperate Repeatedly in Reciprocal Pairs?" *Behavioral Ecology and Sociobiology* 27: 17–23.

Mock, Douglas, Geoffrey Parker, and Patricia Schwagmeyer. 1998. "Game Theory, Sibling Rivalry and Parent-Offspring Conflict." In *Game Theory and Animal Behavior*, edited by L. A. Dugatkin and H. K. Reeve. New York: Oxford University Press.

Pitcher, Anthony. 1992. "Who Dares Wins: The Function and Evolution of Predator Inspection Behaviour in Shoaling Fish." *Netherlands Journal of Zoology* 42: 371–91.

Pitcher, Anthony, David Green, and Anne Magurran. 1986. "Dicing with Death: Predator Inspection Behavior in Minnow Shoals." *Journal of Fish Biology* 28: 439–48.

Ratnieks, Francis, and Paul Visscher. 1988. "Reproductive Harmony Via Mutual Policing by Workers in Eusocial Hymenoptera." *American Naturalist* 132: 217–36.

Reeve, Hudson Kern. 1989. "The Evolution of Conspecific Acceptance Thresholds." *American Naturalist* 133: 407–35.

————. 1998. "Game Theory, Reproductive Skew and Nepotism." In *Game*

Theory and Animal Behavior, edited by L. A. Dugatkin and H. K. Reeve. New York: Oxford University Press.

Reeve, Hudson Kern, and Lee Alan Dugatkin. 1998. "Why We Need Evolutionary Game Theory." In *Game Theory and Animal Behavior*, edited by L. A. Dugatkin and H. K. Reeve. New York: Oxford University Press.

Reeve, Hudson Kern, and Peter Nonacs. 1992. "Social Contracts in Wasp Societies." *Nature* 359: 823–25.

Riechert, Susan. 1998. "Game Theory and Animal Contests." In *Game Theory and Animal Behavior*, edited by L. A. Dugatkin and H. K. Reeve. New York: Oxford University Press.

Rissing, Steven, Gregory Pollock, Michael Higgins, Robert Hagen, and David Smith. 1989. "Foraging Specialization Without Relatedness or Dominance Among Co-founding Ant Queens." *Nature* 338: 420–22.

Scheel, David, and Craig Packer. 1991. "Group Hunting Behaviour of Lions: A Search for Cooperation." *Animal Behaviour* 41: 697–709.

Seger, Jon. 1989. "All for One, One for All, That Is Our Device." *Nature* 338: 374–75.

Sherif, Muzafer. 1966. *Group Conflict and Cooperation: Their Social Psychology*. London: Routledge and Kegan Paul.

Sih, Andrew. 1998. "Game Theory and Predator-Prey Response Races." In *Game Theory and Animal Behavior*, edited by L. A. Dugatkin and H. K. Reeve. New York: Oxford University Press.

Sober, Elliott, and David Sloan Wilson. 1998. *Unto Others*. Cambridge, Mass.: Harvard University Press.

Stephens, David. 1998. "Game Theory and Learning." In *Game Theory and Animal Behavior*, edited by L. A. Dugatkin and H. K. Reeve. New York: Oxford University Press.

Tajfel, Henri. 1970. "Experiments in Intergroup Discrimination." *Scientific American* 223: 96–102.

———, ed. 1978. *Differentiation Between Social Groups*. London: Academic Press.

———, ed. 1981. *Human Groups and Social Categories*. Cambridge: Cambridge University Press.

Trivers, Robert. 1971. "The Evolution of Reciprocal Altruism." *Quarterly Review of Biology* 46: 189–226.

West-Eberhard, Mary Jane. 1975. "The Evolution of Social Behavior by Kin Selection." *Quarterly Review of Biology* 50: 1–35.

Wilson, David Sloan. 1977. "Structured Demes and the Evolution of Group-Advantageous Traits." *American Naturalist* 111: 157–85.

———. 1980. *The Natural Selection of Populations and Communities*. Menlo Park, N.J.: Benjamin Cummings.

———. 1983. "The Group Selection Controversy: History and Current Status." *Annual Review of Ecology and Systematics* 14: 159–87.

———. 1990. "Weak Altruism, Strong Group Selection." *Oikos* 59: 135–40.

Wilson, David Sloan, and Elliott Sober. 1994. "Re-introducing Group Selection to the Human Behavioral Sciences." *Behavioral and Brain Sciences* 17: 585–654.

Zentall, Thomas, and Bennett Galef. 1988. *Social Learning: Psychological and Biological Perspectives*. Hillsdale, N.J.: Lawrence Erlbaum.

Chapter 7

Grunts, Girneys, and Good Intentions: The Origins of Strategic Commitment in Nonhuman Primates

JOAN B. SILK

SOCIAL groups are composed of individuals with very different interests, needs, and abilities. Despite these differences, members of social groups manage to synchronize their activities; negotiate about certain kinds of decisions; anticipate what others will do in certain situations; and broker social transactions that include cooperative and competitive elements. To accomplish these feats, primates somehow must provide information to others about their dispositions and intentions. Detailed observations of the behavior of many species reveal that monkeys and apes use a variety of signals to communicate this information. Some of these signals function as generic commitments, and convey information about what animals will do next (Nesse, ch. 1 herein). Thus many primates use vocalizations to indicate their readiness to travel or the direction in which they intend to move (reviewed by Boinski 2000). These kinds of signals are likely to enhance coordination, even when group members have competing interests. Monkeys also use signals to communicate their intention to behave peacefully toward others and to reconcile disputes with former opponents. These signals may function as strategic commitments, which guarantee that the actor subsequently will behave in ways that are sometimes contrary to its own short-term interests (Nesse, ch. 1 herein).

Strategic commitments can be enforced by external forces, reputational effects, or internal emotional motives (Nesse, ch. 1 herein). The latter constitute subjective commitments. We have no evidence that primates experience the kinds of emotions that are thought to influence subjective commitments in humans (Frank, ch. 3 herein), although some researchers argue for their presence in great apes, particularly chimpanzees (for example, Killen and de Waal 2000). Some emotions, such as sympathy and empathy, may require the ability to understand the perspectives of other individuals. Present evidence suggests that monkeys and apes know very little about what goes on in others' minds, and have limited abilities for empathy, perspective taking, and mind reading (Tomasello and Call 1997, Povinelli and Eddy 1996). It is possible, however, that internal motivational states influence behavior in primates without being mediated by conscious emotions or moral sentiments. Sexually active male elephants, for example, experience a condition called musth (Poole 1989). Males who are in musth signal heightened aggression and intention to fight with glandular secretions, vocalizations, and urine marking. Musth appears to be a costly, honest signal of males' motivation to behave aggressively.

Whether internal motivational states or emotions regulate strategic commitments in primate groups remains unclear. Researchers have not identified any signals in primates that are analogous to musth in elephants. Possibly the behaviors that accompany aggressive displays, such as pilo-erection in chimpanzees or counterchasing in baboons, may communicate information about the intention to fight, regardless of the immediate consequences. These might then constitute subjective commitments. This issue, however, has not been systematically investigated among nonhuman primates.

That strategic commitments in primate groups are enforced by reputational effects is certainly possible. Reputation is likely to be an important factor in shaping signaling strategies in species in which individuals recognize one another, interact repeatedly, and remember their previous encounters. Here I present empirical evidence that primates make use of strategic commitments that are enforced by reputational effects and consider how evolution has shaped the evolution of these kinds of signals. This body of work is useful because it demonstrates that subjective commitments are not the only vehicle for generating behavior that contravenes self-interest.

Listening in on Primate Groups

Observers of primate groups know that monkeys and apes are rarely silent for long. Infant baboons cry loudly and persistently when their mother will not allow them to nurse (Altmann 1980), juvenile ma-caques scream to recruit support in conflicts with other group mem-bers (Gouzoules, Gouzoules, and Marler 1984), gibbons perform com-plex duets at the borders of their territories (Mitani 1985), macaques and baboons give loud copulation calls after mating (O'Connell and Cowlishaw 1994; Hauser 1993), and male chimpanzees pant hoot loudly when they meet members of other traveling parties (Goodall 1986). These are the kinds of calls that most studies of primate com-munication focus on, a bias that reflects the evolutionary design of these signals—they are loud and meant to attract attention. Yet most primates also have a repertoire of quieter and less conspicuous vocal-izations. A growing body of research suggests that some of these kinds of quiet vocalizations provide reliable information about the actor's intentions and disposition and are effective in facilitating so-cial interactions.

Communicating Peaceful Intentions

Monkeys and apes tend to be contentious creatures. Macaques and baboons form strict dominance hierarchies that often remain stable over years or even decades. High rank confers both short-term and long-term advantages upon individuals. Dominance rank acts as an intervening variable that mediates access to resources, so high-ranking individuals gain preferential access to food and mates. As a conse-quence, high-ranking individuals tend to reproduce more successfully than lower-ranking group members (Silk 1987).

In primate groups some conflicts involve contests over food, but in many species the majority of aggressive interactions occur sponta-neously (Walters and Seyfarth 1987). The prevalence of unprovoked aggression generates considerable uncertainty for females whenever they are in proximity to higher-ranking females because there is al-ways some risk of being threatened, chased, or attacked (Aureli, van Schaik, and van Hooff 1989). This may create an obstacle for friendly interactions. A female uncertain about whether she is going to be groomed or bitten may be inclined to take evasive action when she is approached by a more dominant female. While this may limit the risk of being attacked, it also restricts opportunities for friendly interac-tions, such as grooming. A growing body of data suggests that mon-keys have devised an effective solution to this problem. They use quiet calls to communicate their intent to behave peacefully. This con-jecture is based mainly on work conducted on semi-free-ranging rhe-sus macaques on the island of Cayo Santiago (Silk, Kaldor, and Boyd 2000) and free-ranging chacma baboons in the Moremi Reserve of Botswana (Cheney and Seyfarth 1997; Cheney, Seyfarth, and Silk 1995b; Rendall et al. 1999; Silk, Cheney, and Seyfarth 1996).

Figure 7.1   Grunts Inhibit Aggression

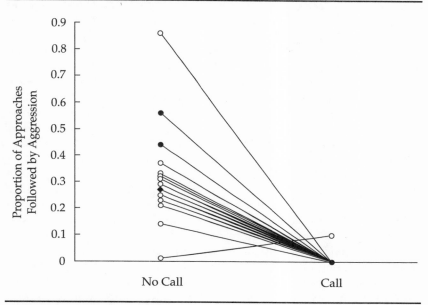

Source: Silk, Kaldor, and Boyd 2000.
Note: Among rhesus macaques, grunts and girneys inhibit aggression. Here the proportions of approaches with and without calls that were followed by aggression are plotted. Each pair of open circles linked by a line represents paired values for a single female. The solid circles represent pairs of females who had identical values, and the solid diamond represents three females who had identical values.

Rhesus macaques have a repertoire of quiet calls, including two calls that frequently are used in affiliative contexts, grunts and gir- neys. These calls are both quiet, low-frequency vocalizations. Grunts are short harsh sounds produced through open lips with a slightly dropped jaw (Hauser, Evans, and Marler 1993). Girneys are soft, low- frequency chewing noises accompanied by rapid lip movement (Green 1975). A careful analysis of the sequence of events that follow grunts and girneys suggests that these calls signal the actor's intention to behave benignly.

For female rhesus macaques, it is often dangerous to be close to higher-ranking females. On Cayo Santiago, nearly one quarter of all approaches by females led to some form of aggression. However, the likelihood that aggression would occur was directly associated with the use of grunts and girneys (Silk, Kaldor, and Boyd 2000). Figure 7.1 demonstrates that females were much less likely to initiate aggression if they called as they approached other lower-ranking females than if they approached and remained silent. The magnitude of the effect was quite substantial: females were nearly thirty times more likely to act aggressively if they approached and remained silent than if they approached and grunted or girneyed.

These results suggest that grunts and girneys provide recipients with reliable evidence that the caller's subsequent behavior will be peaceful. This conjecture is supported by the fact that females were four times more likely to show spontaneous signs of submission when approached by females who did not call as when approached by females who called as they came near. Thus females behaved as if they had some knowledge of what other females would do if they called and what they might do if they remained silent.

Callers did seem to be truly motivated to interact affiliatively when they called. Females who called as they approached subsequently groomed their partners nearly half the time. On average, females who called as they approached were more than twice as likely to groom their partners as females who remained silent as they approached.

Some evidence suggests that grunts and girneys play a similar role in other macaque species. Muroyama (1991) reported that Japanese macaques give girneys during grooming interactions, using one variant when they are attempting to groom others and another variant when they are attempting to solicit grooming from others. Masataka (1989) suggested that monkeys use calls to assess one another's motivation to interact peacefully.

Resolving Conflicts

Grunts seem to have much the same effect among baboons as grunts and girneys have among rhesus monkeys. Analyses of tape-recorded vocalizations indicate that baboon females' grunts carry acoustic information about the identity of the caller (Owren, Seyfarth, and Cheney 1997). Playback experiments conducted in the field show that grunts also carry rudimentary information about the context in which the call was given (Rendall et al. 1999). In the Moremi Reserve grunts facilitate nonaggressive interactions and inhibit supplants among adult females (Cheney, Seyfarth, and Silk 1995b; see also Barton, Byrne, and Whiten 1996).

Grunts evidently play an important role in resolving conflicts among baboons as well (Castles and Whiten 1998; Cheney and Seyfarth 1997; Cheney, Seyfarth, and Silk 1995b; Gore 1994; Silk, Cheney, and Seyfarth 1996). In primate groups former adversaries (or their kin) often interact peacefully with one another soon after conflicts have ended. These interactions are particularly striking because they are so unexpected—one would expect aggression to drive former op-

Figure 7.2   Grunts Predict Nonagressive Interactions

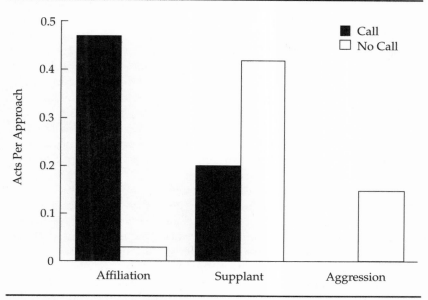

Source: Silk, Cheney, and Seyfarth 1996.
Note: Females who grunted as they approached former opponents were more likely to interact peacefully and less likely to supplant or harass their former opponents than former aggressors who remained silent as they approached.

ponents further apart, not closer together. Nonetheless, former opponents are far more likely to interact nonaggressively in the minutes that follow conflicts than they are at other times (reviewed by de Waal and Aureli 1996). De Waal and van Roosmalen (1979) labeled these peaceful postconflict interactions *reconciliation* because they hypothesized that such interactions helped to mend social relationships that were damaged by conflict. Although some dispute the long-term function of these interactions, there is broad consensus about their immediate effects. Peaceful postconflict interactions relieve former opponents' anxiety that aggression will continue and facilitate affiliative interactions among former opponents (for example, Aureli, van Schaik, and van Hooff 1989; Cheney and Seyfarth 1997; Silk, Cheney, and Seyfarth 1996).

In many primate species, it has proven difficult to identify specific behaviors that produce reconciliatory effects. In baboons, however, both observational and experimental data confirm that they use grunts to signal that conflicts have ended and the callers' intentions are now benign. After conflicts have ended, aggressors sometimes approach and grunt to their former opponents (Castles and Whiten 1998; Gore 1994; Silk, Cheney, and Seyfarth 1996). In Moremi, females who grunt to their former opponents are more likely to interact peacefully with them in the minutes that follow conflicts than females who remain silent. Grunts also reduce the likelihood that aggression will resume (see figure 7.2). The importance of grunts in facilitating peaceful contact after conflicts is further supported by playback experiments in which reconciliation was simulated by playing the aggressor's tape-recorded grunt to her former opponent. After hearing these calls the opponent was more likely to approach and initiate peaceful interactions with her former aggressor (Cheney and Seyfarth 1997).

Grunts may facilitate peaceful interactions among former opponents because they relieve females' anxiety that the aggressor will continue to harass them. Evidence in support of this hypothesis comes from another playback experiment conducted in Moremi (Cheney, Seyfarth, and Silk 1995b). This experiment took advantage of the fact that females sometimes scream when they are attacked by other group members, and victims of aggression sometimes redirect aggression toward lower-ranking individuals. Thus a female who hears the scream of a higher-ranking female may expect to become the target of an attack herself. To determine whether grunting during the post-conflict period reduces females' anxiety about whether former aggressors will redirect aggression toward them, the tape-recorded screams of aggressors were played to their former opponents: (a) shortly after they had fought and the aggressor had grunted to her former opponent; (b) shortly after they had fought but the aggressor had not grunted to her former opponent; and (c) after a period of forty-five minutes in which they had not interacted at all. The last condition functions as a control. Females react most strongly to the screams of aggressors who had not grunted to them. Females' responses to aggressors who subsequently had grunted matched their responses when they had not interacted at all. Thus grunts essentially erased the effects of prior conflicts. This suggests that grunts reassured former opponents that the conflict was over and the aggressor's intentions were peaceful.

Mother, May I?

In most primate species females are intensely interested in other females' infants. They crowd around new mothers, attempting to sniff, nuzzle, touch, inspect, and tug on infants who are still too young to stray from their mothers'embrace. Females groom new mothers assiduously, occasionally pausing long enough to touch the infant or peer at its genitals (Altmann 1980). We do not fully understand the adaptive function of "natal attraction," although a growing body of evidence suggests that it is a by-product of selection for appropriate maternal care (Paul and Kuester 1996; Silk 1999b). Whatever its function, virtually all primate females fall under the thrall of newborn infants.

In macaque and baboon groups infant handling is generally gentle, although females sometimes try to pull infants away from their mothers, creating a tug-of-war over the infant (Maestripieri 1994). Infants sometimes give distress calls when handled, particularly when disturbed while they are nursing or pulled vigorously. In macaque and baboon groups mothers usually are wary when others try to handle their infants. In her classic book on baboon mothers and their infants Jeanne Altmann wrote, "Mothers 'perceived' the mere approach or presence of certain individuals, and certainly handling and pulling of the infant, as a threat or source of distress" (Altmann 1980, 109). In Altmann's study mothers exhibited the highest rates of distress during the months when their infants were the focus of the most intense interest by other females. Mothers' reluctance to allow their infants to be handled is presumably linked to concerns about their infants' welfare (Maestripieri 1994), although risks to infants during infant handling have not been assessed systematically.

In this situation there is a clear conflict of interest between wary mothers and zealous handlers. Female macaques and baboons effectively resolve this impasse by vocalizing to mothers before they attempt to handle their infants. When female baboons approach the mother of a newborn infant, they usually grunt softly to the mother before they reach out to touch or inspect her infant (personal observation). Similarly, stumptailed macaque (*Macaca arctoides*) mothers are less likely to respond aggressively to females who give quiet staccato grunts before they attempt to handle their infants than to females who remain silent (Bauers 1993). These soft grunts seem to act as signals of the callers' intention to behave benignly toward infants (Bauers 1993). Maternal tolerance reflects confidence in the reliability of the potential handler's commitment.

If grunts signal females' benign disposition toward infants, then females who call as they approach mothers of newborns should behave nonaggressively toward their infants. Moreover, these calls should allay mothers' concerns about the safety of their infants. As a consequence, calls should facilitate infant handling interactions. Detailed analyses of infant handling interactions among rhesus macaques confirm all three of these predictions (Silk, Kaldor, and Boyd 2000).

Figure 7.3   Grunts Facilitate Infant Handling

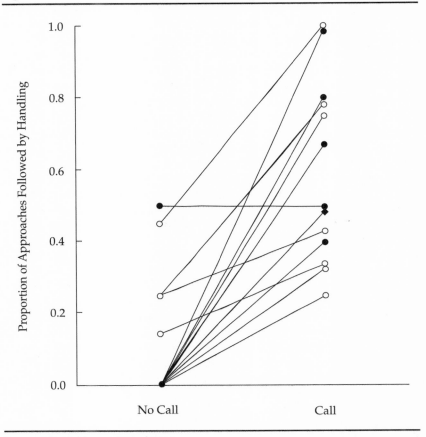

Source: Silk, Kaldor, and Boyd 2000.
Note: Among rhesus macaques, grunts and girneys facilitate infant handling. Here the proportions of approaches with and without calls that were followed by infant handling is compared. Open circles represent individual females, solid circles represent pairs of females with identical values, and the solid diamond represents three females who had identical values.

Females usually handle infants gently, but on some occasions they do treat infants roughly and cause distress. Females who grunt or girney as they approach infants are significantly less likely to handle them roughly and cause distress than females who do not call as they approach. Mothers are less likely to respond aggressively or fearfully if females call before they handle infants than if they remain silent. Finally, females are significantly more likely to handle infants if they call to mothers and their infants than if they remain silent. As can be seen in figure 7.3, the magnitude of this effect is substantial: females who approached and remained silent handled infants 10 percent of the time on average, while females who approached and called handled infants 61 percent of the time on average. Thus for rhesus macaques, who are otherwise contentious and competitive creatures, grunts and girneys seem to convey important information about the caller's disposition and subsequent behavior toward infants.

The Evolution of Low-Cost Signals of Commitment

Biological signaling theory provides a framework for understanding how signals should be designed and what kind of information they should convey. For communication to be effective, signals must convey reliable information, otherwise recipients will stop attending to them. Honesty, however, is not always the best strategy from a signaler's point of view; this is why you don't show your cards when playing poker, and why it is unwise to believe your opponent when he tells you what cards he holds.

When the advantages of deception undermine the credibility of signals, how can honest communication be preserved? Zahavi (1975) suggests that the reliability of signals will be maintained by their cost. Signals that are costly to produce or risky to give cannot be corrupted because it is not profitable for low-quality or poorly motivated individuals to give them. Thus male red deer roar in the early stages of contests. These roars, which are loud and energetically expensive to produce, provide a reliable index of the male's current physical condition (Clutton-Brock, Guinness, and Albon 1982).

By the same logic, when there is no incentive to lie, there is no need for signals to be costly. Suppose that you are engaged in a cooperative venture with a colleague, such as writing a textbook. You probably would decide to divide up the work according to your expertise and interest. It makes no sense to tell your partner you are willing to write the chapter on molecular genetics when you have no intention of doing so. Since you share a common interest in completing the book, you have little reason to deceive your colleague about your intentions. Thus you can send a brief e-mail outlining your plans, and you don't need to work very hard to convince your partner that your message is credible.

This intuition was confirmed by Maynard Smith (1991, 1994), who explored the dynamics of low-cost signaling when there is no conflict of interest between participants (the rationale underlying evolutionary game theory is outlined by Dugatkin in chapter 6 herein). Maynard Smith devised the Philip Sidney game, which takes its name from a famous act of altruism performed by Sir Philip in the battle of Zutphen. Sir Philip, a member of the court of Elizabeth I, was a celebrated poet and diplomat. In the service of the queen, Sir Philip joined a military campaign intended to protect the Netherlands against ongoing attacks by Spain. In 1586 Sir Philip was mortally wounded in the battle of Zutphen, an event that was recorded by his lifelong friend, Sir Fulke Greville:

> An unfortunate hand brake the bone of Sir Philip's thigh with a musket shot. The horse he rode upon, was rather furiously choleric than bravely proud, and so forced him to forsake the field, and being thirsty with excess of bleeding, he called for drink, which was presently brought him; but as he was putting the bottle to his mouth, he saw a poor soldier carried along, who had eaten his last at the same Feast, ghastly casting up his eyes at the bottle. When Sir Philip perceiving, took it from his head, before he drank, and delivered it to the poor man, with these words, Thy necessity is greater than mine. . . . (Greville 1652, 128)

Sir Philip died from his injuries three weeks after the battle at the age of thirty-two.

In the Philip Sidney game a potential donor (Sir Philip) is paired with a potential beneficiary (the soldier). The donor has a resource (water bottle) that can be given to the beneficiary. The donor suffers some cost if he gives up the water bottle, but the beneficiary gains an advantage from obtaining it, particularly if he is thirsty. If donor and recipient have an interest in each other's survival, either because they are kin and share common genes or because they are allies and share a common interest in the outcome of the battle, then evolution can favor cost-free signals of the beneficiary's need for the resource (Maynard Smith 1991) and cost-free signals of the donor's willingness to provide the resource (Maynard Smith 1994).

There are other situations in which deception is unprofitable, and signals may consequently be inexpensive. Suppose that you and your partner want to have dinner together after work. Telling your partner you will meet at the Mexican restaurant downtown makes no sense if you actually intend to go to the Thai restaurant near your office. Since you have no incentive to lie, your partner need not worry about your credibility. Farrel and Rabin (1996) have demonstrated, however, that truthful low-cost signaling does not necessarily depend on both partners having the same preferences. Even if you want to eat at the Thai restaurant and your partner wants to go to the Mexican restaurant, you're better off being truthful if you'd rather eat together than alone.

Again, since you don't benefit by lying, your partner has little concern about your credibility.

The basic logic of this situation is explored in the Battle of the Sexes game. In the traditional version of this game both parties choose their destination without communicating their intentions. The only evolutionary stable strategy then is for both players to choose their own preferred destination with the same probability. If you follow this strategy to decide which restaurant to go to, you and your partner often will end up at different restaurants. Of course, in this situation most people do not rely on chance—they talk. Since they want to eat together, they have no reason to lie about where they intend to go and no reason to doubt their partner's credibility. Farrel and Rabin (1996) have shown that low-cost signals (cheap talk) can be favored when preferences differ as long as coordination is sufficiently valued. (This does not necessarily mean that signalers will obtain their most preferred outcome. When preferences differ, individuals may have to negotiate, sometimes at length, or adopt a conventional asymmetry, such as flipping a coin, to resolve the impasse.)

When monkeys grunt after conflicts or girney before they groom, it is plausible that both partners benefit from the exchange of information, and this explains why the signals that they use in these situations are quiet and inconspicuous. Yet the same kinds of quiet low-cost calls are used to facilitate infant handling, an interaction that seems to represent a real conflict of interest between females who have no interest in coordination. How can this be?

Most of the work on the evolution of communication in conflict situations assumes that individuals interact only once. Yet for animals who live in social groups, meet repeatedly, and remember their interactions this is not a realistic assumption. If individuals use their memory of past experiences to evaluate the reliability of information, then reputation may play an important role in the assessment of signals (Maynard Smith 1982; van Rhijn 1980; van Rhijn and Vodegel 1980). Actors who give false signals may benefit initially from deceiving others, but the benefits of deception will be short-lived if recipients stop believing those who have deceived them in the past (Slater 1983).

The conflict between the short-term benefits of lying and the long-term benefits of telling the truth may be very real for animals living in social groups. The reluctance of mothers to allow their infants to be handled is likely to be based at least partly on the fact that other females sometimes harass and attack infants (Maestripieri 1994). Harassment of infants is generally interpreted as a form of reproductive competition (Silk 1980; Wasser 1983). If females benefit from harassing other females' infants, then they might be able to use grunts to lull mothers of newborns into complacency. A female who grunts as she approaches a mother-infant pair and then bites the infant may be able to catch the mother unawares; but if mothers remember acts of deception, such strategies will only work once. The deceptive female will not be able to use this device again and she won't be able to handle the female's infant either.

My colleagues and I have explored the dynamics of signaling when there is a potential conflict of interest, but individuals meet repeatedly, remember their interactions, and condition their behavior on their prior experience (Silk, Kaldor, and Boyd 2000). We assume a situation in which one individual approaches another individual. The actor's disposition is benign some fraction of the time, but the recipient initially is unaware of the actor's disposition. When the actor approaches the recipient, she can produce a signal that conveys information about her disposition. At this point the recipient can decide to stay and interact or flee. If the actor's disposition is benign and the recipient stays put, then they interact peacefully.

In our model actors have three strategies. Truthful signalers (TF) call when they intend to behave nicely, and otherwise remain silent. Deceptive signalers always signal (AS) no matter what they intend to do. Nonsignalers (NS) remain silent even when they intend to behave benignly. Recipients also have three possible responses: they may always interact (AI) regardless of the signaler's behavior, they may always flee (AF), or they may alter their behavior based on the actor's prior experience. Conditional believers (CB) believe the actor until they are deceived, but once they have been deceived, they always flee. The CB strategy provides a simple way to capture the idea that the recipient's behavior is contingent on their previous experience with the actor. The decision tree shown in figure 7.4 outlines all of the possible combinations of strategies and the behavioral outcomes that result.

The results of this game theory model indicate that if conditional believers are common, truthful signaling is an evolutionary stable strategy whenever the future benefits of being believed exceed the short-term benefits achieved by lying. Moreover, the more often the actor is disposed to behave benignly, the less advantageous it is to lie in any given interaction. Results confirm that it is not necessary for participants to rank outcomes in the same order. Thus low-cost signals can evolve even when there is a conflict of interest between participants, as long as partners interact repeatedly and condition their behavior on the basis of past experience.

Figure 7.4 Payoff Structure Associated with Signalling Intent

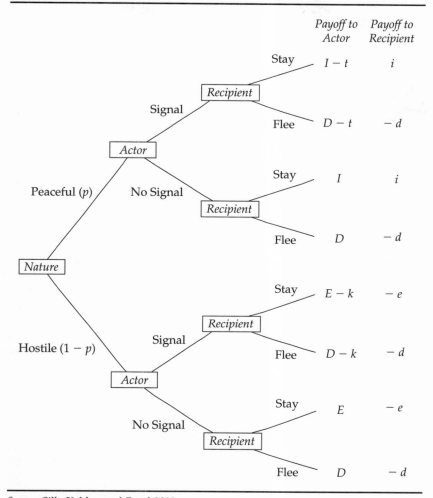

Source: Silk, Kaldor, and Boyd 2000.
Note:This decision tree summarizes the sequence of possible moves and associated payoffs for each player. Jnitially, the actor's disposition is benign or hostile, but this internal state is not known by the recipient. The actor may signal or not signal. The recipient may interact or flee. The behavioral outcomes that result from each sequence of moves are given at the terminal nodes of the tree. The payoffs associated with each sequence are given on the right side of the figure. The actor's payoffs reflect the effects of interacting peacefully (*I*), supplanting the recipient (*D*), or attacking the recipient (*E*) minus the costs of signaling honestly (*t*) or dishonestly (*k*). The payoffs to the recipient reflect the effects of interacting peacefully (*i*), being supplanted (*d*), or being attacked (*e*).

Communicating Commitment

Monkeys who give grunts or girneys typically behave peacefully, while monkeys who do not call in the same contexts are more likely to behave aggressively, cause distress to infants, or resume fighting. Females' responses indicate that they have some awareness of the association between these calls and the kinds of outcomes that typically follow. Monkeys' use of signals of intent does not require any conscious knowledge of the consequences of their behavior, just as males' interest in mating with receptive females does not imply any conscious knowledge of the association between copulation and conception. We have no evidence that female monkeys understand other individuals' intentions or have insight about their internal mental states. The effectiveness of these signals simply implies that they have learned to associate these kinds of calls with benign outcomes (Cheney and Seyfarth 1996).

Nonetheless, signals of intent fit the definition of strategic commitments because they entail an obligation to behave in certain ways and preclude certain alternatives. When females give grunts or girneys, they are effectively guaranteeing that they will behave peacefully. These kinds of calls function as pledges or promises to behave peacefully, even when it might be in their short-term interest to behave aggressively. The females' confidence in the reliability of the promise makes them effective. A female who grunts as she approaches the mother of a newborn infant gives up her option to harass the infant, even though there are some circumstances under which this deception might yield short-term benefits.

Unlike costly signals, which are not profitable to use deceptively, low-cost signals of intent could be faked readily; but deceit may be counterproductive in the long term. "In close-knit groups of animals, where individuals recognise one another and interact with each other over extended periods, the long-term penalties which may arise if deceit is discovered may more than outweigh any short-term gain it makes possible" (Slater 1983). In fact there are very few well-documented examples of tactical deception among monkeys, although apes may be more devious (Whiten and Byrne 1988). This is usually explained as a result of the fact that monkeys do not have the cognitive abilities that are required for deception, such as attribution and perspective taking. Yet it is also possible that deception may be uncommon because it is ultimately an unprofitable tactic for group-living animals with long-term social bonds and good memories.

I have suggested here that strategic commitments are enforced through reputational effects. If this is correct, then it might be productive to study how reputation influences the nature of social interactions within animal groups. Primates seem to know a considerable amount about their own relationships to other group members, including kinship, relative dominance rank, and the quality of social bonds (Tomasello and Call 1997). A growing body of evidence indicates that primates also know something about the same aspects of the relationships among other group members (Bachmann and Kummer 1980; Cheney and Seyfarth 1999; Cheney, Seyfarth, and Silk 1995a; Dasser 1988a, 1988b; Silk 1999a). It is not clear whether or how monkeys use this information to assess the behavioral predispositions of others. We are reasonably certain that monkeys make use of information derived from their own interactions with other group members to regulate their social relationships. Female baboons, for example, selectively groom unrelated females who groom them in return (Silk, Cheney, and Seyfarth 1999); male bonnet macaques are most likely to intervene against males who are most likely to intervene against them (Silk 1992); and female macaques selectively reconcile with kin and close associates (Cords and Aureli 2000). Yet we do not know whether primates' assessments about the behavioral predispositions of their partners are based solely on their own experiences or include information derived from observations of their interactions with others.

It should be possible to design experiments that would address this question empirically. We might, for example, artificially manipulate exchanges of valued food resources, and investigate whether observers were attracted to individuals who reciprocated reliably or were indifferent to this information. We might also evaluate the weight animals placed on their own experiences with particular partners versus the experiences of others. It might also be useful to conduct playback experiments to examine the effects of manipulating the honesty of signals. For example, a dominant baboon's grunt could be paired with a subordinate baboon's scream. This is an anomalous sequence if grunts are reliable signals of peaceful intent (Cheney, Seyfarth, and Silk 1995a). If baboons keep track of the reliability of other animals' signals, then those who hear this sequence of calls would be expected to respond more warily when approached by the "unreliable" dominant female than those who have heard a typical sequence of calls. Such experiments would help us to determine whether primates make use of third-party information about the reputations of other group members.

The mechanisms that underlie strategic commitments in nonhuman primates are not yet fully understood. Detailed ethological observations and carefully designed experimental studies may help to clarify the role of reputational effects and subjective commitments in enforcing strategic commitments among monkeys and apes. By documenting the full range of commitment strategies that we see in nature, we may ultimately be able to trace the evolutionary history of the human capacity for subjective commitment.

The work described here would not have been possible without the contributions of my colleagues. The behavioral work on baboons was conducted in collaboration with Dorothy Cheney and Robert Seyfarth in the Moremi Reserve of Botswana. The empirical work on rhesus macaques was conducted by Elizabeth Kaldor on Cayo Santiago. I thank Randy Nesse for the invitation to participate in the symposium that led to the development of this volume; and Rob Boyd, Eldridge Adams, and several anonymous reviewers for their comments on this chapter.

References

Altmann, Jeanne. 1980. *Baboon Mothers and Infants*. Cambridge, Mass.: Harvard University Press.

Aureli, Felippo, Carel P. van Schaik, and Jan A. R. A. M. van Hooff. 1989. "Functional Aspects of Reconciliation Among Captive Long-Tailed Macaques (*Macaca fasicularis*)." *American Journal of Primatology* 19: 39–51.

Bachmann, Christian, and Hans Kummer. 1980. "Male Assessment of Female Choice in Hamadryas Baboons." *Behavioral Ecology and Sociobiology* 6: 315–21.

Barton, Robert A., Richard W. Byrne, and Andrew Whiten. 1996. "Ecology, Feeding Competition, and Social Structure in Baboons." *Behavioral Ecology and Sociobiology* 38: 321–29.

Bauers, Kim A. 1993. "A Functional Analysis of Staccato Grunt Vocalizations in the Stumptailed Macaque (*Macaca arctoides*)." *Ethology* 94: 147–61.

Boinski, Sue. 2000. "Social Manipulation Within and Between Groups Mediates Primate Group Movement." In *On the Move: How and Why Animals Travel in Groups*, edited by Sue Boinski and Paul A. Garber. Chicago: University of Chicago Press.

Castles, Duncan L., and Andrew Whiten. 1998. "Post-Conflict Behaviour of Wild Olive Baboons. I. Reconciliation, Redirection, and Consolation." *Ethology* 104: 126–47.

Cheney, Dorothy L., and Robert M. Seyfarth. 1996. "Function and Intention in the Calls of Non-Human Primates." In *Evolution of Social Behaviour Patterns in Primates and Man*, edited by W. C. Runciman, John Maynard Smith, and Robin I. M. Dunbar. Oxford: Oxford University Press.

———. 1997. "Reconciliatory Grunts by Dominant Females Influence Victims' Behaviour." *Animal Behaviour* 54: 409–18.

———. 1999. "Recognition of Other Individuals' Social Relationships by Female Baboons." *Animal Behaviour* 58: 67–75.

Cheney, Dorothy L., Robert M. Seyfarth, and Joan B. Silk. 1995a. "The Responses of Female Baboons (*Papio cyncocephalus ursinus*) to Anomalous Social Interactions: Evidence for Causal Reasoning?" *Journal of Comparative Psychology* 109: 134–41.

————. 1995b. "The Role of Grunts in Reconciling Opponents and Facilitating Interactions Among Adult Female Baboons." *Animal Behaviour* 50: 249–57.

Clutton-Brock, T. H., F. E. Guinness, S. D. Albon. 1982. *Red Deer: Behavior and Ecology of Two Sexes*. Chicago: University of Chicago Press.

Cords, Marina, and Felippo Aureli. 2000. "Reconciliation and Relationship Qualities." In *Natural Conflict Resolution*, edited by Felippo Aureli and Frans B. M. de Waal. Berkeley: University of California Press.

Dasser, Verena. 1988a. "Mapping Social Concepts in Monkeys." In *Machiavellian Intelligence: Social Expertise and the Evolution of Intellect in Monkeys, Apes, and Humans*, edited by Richard W. Byrne and Andrew Whiten. New York: Oxford University Press.

————. 1988b. "A Social Concept in Java monkeys." *Animal Behaviour* 36: 225–30.

De Waal, Frans B. M., and Felippo Aureli. 1996. "Consolation, Reconciliation, and a Possible Cognitive Difference Between Macaques and Chimpanzees." In *Reaching into Thought*, edited by Anne E. Russon, Kim A. Bard, and Sue T. Parker. Cambridge: Cambridge University Press.

De Waal, Frans B. M., and Angeline van Roosmalen. 1979. "Reconciliation and Consolation Among Chimpanzees." *Behavioral Ecology and Sociobiology* 5: 55–66.

Farrel, Joseph, and Matthew Rabin. 1996. "Cheap Talk." *Journal of Economic Perspectives* 10: 110–18.

Goodall, Jane. 1986. *The Chimpanzees of Gombe*. Cambridge, Mass.: Harvard University Press.

Gore, Mauvis A. 1994. "Dyadic and Triadic Aggression and Assertiveness in Adult Female Rhesus Monkeys, *Macaca mulatta*, and Hamadryas Baboons, *Papio hamadryas*." *Animal Behaviour* 48: 385–92.

Gouzoules, Sarah, Harold Gouzoules, and Peter Marler. 1984. "Rhesus Monkey (*Macaca mulatta*) Screams: Representational Signaling in the Recruitment of Agonistic Aid." *Animal Behaviour* 32: 182–93.

Green, Steven. 1975. "Variation of Vocal Pattern with Social Situation in the Japanese Macaque (*Macaca mulatta*): A Field Study." In *Primate Behavior*, edited by Leonard A. Rosenblum. Vol. 4. New York: Academic Press.

Greville, Sir Fulke. 1652. *The Life of Sir Philip Sidney*. N.p.

Hauser, Marc D. 1993. "Rhesus Monkey (*Macaca mulatta*) Copulation Calls: Honest Signals for Female Choice?" *Proceedings of the Royal Society, London* 254: 93–96.

Hauser, Marc D., Christopher S. Evans, and Peter Marler. 1993. "The Role of Articulation in the Production of Rhesus Monkey Vocalizations." *Animal Behaviour* 45: 423–33.

Killen, Melanie, and Frans B. M. de Waal. 2000. "The Evolution and Development of Morality." In *Natural Conflict Resolution*, edited by Felippo Aureli and Frans B. M. de Waal. Berkeley: University of California Press.

Maestripieri, Dario. 1994. "Social Structure, Infant Handling, and Mother Styles in Group-Living Old World Monkeys." *International Journal of Primatology* 15: 531–53.

Masataka, Nobuo. 1989. "Motivational Referents of Contact Calls in Japanese Monkeys." *Ethology* 180: 265–73.

Maynard Smith, John. 1982. "Do Animals Convey Information About Their Intentions?" *Journal of Theoretical Biology* 97: 1–5.

———. 1991. "Honest Signalling: The Philip Sidney Game." *Animal Behaviour* 42: 1034–35.

———. 1994. "Must Reliable Signals Always Be Costly?" *Animal Behaviour* 47: 1115–20.

Mitani, John C. 1985. "Responses of Gibbons (*Hylobates muelleri*) to Self, Neighbor, and Stranger Duets." *International Journal of Primatology* 6: 193–200.

Muroyama, Yasuyuki. 1991. "Mutual Reciprocity of Grooming in Female Japanese Macaques (*M. fuscata*)." *Behaviour* 119: 161–70.

O'Connell, Sanjida M., and Guy Cowlishaw. 1994. "Infanticide Avoidance, Sperm Competition and Mate Choice: The Function of Copulation Calls in Female Baboons." *Animal Behaviour* 48: 687–94.

Owren, Michael J., Robert M. Seyfarth, and Dorothy L. Cheney. 1997. "The Acoustic Features of Vowel-like Grunts in Chacma Baboons (*Papio cynocephalus ursinus*): Implications for Production Process and Functions." *Journal of the Acoustical Society of America* 101: 2951–63.

Paul, Andreas, and Jutta Kuester. 1996. "Infant Handling by Female Barbary Macaques (*Macaca sylvanus*) at Affenberg Salem: Testing Functional and Evolutionary Hypotheses." *Behavioral Ecology and Sociobiology* 39: 133–45.

Poole, Joyce H. 1989. "Announcing Intent: The Aggressive State of Musth in African Elephants." *Animal Behaviour* 37: 140–52.

Povinelli, Daniel J., and Timothy J. Eddy. 1996. "What Young Chimpanzees Know About Seeing." *Monographs of the Society for Research in Child Development* 61(3).

Rendall, Drew, Robert M. Seyfarth, Dorothy L. Cheney, and Michael J. Owren. 1999. "The Meaning and Function of Grunt Variants in Baboons." *Animal Behaviour* 57: 583–92.

Silk, Joan B. 1980. "Kidnapping and Female Competition Among Captive Bonnet Macaques." *Primates* 21: 100–10.

———. 1987. "Social Behavior in Evolutionary Perspective." In *Primate Societies*, edited by Barbara B. Smuts, Dorothy L. Cheney, Robert M. Seyfarth, Richard W. Wrangham, and Thomas T. Strudhsaker. Chicago: University of Chicago Press.

———. 1992. "The Patterning of Intervention Among Male Bonnet Macaque: Reciprocity, Revenge, and Loyalty." *Current Anthropology* 33: 318–25.

———. 1999a. "Male Bonnet Macaques Use Information About Third-Party Rank Relationships to Recruit Allies." *Animal Behaviour* 58: 45–51.

———. 1999b. "Why Are Infants So Attractive to Others? The Form and Function of Infant Handling in Bonnet Macaques." *Animal Behaviour* 57: 1021–32.

Silk, Joan B., Dorothy L. Cheney, and Robert M. Seyfarth. 1996. "The Form and Function of Postconflict Interactions Between Female Baboons." *Animal Behaviour* 52: 259–68.

————. 1999. "The Structure of Social Relationships Among Female Savannah Baboons in Moremi Reserve, Botswana." *Behaviour* 136: 679–703.

Silk, Joan B., Elizabeth Kaldor, and Robert Boyd. 2000. "Cheap Talk About Conflicts." *Animal Behaviour* 59: 423–32.

Slater, Peter J. B. 1983. "The Study of Communication." In *Animal Behaviour*, edited by Patrick P. G. Bateson and Peter J. B. Slater. Vol. 2. Oxford: Blackwell Scientific.

Tomasello, Michael, and Josep Call. 1997. *Primate Cognition*. New York: Oxford University Press.

Van Rhijn, Johan G. 1980. "Communication by Agonistic Displays: A Discussion." *Behaviour* 74: 284–93.

Van Rhijn, Johan G., and Ron Vodegel. 1980. "Being Honest About One's Intentions: An Evolutionary Stable Strategy for Animal Conflicts." *Journal of Theoretical Biology* 85: 623–41.

Walters, Jeffrey R., and Robert M. Seyfarth. 1987. "Conflict and Cooperation." In *Primate Societies*, edited by Barbara B. Smuts, Dorothy L. Cheney, Robert M. Seyfarth, Richard W. Wrangham, and Thomas T. Struhsaker. Chicago: University of Chicago Press.

Wasser, Samuel K. 1983. "Reproductive Competition and Cooperation Among Female Yellow Baboons." In *Social Behaviour of Female Vertebrates*, edited by Samuel K. Wasser. New York: Academic Press.

Whiten, Andrew, and Richard W. Byrne. 1988. "Tactical Deception in Primates." *Behavioral and Brain Sciences* 11: 223–44.

Zahavi, Amotz. 1975. "Mate Selection—a Selection for a Handicap." *Journal of Theoretical Biology* 53: 205–14.

PART III

COMMITMENT IN HUMANS

I N ANIMALS, the question is whether the concept of commitment is
necessary to explain observed behavior. In humans, commitment
is ubiquitous. For us, the question is not whether we use commitments but how they work and how we became capable of using and
assessing them. The first chapter in this section, by Cohen and Vandello, offers a detailed examination of a superb example of commitment, the psychology and sociology of honor. The next chapter, by
Richerson and Boyd, tackles the core question of how our individual
psychology has been shaped to a form that makes stable cooperation
possible in human groups. Finally, Ruse addresses the evolutionary
origins and functions of the moral passions and their contribution to
making commitments and cooperation possible.

Research on the psychology of honor and honor cultures offers the
best studied example of how commitment to threats is not only possible but in some social circumstances essential. Where policing is rudimentary, and resources can be stolen, every individual must defend
his or her own turf and possessions. When a stronger individual
makes threats, the rational response is to give in, to yield the goods in
order to avoid being hurt; but people are not like that. If they feel
they are being challenged unfairly or if they feel disrespected, often
they will fight—and far more viciously and longer than would be
justified by the resources at issue. A teenager threatened with having
his new shoes stolen fights the thief and risks death for shoes worth
only a hundred dollars. This seems senseless, and to a rationalist, it is.
Yet rationalists may prove easy prey in settings where the culture
expects a quick response to threats. Failure to respond may risk com-

plete loss of social position and, paradoxically, escalation of provoca-
tion until the situation becomes dangerous. In such cultures security
may require a response to even small provocations that is measured
but prepared for reckless escalation if necessary.

Cohen and Vandello explore this topic in the context of the American South, with its special culture of honor, where careful manners
avoid conflict, but physical violence is quick and deadly when tact
fails. Note that their presentation bridges the gap between culture
and psychology, with its prediction that honor cultures should flourish mainly where individuals must rely on themselves for defense.
What does biology have to do with it? The whole system would not
work without emotional predilections that fuel concern about honor
and desires to maintain respect and exact revenge. As in the animal
studies, the question is why bluffing does not take over. To a considerable extent it does; yet eventually some bluffers will be detected, to
their huge cost. Imagine living in a society in which anyone could
challenge you to a duel, and you would have to show up and risk
your life or else sacrifice your reputation. Historically, that was only
yesterday. Today, at least in suburbs and offices, the dangers are not
bullets but rather debates and takeover attempts and office politics,
perhaps less deadly but no less important. Challenges arouse us to
aggression that we did not know we were capable of.

In honor cultures all parties attend to the subtleties of social norms.
While it might seem burdensome to have to defend constantly any
incursion on those norms of behavior, the existence of understood
rules offers paradoxical benefits as well. So long as they are clear and
well recognized, those who violate them can expect to be challenged.
Thus the war of all against all becomes a society in which every individual enforces the social norms. This reins in the bullies who otherwise would terrorize every person, one by one. Individuals do this
not for the group, but to protect themselves. Yet the impact of these
individual behaviors on the group is substantial, even in the absence
of a higher social power. This is another example of social selection at
work. Individual actions in a social setting create powerful forces that
shape group behaviors and influence gene frequencies as well.

This enforcement of group norms is at the core of Richerson and
Boyd's analysis of how "tribal instincts" make complex group cooperation possible. They use vivid illustrations of the commitments that
unite men in war to disparage the perspective of individual rationalism, and they review many other examples in which people simply
do not do what is in their interests. How, Richerson and Boyd ask, is
it possible that people can sacrifice themselves for the group? Three
possibilities are placed on the table: some variation on methodological
individualism, group selection for genes, and group selection for cul-

tural traits. They argue against the first and second possibilities, and outline evidence from several dimensions that supports their hypothesis that groups with prosocial traits grow faster and displace other groups. Equally important, the norms in such cooperative groups have been a force of natural selection for thousands of generations, thus shaping capacities for commitment. This is a somewhat more specific version of what others have referred to as *social selection* (West-Eberhard 1987; Simon 1990; Jason, Brodie, and Moore 1999).

Interestingly, Richerson and Boyd include the Frank-Hirshleifer model as an example of an individualistic approach and are skeptical of the Alexander model of generalized reciprocity because it does not prove robust in their models. In contrast, their model is resolutely social and depends on phenomena at the level of the group, not just individuals exchanging favors. They present substantial evidence, including the ubiquity of ethnic markers, and the major unsecured commitments that individuals make to their reference groups. Richerson and Boyd are relatively unconcerned about the problem that occupies so many social theorists: why individuals are willing to accept costs to punish cheaters. They simply observe that people do accept these costs and seem to get emotional rewards for doing so, rewards that well could have been shaped by social selection induced by group traits incorporated by cultural group selection.

These are, of course, time-honored questions; at issue is nothing less than the explanation for human society, which requires an explanation for our capacity for moral judgment and moral behavior. Ruse takes us back to Plato and contrasts the rationalist foundations for morality to those based on emotions in his attempt to bring together a naturalist foundation for ethics with a Rawlsian framework for fairness in the context of commitment. In commitment Ruse finds a mechanism by which the moral passions give benefits. Moral actions are not based on rational strategies but rather on emotions, and these emotions had to come from some place. The important possibility is that moral emotions enforce commitments due to the manifold benefits of being capable of using commitment strategies. These emotions are not just crude fast ways of influencing behavior; they are intrinsically opposed to inferior rationalistic strategies. This hearkens back to the prior two chapters in this section, both of which document the severe limitations of social decisions made on the basis of rational calculation. If your group detects that your actions are based only on calculations of what is in your best interest, you are likely to be loathed and excluded. Groups, like individuals, demand emotional commitments.

Taken together, the three chapters in this section provide abundant examples of the importance of commitment in human social life. The evidence is so compelling that one cannot help but wonder why explanations for cooperation have been so narrowly dependent on methodological rationalism and individualism. I suspect the reason is the absence of a framework that can account for actions that seem irrational. In the framework of commitment, such behaviors are not only explicable, they are expected. Certain emotions seem opposed to reason because they are opposed to reason. In the short run they seem mysterious, but in the long run on average they give advantages that shape psychological traits that change the structure of human society. These psychological traits must be incorporated into our model, however difficult that may be. After all, it was Pascal, that most rational philosopher, who said, "The heart has reasons which reason can not understand."

References

Jason, B. Wolf, Edmund D. Brodie III, and Allen J. Moore. 1999. "Interacting Phenotypes and the Evolutionary Process II. Selection Resulting from Social Interactions." *American Naturalist* 153: 254–66.

Simon, Herbert A. 1990. "A Mechanism for Social Selection and Successful Altruism." *Science* 250: 1665–68.

West-Eberhard, Mary Jane. 1987. "Sexual Selection, Social Competition, and Speciation." *Quarterly Review of Biology* 58: 155–83.

Chapter 8

Honor and "Faking" Honorability

Dov Cohen and Joseph Vandello

F OR OVER 200 years, Southerners of the United States have been known to be pricklish about their sense of honor. As an observer in the 1700s noted, quarrels in the South developed when one party

> Has in a merry hour called [the other] a Lubber or a thick-Skull or a Buckskin, or a Scotsman, or perhaps one has mislaid the other's hat, or knocked a peach out of his Hand, or offered him a dram without wiping the mouth of the Bottle; all these, and ten thousand more quite as trifling and ridiculous are thought and accepted as just Causes of immediate Quarrels. (Fithian 1774, quoted in Gorn 1985, 19)

In response to insults that a Northerner was supposed to turn a deaf ear to, Southerners were supposed to retaliate with physical violence. "'Call a man a liar in Mississippi,' an old saying went, 'and he will knock you down; in Kentucky, he will shoot you; in Indiana, he will say you are another'" (Ayers 1984, 20).

The reason for responding with violence to such insults in the Old South had to do with *honor* and maintaining a reputation for being one who will stand up for himself. Having a reputation as someone who could not be trifled with on "small" matters such as insults served as a warning that one certainly couldn't be trifled with on big ones either. As will be seen, present-day Southerners still act in accord with culture of honor norms, but whether they are privately committed to such norms and to short run "irrationality" in defense of their honor is another matter altogether.

In this chapter we note briefly the reasons for why such a seemingly irrational concern with honor may have developed in the Old South in the first place, describe its manifestation in the South today, and then show through experiments some possible mechanisms by which honor norms can be perpetuated among Southerners—regardless of whether people today privately subscribe to such norms. We then describe the conditions that make it more or less *difficult* and more or less *important* to identify those who have not truly internalized the culture of honor code. In closing we speculate a bit on the arms races and stalemates that can develop between those "faking" an honor stance versus the ability of others to detect such faking in the U.S. South, as well as in other cultures of honor.

Short-Run "Irrationality" and Lawless Environments

In some senses irrationality or at least the appearance of irrationality is the essence of honor. The willingness to risk everything, including one's life, over a matter of principle is central to many culture-of-honor concerns. Men are expected to fight and even to die over affronts that are sometimes dismissed as trivial or that start as "little ol' arguments over nothing at all" (Daly and Wilson 1988, 127). The short-run calculation that a fight over some affront could not be "worth" the risk to participants misses the point. That is, it misses the intangible value of honor and misses the extent to which honorable men are willing (and sometimes eager) to risk their lives (Ayers 1984, 16). As the anthropologist David Gilmore (1990) has concluded, the "acceptance of *expendability* constitutes the basis of the manly pose everywhere it is encountered" (223). "Disdain for personal injury" is the quality "upon which all feats of daring rest" (70); and as Elijah Anderson notes, "not to be afraid to die is the quid pro quo of being able to take someone else's life" (1994, 92).

Such concerns with honor may seem irrational. Yet in the environments where cultures of honor usually develop, a commitment to "irrationally" defend one's honor—backed by a "pledge of reputation" or "internal emotional motives" or both (Nesse 2001)—may be quite adaptive indeed. That is, such honor cultures tend to develop in places where there is a weak state that is unable to enforce the law. In such environments with inadequate law enforcement people need to establish reputations that they are not to be messed with. Especially in cases where wealth is portable or one is subject to predation, it is very important to be known as someone who can protect himself, his family, and his possessions (Nisbett and Cohen 1996). If insults and small affronts are the probes by which one person tests another, then answering such small affronts becomes essential to warding off larger threats. Being known as one who will "irrationally" defend his honor can have a very rational deterrent value in keeping others at bay. As Pitt-Rivers has written,

> whenever the authority of law is questioned or ignored, the code of honor re-emerges to allocate the right to precedence and dictate the principles of conduct . . . [as] among aristocracies and criminal underworlds, school boy and street-corner societies, open frontiers and the closed communities where reigns "The Honorable Society" as the Mafia calls itself. (Pitt-Rivers 1968, 510)[1]

The cases of the Old South (and the Old West) fit well with these characterizations as lawless environments (Gastil 1971; McWhiney 1988). Both regions were frontiers with inadequate law enforcement during their development and, in addition, both had economies based on the keeping of animals—a very portable and hence easily stealable form of wealth. Thus, as historian David Hackett Fischer (1989) wrote of the South,

> In the absence of any strong sense of order as unity, hierarchy, or social peace, backsettlers shared an idea of order as a system of retributive justice. The prevailing principle was lex talionis, the rule of retaliation. It held that a good man must seek to do right in the world, but when wrong was done to him, he must punish the wrongdoer himself by an act of retribution that restored order and justice in the world. (765)

Or as a North Carolina proverb put it, "every man should be sheriff on his own hearth" (765).

Over and above the practical concerns of deterring others, these honor norms were internalized by Southerners and embedded in the code of what it meant to be a man. That is, actions to defend honor were valued for more than just their rational deterrent value; they were meant to be valued in and of themselves. According to historians, Southerners were committed to honor in the sense that they had internalized its value and were determined to maintain it on pain of death. Sam Houston recalled his mother telling him when she presented him a musket for his use in the army, " 'Never disgrace it; for remember, I had rather all my sons should fill one honorable grave, than that one of them should turn his back to save his life.' She then gave him a plain gold ring with the word 'Honor' engraved inside it." (Wyatt-Brown 1982, 51).

As Gilmore (1990) has written about other such honor cultures, adherence to proper masculine ideals often requires a deep subjective commitment. "Simple acquiescence [to the norms] will not do. To be socially meaningful the decision for manhood must be characterized by enthusiasm combined with stoic resolve or perhaps 'grace.' It must show a public demonstration of positive choice, of jubilation even in pain . . ." (224). Or as one contemporary wrote about Southerners after the Civil War,

> Self-respect, as the southerners understand it, has always demanded much fighting. . . . A pugnacity which is not merely war paint, but is, so to speak, tattooed into the character, has resulted from this high sentiment of personal value. . . . It permeates all society; it has infected all individualities. The meekest man by nature, the man who at the North would no more fight than he would jump out of a second story window, may at the South resent an insult by a blow, or perhaps a stab or pistol shot. (Ayers 1984, 10)[2]

Research on the present-day South seems to indicate that white male Southerners do at least act as if they subscribe to such culture of honor norms, even today. Yet the issue of whether they have internalized such norms and truly believe them, or are committed to them in the sense that people of the Old South were supposed to have been, is another question.

Evidence for Culture of Honor Norms in the Present-Day South

Ample evidence shows that the contemporary South indeed does have a version of the culture of honor. Such evidence comes from analyses of homicide rates, social policies, attitude surveys, and lab experiments.

Southern white homicide rates continue to be far higher than those of the North (Reaves and Nisbett 1999). More pertinent to the present concerns, the South seems to exceed the North especially in homicides of a certain type. Nisbett, Polly, and Lang (1995) found that homicide rates for murders that occurred in the context of another felony (such as burglary or robbery) tended to be no higher in the South than in the North. Yet the South far exceeds the North in those sorts of homicides where arguments and affronts were the precipitating cause. Such homicides are more likely to center around insults and honor-related concerns (see also Cohen 1998a; Daly and Wilson 1988; Reed 1981).

Social policies too reflect a greater concern for honor among Southerners. The states of the South and the West are likely to have far looser gun control laws and are likely to have senators and representatives who are more likely to be hawkish in their foreign policies, as compared to northern states. Further, in their self-defense rules, southern and western states are likely to give citizens a freer hand in defending themselves. Unlike most northern states that require a person to first retreat "until their back is to the wall," southern and western states are more likely to have "true man" rules that require no such "cowardly" maneuvering and instead allow a person to stand their ground and kill to defend themselves (Cohen 1996, 1998a; Cohen and Vandello 1998). As an Oklahoma court ruled, "Here the wall is to every man's back. It is the wall of his rights; and when he is [assailed] at a place where he has a right to be . . . he may stand and defend himself" (*Fowler v. State*, 1912, 126 Pacific 831, cited in Mischke 1981, 1007).

Attitude surveys also are likely to show that southern whites hold to a culture-of-honor stance. Southerners and Westerners are not more likely to approve of violence in the abstract or in general. They are, however, more likely to show greater tolerance for violence when it is used for honor-related concerns. Thus Southerners were twice as likely as Northerners to approve of a man punching a drunk stranger who bumped into him and his wife on the street (15 percent versus 8 percent), and they were nearly twice as likely to think that a man would be "extremely justified" in shooting a person who had sexually assaulted the man's sixteen-year-old daughter (47 percent versus 26 percent) (Cohen and Nisbett 1994; Cohen, Vandello, and Rantilla 1998; Ellison 1991).

These differences also show up in laboratory experiments where southern white males are more likely to act aggressively in response to affronts. In a series of experiments we invited southern and northern students to the lab where they were provoked—either repeatedly (Cohen et al. 1999) or with a single unambiguous insult (Cohen et al. 1996). In a typical study, subjects invited to the lab were given a brief cover story, then were sent down a long hallway to drop off a form. As they did this, a confederate, who was allegedly unrelated to the experiment, bumped into the subject with his shoulder and then rudely called him an "asshole." In response to this, subjects from the South were far more likely to show angry emotional reactions than were subjects from the North. Further, using tests done on their saliva samples taken before and after the insult, we found that Southerners responded to the insult with increases in their levels of cortisol (a hormone associated with stress) and testosterone (a hormone associated with competition, aggression, and dominance). Such an increase did not occur for Northerners.

Moreover, after being insulted, Southerners were more likely than Northerners to act out aggressive or domineering tendencies with other people. That is, whereas uninsulted Southerners were the most polite and deferential group, Southerners who had been insulted were subsequently most domineering in an interpersonal encounter with another experimental participant, and most aggressive when they later encountered another confederate who walked toward them in the long narrow hallway. Essentially a Chicken game had been set up farther down in the hallway as a six-foot, three-inch 250-pound confederate walked rapidly toward the subject, there being only room for one to comfortably pass in the narrow corridor. After being insulted, southern subjects waited longest to give ground to the man and were most likely to try to face him down (Cohen et al. 1996).

Thus culture of honor norms clearly can characterize southern white male behavior. Less clear, however, is the extent to which southern white men really are strongly subjectively committed to those norms. As scholars such as Miller and Prentice (1994), Kuran (1995), Kahan (1997), and McAdams (1997) have noted, norms sometimes hold sway over people's behavior without people being particularly committed to them. In this case many contemporary Southerners may pay lip service to and even act in accord with a culture of honor stance while perhaps not embracing it with the sort of "jubilation" and "enthusiasm" that Gilmore describes. Specifically, in our work, we have found at least one subpopulation of the South—southern college students—who do seem to follow culture of honor norms but who are not particularly committed to such aggression and seem to prefer a far less macho stance than their behavior would indicate.

Internalization and Commitment to Culture of Honor Norms

While we believe there is some subjective commitment on the part of southern white male college students to a culture-of-honor stance, evidence suggests that their commitment to such norms is not as great as it seems. At least some of their aggressive behavior in fact may be attributable to Southerners assuming mistakenly that *their peers* hold to aggressive norms and subjective commitments (Vandello and Cohen 1999c).

The Insult and the Impartial Spectator

In one experiment we showed that southern white male college students who were bumped into and called an "asshole" believed that their manly image had been tarnished in front of someone who witnessed the insult (Cohen et al. 1996). Following the usual procedure, subjects were bumped into and called an "asshole" (or not). In some cases this bump and insult happened in front of another confederate whom the subject later interacted with and in other cases it did not. Toward the end of the study, the subject and the other confederate were given a chance to get acquainted very briefly. Under the guise that this was a person perception study, the subject was asked to fill out a questionnaire asking him (a) to rate himself on a number of personality dimensions, and (b) to guess how the *other* person would rate him on these same dimensions.

The eight dimensions of interest were those that had to do with masculine reputation (manly–not manly, courageous–cowardly, tough–wimpy, aggressive–passive, strong–weak, and so on). On these dimensions, southern subjects who were insulted did not appear to think less of themselves after they had been bumped. Yet southern subjects who had been insulted in front of the other confederate believed that their masculine reputation had suffered dramatically in that other person's eyes. That is, compared to southern subjects who were not insulted and northern subjects who were and were not insulted, Southerners who were insulted in front of another person believed that this person saw them as less manly, more cowardly, weaker, and so on. Insulted Southerners thus seemed to believe that the *generalized other* or the *impartial spectator*—in this case, as personified by the other man in the hallway—thought less of them after the incident (Cooley 1902; Mead 1934; Smith 1976 [1759]).

Our southern subjects may have been quite wrong, however. In a follow-up to this study we created videotape reenactments of the bump-and-insult scenario and showed them to southern and northern judges. Unlike the previous study in which subjects were bumped and then had to guess how the impartial spectator saw them, in this study subjects were the impartial spectator. They watched the videotapes of people getting insulted and then either shrugging off the insult or responding aggressively to their insulter. If subjects in the original study (Cohen et al. 1996) were being realistic in their assessments, one would expect that at least the southern judges in this follow-up study would actually think less of the man who did nothing after the incident.

This did not happen, however. Both northern and southern judges rated the persons on the tapes similarly and in fact both groups showed some preference for the passive person (Vandello and Cohen 1999c). The expected "loss of manhood" effect that insulted southern subjects feared did not occur. Subjects in the original study seemed to think that others had internalized culture of honor standards that they were being held to. Yet the subsequent study suggests that this might have been more imagined than real.

Aggressiveness of the Self and Other

In another study male students from three campuses (the Universities of Illinois, Kentucky, and Florida) were asked about their own aggressiveness and were asked to compare their responses to how they thought a random sample of 100 male students at their university would respond (Vandello and Cohen 1999c). Participants were given five short scenarios that involved incidents in which the protagonist was ridiculed or in some way affronted (for example, another person whistles at the man and his girlfriend as they are walking down the street). Subjects were asked to rate their own likelihood of responding with violence to the affront as well as the likelihood that a random sample of 100 men from their university would respond with violence. On all three campuses, subjects believed that they were much less aggressive than average. Yet the perceived disparity between self and others was much greater for Southerners. That is, southern men seemed to be particularly likely to project an aggressive stance onto other people in their environment.

Enforcement and the Generalized Other

In another pair of studies we found that these same tendencies occurred with respect to the issue of norm enforcement (Vandello and Cohen 1999c). That is, while Southerners don't seem particularly committed to enforcing culture of honor norms themselves, they believe that others are committed and therefore project enforcement behavior onto them.

The first study in the pair of experiments looked at the extent to which Southerners put in a live conflict situation would goad others in that conflict situation to be aggressive. This issue is particularly important because, as Miller has suggested, being honorable often involves risks that people are not always eager to take. In his work on the honor culture of Saga Iceland, Miller (1990, 1993) argues that many times people have to be goaded into action. "The saga woman provoked her reluctant men to action by impugning their manhood. They were no better than women, they would better have been their father's daughters, they have the memories of pigs, or they are merely contemptible" (Miller 1990, 212). (In one particular ceremony the corpse of the person to be revenged is dismembered, and "the threat of shame is made explicit by the person [usually a woman] bearing the pieces of the dead man, 'If you don't take revenge, you will be an object of contempt to all men'" [Miller 1993, 162]).

Modern criminologists too, such as Luckenbill (1977), also argue that the incitement to violence by an audience often is a crucial factor in leading a situation to boil over. Bystanders send signals that can escalate or deescalate a conflict, that can define an action as either a serious affront to honor that must be avenged or one that is "no big deal." Thus they can dramatically influence whether a situation erupts in violence or is peacefully resolved (see also Pitt-Rivers 1968).

In our laboratory study we brought northern and southern subjects into the lab, put them in the middle of a conflict between two men, and examined the extent to which they would either encourage aggressive responding, bringing honor concerns to the fore, or try to minimize these concerns and deescalate the situation. In this study the subject was seated with other "subjects" (actually confederates). As one of the men got up to go to the bathroom he stepped on another person's eyeglass case that was on the floor. (Actually the case contained dried rigatoni pasta to give the incident a suitably dramatic crunching sound.)

The confederate "victim" pulled out a pair of cracked and deformed glasses; and when he pointed this out to the confederate "perpetrator," the perpetrator refused to apologize. The two exchanged hostile words, and after the perpetrator left to go to the bathroom, the victim then probed the subject for coaching as to what he should do. The series of probes themselves were either belligerent ("I'm tempted to go in there and kick his ass. Wouldn't you be pissed?") or less belligerent ("Do you think I should go in and apologize before this gets out of hand?").

There was certainly variability in subjects' responses, with a few at least spontaneously telling the victim to "go kick his ass" as well as a few who practically delivered sermons on nonviolence. And the gender effect that one might predict (that is, men being more encouraging of aggression) emerged. There was no difference, however, in how our northern and southern subjects responded. That is, southern subjects were no more likely to enforce aggressive norms or bring honor concerns into this conflict than were their northern counterparts.

Importantly, a regional difference did emerge in our next study. In this study we switched subjects' perspectives by having them now act as judges and try to read the signaling of the subjects who were bystanders in the first study. That is, while the first study examined what sort of signals Northerners and Southerners send as bystanders, the second study examined how Northerners and Southerners actually interpret the behavior of these bystanders.

We therefore brought northern and southern judges into the lab, explained the first study to them and, as they watched actual videotapes from this study, asked them to rate what sort of signals they thought the bystanders were sending and what behavior they were encouraging. In this case Southerners watching the same videotapes as Northerners were more likely to think that the bystanders were encouraging the parties to be aggressive. That is, Southerners seemed to project aggressive signaling onto the generalized other—in this case, personified by the bystander to the conflict—just as they had projected a culture of honor stance onto the hallway observer in the earlier study (Cohen et al. 1996). Interestingly, this seemed to be especially the case when the signaling that the bystanders were sending was relatively ambiguous. Tapes in which the subject pleaded with our confederate not to use violence or tapes in which the subject encouraged our confederate to "jack him up" seemed to leave little room for interpretation. In cases that were less clear-cut, however, regional differences emerged as expectations seemed to guide perceptions of what this impartial spectator was signaling.

In sum, Southerners were no more likely than Northerners to enforce aggressive norms on their peers. When it came to reading the signals that others were sending, however, Southerners seemed more likely to think that *other* people were encouraging aggression and enforcing culture of honor norms. Our Southerners may not have been totally subjectively committed to the culture of honor stance, but they tended to assume that other people were.

Public Behavior and Pluralistic Ignorance

The findings from the previously described five studies actually help to make sense of some of the other patterns of results we have found in previous research. While finding, for example, that southern private attitudes about honor-related violence are somewhat more condoning of aggression than northern attitudes, these regional differences found on attitude surveys tend to pale in comparison to the differences found when public behaviors and public representations are examined (see Cohen 1996, 1998a; Cohen and Nisbett 1994, 1997; Cohen et al. 1996, 1999). Some of the reason for this is probably methodological (Cohen 1997; Peng, Nisbett, and Wong 1997); but some of the reason probably goes beyond methodological considerations and points to a real disjunction between privately held attitudes and publicly performed behavior. Perhaps Southerners are more publicly aggressive than they would privately like to be, because they (perhaps mistakenly) believe that others expect aggressive or "honorable" behavior from them. (Writing about the inner city, for example, Anderson [1994, 89] makes a similar observation when he notes that many people "adopt the code [of the streets] as a kind of shield really—to prevent others from 'messing with [them].'" As with at least some portion of the southern white male subpopulation, such people may not believe in the code of honor themselves but may play by its rules because they believe the street requires it of them.)

The consequence of this sort of "pluralistic ignorance"—in which everyone is unclear about what everyone else is thinking and feeling—is that it can lead to self-fulfilling prophecies in which people in a culture act aggressively merely because they think others support violence. People may use violence in an attempt to live up to what is expected of them, or as a matter purely of perceived "self-defense" if they anticipate that others will use violence against them. For either reason, if people view the prevailing norms of a community as encouraging violence, they will be more likely to act violently. Such violence in turn helps reinforce the perception that violence is indeed the norm or is condoned in the community (Bikchandani, Hirshleifer, and Welch 1992; Gladwell 2000; Kuran 1995; Miller and Prentice 1994; Picker 1997; Prentice and Miller 1993, 1996; Schelling 1978; Wilson and Kelling 1982). In this case the mutual interdependence of actors creates possibilities for multiple equilibria, in which societal norms for aggression can settle at either low or high levels, depending on what people think everyone else is thinking (Cohen 2000; Cohen et al. 1999; Cohen and Vandello in press; Daly and Wilson 1988; Vandello and Cohen 1999c). In a simple two-person example, person A may behave aggressively because he believes that person B endorses aggression; and person B may behave aggressively because he believes person A endorses aggression. In turn, the public behavior of A and B makes each (as well as others observing them) think that aggressive norms hold sway, when in fact neither may believe in aggression in their heart of hearts in the first place (Cohen and Nisbett 1994; Daly and Wilson 1988; McWhiney 1988).

Expectations about what others think play an important role in creating public behaviors and establishing public norms—perhaps sometimes a more important role than private internal dispositions or subjective commitments. Sorting out when behavior comes from private subjective commitments and when it comes from outward conformity due to reputational concerns can be a difficult task, and is one of the issues addressed in the next section.

Some Puzzles

There remain serious puzzles in the account just given of how at least some parts of the southern subpopulation may not have really internalized culture of honor norms with the "enthusiasm" that Gilmore describes, but rather reluctantly behave in accord with them because they think others expect it. The puzzles have to do with the following findings:

Some private attitude differences exist between Northerners and Southerners. These differences tend to be smaller in magnitude than other regional differences, but they are reliable across a number of honor-related questions (Cohen and Nisbett 1994).

Southern college students who are insulted show rises in their testosterone and cortisol levels in a way that Northerners do not when insulted (Cohen et al. 1996). (Such a reaction would seem relatively uncontrollable or odd to "fake," unless, of course, Southerners were getting ready for a battle that they expected would ensue, even if they didn't believe in the cause [Cohen 1998b; Mazur and Booth 1998].)

Currently, Vandello and Cohen (1999b) have collected data on domestic violence that appear to show that southern whites are more likely than Northerners to endorse violence against women to enforce their fidelity. Such a pattern would at the least be consistent with some versions of a culture of honor stance.

Perhaps most troublingly, one probably would not expect that such a large proportion of the southern population (or at least the southern college student population) should be getting away with "faking it." In this context faking it does not mean that the person won't ever act honorably and aggressively; it only means that their "honorable" behavior seems adventitious and that culture of honor beliefs do not seem very internalized or privately committed to (Cooter 1998).

The Arms Race:
Faking and Detecting Fakes

In terms of the issue of fakery it is necessary to consider the analogy of the evolutionary "arms race" that theorists such as Krebs and Dawkins (1984) and Frank (1988) have discussed. In such a race a battle constantly escalates between organisms that become increasingly adept at being able to fake certain desirable characteristics and other organisms that become increasingly able to detect these fakes (see also Pinker and Bloom 1992, 483; Nesse and Lloyd 1992, 606). Applied by analogy to the culture of honor context, a race would escalate between abilities to fake or mimic being honorable and tough versus abilities to detect who is faking or merely mimicking honorability.

Thus at step 1 in the arms race that might develop in a culture of honor, rewards would go to those who take risks and actually incur the costs of being macho. Being honorable entails taking certain risks, and the rewards would go to those who take those risks (Gilmore 1990). At step 2, some people would learn how to fake being honorable or macho, in which case they would get the benefits of being seen as manly without having to incur the associated costs and risks. That is, they could have a reputation for being honorable (or at least for not being a wimp) without doing all the things that a strong culture of honor stance would entail. At step 3, people's ability to detect the fakers would increase and the fakers no longer would be able to get away with it (and the cycle, of course, would continue with the ability to fake improving and the techniques for detecting fakes improving in serial fashion).

Bluffing and Micro-Level Factors That Allow for Faking

At the moment, however, the arms race may not be in this escalating cycle. That is, the process of the arms race may be stuck at step 2, where some people are able to get away with faking honorability and not being internally committed to the honor stance. This would be a conjecture that might help to explain one of the theoretical puzzles outlined earlier concerning the high proportion of fakers.

We also have independent evidence, however, that such faking potentially can be quite successful because southern white male college students are not particularly adept at sorting out who is truly honorable and who is merely bluffing. Another set of studies shows that because of some complicated signaling and coordination issues (to be described further), Southerners probably are less adept than Northerners at picking up cues for who is getting angry enough to become violent and who is not (Cohen et al. 1999).

Specifically, in one study we brought subjects into the lab and exposed them to a series of annoyances perpetrated by a confederate. Unfortunately, the procedure brought on anger that was far more sudden and unpredictable than we initially had expected, and we stopped running the study after two subjects (both Southerners) attempted to physically make contact with our confederates. In a follow-up study we took videotapes of these two experimental sessions—along with videos from other experimental sessions that did not have to be stopped—and showed them to other northern and southern subjects. In watching these tapes, Northerners were far more likely than Southerners to assess correctly which participants would end the study by "blowing up" and which would not. Southern white males in fact were five times as likely as their northern counterparts to miss the relevant cues and think that the wrong person would explode (21 percent incorrect for Southerners versus 4 percent for Northerners in a forced choice between four tapes). In such cases where their fellow Southerners have trouble correctly reading the signals of who truly will become violent and who will not, many Southerners may find that they can get away with bluffing.

As Schelling (1966) notes, many conflicts amount to Coordination games in which two parties have to figure out what will be tolerated and what constitutes an affront that calls for retaliation. Complicating these coordination difficulties for Southerners are rules for politeness

that make Southerners slower to express their anger when responding to situations that are not clearly honor related or a direct challenge (Cohen et al. 1999). As Carter (1963, 59) notes, "the southerner
is proverbially gentle in manner. It has been said that until he is angered enough to kill you he will treat you politely." (Or as Andrew
Jackson's mother advised him, "If ever you have to vindicate your
feelings or your honor, do it calmly" [Curtis 1976, 36].) Such politeness, apparent equanimity, and slowness to anger make it extremely
hard to guess just how angry and how willing someone is to commit
violence, renders nonaction relatively ambiguous because the person
simply could be biding his time until he explodes, and also conversely would allow either party to do a lot of huffing and puffing
before the other determines that he has "crossed the line" and a
gauntlet has been thrown down. Thus if A and B are in a conflict,
southern norms of politeness can make it so that: A and B cannot tell
how annoyed the other party is becoming; inaction by either party
becomes nondiagnostic about whether the other will ultimately blow
up; and either party is relatively free to bluff and engage in "cheap
talk," so long as a direct and clear-cut challenge is not made. Coupled
with southern white male college students being less adept at detecting who truly will become violent, these rules for being slow to anger
may make it so that at least some Southerners can bluff or fake their
honorability quite successfully.

Environmental Contingencies and Arms Race Escalation

One macro-level question concerns the distal reasons for why the
arms race would be stuck at step 2—with people getting away with
faking—and would not proceed further. One plausible answer is that
perhaps it is not of crucial importance right now for Southerners in at
least some subpopulations to be able to detect fakers. The environmental circumstances that gave rise to the culture of honor in the first
place and that made such a stance adaptive are largely gone (Vandello and Cohen 1999a, 2000). The South is not a lawless frontier with
a primarily herding economy anymore, Southerners are not in danger
of having their herds (their wealth) rustled away from them and,
while the base rate for aggression may be higher in the South than the
North, it is still not exceedingly high.

All of these conditions can be contrasted with those of the inner-
city gang culture. There is inadequate law enforcement in the inner
city. (As the saying goes, "Call for a cop, call for an ambulance, and
call for a pizza. See which comes first" [Will 1993].) There is a port-

ability of wealth with the drug trade and cash economy of inner-city gangs. And there is a higher base rate of aggression.

In these circumstances the arms race has escalated, and as Anderson (1994) notes, when push comes to shove, the fakers versus those with real "juice" can be sorted out in the inner city. "The youths who have internalized this attitude and convincingly display it in their public bearing are among the most threatening people of all, for it is commonly assumed that they fear no man. As the people in the community say, 'They are the baddest dudes on the street'" (Anderson 1994, 92).

Anderson argues that in the inner city signaling systems and rituals have developed that sort out fakers from nonfakers. As an example, Anderson argues that possessing the right sort of material objects is not just a matter of fashion—a matter which many teenagers both inside and outside the inner city care about. It is also a signal; and importantly, it is a "costly to fake" (and thus a potentially reliable) signal that a person is willing and able to defend himself. "Jackets, sneakers, gold jewelry reflect not just a person's taste . . . but also a willingness to possess things that may require defending. [A person] wearing a fashionable, expensive jacket, for example, is vulnerable to attack by another who covets the jacket and either cannot afford to buy one or wants the added satisfaction of depriving someone of his" (Anderson 1994, 88).

Other related signals include:

The taking of other people's "trophies": "One way of campaigning for status is by taking the possessions of others. . . . Sneakers, a pistol, even somebody else's girlfriend can become a trophy. When a person can take something from another and then flaunt it, he gains a certain regard by being the owner, or the controller of that thing. But this display of ownership can then provoke other people to challenge him. The game of who controls what is thus constantly being played out on inner city streets, and the trophy—extrinsic or intrinsic, tangible or intangible—identifies the current winner" (Anderson 1994, 88–89).

Displaying "nerve" as one takes another's property, "'messes with' someone's woman, throws the first punch, 'gets in someone's face,' or pulls a trigger. Its proper display helps on the spot to check others who would violate one's person and also helps to build a reputation that works to prevent future challenges" (Anderson 1994, 92).

Experience in prison: "Many people feel not only that they have little to lose by going to prison but they have something to gain. The toughening-up one experiences in prison can actually enhance one's reputation on the street" (Anderson 1994, 94).

These signals are all costly to fake in that they all require the signaler to take a considerable risk or pay a heavy cost.[3] As such, such signals may serve as a reliable indicator for who has "juice" in the inner city and who does not. Due to environmental contingencies of inadequate law enforcement, portable wealth, and a currently high base rate for aggression, there are real rewards in inner-city gang culture for being known as someone with "nerve" or "heart," and there can be very severe costs for being seen as someone without these qualities.

The contrast with the present-day South is informative. Now that the initial conditions that made a culture of honor stance functional are gone, it may not be tremendously important to be able to sort out the fakers from the nonfakers, and thus contemporary southern culture may have fewer of the rituals and signaling games that help sort out the truly honorable from the adventitious.

It would be interesting to see if such rituals were developed in the Old South, when the environmental contingencies still made it very important to sort out the tough from those who were just trying to pass. The historical record in fact suggests that these rituals probably did exist. Pastimes in the Old South often tested one's physical endurance and courage. The game called Purring, for example, involved two opponents grabbing each other by the shoulders and then kicking each other in the shins at the starting signal. The loser was the one who let go first (McWhiney 1988). "Wrassling" or fighting in the backcountry could be done either "fair" (according to standard boxing rules) or "rough and tumble" (Fischer 1989, 736). The latter option meant that weapons were not allowed but everything else was; and participants often left the contests with parts of their noses, ears, or lips bitten off or with other injuries deriving from the opponents attempting to "tear out each other's testicles" (Gorn 1985, 20; Fischer 1989, 737). "To feel for a feller's eyestrings and make him tell the news" was part of the game and "gouging out an opponent's eye became the sine qua non of rough-and-tumble fighting," according to historian Elliot Gorn (1985, 18, 20). Further, on the more formal level, the institution of the duel had its own set of rituals and tests that were costly to fake. Sometimes the "affronted party printed his 'card' in a newspaper so that as many people as possible, including strangers, would know of his willingness to defend his honor—and know also that he possessed honor worthy of defense. . . . An ambitious young man might make a name for himself by challenging the right opponent in the fluid society of the Old Southwest" (Ayers 1984, 17). The challenge of a duel could not be turned down without "loss of respect, loss of reputation, [a] loss of standing in the community" and potentially a "ruining of [one's] future prospects" (Curtis 1976, 17; Wyatt-Brown 1986, 150).

These rituals that sorted out the honorable from the not honorable are now in the past for the South (Ayers 1984); and thus, as Richerson has suggested, there may have been an actual *deescalation* of the faking-and-detecting arms race. Whereas the Old South may have developed rituals for sorting out fakes (step 3 in the arms race), these rituals seem to have disappeared from the landscape as the need to do such sorting declined. Thus the current state (step 2) in which people are getting away with faking honorability may in fact represent a deescalation of the arms race, as such rituals as purring, gouging matches, gander pulls, duels, and so on have disappeared.

The contrast between the South and the inner-city gang culture is informative in that it adds a contingency to the arms race model. The contingency is that a social system may only go on in the spiraling arms race between better faking and better detecting when environmental factors make it pay to catch the cheaters. When it is not particularly important to catch the fakers, the arms race may not escalate—or it may even deescalate. As game theorists and legal scholars such as Cooter, Posner, and Lessig point out, enforcing a norm, detecting cheaters, or engaging in the sorts of rituals here described can be a very costly practice (Cooter 1996, 1997, 1998; Lessig 1995; Posner 1996, 1998; see also Fudenberg and Maskin 1986). (In the case of aggression, testing for fakers also can be a particularly risky activity if a person attempts to "call another's bluff" and then discovers that it was no bluff.) Thus, on balance, in circumstances where there is little benefit to catching cheaters, it may be more beneficial to just let them go.

The natural world, of course, has its own parallels to this phenomena. Authors such as Tinbergen (1974, 134–37), Zahavi and Zahavi (1997, 9–10, 185–95), and Dawkins (1989, 248–52) have argued that arms races involving mimicry and the ability to detect mimicry need not spiral out of control endlessly. Depending on how costly or risky it is to detect mimics versus how costly it is to simply let them go, a certain amount of mimicry or fakery can persist in the system. Zahavi and Zahavi (1997, 185, 195) characterize this as a "stalemate" in the arms race, where a "dynamic state of equilibrium" has been reached between organisms in the system. Both biological and social systems may find themselves in either escalating arms races or in these relatively stable states of equilibrium, depending on the costs, benefits, and probabilities of faking or detecting fakes.[4]

Continuity and Change

The major drawback to the bluffing and "cheating" going on in the South is that it prevents Southerners from understanding that their peers do not actually strongly subscribe to culture of honor norms. Southerners may not be subjectively committed to honor norms, but they believe that *others* are, and this may guide their behavior, particularly when the signaling from these others is relatively ambiguous.

To reiterate, we do believe that honor norms are internalized by Southerners to some extent (Cohen, Vandello, and Rantilla 1998; Vandello and Cohen 1999b). We also believe, however, that the cultural system of Southerners is at a relatively awkward stage. On the one hand, Southerners probably are not as internally committed to honor norms as they were in the past, and thus violence deriving from an "irrational" inflexible sense of honor is probably lessened. On the other hand, the model of the generalized other or the impartial spectator for Southerners may not have caught up. Thus a good deal of contemporary violence probably stems from mistaken beliefs about what others expect, rather than truly aggressive tendencies. The problem then is that some of the same mechanisms that allow people to "cheat" and "get away" with not internalizing honor beliefs also are the same mechanisms that allow the system of misperceptions about others to continue. Thus the factors that allow Southerners to fake their honorability also contribute to a system of "shared misunderstanding" (Matza 1964) that keeps them from recognizing that *others* are faking their own honorability. Public norms for honor remain strong because people's private beliefs about honor can remain unexposed. Ironically, the same factors that allow people's private beliefs to diverge from public stances also maintain the longevity of such potentially dysfunctional public stances themselves. One would expect that public honor-related norms would fade as environmental circumstances changed and made them less functional (Nisbett and Cohen 1996); yet this "stalemate" allowing mimicry to be sustained possibly has helped keep these public norms alive and prevents—or at least slows—their dismantling.

Here the practical challenge is to develop interventions that can prevent the system of "shared misunderstandings" from continuing. The theoretical challenges are to identify the micro- and macro-level forces that are conducive to strong public norms about honor as well as strong or weak internal subjective commitments. Comparisons and contrasts between the contingencies and environmental circumstances that have developed in the U.S. South and those that have developed in other cultures of honor (in other times and other places) should prove informative.

Notes

1. This sense of the willingness to risk all, the importance of principle, and the practical benefits of "irrationally" upholding one's honor at all costs

were captured memorably in a passage from Mario Puzo's *The Godfather*. In the passage, Puzo (1985 [1969], 91–93) describes how the Mafia Don— head of "the Honorable Society"—sized up his opponents. In thinking about how to deal with his adversary Jack Woltz, the Don asked his advisor Tom Hagen whether Woltz had "real balls."

> Hagen had learned that the Don's values were so different from those of most people that his words also could have a different meaning. Did Woltz have character? Did he have a strong will? He most certainly did, but that was not what the Don was asking. Did the movie producer have the courage not to be bluffed? Did he have the willingness to suffer heavy financial loss delay on his movies would mean, the scandal of his big star exposed as a user of heroin? Again the answer was yes. But again this was not what the Don meant. Finally Hagen translated the question properly in his mind. *Did Jack Woltz have the balls to risk everything, to run the chance of losing all on a matter of principle, on a matter of honor; for revenge?*
>
> Hagen smiled. He did it rarely but now he could not resist jesting with the Don. "You're asking if he is a Sicilian." The Don nodded his head pleasantly, acknowledging the flattering witticism and its truth. "No," Hagen said.
>
> That had been all.

And at that point the Godfather knows how to respond.

2. In a similar vein, it has been argued that notions of morality and justice generally must be embraced with passion rather than simply recognized. As Hume (1996 [1777], 172) noted,

> [W]hat is honourable, what is fair, what is becoming, what is noble, what is generous, takes possession of the heart, and animates us to embrace and maintain it. What is intelligible, what is evident, what is probable, what is true, procures only the cool assent of the understanding; and gratifying a speculative curiosity, puts an end to our researches.

3. Costly to fake signals, of course, have their power because they signal something about those making the display and their willingness and ability to pay the costs. In many cultures physical symbols such as scars can serve the purpose of signaling toughness. Dueling scars of Prussian and Austrian men were "shown off as proofs not necessarily of victory but of bravery and self-discipline" (Gilmore 1990, 70).

    Truk Islanders today also wear their scars "proudly . . . They may even be self-inflicted for show as well as earned in fights. In the old days, for example, Trukese warriors used to intimidate opponents by slowly and ostentatiously cutting their own arms to show their unflinching bravery. Obviously they cared more to make an impression on enemies than to win, as wounding themselves could not have enhanced their fighting capability" (Gilmore 1990, 69–70). As Zahavi and Zahavi (1997, 229) argue, risk or "waste can make sense, because by wasting one proves conclusively that one has enough assets to waste and more. The investment—the waste itself—is just what makes the advertisement [the signal] reliable."

4. Dawkins and Krebs memorably made this point about arms races failing to escalate interminably owing to what they called the "life/dinner principle." The principle comes from Aesop's fables: "The rabbit runs faster than the fox, because the rabbit is running for his life while the fox is only running for his dinner" (Dawkins 1989, 250). The point is that there may be an "asymmetry in the cost of failure" such that one organism has a huge incentive to improve its capabilities in the "arms race," while the other can opt out without losing too much.

References

Anderson, Elijah. 1994. "The Code of the Streets." *Atlantic Monthly* 5: 81–94.

Ayers, Edward. 1984. *Vengeance and Justice*. New York: Oxford University Press.

Bikhchandani, Sushil, David Hirshleifer, and Ivo Welch. 1992. "A Theory of Fads, Fashion, Customs, and Culture as Informational Cascades." *Journal of Political Economy* 100: 992–1026.

Carter, Hodding. 1963. *First Person Rural*. Garden City, N.Y.: Doubleday.

Cohen, Dov. 1996. "Law, Social Policy, and Violence: The Impact of Regional Cultures." *Journal of Personality and Social Psychology* 70: 961–78.

———. 1997. "Ifs and Thens in Cultural Psychology." In *Advances in Social Cognition*, edited by Robert Wyer. Vol. 10 (121–31). Mahwah, N.J.: Lawrence Erlbaum.

———. 1998a. "Culture, Social Organization, and Patterns of Violence." *Journal of Personality and Social Psychology* 75: 408–19.

———. 1998b. "Shaping, Channeling, and Distributing Testosterone in Social Systems." *Behavioral and Brain Sciences* 21: 367–68.

———. 2001. "Cultural Variation: Considerations and Implications." *Psychological Bulletin* 127: 451–71.

Cohen, Dov, and Richard Nisbett. 1994. "Self-Protection and the Culture of Honor: Explaining Southern Violence." *Personality and Social Psychology Bulletin* 20: 551–67.

———. 1997. "Field Experiments Examining the Culture of Honor: The Role of Institutions in Perpetuating Norms About Violence." *Personality and Social Psychology Bulletin* 23: 1188–99.

Cohen, Dov, Richard Nisbett, Brian Bowdle, and Norbert Schwarz. 1996. "Insult, Aggression, and the Southern Culture of Honor: An 'Experimental Ethnography.'" *Journal of Personality and Social Psychology* 70: 945–60.

Cohen, Dov, and Joseph Vandello. 1998. "Meanings of Violence." *Journal of Legal Studies* 27: 567–84.

———. Forthcoming. "The Paradox of Politeness." In *Cultural Shaping of Violence*, edited by Myrdene Anderson.

Cohen, Dov, Joseph Vandello, Sylvia Puente, and Adrian Rantilla. 1999.

"'When You Call Me That, Smile!': How Norms for Politeness, Interaction Styles, and Aggression Work Together in Southern Culture." *Social Psychology Quarterly* 62: 257–75.

Cohen, Dov, Joseph Vandello, and Adrian Rantilla. 1998. "The Sacred and the Social: Cultures of Honor and Violence." In *Shame*, edited by Paul Gilbert and Bernice Andrews (261–82). New York: Oxford University Press.

Cooley, Charles. 1902. *Human Nature and the Social Order*. New York: Scribner.

Cooter, Robert. 1996. "Decentralized Law for a Complex Economy: The Structural Approach to Adjudicating the New Law Merchant." *University of Pennsylvania Law Review* 144: 1643–96.

———. 1997. "Normative Failure Theory of Law." *Cornell Law Review* 82: 947–79.

———. 1998. "Expressive Law and Economics." *Journal of Legal Studies* 27: 585–608.

Curtis, James. 1976. *Andrew Jackson and the Search for Vindication*. Boston: Little, Brown.

Daly, Martin, and Margo Wilson. 1988. *Homicide*. Hawthorne, N.Y.: Aldine.

Dawkins, Richard. 1989. *The Selfish Gene*. Oxford: Oxford University Press.

Ellison, Christopher. 1991. "An Eye for an Eye?" *Social Forces* 69: 1223–39.

Fischer, David. 1989. *Albion's Seed: Four British Folkways in America*. New York: Oxford University Press.

Frank, Robert. 1988. *Passions Within Reason: The Strategic Role of the Emotions*. New York: Norton.

Fudenberg, Drew, and Eric Maskin. 1986. "The Folk Theorem in Repeated Games with Discounting or with Incomplete Information." *Econometrica* 54: 533–54.

Gastil, Raymond. 1971. "Homicide and a Regional Culture of Violence." *American Sociological Review* 36: 412–27.

Gilmore, David. 1990. *Manhood in the Making*. New Haven: Yale University Press.

Gladwell, Malcolm. 2000. *The Tipping Point*. Boston: Little, Brown.

Gorn, Elliot. 1985. "Gouge and Bite, Pull Hair and Scratch: The Social Significance of Fighting in the Southern Backcountry." *American Historical Review* 90: 18–43.

Hume, David. 1777. *Enquiries Concerning Human Understanding and Concerning the Principles of Morals*. Reprint. New York: Oxford University Press, 1996.

Kahan, Dan. 1997. "Social Influence, Social Meaning, and Deterrence." *Virginia Law Review* 83: 349–95.

———. 1998. "Social Meaning and the Economic Analysis of Crime." *Journal of Legal Studies* 27: 609–22.

Krebs, John, and Richard Dawkins. 1984. "Animal Signals." In John Krebs and Nicholas Davies, eds., *Behavioral Ecology: An Evolutionary Approach* (380–402). Sunderland, Mass.: Sinauer.

Kuran, Timur. 1995. *Private Truths, Public Lies: The Social Consequences of Preference Falsification*. Cambridge, Mass.: Harvard University Press.

Lessig, Lawrence. 1995. "The Regulation of Social Meaning." *University of Chicago Law Review* 62: 943–1045.

Luckenbill, David. 1977. "Criminal Homicide as a Situated Transaction." *Social Problems* 25: 176–86.

Matza, David. 1964. *Delinquency and Drift*. New York: Wiley.

Mazur, Allan, and Alan Booth. 1998. "Testosterone and Dominance in Men." *Behavioral and Brain Sciences* 21: 353–97.

McAdams, Richard. 1997. "The Origin, Development, and Regulation of Norms." *Michigan Law Review* 96: 338–433.

McWhiney, Grady. 1988. *Cracker Culture*. Tuscaloosa: University of Alabama Press.

Mead, George. 1934. *On Social Psychology*. Chicago: University of Chicago Press.

Miller, Dale, and Deborah Prentice. 1994. "Collective Errors and Errors About the Collective." *Personality and Social Psychology Bulletin* 20: 541–50.

Miller, William. 1990. *Bloodtaking and Peacemaking: Feud, Law, and Society in Saga Iceland*. Chicago: University of Chicago Press.

———. 1993. *Humiliation*. Ithaca, N.Y.: Cornell University Press.

Mischke, P. 1981. "Criminal-Law-Homicide-Self-Defense-Duty-to-Retreat." *Tennessee Law Review* 48: 1000–23.

Nesse, Randolph M. 2001. "Natural Selection and the Capacity for Subjective Commitment." In *Evolution and the Capacity for Commitment*, edited by Randolph Nesse. New York: Russell Sage Foundation.

Nesse, Randolph M., and Alan T. Lloyd. 1992. "The Evolution of Psychodynamic Mechanisms." In *The Adapted Mind*, edited by Jerome Barkow, Leda Cosmides, and John Tooby (601–24). New York: Oxford University Press.

Nisbett, Richard, and Dov Cohen. 1996. *Culture of Honor: The Psychology of Violence in the South*. Boulder, Colo.: Westview Press.

Nisbett, Richard, Greg Polly, and Sylvia Lang. 1995. "Homicide and U.S. Regional Culture." In *Interpersonal Violent Behaviors*, edited by R. Barry Ruback and Neil Weiner (135–51). New York: Springer.

Peng, Kaiping, Richard Nisbett, and Nancy Wong. 1997. "Validity Problems in Cross-Cultural Value Comparisons and Possible Solutions." *Psychological Methods* 2: 329–44.

Picker, Randal. 1997. "Simple Games in a Complex World: A Generative Approach to the Adoption of Norms." *University of Chicago Law Review* 64: 1225–88.

Pinker, Steven, and Paul Bloom. 1992. "Natural Language and Natural Selection." In *The Adapted Mind*, edited by Jerome Barkow, Leda Cosmides, and John Tooby (451–93). New York: Oxford University Press.

Pitt-Rivers, Julian. 1968. "Honor." In *International Encyclopedia of the Social Sciences*, edited by David Sills (503–11). New York: Macmillan.

Posner, Eric. 1996. "Law, Economics, and Inefficient Norms." *University of Pennsylvania Law Review* 144: 1697–1744.

———. 1998. "Symbols, Signals, and Social Norms in Politics and Law." *Journal of Legal Studies* 27: 765–98.

Prentice, Deborah, and Dale Miller. 1993. "Pluralistic Ignorance and Alcohol Use on Campus: Some Consequences of Misperceiving the Social Norm." *Journal of Personality and Social Psychology* 64: 243–56.

———. 1996. "Pluralistic Ignorance and the Perpetuation of Social Norms by

Unwitting Actors." In *Advances in Experimental Social Psychology*, edited by Mark Zanna (161–209). San Diego: Academic Press.

Puzo, Mario. 1985 [1969]. *The Godfather*. New York: Daw.

Reaves, Andrew, and Richard Nisbett. 1999. *The Cultural Ecology of White Homicide*. Typescript. University of Alabama.

Reed, John. 1981. "Below the Smith and Wesson Line." In *Perspectives on the American South*, edited by Merle Black and John Reed (9–22). New York: Cordon and Breach.

Rosen, Jeffrey. 1997. "The Social Police." *The New Yorker*, 20 October, 170–81.

Schelling, Thomas. 1966. *The Strategy of Conflict*. New York: Oxford.

———. 1978. *Micromotives and Macrobehavior*. New York: Norton.

Smith, Adam. 1759. *The Theory of Moral Sentiments*, edited by D. Raphael and A. Macfie. Reprint. Oxford: Clarendon Press, 1976.

Tinbergen, Niko. 1974. *Curious Naturalists*. Baltimore: Penguin.

Vandello, Joseph, and Dov Cohen. 1999a. "Patterns of Individualism and Collectivism Across the United States." *Journal of Personality and Social Psychology* 77: 279–92.

———. 1999b. "Honor and Domestic Violence." Typescript, Princeton University.

———. 1999c. "Pluralistic Ignorance and the Perception of Norms About Male Aggression." Typescript.

———. 2000. "When Believing Is Seeing." In *The Psychological Foundations of Culture*, edited by Mark Schaller and Chris Crandall, forthcoming. Mahwah, N.J.: Lawrence Erlbaum.

Will, George. 1993. "Are We a 'Nation of Cowards'?" *Newsweek*, 15 November, 93–94.

Wilson, James, and George Kelling. 1982. "Broken Windows." *Atlantic Monthly* 249: 29–38.

Wyatt-Brown, Bertram. 1982. *Southern Honor*. New York: Oxford University Press.

———. 1986. *Honor and Violence in the Old South*. New York: Oxford University Press.

Zahavi, Amotz, and Avishag Zahavi. 1997. *The Handicap Principle*. New York: Oxford University Press.

Chapter 9

The Evolution of Subjective Commitment to Groups: A Tribal Instincts Hypothesis

PETER J. RICHERSON AND ROBERT BOYD

> In August 1914 I was torn between an intense curiosity to see war at close quarters, an intense objection to killing people, both mixed with ideas of public duty and doubt as to whether I could endure danger.
> —Lewis F. Richardson, turbulence theorist, Quaker pacifist, ambulance driver in France, posthumous author of
> *Statistics of Deadly Quarrels*, 1960

EXPRESSIONS of commitment to group goals are commonplace. At the time of this writing, the daily newspaper reports that several foreign affairs departments from Western nations are exerting pressure on Russia to suspend its offensive in Chechnya and begin peace negotiations. The Chechen president is committed to peace talks, but the current war seemingly has begun because Russia doubts his government's commitment to control Islamic revolutionaries apparently committed to the armed expansion of their style of regime into neighboring Dagestan. The president of Syria and the prime minister of Israel have expressed commitments to peace between their nations and the U.S. president is entertaining them in Washington to demonstrate American commitment to brokering the peace process. A presidential candidate promises to commit the U.S. military to a more liberal policy toward gay soldiers if elected. Democrats in California are committed to using their hold on the state legislature and governor's office to redistrict the state's legislative districts as much in their favor as possible, while Republicans are committed to an initiative to place redistricting in the hands of the state supreme court.

Indeed, speaking of whole nations as having policies and strategies as if they were individual actors is commonplace. Leaders commonly articulate promises and threats on behalf of their nations. Schelling's (1966) classic on the logic of commitment, *Arms and Influence*, speaks almost entirely in this idiom, although he is perfectly clear that the same principles apply to person-to-person negotiation. Of course we know that the reality is more complex. The Israeli prime minister left for Washington with the support of only the bare majority of his cabinet for peace talks with Syria. Incumbent Republicans, if history is any indication, will fight Democratic redistricting with big words and little action because the Democrats will induce their personal acquiescence by creating safe districts for them. Nevertheless, the fact that we can speak so casually about commitment to group goals suggests that they really do exist. Doubting them is frequently a recipe for hurt. California voters recently passed a medical marijuana law, but the commitment of federal prosecutors to rigorous enforcement of the national marijuana prohibition laws in the name of the so-called War on Drugs still lands open medical users in trouble with the law.

As L. F. Richardson's reminiscence suggests, commitments to group goals are deeply rooted in the emotions of individual humans who make up groups. The threats and promises of leaders are only credible to the extent that followers will collectively back them up with passionate action. Richardson's own uncommon commitment to pacifism was felt deeply enough to cause him to risk ostracism for failure of patriotism, but also to volunteer for near-frontline service in the medical corps, and later to turn from his illustrious career as a fluid dynamicist to the study of the causes of war. Millions of Richardson's contemporaries were motivated by patriotic sentiments to volunteer to serve in their nation's fighting services. No doubt few indeed envisioned just how terrible trench warfare would prove to be, but no doubt their feelings of duty were, even at the outset, normally mixed with the same trepidation as Richardson. In the event, most served, suffered, and died faithfully through the horrors of World War I.

Richardson's emotional commitments and the actions they led to illustrate some stylized facts about human commitments to the groups in which they live. To begin with, they are of enormous subjective import. Dramas such as *Henry V*, *Saving Private Ryan*, *The Cross of Iron*, and less dramatic but more realistic pieces are often recommended by veterans to civilians to give them some insight into extraordinary emotions that bind soldiers to one another and to their duty—feelings that many find very difficult to share with those who have not experienced them. Moreover, one of the reasons these emotions are so powerful is that they are highly conflicted. Duty struggles with terror in the hearts of soldiers. Not uncommonly, fear wins and soldiers run away. Individuals' commitments to their groups are highly contingent. Clausewitz's famous dictum that the moral is to the physical as three to one expresses the military analysts's finding that the morale of an army is its most important single attribute. As long as soldiers feel that they are doing good in a common cause, their commitment to their army is likely to be high. Morale evaporates when soldiers feel they are misused, abused, or exploited for others' personal gain. Furthermore, the group toward which individuals feel an emotional attachment is highly variable: some people feel slight commitment to any group; some give their families pride of place; some their town, class, or caste; some their nation or religion; and some to all humanity or even all sentient life. Finally, a given culture generally has a consensus on the nature of the groups to which commitments of various kinds are expected. Most Europeans in 1914 agreed that young men should fight for their nation, most of all the young men themselves. Honorable dissenters such as Richardson had the choice of a few tolerated options, such as service in the medical corps. Those who were perceived as avoiding service for selfish motives or fear were subject to informal suasion, conscription, and coercive discipline. Early twentieth-century nationalism had, of course, a rather short history in 1914. In the sixteenth century the most enthusiastic bloodletting in Europe was motivated by religion, not nation.

War is an extreme case. Yet everyday life is full of behavior that confronts individuals with the dilemma of commitment to groups at personal expense. Voting in elections is a classic example. The chance of anyone's vote actually affecting the outcome of an election is very small, and the costs of casting a vote, particularly an informed vote, are significant. Most votes appear to be cast in voters' conception of the common good, not from selfish motives (Sears and Funk 1990). Temptations to selfish behavior do abound and many do succumb. Many more cooperate, especially when cajoled into arrangements of more secured commitment by those with less secured commitments.

In this chapter we will review empirical evidence that many people have unsecured commitments to groups, and advance a theory to explain the data. We know that many if not most readers will bring a large dose of skepticism to this argument; we ask only that such skeptics give us a fair hearing. As Miller (1999) observes, people in the rational individualist Western tradition have a strong folk belief in selfish rationality. The scientific versions of the folk belief—rational choice theory and the evolutionary theory of individual fitness—

make strong predictions that hold in the case of most nonhuman species studied. Yet when taken into the laboratory, most human folk individualists violate the canons of formal individualism. As we will see, folk individualists show high rates of cooperation in one-shot, anonymous prisoner's dilemma games, high rates of participation in commons games, and high rates of fair treatment of others in resource division games such as the one-shot anonymous Ultimatum and Dictator games. We think that this evidence alone ought to shake individualists' belief in their intuitions.

We argue that unsecured commitments to social groups arose by coevolution with cultural institutions subject to group selection. We will refer to the emotions and cognitive mechanisms that give rise to group cohesion and strategic action as *tribal social instincts* and distinguish them from the more ancient social instincts that underpin cooperation in smaller-scale groups based on nepotism and reciprocity. Cultural variation is much more easily subject to group selection than are genes, because the properties of the cultural inheritance allow persistent, heritable difference between groups. Once culture became subject to group selection, prosocial tribal instincts arose by coevolution with group-selected cultural institutions.

One of the great attractions of evolutionary theories is that they are maximally vulnerable to the consilient properties of nature (Wilson 1998). Many different disciplines command data with which an evolutionary explanation must be consistent to be plausible. Five different domains of evidence can be used to test our social instincts explanation of commitments to groups:

Checks for logical coherence, typically using mathematical models. Unless we can make a mathematical model of cultural group selection work on paper or in the computer, it probably doesn't work in nature.

Verification that the proximal mechanisms entailed by the hypothesis actually exist. If we cannot find evidence for proximal psychological mechanisms that produce a measure of unsecured commitment to aid group members, we should doubt that the postulated group recognition and altruism could or did evolve.

Tests for the existence of the necessary microevolutionary processes. If operation of cultural group selection can't be detected in the field, it probably doesn't exist.

Examinations of the large-scale and comparative evidence. Are the differences between human sociality and sociality in other species consistent with the operation of cultural group selection? Have the revolutions in human social organization during the rise of "civilization" been constrained by social instincts?

Searches for predicted patterns of adaptation and maladaptation. Natural selection and derivative processes produce characteristic patterns of adaptation and maladaptation. Thus Hamilton's (1964) famous theory of inclusive fitness shows how selection can shape altruistic adaptations among relatives. It is equally a theory of why selection cannot perfect these adaptations. Reproductive conflicts among kin groups means that cooperation on a larger scale between distantly related individuals cannot evolve, even if participants' fitness would increase if it could.

We argue that our tribal instincts hypothesis is more plausible than its competitors in all five domains of evidence.

The Tribal Social Instincts Hypothesis and Its Competitors

The tribal social instincts hypothesis is based on the idea that group selection plays a more important role in shaping culturally transmitted variation than it does in shaping genetic variation and, as a result, that humans have lived in social environments characterized by high levels of cooperation for as long as culture has played an important role in human adaptation. The archaeological record has evidence of our use of symbols—probably to mark social groups, among other functions (Bettinger 1991, 203–8; Bettinger, Boyd, and Richerson 1996)—for the last fifty thousand years, and nascent tribes were presumably a still more ancient phenomenon, perhaps two hundred fifty thousand to three hundred fifty thousand years old (Klein 1999, chs. 6 and 7). So human minds have been selected for between two thousand and ten thousand generations in social environments in which the innate willingness to recognize, aid and, if necessary, punish fellow group members was favored by ordinary natural selection (see Richerson and Boyd 1998 for a fuller treatment). We suppose that the resulting tribal instincts are something akin to principles in the Chomskyan linguists' "principles and parameters" view of language (Pinker 1994). The innate principles furnish people with basic predispositions, emotional capacities, and social skills that are implemented in practice through highly variable cultural institutions, the parameters. Humans evolved to be innately prepared to commit to the institutions and projects of their tribes, but culture dictates how to recognize who belongs to the tribes, what schedules of aid, praise, and punishment is due to tribal fellows, and how the tribe is to deal with other tribes—allies, enemies, and clients.

Since tribal instincts are of relatively recent origin, they are not the sole regulators of human social life. Tribal instincts are laid on top of more ancient social instincts rooted in kin selection and reciprocal altruism. These ancient social instincts conflict with our tribal impulses. We are simultaneously committed to tribes, family, and self, even though our simultaneous and conflicting commitments very often cause us the great anguish Freud (1930) described in *Civilization and Its Discontents* and Graham Greene portrayed in novels such as *The Honorary Consul*.

We have not the space to review in detail all the competing hypotheses to explain the evolution of human social organization. Broadly speaking, however, the arguments fall into two classes: those that emphasize individual-level processes and those that emphasize group function. Methodological individualists in the social sciences are deeply skeptical of the group-functional picture of human behavior, and wish to ground the social sciences on the postulate of self-interested rational choice (for example, Coleman 1991). Evolutionary biologists by and large follow Williams's (1966) lead in rejecting group selection as an important force in nature. In the case of humans, not to mention other animals, selfish behavior and very small-scale altruism—for example, among close relatives—is common and in accord with methodological individualists' theoretical models. Following Axelrod and Hamilton (1981) and Alexander (1987), individualists reckon that the logic of small-scale reciprocity can be scaled up to explain human cooperation on the large scale without violating any of the standard assumptions of methodological individualism, such as postulating a strong role for group selection. Evolutionary theories of subjective commitment deriving from these theories imagine that emotions essentially act to buttress individual contracts with other individuals (Hirshleifer 1987; Frank 1988).

The relationship between rational choice theory and cultural evolution theory is complex because we assume that individual choice exists, acts as a force shaping cultural evolution, and in some measure follows ends prescribed by the ancient social instincts (Boyd and Richerson 1993). We hold, however, that choice is boundedly rational and does not normally follow the canons of formal rationality—that is, people form their repertoires of behavior mostly by imitating others, making adaptive but myopic choices among the cultural variants they observe. More rarely, people independently invent new adaptive behaviors. When the results of such myopic decision making are accumulated over a population of people and many cycles of imitation and decision making, they indeed become potent evolutionary forces. However, we also suppose that such forces are not sufficiently powerful to obviate the effects of natural selection *on cultural variation*. Our social instincts hypothesis requires that cultural group selection be strong enough to counter individualistically motivated selfish decision making in order to favor tribal-scale cooperation and, as a corollary, to favor a measure of unsecured commitment to the group's practices and projects.

Group functionalism remains a prominent theory in sociology and anthropology. According to Turner (1995), plausible evolutionary models underlie the classic functionalist theories of Durkheim and Spencer and their successors, but these ideas have not been formally elaborated and tested in the style of evolutionary theory in biology, so little more can be said about these contributions. Darwin (1902 [1874], 179) himself articulated a clear group-selection argument to account for human cooperation: "A tribe including many members who, from possessing in a high degree the spirit of patriotism, fidelity, obedience, courage, and sympathy, were always ready to aid one another, and to sacrifice themselves for the common good, would be victorious over most other tribes; and this would be natural selection." Darwin's list of prosocial virtues is easily read as a list of unsecured or weakly secured subjective commitments to group welfare. (We will later discuss what we mean by "weakly secured.") One possibility is that humans are genetically group selected. Several prominent modern Darwinians (Hamilton 1975; Wilson 1975, 561–62; Alexander 1974; Eibl-Eibesfeldt 1982) have given serious consideration to group selection as a force *in the special case* of human ultrasociality. They are impressed, as we are, by the organization of human populations into units that engage in highly organized, lethal competition with other groups, not to mention other forms of cooperation. Direct group selection on genes is a process that could give human groups a degree of functional integration. A second view is that processes peculiar to culture are prone to group selection. This idea is the root of our tribal instincts hypothesis. A third possibility is that human propensities to cooperate are a by-product or accident of some other process. Simon (1990) proposed that human cooperation is a by-product of our docility and that docility is necessary to take advantage of cultural transmission. Van den Berghe (1981) argued that in small-scale societies cultural similarity in dialect, clothing, and so forth is used as a sensitive marker of genetic relatedness. The relative isolation of families and bands set up sharp cultural gradients that would measure genetic distance more effectively than innate characters, for which the gradient at the small scale is likely to be very small. In the much larger, denser societies made possible by agriculture, people with very similar culture might come to number thousands and, with mass media, millions. Such cultural similarity may trigger kin-selected social instincts so that we have unsecured subjective commitments to the welfare of our fellow tribals as if they were close kin.

Tests in Five Domains

Sufficient data are available in the literature to make a preliminary test of the competing hypotheses about the nature of human sociality. To be sure, none of the competitors can be entirely ruled out, and no doubt both new hypotheses and new data will shed new light. Of the existing conjectures, however, we believe the tribal instincts hypothesis is the most likely to survive further tests.

Logical Cogency

The tribal social instincts hypothesis is inspired largely by work on mathematical models of cultural evolution. We have modeled five facets of the evolution of cooperation in human societies: the plausibility of group selection on cultural variation; the dynamics of boundary formation in human groups; the role of moralistic punishment in human social systems; the potential for social norms to exert coevolutionary pressures on genes; and finally, the power of indirect reciprocity to support cooperation in large groups.

Models of Cultural Group Selection   We have studied the effects of conformist transmission. In most societies individuals observe the behavior of many other people, and hence can estimate the frequency of traits in the population. Our theoretical work suggests that imitating the commoner type is adaptive under a wide range of spatially and temporally variable environments (Boyd and Richerson 1985, ch. 7; Henrich and Boyd 1998). In the models various learning mechanisms in addition to selection tend to make adaptive behavior more common than maladaptive behavior. In a world where information is costly and individual learning therefore error prone, imitating common behaviors is a simple heuristic that will get you the correct behavior most of the time at a smaller cost than subjecting alternative behaviors to more rigorous test. Conformity probably evolved in concert with human capacities for imitation. In theoretical models at least, conformity is an advantage even when reliance on social learning is scant.

Conformist imitation has the by-product of reducing variation within groups and preserving variation between groups. Once a cooperative variant becomes the commonest variant in a local group, the conformist effect will favor its further increase by group selection. Once a local group has a given trait maintained at high frequency partly by conformity, rather large rates of migration will not perturb it sufficiently to flip to another trait. This is just the sort of difference from genetic inheritance that in theory should make group selection a strong force. The reason that group selection tends to be a weak force on genes is that migration between groups has a strong tendency to erode variation between them. Conformity solves this problem.

Cultural group selection does not have to result in the physical extinction of losing groups. The process works if groups merely become socially extinct by breaking up and joining other groups as refugees. So long as not too many refugees join any one group, the host group's culture is not likely to change.

The models are quite abstract and do not themselves say anything about the mechanisms by which progroup altruism will be motivated by proximal psychological processes, such as subjective commitments. They do provide an explanation consistent with folk models of subjective motivations, such as those enumerated by Darwin.

Symbolic Marking of Cultural Group Boundaries   We have studied models of a process we term *indirect bias* (Boyd and Richerson 1985, ch. 8), in which individual imitators use one attribute of potential cultural models to weight that individual in the socialization process. For example, young people pick adult role models on the basis of charm, prestige, or power and, once a role model is chosen, youngsters may pick up a number of other ideas, norms, skills, and attitudes from that individual. If any of these other traits happens to be correlated with indices of prestige or charm that youngsters are using to choose role models, then the correlated variants will increase in frequency.

The evolution of symbolic, stylistic markers of group boundaries is an interesting special case of cultural evolution under indirect bias. We (Boyd and Richerson 1987) investigated a model of the evolution of "ethnic" markers motivated by these observations. Assume, for example, both child and subadult phases of transmission. In the child phase children learn some neutral marker trait, such as a speech dialect, from their parents and other local adults. In the later subadult phase they learn a subsistence trait and modify their dialect by selecting among a larger set of adult models. In the first phase children just copy blindly. Subadults weight models by both their symbolic trait and their subsistence success. Subadult imitators prefer models with the dialect they learned as children, but also prefer successful models. The larger set of models in the subadult phase is meant to mimic the effects of cultural diffusion from one environment to another; wide-ranging subadults are influenced by a much wider social world than are children. The question is, in an environment in which the best subsistence strategy is variable from place to place, can a symbolic marker reducing the effect of cultural diffusion of locally maladaptive traits from neighboring environments arise? The answer is yes. Given a sharp environmental gradient, a dialect difference will emerge and continue to grow more extreme until the degree of cultural isolation is sufficient to allow the population to locally optimize the mean subsistence behavior. Thus to the picture of a culturally group-selected hominid from the previous section, we can also imagine in theory that the boundaries between groups are formally marked by symbolic and stylistic changes. Much as in the case of group selection on culture, the evolution of markers of group boundaries is easier than in the analogous genetic case. Premating isolating barriers arise with difficulty under selection. Our ethnic markers model works assuming two phases of transmission. Although symbolic boundaries arise in this model for ordinary adaptive reasons, their isolating tendency will, like conformity, tend to aid the group-selection process by protecting any group-level variation that arises from the variation-reducing effects of migration.

One might think that ethnic boundaries could arise directly to mark groups of cooperators, but this does not seem to be the case (McElreath, Boyd, and Richerson n.d.). The reason is clear. In a simple world in which cooperation is the only behavior correlated with a marker, selection will strongly favor defectors who carry the marker, deceiving cooperators in order to victimize them. Behaviors for which coordination is important do support the evolution of markers. Coordination involves no dilemma of group versus individual interest; everyone is better off to conform to the common type. Money is an example. Many things—gold, silver, paper, scarce seashells—will more or less equally serve the functions of store of wealth and medium of exchange, but these functions are best served if everyone agrees to use the same standard. Games of coordination will favor the evolution of norms and subjective commitment to group norms, especially in complex cases where individuals cannot easily perceive the nature of the coordination solution. If some coordination equilibria are superior to others, group selection will favor those.

Moralistic Punishment   Moralistic punishment is the strategy of punishing others who disobey a moral rule and also sanctioning those who do not punish others for breaking the rule. In principle, moralistic punishment strategies could create cooperation in large groups. However, this mechanism will stabilize any norm that becomes common, whether adaptive or not (wearing ties to work is a humble example of the latter) (Boyd and Richerson 1992). Once a moralistic strategy becomes common, those who do not follow the rule are at a considerable disadvantage. In the pure moralistic punishment model no force acts to make moralistic rules prosocial. If we suppose that the evolution of moralistic strategies is guided to a significant extent by cultural group selection, then those groups that have prosocial moralistic norms for cooperation will have a considerable advantage over those with no norms, arbitrary norms, or only norms for coordination.

Once more, subjective commitments are a potential proximal mechanism to implement moralistic punishment. In one model we studied one equilibrium was a mixture of cooperator-punishers and reluctant cooperators who could be coerced into cooperating by a cooperator-punisher. The equilibrium number of cooperator-punishers was enough so that each interacting group on average had about one punisher, just enough to induce complete cooperation in most groups. Even a relatively small minority of individuals with unsecured commitments to group welfare can move a much larger mass by generating incentives that secure the cooperation of many more. For this to happen, the majority must be rather prone to being coerced into cooperating and punishing, or else the costs of punishing to the cooperator-punishers will be too high for this type to evolve at all.

We might call this a system sustained mainly by *weakly secured* commitments. The unsecured commitments of the few can act to secure the commitments of the many, but only if the cost of providing such security is low. Frequency-dependent effects are liable to drive up the frequency of defectors in any system in which unconditional cooperation becomes common, so some sort of policing system must evolve to counteract this threat. A commitment to police is itself an altruistic propensity. Moralistic strategies can act to spread the costs of policing very widely by leveraging a small amount of unsecured commitment.

Genes Coevolve with Culture   Culture can create coevolutionary pressure by social selection against genotypes that are ill adapted to cultural institutions and by favoring ones that are well adapted. We have modeled a case in which males acquire prestige in a culturally determined competition and asked if females will evolve to prefer to mate with prestigious males, even if prestigious males have lower genetic fitness than males who do not invest resources in conforming to prestige norms (Richerson and Boyd 1989). If prestige has an important effect on *cultural* fitness then the evolution of females with a *genetic* predisposition to mate with prestigious males can evolve. As with the punishment model, this process does not intrinsically favor prosocial prestige norms. Yet, in conjunction with cultural group selection, we believe that social institutions will tend to be prosocial and thus the mate choices and moralistic punishments people make will tend to grant prestige to people with prosocial dispositions and stigmatize those with antisocial ones.

Models of Indirect Reciprocity   Trivers (1971) described a mechanism whereby long-continued interactions between partners might lead to the development of sufficient trust in reciprocation of acts of aid to make such acts routine. Axelrod and Hamilton (1981) analyzed the case of pairwise interactions of players of prisoner's dilemma in their important contribution to the theory of reciprocity. In their model the interaction has a given, usually large, probability of continuing for another turn. In this situation strategies such as tit for tat (cooperate on the first round of the game, and then do whatever your partners did on the previous round of the game) easily evolve. If two players of this strategy meet, they cooperate from the first. If tit-for-tat players play against an unconditional noncooperator, they receive the worst possible sucker's payoff on the first round of the game, but are only victimized once. If payoffs to cooperation are relatively high and games go on for many rounds, then selection can prevent unconditional defectors from invading a population of tit-for-tat strategists.

Alexander (1987) proposed that Axelrod and Hamilton's result could be extended to very large societies by what he calls *indirect reciprocity*. If one of us helps you, you may help some third person who in turn helps the other of us, who helps the original helper. Rather than being restricted to pairwise interactions, perhaps reciprocity can encourage cooperation among large, diffuse networks of reciprocators. We have studied mathematical models of the effects of group size on the evolution of strategies such as tit for tat. In one series of models we considered unstructured groups in which all individuals in the group simultaneously played repeated turns of prisoner's dilemma (Boyd and Richerson 1988). We generalized the idea of tit for tat to large groups by studying rules of the form "cooperate if k out of the other n individuals cooperated on the last iteration of the game." The tit-for-tat results do not generalize to large groups. As group size increases, the threshold frequency above which reciprocity can increase in a population dominated by unconditional defection rapidly becomes very large. This makes sense. In a situation where interacting groups are of size ten and your rule is to cooperate if five others do, it is highly improbable that the five others with the same rule, when rare, will be in any given group. Only when such a rule is already quite common can it have a positive payoff. Alexander's idea involves indirect reciprocity flowing along fairly stable networks— that is, what goes around eventually comes around. Adding a ring structure to groups to organize reciprocity in larger groups helps, but not much (Boyd and Richerson 1989).

If cooperation does occasionally get started in large groups due to indirect reciprocity, individuals, cabals of relatives, and small-group reciprocators should quickly arise to selfishly appropriate any benefits of cooperation arising in the larger group, thereby causing its collapse. The strength of ties between close relatives and intimate reciprocators should always trump weaker ties to more distantly affiliated others. The model of Nowak and Sigmund (1998) produces cooperation among strangers based on a reciprocity mechanism, but it depends on each individual costlessly and accurately knowing the "image score" (average propensity to cooperate) of everyone with whom they interact. Cooperators can interact selectively with other cooperators, but only because implausibly perfect information eliminates the possibility of deceptive signaling. This scenario is also limited to cooperation in pairs of individuals. Thus, so far the concept of large-scale indirect reciprocity lacks a credible mechanism to increase when rare and to defend itself against the rapid evolution of counterstrategies and false signals of benign intent. We believe that indirect reciprocity has intuitive appeal because in most societies most people do have cautiously benign intent toward strangers—at least toward strangers that do not belong to a hostile group—because group selection has resulted in cooperative institutions and cooperative predispositions. People who do good *are* frequently rewarded by third parties, as the group-selection model predicts, without the need for closed chains of reciprocation. Folk individualism gives indirect reciprocity an intuitive appeal not supported by formal modeling.

The modeling work to date suggests that the tribal instincts hypothesis is cogent, and the main competitors suffer serious problems. We can imagine a population evolving social institutions that encourage altruism toward fellow group members, define which are the relevant groups for cooperation, and mandate punishment of transgressions of socially sanctioned rules. We may very well be innately adapted to function in societies with such institutions. Having unsecured prosocial commitments can be favored under the circumstances envisioned in these models. Once some unsecured commitment exists, moralistic strategies can secure widespread commitment to groups so long as most people are not too reluctant to cooperate. The cultural case is quite different from its genetic analogs, where models of group-selected altruism and symbolic isolating mechanisms encourage us to think that such things are unlikely to evolve. One of the strongest reasons for doubting that selection among large groups of individuals is an effective force in nature is the narrow range of assumptions that allow genetic group selection for altruism to work in mathematical models. *The same logic does* not *apply to the cultural case.*

Proximate Mechanisms

Does evidence exist for prosocial impulses such as unsecured subjective commitments to groups and their projects?

Altruistic Propensities A wide range of evidence suggests that humans routinely engage in altruistic behavior toward unrelated and very distantly related people even in the absence of rewards and punishments (Mansbridge 1990). The experimental data on what motivates people to cooperate in social dilemma games, such as laboratory realizations of commons exploitation, is quite extensive (Kopelman, Weber, and Messick n.d.). We focus here on social psychologist Daniel Batson's (1991) wonderful series of experiments designed to distinguish between the "empathy-altruism" hypothesis and competing hypotheses asserting that altruistic behavior results from egoistic motives. According to the empathy-altruism hypothesis, once a potential helper's empathy for a sufferer is engaged, helping behavior is the result of a genuinely unselfish desire to relieve the victim's suffering. Competing egoistic hypotheses propose that seeming altruists give aid in the expectation of some form of personal reward. Egoistic hypotheses come in many flavors. Individuals may help others to gain rewards or avoid punishment. Rewards and punishments may be external or internal—that is, people may expect others to give rewards or administer punishments, or it may be a matter of conscience, self-administered rewards and punishments. In our terms here, Batson asks if emotionally motivated commitments to aid others exist. Expected external rewards or punishments may be material (soldiers' pensions, for example) or social (such as enhanced prestige). Batson sought to determine whether fundamentally nonegoistic motivation plays a significant role in decisions to help others.

The experiments encouraged empathy on the part of subjects by asking them to take the victim's point of view while nonempathetic controls were asked to view the situation objectively. Then conditions were manipulated to control for one or another egoistic motivation and to test whether subjects in the empathy condition were still willing to provide aid to the victim. For example, one egoistic motivation for aiding a victim might be to relieve one's own suffering at having to watch the victim suffer. To test this possibility, Elaine, acting the sham victim in one experiment, was to suffer a series of moderately painful shocks. The subjects were told at the beginning of the experiment that Elaine is unusually sensitive to shocks due to a traumatic childhood experience. The experimenter expresses concern about this, and offers the real subjects the chance to continue the experiment in place of Elaine. The shocks will be uncomfortable for them, but not nearly so painful as for Elaine. If helping is motivated by the desire to avoid viewing someone else suffering, Batson reasoned that allowing the subjects to escape (that is, watch only two trials of the experiment on Elaine instead of all ten) should reduce the tendency to help, whereas if subjects had a genuine desire to help Elaine, even those allowed escape should offer to help. In this experiment difficult escape had a dramatic effect on helping in the low-empathy condition, raising the proportion helping from about 0.2 to 0.6. The high-empathy condition showed no significant difference in helping; in the easy-escape condition the proportion offering to help was 0.9, and in the difficult escape, 0.8. While the egoistic motivation clearly had an effect, the helping in the empathy condition is consistent with the empathy-altruism hypothesis.

Batson even produced evidence that people's desires to aid others go beyond conscience and pride, the most commonly mentioned internal psychological punishments and rewards motivating prosocial commitments. In experiments in which the desire to help was aroused and then frustrated by someone else getting to do the helping, an internal reward system would elevate the mood of those who got to help, but not those who did not. Contrary to this hypothesis, subjects who saw help provided but didn't have to provide it themselves had the greatest mood increase, and those who were prevented from helping when no one else did had the lowest mood. People who actually got to help were intermediate. This finding is neatly consistent with our hypothesis that humans experience conflict between individualistic and prosocial motivations. We do not argue that normal humans have the extreme self-sacrificial propensities of honeybees that "think" little of sacrificing their lives to sting an enemy of their colony. Batson's experiments provide ample evidence that people also are motivated by individual interest.

This experiment also suggests that most people have subjective commitments to help those who have engaged their sympathy that go beyond even internal rewards and punishments. People are prepared to take actions that are objectively and subjectively costly to aid others. Those who rescue people from perilous perches and burning houses generally do so with sober determination and often fade away anonymously when the job is done. Publicly recognized heroes often remark that anyone would have done the same, implying that they take no special pride in their act. Few veterans of heavy military combat seem to view it as better than a grim duty to be endured, something with no *net* subjective or objective personal rewards.

Batson's findings do not decisively reject *evolutionary* individualist hypotheses. Subjectively altruistic motivations of individuals might merely have the effect of advertising their reliability and earnestness as reciprocity partners (Hirshleifer 1987; Frank 1988). As always, when signaling models are applied to altruism, we need to worry about advertising a willingness to help without reward in a world where this trait is liable to make you more false than true friends. The existence of psychological altruism is a serious problem for the pure individualist hypothesis, though it may not be fatal.

Kinship   No doubt propensities to cooperate with kin are deeply ingrained in human emotions. One excellent body of evidence comes from the seemingly tangential literature on incest avoidance. Westermarck (1894) suggested that avoidance of inbreeding is innate. If so, humans must have an innate kin-recognition system. The operation of this device is nicely illustrated by the rarity of marriage among Israeli kibbutz agemates (Sepher 1983) and the poor success of Taiwanese minor marriages (Wolf 1970). In these famous examples potential husbands and wives are raised in close companionship as children, much as siblings typically are, even though unrelated in fact. Coresident agemates apparently have an innate algorithm that invokes a mating-avoidance mechanism. The kin-recognition system fails in the rather unusual circumstances discovered by Sepher and Wolf but in most families will function properly as an incest-avoidance mechanism.

Daly and Wilson (1988) explore a useful set of data on patterns of homicide. Family members living in close proximity have the maximum opportunity to kill one another, and family homicides are a large fraction of the total. Nevertheless, consanguineous relatives show a striking tendency to refrain from killing each other, compared to affinal family members. For example, child abuses and child murders are disproportionately committed by stepparents. The homicide data, like that from incest avoidance, strongly suggest that humans have deep-seated psychological mechanisms for kin recognition and for motivating kin-appropriate behavior, as predicted by Hamilton's theory of inclusive fitness. Sahlins (1976) argued that Polynesian adoption practices show that human kin behavior is overwhelmingly modified by cultural practices. However, Silk's (1980) detailed analysis of the ethnographic data shows that Polynesians do generally adopt biological kin whose parents are unable to provide proper care for them. Kin altruism no doubt has deep roots in the vertebrate order, and human examples of nepotistic behavior can be multiplied at will.

These data suggest that people are normally quite aware of who their biological kin are. If so, van den Berghe's (1981) hypothesized extension of altruism to culturally similar individuals due to erroneous assignment of kinship is implausible. The human subjective commitment to aid kin apparently operates accurately enough to generate real conflicts between loyalties to kin and loyalties to larger groups. Teamsters know that their International Brotherhood is composed of strictly fictive kin, though they may show some *tribal* loyalty to the organization. Thus we suppose that the frequent usage of kin terms in the context of nonkin groups (fraternity, sorority, and so on) is metaphorical, and that few are fooled (either consciously or unconsciously) about who are kin and who are fellow members of a tribal or quasi-tribal group. More refined experiments are, we acknowledge, desirable to be sure that metaphorical usages tap little real force from predispositions to kin compared to tribal commitments.

Ethnic Markers   Larger human groups that cooperate are typically explicitly defined and marked by symbolic boundaries. Some of these markers are relatively simple badges, such as styles of body ornamentation or dialects. Others are complex ritual systems accompanied by elaborate belief systems. Such systems usually contain ethical injunctions. Ritual and belief seem commonly to act as vehicles for inducing subjective commitment to group goals (Rappaport 1979; Richerson and Boyd 1989; Hinde 1999). Even in simple hunting and gathering societies, the groups so marked are rather large, as previously noted. This section reviews evidence that symbolic cultural markers are potent factors dividing in-groups from out-groups, sharpening the boundaries between social units subject to cultural group selection and regulating subjective commitment and hence altruism.

The minimal-group experimental system developed by Tajfel (1981) provides insight into the cognitive mechanisms involved in the use of symbols to demarcate groups and the actions people take based on group membership. Social psychologists commonly find in the laboratory, as in life, that members of groups favor one another and discriminate against out-groups. Social psychologists in Tajfel's tradition were interested in separating the effects of group membership per se from the personal attachments that form in groups. Turner (1984) contrasts two sorts of hypotheses to explain group-oriented behavior. Functional social groups might be composed entirely of networks of individuals who are linked by personal ties, shared fate, or other individual-centered ties, much as the indirect reciprocity hypothesis imagines. Groups, in this hypothesis, are "some collection of individuals characterized by mutual interpersonal attraction reflecting some degree of interdependence and mutual need-satisfaction." The contrasting hypothesis is that identity symbols alone are sufficient to induce humans to accept membership in a group, creating positive commitments toward anonymous in-group members, and neutral or negative ones toward out-groups.

In his prototypical experiments, Tajfel (1981) told subjects that they were participating in a test of aesthetic judgment. They were shown pictures of paintings by Klee and Kandinsky and asked to indicate which they preferred. Subjects then were divided into two groups, supposedly on the basis of their aesthetic preferences, but in fact at random. The subjects' task then was to divide a sum of money among members of their own group or the other group. Subjects discriminated in favor of the sham in-group members. Tajfel interpreted these experiments as tapping, in our terms here, unsecured subjective commitments to discriminate in favor of in-group members and against out-groups.

Turner (1984) was interested in whether an extreme case of categorization would generate group-oriented cooperative behaviors. Children were shown their picture paired with others and asked to rate the others as liked or disliked. When they were explicitly grouped into liked or disliked subjects, those led to believe that they were now members of a pariah group of disliked others discriminated almost as much as liked group members in favor of their fellow pariahs. In the ungrouped condition disliked children discriminated in favor of liked others. Turner (1984) argues that such experiments show that even shared membership in a group of unattractive others can induce a commitment to the group (recall films such as *The Seven Samurai* and *The Dirty Dozen*, where the plot turns on the bonding among a group of initially hostile outcasts). Categorization per se does have a strong effect, independent of interpersonal bonds.

Other social psychologists have objected that Tajfel and Turner overemphasized the raw categorization effect in interpreting their experiments. Rabbie (1991) argues that no experimental system implying that people belong to a group can control away people's expectation that the group membership imposed by experimenters implies instrumental interdependence. From an evolutionary point of view especially, Rabbie's point is well taken; people presumably only react to symbolic badges of group membership because in the evolutionary past they generally signal politically important social units. In the politically complex world outside the lab, where many groupings are abstractly possible, people no doubt attempt to make sensible decisions about which to take seriously in any given circumstance. Nevertheless, humans are strikingly prone to give rather abstract, large, impersonal, marked groups (Protestant, Irish, Serb, Jew, German, and so on) great emotional salience that in turn motivates desperate deeds of great risk to participants (Stern 1995). The experimental evidence and such observations are consistent with the view that humans can develop strong subjective commitments to the symbolically marked groups of which they are members, and that the symbols motivate behavior in the absence of any personal knowledge of the individuals with whom one is interacting. The evidence and observations are not consistent with an exclusively individualistic hypothesis of human social commitments. We imagine that common group membership will generate the empathy Batson observes to tap unsecured commitments. This hypothesis ought to be tested.

Prosocial Punishment (or Reward)   That humans are capable of using rules about appropriate behavior in partners as a basis for social decisions and actions is beyond doubt. Cosmides (1989) conducted a series of experiments to test the hypothesis that at least one of the kinds of problems that people evolved to solve is that which involves social contracts. She supposed that human cognition includes the rule, "if you take the benefit, then you must pay the cost." Of many simple rules that humans might use in social or more general decision making, this one is uniquely suited to detecting defection in games such as repeated prisoner's dilemma. Cosmides then tested subjects' abilities to solve a logical problem when couched as a social contract, compared to their abilities to solve it couched as some simple nonsocial problem. For example, the rule "if a man eats cassava, he has a tattoo on his face" can be framed as a social rule ("only men who have undergone the painful ritual of tattooing can eat cassava") or as a mere contingent empirical fact ("tribes that eat cassava also happen to tattoo"). Framed as a cheater detection problem, success rates were in excess of 70 percent, while less than 25 percent solved the problem in its empirical guise. Cosmides interprets these results to mean that people have an innate decision-making module devoted to detecting cheaters on social contracts. Whatever one might think of the inference that this data indicates the existence of an innate module, humans certainly appear to be very efficient decision makers when it comes to detecting defectors on social contracts.

In addition to recognizing cheaters in social games, people seem psychologically prepared to exact retribution even when costs to themselves are likely to be high. Daly and Wilson (1988) report high rates of spousal homicide in some modern communities. Suspicion of infidelity and sexual rivalry are very common motives for murder. Cohen's elegant studies of the southern culture of honor reported in this volume illustrate how cultural institutions can manipulate the raw biology of emotions to create culture-specific subjective commitments. Southerners are not only more committed to use violence to settle personal disputes but also more committed to act violently on behalf of social goals. Southerners are more prone to join the military and more prone to have hawkish views on foreign policy issues than Northerners (Nisbett and Cohen 1996, 2, 63–65).

The capacity of people to be coerced is strikingly demonstrated in experimental settings such as those constructed by Milgram (1974) and Nuttin and Beckers (1975). Experimenters, carrying the institutional charisma of scientists, obtain compliance to quite striking requests. In one of Nuttin and Beckers's experiments Belgian college students were asked by the experimenters to give arguments *in favor* of a hated exam system to which they were subjected. Virtually all students supported a strenuous protest movement *against* the system. In the most extreme experimental condition used, all eleven students assigned to experimental treatment requesting students to give a televised speech favoring the exam system complied with Beckers's request for cooperation. Twenty-two fellow students were asked how many students would comply with such a request; the majority thought less than 5 percent, and the most cynical guessed 30 percent!

If the tribal instincts hypothesis is correct, we expect that people will spontaneously act as third-party rewarder-punishers under much the same conditions that they will act as ordinary altruists. The literature, to our knowledge, contains few studies indicating the extent to which people are willing to punish altruistically. Are some people subjectively committed—at a greater cost to themselves than their expected private benefit—to punish those who transgress social rules? An experiment reported by Fehr and Tyran (1996) illustrates how moralistic punishment might act to permit cooperation in human societies. They used a voluntary-contribution public goods game often used by experimental economists. On each round of the game the players were each given a sum of money that they could keep or contribute to a common pool. The experimenters doubled the size of the common pool and redistributed it equally to all players, regardless of contribution. Players collectively could earn most by contributing all their resources to the common pool, but contributing players were vulnerable to being exploited by selfish individuals who kept their original endowment, contributed little or nothing to the common pool, but reaped their share of rewards from the suckers who did invest in the common pool. The results of the basic version of this experiment were that initial contributions to the common pool are substantial—50 to 60 percent of their income—but that some individuals contributed nothing. The initial level of trust that subjects brought to the game eroded, and contributions to the common pool declined toward zero in subsequent rounds. In some experiments subjects had the opportunity to anonymously assign punishment points to individuals who made small contributions to the common pool, at considerable cost to themselves. Some subjects did punish low contributors to the common pool, and contributions subsequently rose from initial levels to about 90 percent of each period's income.

Note that second-order defection was possible in this experiment; nonpunishers could free ride on the costly punishment of others. This kind of punishing is a form of altruism because it increases the payoff to the group but not the individual—sufficiently to induce large contributions from those who would otherwise free ride. Despite the lack of security for the commitment to punish in this experiment, sufficient people spontaneously punished to ensure that eventually the group took almost all of the money the experimenters were willing to pay.

More generally, experimental evidence on the wellsprings of successful collective action shows that many individuals bring a considerable number of strategies resting on subjective commitment into the laboratory that are quite successful in facilitating prosocial behavior and controlling temptations to defect (Ostrom 1998; Kopelman, Weber, and Messick n.d.). For example, communication—especially in the form of subjectively earnest but objectively "cheap talk" promises to cooperate in commons games—is as effective as punishment in leading to successful commons management. Ample field observations attest to successful community-level management of commons using seemingly the same commitments experimenters find successful in the lab (Baland and Platteau 1996, part 2).

Microevolution

The bread and butter of evolutionary biologists is the estimation of the strength of evolutionary forces in wild and laboratory populations. Endler (1986) reviewed the several hundred studies of natural selection in the wild and conducted a meta-analysis of the hundred or so studies he considered sophisticated enough to be included in his sample. Selection is often surprisingly strong. Although analogous studies of cultural evolution are still quite rare, several research programs in historical linguistics, sociolinguistics, organizational ecology, art history, the diffusion of innovations, and demography have converged independently on Darwinian methods and concepts (Weingart et al. 1997, 292–97). Some of these convergent programs will be further discussed. The practicality of Darwinian investigations of cultural evolution is clearly demonstrated by these convergent studies, even if the range of questions so far tackled is limited. We believe that existing microevolutionary evidence is easier on the tribal instincts hypothesis than its rivals.

The Strength of Cultural Group Selection   Soltis, Boyd, and Richerson (1995) assembled data from reports of group extinctions by early ethnographers in the New Guinea Highlands. Anthropologists first visited the Highlands just after World War II during the first generation of contact with Europeans. Highland New Guinea societies comprise the only large sample of simple societies studied by anthropologists before major changes occurred due to contact with Europeans. Although horticulturalists rather than hunter-gatherers, Highlanders lived in simple tribal societies much as many hunter-gatherers did. (Unfortunately, our sample of hunter-gatherers is far too poor and too influenced by contact with colonial powers to support a quantitative analysis of group extinction rates. Such societies, contrary to some romanticized accounts, are not usually pacifist: see Keeley 1996.) Patterns of intergroup competition were still quite fresh in informants' minds. Many studies report appreciable intergroup conflict, and about half mention cases of the social extinction of local groups. Five studies contained enough information to estimate the rates of extinction of such groups. The rate of extinction varies greatly from a few percent to a few tens of percent per generation; 10 to 15 percent perhaps represents the central tendency. The typical pattern is for groups to be weakened over a period of time by conflict with neighbors, and finally to suffer a sharp defeat. When enough members become convinced of the group's vulnerability to further attack, members flee to other groups, where relatives and friends will give them shelter. On the other side of the coin, successful groups grow and eventually fission. Rates of death in Highland war were not negligible, but neither was the physical extirpation of groups common. The social extinction of groups was rather common, however. In addition to the role we hypothesize for conformist transmission, the fissioning mode of new group formation also tends to preserve variation at the group level compared to a system where migrants from many communities combine to colonize open lands. At the rates of group extinction that characterized Highland New Guinea, the spread of some group selection favored innovation to most of the local groups in a region would take about forty generations, or one thousand years.

Genes and Culture Do Coevolve   The best-documented example of an organic response to cultural selection pressures is the evolution of adult lactose (milk sugar) absorption in dairying populations (Durham 1991, ch. 5). In human populations that lack a tradition of dairying, such as those in Eastern Asia, very few adults retain the ability to digest lactose beyond infancy. The pattern of loss of lactase activity in the guts of adults is the mammalian norm. In those populations with a tradition of dairying, such as those in Western Europe and parts of India and Africa, most adults retain lactase activity. The ability to digest lactase as an adult is transmitted as an autosomal dominant locus. As Durham notes, many other innate characters are candidates for having evolved under coevolutionary pressures from cultural practices. Human societies apparently have had symbolically marked cultural groups for more than forty thousand years (Bettinger 1991), or about ten times as long as dairying populations have existed. The roots of cultural group selection could go back much further. Ample time exists for humans to have evolved prosocial subjective commitments by coevolution with cooperative cultural institutions.

Group Ideologies Evolve in the Laboratory   Insko and colleagues (1983) studied the evolution of intergroup relations in laboratory microsocieties. They established groups of four people, removing and adding one person per "generation" to mimic death and birth. In one series of experiments subjects were given a sham IQ test, and subjects with a purportedly higher IQ (they were actually given an easier test) were placed in one group while those given the harder test were placed in other groups. The "smart" groups were also allowed to dominate the model economic system that earned subjects money from the experimenters. The objective of this treatment was to mimic the conquest of one group by another. The sham IQ treatment was meant to give subjects in the dominant group a plausible basis for feeling superior to subordinate groups. Over the course of the experiment members of the dominant group did evolve increasingly reassuring rationalizations for their quite unfair treatment of subordinate groups, while subordinate groups evolved counterstrategies of strike, sabotage, and slowdown. The emotions generated by these experiments were quite noticeable in the laboratory and the authors report that they led to one volatile confrontation between participants in a chance encounter outside the laboratory.

The Evolution of Dialect   Sociolinguists have studied the generation-to-generation evolution of dialect (Labov 1972). One of Labov's own studies was of the changes in diphthong pronunciation on Martha's Vineyard. On this dimension Martha's Vineyard speech has diverged detectably from New England speech over the last three generations. Labov argues that the advent of the tourist industry on the island led to a sense of social distinction between relatively wealthy tourists and working-class natives. Natives came to model their speech on the patterns of local fishermen, the most independent and traditional islanders. The fishermen thus came to lead the gradual divergence of Martha's Vineyard dialect away from regional norms. More generally, dialect evolution seems to be set in motion whenever social cleavages form, resulting in the linguistic marking of many social boundaries. Emotional reactions to dialect variation are striking and quite likely to tap subjective commitments. A black youth, when played a recording of Black English Vernacular, will stigmatize the speaker as low class, but simultaneously will pick the speaker as a likely source of support in a fight, compared to a recorded speaker of standard English (Labov 1972, ch. 6).

The Diffusion of Innovations   Rogers (1983, 274–77, 321–31) discussed the flow of information about potentially useful innovations in terms of homophily. He found strong empirical support for the proposition that most information flows between people who are socially rather similar. This effect creates a barrier that retards the rate of spread of innovations from one group to a socially different one, much as in the models of ethnic markers described earlier. Very often "change agents" (for example, extension workers, NGO [nongovernmental organization] workers, teachers, health practitioners) are socially remote from their clients and their proffered innovations are ignored.

Henrich (1999) analyzed the time course of many cases of diffusions of innovations to test the cultural evolutionary and rational-choice explanations for this phenomenon. If innovations spread mainly by independent rational choices, the curve of increase should be R shaped, with the maximum rate of increase at the beginning of the process when the largest number of rational choosers has yet to adopt the innovation. If innovations spread by cultural transmission, however, with choice playing a more or less marginal role, then the curve of increase should be S shaped, with a maximum rate of spread when the innovation is used by about half the population. The contagion effect of cultural transmission is maximal when adopters and non-adopters are present in equal numbers. Most cases examined exhibited S shapes.

Rational choice theorists in fact often seem to be cryptic cultural evolutionists. Finke and Stark (1992), for example, outline the history of religion in the United States from 1776 to 1990. The main trends are a steady *increase* in church affiliation, rising from 17 percent of the population in 1776 to 62 percent in 1980, and a tendency for strict churches to prosper while liberal ones wither. The current success of many Fundamentalist churches relative to liberal Protestant ones is thus part of a long history. Finke and Stark believe two factors explain this change. First, the "free market" for religion in the United States as opposed to established churches in the European homeland gives rise to innovative religious entrepreneurs who create churches that are attractive to their parishioners. Second, strong beliefs—often objectively dubious and widely stigmatized beliefs—weed out the lightly committed, who are likely to take more than they give to the religious community. Thus, stricter churches are better providers of the collective benefits of strong commitments to the community. The explanation may well be true, but the timescales of these changes are measured in generations. For example, it took eighty years for the rather successful Church of the Nazarene to grow from 6,600 to 530,000 members. Demographic data suggest that differential birth-rates are as important as joining and leaving decisions in explaining changes in religion in the United States (Roof and McKinney 1987, ch. 5). This pattern is consistent with our picture of individuals inheriting patterns of behavior by cultural transmission, often with some bias, and perhaps modifying them slightly, all the while subject to appreciable effects of natural selection. The pattern is not consistent with standard rational choice theory that has no place for cultural continuity and hence no place for processes with timescales of generations or centuries. More likely, as is true of the Southern culture of honor, the doctrines of strict churches have evolved to create weakly secured and unsecured commitments to the community of faithful.

The evolutionary mechanisms that would favor the proximal mechanism of emotional commitment to group goals apparently exist. On the other hand, few known intertribal interactions are sufficiently genocidal to support genetic group selection. Intermarriage, not to mention rape, wife capture, and child abductions, seem to ensure that all ethnic boundaries are genetically leaky, while the rapid evolution of dialect and tendency of cultural transmission to be restricted by cultural boundaries is consistent with the cultural evolution of cooperation. Microevolutionary studies seem to conflict with the idea that social change occurs entirely by rational choice, unless rational choice is understood to be a weak process relative to cultural transmission in the construction of individual behavioral repertoires.

Macroevolution

Macroevolution covers the sweep of evolutionary history from the few-generation timescales that begin to elude microevolutionary analysis to considerations of organic change on the geological timescale. Typically we know little of the details of macroevolution because the fossil and historical records are poor compared to observations of current behavior. Macroevolutionary data are nonetheless interesting because over the long run, big changes occur, generating much larger-scale natural "experiments" than we can ever hope to conduct on living populations. Four macroevolutionary phenomena provide reasonably sharp tests of the social instincts hypothesis and its competitors.

Rates of Evolution Due to Cultural Group Selection   Cultural group selection is a relatively slow process if the data of Soltis, Boyd, and

Richerson (1995) are indicative; but so then are the actual rates of increase in the scale of commitments to group goals we observe in the historical and archaeological records. New Guinea societies no doubt were actively evolving systems (Wiessner and Tumu 1998), but the net increase in their social complexity during the eleven thousand years since the Pleistocene is modest. In cultural traditions that did lead eventually to the large-scale social systems of our own experience, involving ultimately widespread subjective commitment to groups on the scale of nations, change within any one millennium was modest. If cultural evolution due to group selection appeared to be appreciably more rapid than Soltis, Boyd, and Richerson's (1995) estimate, we would have trouble accounting for such facts as the five-thousand-year lag between the beginnings of agriculture and the first primitive city-states, and another five millennia to get from simple states to modern complex societies.

The Uniqueness of Tribes   One method of using macroevolutionary patterns to test hypotheses is comparative natural history. One of the most striking tests of Hamilton's (1964) theory of inclusive fitness is its high rate of concordance with patterns of ultrasociality in animals across a wide range of taxa. As Wilson noted in his 1975 treatise, inclusive fitness theory explains three of the four pinnacles of social evolution quite well: colonial invertebrates, eusocial insects, and non-human mammalian societies. Since he wrote, investigations have uncovered the kin-selected, social-insectlike eusociality of naked mole rat societies. In all species except humans complex societies are built on a foundation of commitment to the welfare of close kin. Human societies clearly have not taken this otherwise universal path to complex sociality (Campbell 1983). We live in small family units that differ little from those of our primate ancestors. Hunter-gatherer bands are not drastically larger or different in degree of relatedness among members than the troops of the more social apes and monkeys (Dunbar 1995). Human hunter-gatherers do differ in typically having cooperation at the tribal scale among residential bands of the same ethnolinguistic group. We know of no close analog of tribes in other species. The unique features of a species ought to derive from living in a unique niche or in having some historically derived unique feature of their biology. Humans adapt to an unusually diverse array of environments using cultural adaptations. Our unique dependence on culture makes it a plausible candidate to explain the unique form of our social commitments.

This argument is weak because any other unique feature of our biology, such as language or our purportedly extraordinary intelligence, is also a candidate to explain our social commitments. The unique structure of our social systems does, however, cast into question explanations that should apply widely to many other species. For example, many explanations for human sociality involve some sort of "green beard" effect (for example, Frank 1988; Nowak and Sigmund 1998). Such hypotheses, as noted earlier, are suspect for not accounting for the possibility of deceptive signals of cooperative intent. If a cheap, honest, cooperative signaling system evolves in a straightforward way, then we should expect many species to use it, and cooperation on the human pattern should be relatively common. The comparative natural history test thus rules out excessively general explanations of human commitments to tribes and similar groups.

Work-Arounds and the Evolution of Complex Societies   Contemporary human societies differ drastically from those under which our social instincts presumably evolved. Until a few thousand years ago humans lived in relatively small societies with a modest division of labor. Typical tribes consisted of a few hundred to a few thousand individuals. Tribal leadership was informal and leaders had only personal charisma to secure commitments of others. An egalitarian ethos was typically well developed. Division of labor by age and sex was important, but family, band, and village units were largely self-sufficient except in subsistence or political emergencies. After the domestication of plants and animals, beginning about eleven thousand five hundred years ago, human densities rose substantially and the potential for an expanded division of labor grew. Beginning about five thousand years ago, complex societies began to emerge. Hierarchical states arose to administer the increasingly minute division of labor. Families became dependent on the products of strangers for routine subsistence. Leaders came to have great and sometimes quite arbitrary authority to coerce common citizens. Stratification emerged, with elites having highly disproportionate access to power and wealth.

If our tribal social instincts hypothesis is correct, complex societies would have evolved under the constraints and possibilities offered by our evolved social psychology. The rapid social changes of the last few thousand years should throw our social instincts into high relief. Cultural evolution should have produced institutions that conspicuously work around the constraints imposed by a psychology adapted to relatively small-scale egalitarian societies. Institutions should evolve to take advantage of the progroup commitments the tribal instincts make possible, and finesse the conflict between egalitarian impulses and the stratification and command and control ubiquitous in complex societies. One of the most striking features of complex societies, including modern societies, is the persistence of tribal-scale social institutions and the elaboration of institutions such as nationalism that utilize mass media to simulate tribes on a larger scale. Business organizations, schools, religions, and government bureaucracies generally contain features that tap or respond to our propensity to commit to tribes or reasonable facsimiles. The persistence of ethnic sentiments in a large-scale modern world that would seem to make them obsolete is an example (Glazer and Moynihan 1975).

We develop this argument in detail elsewhere using the differential performance of armies in World War II as a specific test (Richerson and Boyd 1999). Suffice it to say here that analysts of the performance of World War II armies have discovered striking differences in the fighting power of individual soldiers from different units and appreciable average differences from nation to nation, after controlling for such factors as the quality and amount of equipment available to them. The explanations scholars offer for these differences boil down to more and less effective means of developing unsecured and weakly secured commitments to close comrades and to larger units such as regiments and divisions. Some analysts believe that differences in the level of patriotic commitments to national goals also played a role.

Patterns of Adaptation and Maladaptation

The adaptive consequences of human cooperation, resting in large part on our subjective commitment to our tribes and quasi- or pseudo-tribal groups, are not far to seek. In the small-scale hunter-gatherer societies of our past, cooperation likely furnished aid in emergencies and local social peace (Cashdan 1990; Wiessner 1996). The development of more sophisticated subsistence and social institutions in the last ten thousand years has rapidly made our species the earth's dominant species. In a world where the limitations of kin selection mean that most animal species are (from the viewpoint of mean fitness optimization) maladaptively uncooperative, a cooperative species has many advantages. Since culture also furnishes the means to rapidly evolve new social and subsistence systems, human populations were relatively dense and extremely widespread by the late Pleistocene. Partitioning our success into subsistence and social components is probably impossible, since everywhere subsistence production is a highly social activity (Steward 1955; see also Byrne 1997).

One of the most interesting things that a commitment to group goals makes possible is collectively organized cultural evolution in pursuit of group goals and to avoid the impact of natural selection by the activities of proactive institutions (Turner 1995, 134–37). The anthropologist Christopher Boehm (1996) argues that simple societies routinely use more or less formal institutions of discussion and consensus seeking to reach the same ends. In modern complex societies specialized institutions engage in various parts of the innovation process. Universities and other research institutions create and test new ideas. Marketing systems spread the word. Governments pass laws to implement new ideas (or to forbid their use) based on some assessment of the needs of society as a whole. Think of the effort that the biomedical innovation system mounted to address the AIDS epidemic. Trust in these collective institutions is built via patriotic sentiments and the use of rules that we feel are fair, such as secret balloting to choose leaders. As our feelings of trust reach their limits or as they begin to falter because experience teaches cynicism, so too does the capacity of collective institutions to function (Fukuyama 1995). Conflicts between individual, kin, and friendship-based commitments and group-oriented goals are ever-present in human societies, and the functionality of tribal and larger-scale institutions is always an issue (Edgerton 1992), but the fact that human societies often successfully can use collective action to solve problems is a most striking adaptation consistent with the existence of tribal instincts and the subjective commitments to groups they make possible.

The frequently maladaptive consequences of commitments to tribal and larger-scale institutions are also a clear indication of their importance. Departures from group functionality in human social systems are not only due to individual self-interest. A great many disasters result from poor management of intergroup conflict, often because passionate commitments to the group drive reason from political discourse. The path of Japan to devastation by the United States in World War II is a classic example (Toland 1970). Whether at the scale of nation-states or local street gangs, tribal and tribal-analog loyalties provide social cleavages that easily escalate into lethal violence. Human societies are more or less successful at suppressing intrasocietal violence (Knauft 1987), but the intersocietal rule of law remains weak. The most murderous forms of intrasocietal violence in modern societies involve civil conflicts between tribal or tribe-mimicking factions. Ethnic conflicts are frequent. Religious communities often engage in conflicts with each other. Abusive rule by upper classes, military elites, and ideological parties is common. Terrorists conduct their violence on behalf of symbolically and ideologically marked groups of diverse sorts. The struggles between interest groups in open political systems involve an even more diverse set of groups.

Humans take great pride in fighting on behalf of their groups and are accorded great prestige for doing so. In sports, athletes and fans take up pretend tribal identities, fight mock good fights and nurse sham grudges. In cases such as European football hooliganism, the acting-out of pseudo-tribal commitments is quite extreme (Buford

1991). Commonly the admiration of the fan for the superlative performer and other emotions associated with sports are heartfelt. The rewards that stars gain as a consequence in such currencies as money and sexual access are substantial. In the hard-nosed business of professional athletics fortunes are made by exploiting for profit and pay our pleasure in having tribal or tribelike commitments.

Few men and fewer women will commit murder in pursuit of personal goals, to advance their families' interests, or to help a friend, except in defense against murder by another. Those who do kill for such low motives we stigmatize as criminal. Yet most men—women have not been so well tested—will kill their group's enemies with relatively little reluctance, without being personally provoked, and at grave risk to their own safety. The military analyst van Creveld (1991) argues that soldiers will remain committed to fighting as long as they *believe* their cause just. Beliefs, however, are products of culture and cultural evolution can easily lead to conflicts that seem not to be in the objective interests of the fighters. According to Fritz (1995) and Bartov (1991), by skillfully exploiting a German tradition of anti-Semitism, Hitler and the Nazis were able to sustain a weakly secured faith among German soldiers that war on the horrific Eastern Front was a legitimate crusade to save Europe from a Jewish-Bolshevik conspiracy. Commitment to such an objectively outlandish, morally repellant, and brutally self-destructive goal seems from the diaries and letters soldiers wrote to have played a significant role in sustaining the morale and exemplary performance of German soldiers. Commitment to tribes and larger-scale institutions not infrequently serves badly chosen if not utterly wicked ends.

The existence of a tribal level of organization is the most striking derived feature of human social organization. It has no close analog in other animals. It is fundamental to our adaptations to the environments in which we have lived. We make our livings in a staggering diversity of ways, but a common thread running through the gamut is the use of symbolically marked groups as foci of cooperation, coordination, and the division of labor. The tribal instincts hypothesis proposes that innate human predispositions to commit to their in-groups arose by coevolution with group-selected cultural institutions. We are adapted to living in tribes, and the social institutions of tribes elicit strong—sometimes fanatical—commitment. The instincts themselves we think of as being on the model of the principles of the Chomskyan "principles and parameters" model of language. The instincts constrain the kinds of societies humans can evolve, but alone they are not a complete explanation of our social organization. The nature of the tribes to which we commit, the kinds of commitments we make, and the strength of those commitments all depend on the cultural traditions that define the group and its institutions. Through the evolution of work-arounds in the last few thousand years, institutions have evolved that recruit the tribal subjective commitment to far larger and very different social systems than the tribe as the concept is understood by anthropologists.

We submit that the totality of the evidence reviewed here is consistent with the social instincts hypothesis and that its competitors all have serious trouble with at least some of the data reviewed. Ancillary hypotheses, of course, may shore up some of the weaker proposals, evidence embarrassing to the tribal instincts idea may be forthcoming from its critics, and competitive hypotheses may be framed in the future. We find it very hard to doubt the existence of unsecured subjective commitments to tribes and their analogs. At minimum, their *apparent* reality is surely one of the prime challenges for explanations of human behavior.

References

Alexander, Richard D. 1974. "The Evolution of Social Behavior." *Annual Review of Ecology and Systematics* 5: 325–83.

———. 1987. *The Biology of Moral Systems*. New York: Aldine de Gruyter.

Axelrod, Robert, and William D. Hamilton. 1981. "The Evolution of Cooperation." *Science* 211(4489): 1390–96.

Baland, Jean-Marie, and Jean-Philippe Platteau. 1996. *Halting the Degradation of Natural Resources: Is There a Role for Rural Communities?* Oxford: Clarendon Press.

Bartov, Omer. 1991. *Hitler's Army: Soldiers, Nazis, and War in the Third Reich.* Oxford: Oxford University Press.

Batson, C. Daniel. 1991. *The Altruism Question: Toward a Social Psychological Answer.* Hillsdale, N.J.: Lawrence Erlbaum.

Bettinger, Robert L. 1991. *Hunter-Gatherers: Archaeological and Evolutionary Theory.* New York: Plenum Press.

Bettinger, Robert L., Robert Boyd, and Peter J. Richerson. 1996. "Style, Function, and the Cultural Evolutionary Process." In *Darwinian Archaeologies*, edited by Herbert D. G. Maschner. New York: Plenum Press.

Boehm, Christopher. 1996 "Emergency Decisions, Cultural-Selection Mechanics, and Group Selection." *Current Anthropology* 37(5): 763–93.

Boyd, Robert, and Peter J. Richerson. 1985. *Culture and the Evolutionary Process.* Chicago: University of Chicago Press.

———. 1987. "The Evolution of Ethnic Markers." *Cultural Anthropology* 2(1): 65–79.

———. 1988. "The Evolution of Reciprocity in Sizable Groups." *Journal of Theoretical Biology* 132(3): 337–56.

———. 1989. "The Evolution of Indirect Reciprocity." *Social Networks* 11(3): 213–36.

————. 1992. "Punishment Allows the Evolution of Cooperation (or Anything Else) in Sizable Groups." *Ethology and Sociobiology* 13(3): 171–95.

————. 1993. "Rationality, Imitation, and Tradition." In *Nonlinear Dynamics and Evolutionary Economics*, edited by Richard H. Day and Ping Chen. New York: Oxford University Press.

Buford, Bill. 1991. *Among the Thugs*. London: Secker & Warburg.

Byrne, Richard W. 1997. "The Technical Intelligence Hypothesis: An Additional Evolutionary Stimulus to Intelligence?" In *Machiavellian Intelligence II: Extensions and Evaluations*, edited by Andrew Whiten and Richard W. Byrne. Cambridge: Cambridge University Press.

Campbell, Donald T. 1983. "The Two Distinct Routes Beyond Kin Selection to Ultrasociality: Implications for the Humanities and Social Sciences." In *The Nature of Prosocial Development: Theories and Strategies*, edited by Diane L. Bridgeman. New York: Academic Press.

Cashdan, Elizabeth. 1990. *Risk and Uncertainty in Tribal and Peasant Economies*. Boulder, Colo.: Westview Press.

Coleman, James S. 1991. *Foundations of Social Theory*. Cambridge, Mass.: Harvard University Press.

Cosmides, Leda. 1989. "The Logic of Social Exchange: Has Natural Selection Shaped How Humans Reason? Studies with the Wason Selection Task." *Cognition* 31(3): 187–276.

Daly, Martin, and Margo Wilson. 1988. *Homicide*. New York: Aldine de Gruyter.

Darwin, Charles. 1874. *The Descent of Man*. 2d ed. Reprint. New York: American Home Library, 1902.

Dunbar, Robin I. M. 1995. "Neocortex Size and Group Size in Primates: A Test of the Hypothesis." *Journal of Human Evolution* 28(3): 287–96.

Durham, William H. 1991. *Coevolution: Genes, Culture, and Human Diversity*. Stanford, Calif.: Stanford University Press.

Edgerton, Robert B. 1992. *Sick Societies: Challenging the Myth of Primitive Harmony*. New York: Maxwell Macmillan.

Eibl-Eibesfeldt, Irenäus. 1982. "Warfare, Man's Indoctrinability, and Group Selection." *Zeitschrift für Tierpsychologie* 67(3): 177–98.

Endler, John. 1986. *Natural Selection in the Wild*. Princeton, N.J.: Princeton University Press.

Fehr, Ernst, and Jean-Robert Tyran. 1996. "Institutions and Reciprocal Fairness." *Nordic Journal of Political Economy* 23(2): 133–44.

Finke, Roger, and Rodney Stark. 1992. *The Churching of America, 1776–1990*. New Brunswick, N.J.: Rutgers University Press.

Frank, Robert H. 1988. *Passions Within Reason: The Strategic Role of the Emotions*. New York: Norton.

Freud, Sigmund. 1930. *Civilization and Its Discontents*. New York: Norton.

Fritz, Stephen G. 1995. *Frontsoldaten: The German Soldier in World War II*. Lexington: University of Kentucky Press.

Fukuyama, Francis. 1995. *Trust: Social Virtues and the Creation of Prosperity*. New York: Free Press.

Glazer, Nathan, and Daniel P. Moynihan. 1975. *Ethnicity: Theory and Experience*. Cambridge, Mass.: Harvard University Press.

Hamilton, William D. 1964. "Genetical Evolution of Social Behavior I, II." *Journal of Theoretical Biology* 7(1): 1–52.

———. 1975. "Innate Social Aptitudes of Man: An Approach from Evolutionary Genetics." In *Biosocial Anthropology*, edited by Robin Fox. London: Malaby.

Henrich, Joseph P. 1999. "Cultural Evolutionary Approaches to Adaptation, Rationality, Evolutionary Psychology and Economic Behavior." Ph.D. diss., University of California, Los Angeles.

Henrich, Joe, and Robert Boyd. 1998. "The Evolution of Conformist Transmission and the Emergence of Between-Group Differences." *Evolution and Human Behavior* 19(4): 215–41.

Hinde, Robert A. 1999. *Why Gods Persist: A Scientific Approach to Religion*. London: Routledge.

Hirshleifer, Jack. 1987. "On Emotions as Guarantors of Threats and Promises." In *The Latest on the Best: Essays on Evolution and Optimality*, edited by J. Dupre (307–26). Cambridge, Mass.: MIT Press.

Insko, Chester A., Robert Gilmore, Sarah Drenan, Angela Lipsitz, Debra Moehle, and John Thibaut. 1983. "Trade Versus Expropriation in Open Groups: A Comparison of Two Types of Social Power." *Journal of Personality and Social Psychology* 44(5): 977–99.

Keeley, Lawrence H. 1996. *War Before Civilization*. New York: Oxford University Press.

Klein, Richard G. 1999. *The Human Career: Human Biological and Cultural Origins*. 2d ed. Chicago: University of Chicago Press.

Knauft, Bruce M. 1987. "Reconsidering Violence in Simple Human Societies: Homicide Among the Gebusi of New Guinea." *Current Anthropology* 28(4): 457–500.

Kopelman, Shirli, J. Mark Weber, and David M. Messick. N.d. "Commons Dilemma Management: Implications of Experimental Research." Submitted for inclusion in *Drama of the Commons*, edited by Thomas Dietz, Nives Dolšak, Elinor Ostrom, Paul Stern, Susan Stonich, and Elke Weber. Washington, D.C.: National Academy Press.

Labov, William. 1972. *Sociolinguistic Patterns*. Philadephia: University of Pennsylvania Press.

Mansbridge, Jane J. 1990. *Beyond Self-Interest*. Chicago: University of Chicago Press.

McElreath, Richard, Robert Boyd, and Peter J. Richerson. N.d. "Shared Norms Can Lead to the Evolution of Ethnic Markers." Submitted to *Current Anthropology*.

Milgram, Stanley. 1974. *Obedience to Authority: An Experimental View*. New York: Harper and Row.

Miller, David T. 1999. "The Norm of Self-Interest." *American Psychologist* 54(12): 1053–60.

Nisbett, Richard E., and Dov Cohen. 1996. *Culture of Honor: The Psychology of Violence in the South*. Boulder, Colo.: Westview Press.

Nowak, Martin A., and Karl Sigmund. 1998. "Evolution of Indirect Reciprocity by Image Scoring." *Nature* 393(6685): 573–77.

Nuttin, Jozef M., Jr., and Annie Beckers. 1975. *The Illusion of Attitude Change: Towards a Response Contagion Theory of Persuasion*. London: Academic Press.

Ostrom, Elinor. 1998. "A Behavioral Approach to the Rational Choice Theory of Collective Action." *American Political Science Review* 92(1): 1–22.

Pinker, Stephen. 1994. *The Language Instinct: How the Mind Creates Language*. New York: William Morrow.

Rabbie, Jacob M. 1991. "Determinants of Instrumental Intra-Group Cooperation." In *Cooperation and Prosocial Behavior*, edited by Robert A. Hinde and Jo Groebel. Cambridge: Cambridge University Press.

Rappaport, Roy A. 1979. *Ecology, Meaning, and Religion*. Richmond: North Atlantic Books.

Richardson, Lewis F. 1960. *Statistics of Deadly Quarrels*, edited by Quincy Wright and C. C. Lienau. Pittsburgh: Boxwood Press.

Richerson, Peter J., and Robert Boyd. 1989. "The Role of Evolved Predispositions in Cultural Evolution: Or Human Sociobiology Meets Pascal's Wager." *Ethology and Sociobiology* 10(1–3): 195–219.

———. 1998. "The Evolution of Human Ultra-sociality." In *Indoctrinability, Ideology, and Warfare*, edited by Irenäus Eibl-Eibesfeldt and Frank K. Salter. New York: Berghahn.

———. 1999. "Complex Societies: The Evolutionary Origins of a Crude Superorganism." *Human Nature* 10(3): 253–89.

Rogers, Everett M. 1983. *Diffusion of Innovations*. 3d ed. New York: Macmillan.

Roof, Wade Clark, and William McKinney. 1987. *American Mainline Religion: Its Changing Shape and Future*. New Brunswick: Rutgers University Press.

Sahlins, Marshall. 1976. *The Use and Abuse of Biology: An Anthropological Critique of Sociobiology*. Ann Arbor, Mich.: University of Michigan Press.

Schelling, Thomas C. 1966. *Arms and Influence*. New Haven: Yale University Press.

Sears, David O., and Carolyn L. Funk. 1990. "Self-Interest in Americans' Political Opinions." In *Beyond Self-Interest*, edited by Jane J. Mansbridge. Chicago: University of Chicago Press.

Sepher, Joseph. 1983. *Incest, the Biosocial View*. New York: Academic Press.

Silk, Joan B. 1980. "Adoption and Kinship in Oceania." *American Anthropologist* 82(4): 799–820.

Simon, Herbert A. 1990. "A Mechanism for Social Selection and Successful Altruism." *Science* 250(4988): 1665–68.

Soltis, Joseph R., Robert Boyd, and Peter J. Richerson. 1995. "Can Group-Functional Behaviors Evolve by Cultural Group Selection? An Empirical Test." *Current Anthropology* 36(3): 437–94.

Stern, Paul C. 1995. "Why Do People Sacrifice for Their Nations?" *Political Psychology* 16(2): 217–35.

Steward, Julian H. 1955. *Theory of Culture Change: The Methodology of Multilinear Evolution*. Urbana, Ill.: University of Illinois Press.

Tajfel, Henri. 1981. *Human Groups and Social Categories: Studies in Social Psychology*. Cambridge: Cambridge University Press.

Toland, John. 1970. *The Rising Sun: The Decline and Fall of the Japanese Empire*. New York: Random House.

Trivers, Robert L. 1971. "The Evolution of Reciprocal Altruism." *Quarterly Review of Biology* 46(1): 35–57.

Turner, John C. 1984. "Social Identification and Psychological Group Formation." In *The Social Dimension: European Developments in Social Psychology.* Vol. 2, edited by Henri Tajfel. Cambridge: Cambridge University Press.

Turner, Jonathan H. 1995. *Macrodynamics: Toward a Theory on the Organization of Human Populations.* New Brunswick, N.J.: Rutgers University Press.

van Creveld, Martin L. 1982. *Fighting Power: German and U.S. Army Performance, 1939–1945.* Westport, Conn.: Greenwood Press.

———. 1991. *The Transformation of War.* New York: Free Press.

van den Berghe, Pierre L. 1981. *The Ethnic Phenomenon.* New York: Elsevier.

Weingart, Peter, Sandra D. Mitchell, Peter J. Richerson, and Sabine Maasen. 1997. *Human by Nature: Between Biology and the Social Sciences.* Mahwah, N.J.: Lawrence Erlbaum.

Westermarck, Edward. 1894. *The History of Human Marriage.* London: Macmillan.

Wiessner, Polly. 1996. "Leveling the Hunter: Constraints on the Status Quest in Foraging Societies." In *Food and the Status Quest*, edited by Pauline Wiessner and Wulf Schiefenhovel. Oxford: Berghahn.

Wiessner, Polly, and Akii Tumu. 1998. "Historical Vines: Enga Networks of Exchange, Ritual, and Warfare in Papua New Guinea." Washington, D.C.: Smithsonian.

Williams, George C. 1966. *Adaptation and Natural Selection.* Princeton, N.J.: Princeton University Press.

Wilson, Edward O. 1975. *Sociobiology: The New Synthesis.* Cambridge, Mass.: Harvard University Press.

———. 1998. *Consilience: The Unity of Knowledge.* New York: Knopf.

Wolf, Arthur P. 1970. "Childhood Association and Sexual Attraction: A Further Test of the Westermarck Hypothesis." *American Anthropologist* 72(3): 503–15.

Chapter 10

Morality and Commitment

MICHAEL RUSE

We may call that part of the soul whereby it reflects, rational; and the other, with which it feels hunger and thirst and is distracted by sexual passion and all the other desires, we will call irrational appetite, associated with pleasure in the replenishment of certain wants.

Yes, there is good ground for that view.

Let us take it, then, that we have now distinguished two elements in the soul. What of that passionate element which makes us feel angry and indignant? Is that a third, or identical in nature with one of those two?

It might perhaps be identified with appetite.

I am more inclined to put my faith in a story I once heard about Leontius, son of Aglaion. On his way up from the Piraeus outside the north wall, he noticed the bodies of some criminals lying on the ground, with the executioner standing by them. He wanted to go and look at them, but at the same time he was disgusted and tried to turn away. He struggled for some time and covered his eyes, but at last the desire was too much for him. Opening his eyes wide, he ran up to the bodies and cried, "There you are, curse you; feast yourselves on this lovely sight!"

Yes, I have heard that story too.

The point of it surely is that anger is sometimes in conflict with appetite, as if they were two distinct principles. Do we not often find a man whose desires would force him to go against his reason, reviling himself and indignant with this part of his nature which is trying to put constraint on him? It is like a struggle between two factions, in which indignation takes the side of reason. But I believe you have never observed, in yourself or anyone else, indignation make common cause with appetite in behavior which reason decides to be wrong.

—Plato, *The Republic*

TODAY MUCH interest has been shown in naturalistic approaches to ethics, particularly in bringing evolutionary thinking (Darwinian evolutionary thinking in particular) to bear on our understanding of morality. Especially with the coming of human sociobiology and the attempt to explain human social behavior in Darwinian terms of natural selection, a growing number of scientists and philosophers has argued that morality—this most important, defining feature of what it is to be human—simply must yield to evolutionary analysis (Wilson 1978; Alexander 1987; Mackie 1978; Murphy 1982; Ruse 1986, 1989, 1995). In the hope of carrying discussion further, here the focus will be on what has been called the commitment problem and if and how this has significant implications for our thinking about evolutionary ethics. Let us begin with some background and move then to commitment, asking if it challenges and extends our thinking.

A Naturalistic Approach to Ethics

What will be the basic outline of a naturalistic approach to ethics—a Darwinian approach to ethics? Start with the fact that humans have evolved through natural selection to be social, and combine this with the fact that selection works for the individual rather than the group. This means, to use Richard Dawkins's (1976) felicitous metaphor, that at bottom everything is a function of *selfish genes*—one's biology is working for oneself and not for others. Hence any interaction between organisms which may involve one organism doing something for another (what evolutionists call *altruism*) must be understood ultimately in terms of the reproductive benefit or ends of the actor doing the favor for the other. Consider then how it is that sociality among humans might have come into being and be continued on an ongoing basis.

One possibility is that which is pursued by the social insects, the hymenoptera, for instance. Here everything works by instinct. The ants, the bees, and the wasps are not thinking beings. They do not calculate relationships and determine what they should do. Nor do they act out of moral sentiment. They are, to use another metaphor, programmed to do what they do, and there is an end to it—or rather, there is a beginning to it for humans. Clearly in some respects our sociality, our biological altruism, works through instinct. The love of a mother for her children, for instance. Biologically the mother's interest is to care for her children, but she does not do so for conscious biological interest. She does so out of love! Note, however, that this instinctive sociality can only go so far and that very good reasons exist as to why organisms such as humans cannot rely on instinct alone. The virtue of instinct is that no training is necessary. The cost of instinct is that if something goes wrong, one has no ready recourse. For ants this is fine. The queen produces millions of offspring and no training is needed. If something goes wrong (a rainstorm destroying pheromone trails back to the nest) she can afford to lose a few thousand—millions more are always available. In the case of humans, which have evolved so that they produce few offspring but demand much parental care, one simply cannot afford to make mistakes or get into situations that cannot be remedied. One must have ways of getting around problems, and instinct alone will not do this. Something more is needed.

The most obvious lead to something more takes you to the other end of the spectrum. Perhaps this is where intelligence comes in. Could we not just be rational superbrains who calculate self-interest and act on it when there is a positive payoff and not otherwise? We are both in danger: Should we, as Benjamin Franklin graphically put it, hang together or assuredly we will all hang separately? Or should we look after ourselves and let others attend to their own fates? Morality is not at work here, but neither necessarily is nastiness. One calculates one's own interests as does everyone else, and acts accordingly. Everyone acts socially, but in this instance the altruism is indeed selfishness or at least self-regard—and no doubt that, like instinct, this too is true in part of humans. In the memorable words of Adam Smith, "It is not from the benevolence of the butcher, the brewer, or the baker that we expect our dinner, but from their regard of their own interest. We address ourselves not to their humanity, but to their self-love, and never talk to them of our necessities, but of their advantage" (Smith 1976 [1759], quoted in Frank 1988, 21).

Yet why would this rationality not generally be the case? The obvious answer is that—physiological and other constraints aside (to produce a brain costs a lot and a supercalculating brain simply might be too expensive)—calculation in itself has costs, most particularly time. In getting on with daily life time is valuable, and the time needed for perfect calculation just might collapse down everything into total inaction. Such a situation can be likened to early chess-playing machines, which were absolutely useless because after one or two moves they took infinitely long periods of time running through all of the possibilities until they were ready to make the next move. This analogy brings us to the third option, morality—genuine or literal altruism. The new chess machines, machines such as Deep Blue, which beat the best humans in the world, succeed not because they never make mistakes but because they can get on very well at a brisk clip. They have certain strategies preprogrammed, and when the appropriate configuration appears they can make a move accordingly. Thus they have certain instinctual patterns, but they are more than mere creatures of instinct, for these machines can respond to different situations. This is the third option for humans. Certain strategies or patterns are built in by instinct, and as various situations arise we humans think and act accordingly.

Here—and this is an empirical claim—is where we find morality. Selfish genes do tend, all other things being equal, to make selfish people or at least self-centered people. Sociality is of biological value and so we have moral feelings or sentiments to make us (or help us) break through the selfishness. So we act morally. Not all the time, but enough of the time for things to function. Indeed this is a *genuine* morality—we do feel that we ought to do things, although as Plato realized, such sentiments are backed by passions. Self-disgust, for example, for looking at revolting objects such as executed criminals.

Rawls and Rationality

One more point before we turn to the commitment problem. The just-sketched naturalistic approach to morality puts one very much in the tradition of British moral philosophy of the seventeenth and eighteenth centuries—from Hobbes to Hume and beyond. Morality is seen as a matter of emotion or passion or sentiment or feeling, rather than some special product of a rational intuitive faculty. For this reason, at a certain level one sees morality as a matter of rules of thumb, of commonsense or everyday motives, rather than as some grand overarching system. Be kind to kids. Don't beat up your wife. Try not to cheat. Give a few bucks when the Salvation Army comes calling. And so forth.

Indeed even in the big things one sees the rules of thumb rather than systems. One oft-versed criticism of an evolutionary account of morality refers to the soldier in battle who gives his life for his country, even though doing so results in no payoff for him and probably not much for relatives either. How could this sacrifice be justified from an individual selection view? The answer is that perhaps it cannot—perhaps modern warfare distorts things so that one cannot see biology in action. Yet when you read accounts of soldiers in battle—the British in the Battle of the Somme in the First World War or the Americans in Vietnam—what is striking is just how little motivation is provided by the big things (Ferguson 1998). Right at the crunch point, God and country seem not to count for much. Few if any went over the top to promote the virtues of the Church of England, or to honor king and country. They fought to be alongside their pals and buddies—not to let the side down, as well as to avenge themselves for the chum killed last week or the women and children raped by the Huns in Belgium or some such thing. The soldiers acted for every-day things, not for philosophers' systems.

Not that systems are irrelevant or that philosophers are wasting their time. Systematization has its virtues—trying, as the philosopher John Rawls (1971) has said, to get the various parts of one's thinking into "reflective equilibrium." If you are against capital punishment, should you also be against abortion, for instance? Or can one hold consistently to the two prima facie opposing positions? Here system building can be of great value as one tries to make sense of the whole. This is just as much a virtue in morality as system building in science. One has various bits and pieces of information about planets and pendulums and flying bodies, and one puts them all together in New-ton's theory. Thus one finds, for instance, no inconsistency in suppos-ing that the planets in the heavens go in ellipses whereas cannonballs here on earth go in parabolas. Likewise in morality. One has various bits and pieces of information about killing and mercy and justice, and one puts them all together in the theory one favors—utilitarian-ism or Kantianism or some such thing. Thus one finds, for instance, no inconsistency in supposing that capital punishment is wrong but abortion is sometimes morally acceptable.

Indeed one might say that the neo-Kantian system of Rawls him-self is a good model for the Darwinian moralist looking for an overall system. Rawls argues that one ought to be just, and to be just one should be fair. Fairness Rawls finds by pretending one does not know what position one might find oneself in society—getting behind a "veil of ignorance"—then asking how the goodies of society should be distributed. Here he argues that the distribution should be such as to benefit everyone to the maximum. This does not necessarily mean equality. If the only way to get the best people to be doctors rather than philosophers is to pay them twice as much, then so be it. The worst-off people will benefit by the best people being doctors. We should not, however, simply assign benefits on people's talents or position or whatever. Being born strong and handsome does not enti-tle one to more than a person who is born weak and ugly. This is not fair and hence not just. Note that fairness in this instance does not say that the strong and handsome do not get more than the weak and ugly; probably they usually do. The point is that this happens, not that this is fair and just.

This kind of social morality is what one might expect to find put in place by natural selection—it does in basic respects spell out and sys-tematize our commonsense morality—and therefore conclude that no conflict or contradiction exists between the rationalist such as Rawls and the evolutionary naturalist. In this context interesting and suggestive is that Rawls himself suggests that morality might have been created by natural selection. The social contract at the heart of his system was produced by selection working on the genes rather than by a group of village elders sitting around and deciding how the benefits of society should be divided up. This is not to say that there are no philosophical differences between a neo-Kantian such as Rawls and an evolutionary ethicist. Rawls (1980) sees the metaethical foundation of morality as lying in the contradictions that obtain if rational beings do not pay heed to the moral norms he articulates. The naturalist finds no such foundations and does not think that substantive morality has quite the necessity he thinks obtains.

Commitment

Let us turn now to the commitment problem. The definitive discussion comes in *Passions Within Reason*, where the economist Robert Frank sets the problem as follows. A kidnapper gets cold feet and wants to release his victim. Yet he knows that if he does release the victim, any promises made now not to tell will at once be broken. If the victim could give the kidnapper some hold, however, such as a deadly secret that the victim could not afford to have released, then the victim might now walk free because the kidnapper would be sure that he has sufficient hold over the victim that the victim will not release his identity. "The blackmailable act serves here as a *commitment* device, something that provides the victim with an incentive to keep his promise. Keeping it will still be unpleasant for him once he is freed; but clearly less so than not being able to make a credible promise in the first place" (Frank 1988, 4).

Brian Skyrms, making a similar point in *Evolution of the Social Contract* (1998), uses the example of the doomsday device in the movie *Dr. Strangelove*. The device is made by the Russians in such a fashion that if detonated it will destroy the whole world, Americans and Russians alike; it will be set off in the event of a nuclear explosion or if someone tampers with it trying to defuse it. Obviously if the Americans attack first (which in the movie is precisely what they end up doing, thanks to the madness of one American general), then the Russians will regret bitterly that they cannot defuse the weapon. Yet at this point they are committed—and the reason is that, in a sane world, knowing that they will be committed is sufficient to deter the attack in the first place.

From an overall perspective this kind of commitment, although at some later point we may regret it, serves us well. However, in real life a blackmailing hold on us rarely makes us committed. Rather, what makes us committed is emotion of some kind. Anger, for instance, for (to return to Frank) when the Argentinians invaded the Falklands, to reclaim them cost Britain more than could ever possibly be returned by renewed possession of the islands. The British were not particularly rational at this point, but they were incredibly angry, and simply were not prepared to be pushed around by a bunch of foreigners. Indeed the point Frank and Skyrms stress is that the willingness to make such a commitment, a willingness that one is prepared to follow through no matter what the costs, can in an overall way pay off dividends for the individual—the individual country, in the case of the Falklands. Spain would think twice before it contemplated invading Gibraltar, for instance, even though the cost of its defense would be ludicrous for the British.

> Being known to experience certain emotions enables us to make commitments that would otherwise not be credible. The clear irony here is that this ability, which springs from a *failure* to pursue self-interest, confers genuine advantages. Granted, following through on these commitments will always involve avoidable losses—not cheating when there is a chance to, retaliating at great cost even after the damage is done, and so on. The problem, however, is that being unable to make credible commitments will often be even more costly. Confronted with the commitment problem, an opportunistic person fares poorly. (Frank 1988, 5)

From here Frank launches right into a full-blown account of morality, arguing that it is driven by passions or feelings or sentiments (to use the old-fashioned eighteenth-century term) in acts that are not rational in the sense of calculating the odds every time—where it simply would not pay us to calculate the odds every time—and that we make commitments based on these feelings or sentiments. Thus, for instance, a couple of businessmen set up a going concern, say a restaurant. Bringing diverse talents they flourish, or at least have the potential to flourish. Either could cheat on the other. If both cheated then both would suffer. If one cheated then he or she would do even better than if neither cheated; but they do not cheat. They make a commitment, trusting each other, feeling that it would be wrong if they were to cheat—and so the potentially flourishing restaurant actually does flourish. (The reader will recognize this as an example of the prisoner's dilemma situation, with the dilemma being solved by an emotion—a feeling that it would not be right to cheat on one's partner.)

Another example is marriage. Two people hitch up, promising to love and cherish right through life, in sickness and in health and so forth. So long as they are both fit and healthy, they are both gaining from the relationship—companionship, a home, a family, and so forth. Then one falls sick. Why not break the commitment and move out? From a personal point of view it would seem to pay. What is the point now of devoting all of your energies to a relationship where one is going to gain nothing? One does not pull out, however, because a commitment has been made—with a resultant feeling of guilt if one did break out. In any case, importantly, one loves one's partner even though that person is broken down and sick. One wants to be with and help the partner even though he or she can give little or nothing in return. The sentiments pull one along and over the problems. Ultimately this is in one's biological interests, even though on a specific occasion one might lose out. One will be, and show oneself to be, the kind of person who does make and keep commitments and so others with be likely (or more likely) to make and keep commitments to you.

Not that Frank wants to argue that no one ever cheats on any occasion; obviously they do. People take money out of the till, thereby reducing the overall profits, with the consequence that their partners get less than their full share. Marriages do break up significantly owing to the sickness or other misfortune of a partner. Such acts may be mean and horrible, but people are sometimes mean and horrible. In every war one finds cowards and deserters. You may try to put the fear of God into them, but sometimes not even that is enough. Yet here we have a situation very much like that explored by students of animal mimicry. A mimic is a freeloader, perhaps a harmless and tasty butterfly mimicking a nasty-tasting, poisonous butterfly. So long as the mimics are rare enough, their camouflage will work and the predators (birds) will not cotton on to the trick and everyone will be protected. When the mimics become too common, however, the birds start to pounce yet again and so soon it becomes in the interests of the nasties to show some difference so that they uniquely will be protected. Likewise with cheats and cowards. Some are going to get away with it, but so long as they are not too common they will be tolerated. Car thieves are a nuisance, but so long as every other person is not a car thief it is hardly worth removing the battery every time one leaves the car in a parking lot. If the thieves get too common, then one will start to take ever-increasing countermeasures. One looks for some kind of balance or equilibrium between those who play fair and try to keep to their commitments and those who cheat and try to benefit from the fairness of others. Further, one looks for a kind of arms race between the detection of cheaters—to be honest is one thing, to be stupid is another—and the concealment of cheating and dishonesty.

Summing up, Frank writes:

> The commitment model is like the conventional evolutionary account in that it predicts the inevitability of opportunistic behavior. In at least one

critical respect, however, it differs: opportunistic behavior here is not the *only* viable strategy. There is also room, possibly even a wide berth, for behavior that is unopportunistic in the truest sense. . . .

The honest individual in the commitment model is someone who values trustworthiness for its own sake. That he might receive a material payoff for such behavior is completely beyond his concern. And it is precisely because he has this attitude that he can be trusted in situations where his behavior cannot be monitored.

Trustworthiness, provided it is recognizable, creates valuable opportunities that would not otherwise be available. The fact that trustworthy persons *do* receive a material payoff is of course what sustains the trait within the individual selectionist framework. But even if the world were to end at midnight, thus eliminating all possibility of penalty for defection, the genuinely trustworthy person would not be motivated to cheat. (Frank 1988, 68–69)

Rationality Again

The basic problem of commitment and the proposed solution are now before us. (See also Schelling 1960; Hirshleifer 1987.) Our question must be about how this discussion on commitment sits with the earlier-sketched, evolution-based, naturalistic approach to ethics. In many respects, very well indeed. Frank's ideas are enthusiastically welcomed (and those of others such as Skyrms). Everyone is trying for a naturalistic position within an evolutionary context, seeing the ultimate nature of morality as reducing to emotions or sentiments as produced and refined by natural selection. Not all sentiments or emotions are necessarily moral ones. I feel sexual stirrings at the sight of a naked beautiful woman, but in themselves they are not particularly moral or immoral. (These would be Plato's appetitive feedings, as opposed to passions.) The morality comes in when these basic stirrings are mixed with guilt or joy or whatever, setting up desires or intentions or behavior or whatever. On my wedding night, I presume that the moral issues are positive. With a student desperate for a good mark, I presume that the moral issues are otherwise. The point of concern here—agreement between my evolutionary ethicist and Frank—is that inasmuch as we do have morality we have feelings and sentiments in action.

Yet a difference exists, most obviously over the rationality question, particularly over the proper approach to be taken toward the work of someone such as Rawls. My evolutionary ethicist wants to draw upon and endorse the neo-Kantian thinking of Rawls. Justice as fairness makes good sense to such a person. Frank is certainly not against rationality as such. He agrees that sometimes humans do interact on a rational basis—they reason out what is in their best interests and act

accordingly. (This is the second option for producing biologically altruistic behavior.) Frank gives the instance of the soldiers from the
two sides in the First World War out on patrol in no-man's-land. If a
party from one side bumped into a party from the other side, by tacit
agreement the two groups would move away without interaction.
This, Frank agrees, seems to fit Axelrod's (1984) model of tit for tat,
where one side responds to the other side with imitative behavior—
friendliness with friendliness and hostility with hostility.

> The conditions called for by the tit-for-tat model are often met in hu-
> man populations. Many people do interact repeatedly and most keep
> track of how others treat them. Axelrod has assembled persuasive evi-
> dence that these forces help explain how people actually behave. Per-
> haps the most impressive of all this evidence comes from accounts of
> the "live-and-let-live" system that developed in the trench warfare in
> Europe during World War I. In many areas of the war the same units
> lay encamped opposite one another in the trenches over a period of
> several years. Units were often closely matched, with the result that
> neither side had much hope of quickly eliminating the other. Their
> choices were to fight intensively, with both sides sustaining heavy casu-
> alties, or to exercise restraint. . . .
>   There is little doubt that tit-for-tat often did emerge as the strategy of
> choice for both Allied and German fighting units. Although strongly
> discouraged as a matter of official policy, restraint was sometimes con-
> spicuously apparent. (Frank 1988, 32–33)

Generally, however—unlike my evolutionary ethicist—Frank sees
his sentiment-based approach and a rationality-based approach as being in opposition. They do not turn up the same kinds of results at all.
Here then is not simply a question of morality being a quick and dirty
solution to rationality problems, but of action that is purely rational
leading to radically different solutions to action that is sentiment
based. One of Frank's (1999) examples is of leaving a tip at a roadside
café where never again will one be a customer. Rationality says leave
without tipping, whereas sentiment says leave a tip (you cheap fellow
you). Sometimes indeed the passions get in the way of rationality. To
make a prenuptial contract is wise and sensible, and in the old days
fathers or guardians used to do just this for heiresses. Yet the very act
of making a prenuptial contract between two autonomous beings
rather casts a chill on the whole (passion-based) relationship and, in a
way, could backfire, making a failure of that which both parties passionately (and perhaps rationally) desired.

Now some of these problems can be answered fairly readily. At
one level the commitment problem and the sentiment solution truly
do point to places where (along the way) the sentiment solution will

point to different actions from a rationality-based approach. Those who assume otherwise (that passions will always support reason), such as Plato in the opening quotation, are wrong. Suppose you have a couple setting up a business in a somewhat risky area, where big gains can be made but with the risk of losses as well, and long-term prospects may be rather dim. Rationality might dictate that you should grab what you can when you can. If things go well from the start, then maximize your profits and withdrawals. Yet your partner needs a long-term policy (unlike you, he is supporting children and aged parents). So he needs a commitment, to which you agree (otherwise he would not get into business with you). Rationality, however, dictates that you be self-centered and help yourself, even to the point of concealment or cheating. Tell him that you will stay with him and then break your word. Sentimentality dictates otherwise. You made a deal and you must stick with it. A promise is a promise, even though it costs you (and let us assume that you will never again get such a chance of profit, so staying true carries no payoff). Obviously, inasmuch as we would want to say that sentiments differ from rationality here, that is surely true.

A second question centers on that of motivation. Frank rightly points out that rationality in itself simply cannot produce morality.

It is impossible to quarrel with the notion that trust and cooperation often emerge for the reasons suggested by these authors. The material world is a difficult environment, and the penalty for uncritically charitable behavior will often be failure to survive.

But again, the difficulty, for our purposes, is that tit-for-tat is simply not genuinely *altruistic* behavior. Rather, it is, like reciprocal altruism, a straightforward illustration of prudent behavior—enlightened prudence, to be sure, but self-interested behavior all the same. The person whose cooperation is summoned only by the conditions specified by these theories can hardly lay claim to the moral high ground. Those who would search for deeper, more noble impulses in people must look elsewhere. (Frank 1988, 34–35)

Then again, about Rawls's thinking, Frank writes:

Even the humane moral philosophy of John Rawls, so influential in our own time, is derived from a quintessentially rationalist thought experiment in which self-interest is the primary human motive. In this landmark treatise, A Theory of Justice, people are asked to decide upon the rules of social justice by imagining themselves in an "original position" in which they lack knowledge of their own specific talents and abilities. Rawls accords no appreciable role to sentiments such as sympathy, charity, or envy in the choices made by his social contractors. (Frank 1988, 146)

This is a problem faced by all who would derive morality from reason, and was faced by Kant—who recognized it, although whether he solved it is uncertain. The rationalist must agree that we need feelings to drive us. Take the Rawlsian situation in which we are born with unequal talents and opportunities. At such a point, without anything else we would simply grab what we can and those born more fortunate than others would do better than others. Theoretical discussions about justice would cut no ice whatsoever. We must have human emotions that drive us to behave morally. In all fairness to Rawls (and contra Frank) he recognizes this and has a place for the sentiments. Indeed he goes so far as to argue that feelings and sentiments are put in place by good sociobiological factors—yet he does not think that they justify morality.

> The crucial question here, however, is whether the principles of justice are closer to the tendency of evolution than the principle of utility. Offhand it would seem that if selection is always of individuals and of their genetic lines, and if the capacity for the various forms of moral behavior has some genetic basis, then altruism in the strict sense would generally be limited to kin and the smaller face-to-face groups. In these cases the willingness to make considerable self-sacrifice would favor one's descendants and tend to be selected. Turning to the other extreme, a society which had a strong propensity to supererogatory conduct in its relations with other societies would jeopardize the existence of its own distinctive culture and its members would risk domination. Therefore one might conjecture that the capacity to act from the more universal forms of rational benevolence is likely to be eliminated, whereas the capacity to follow the principles of justice and natural duty in relations between groups and individuals other than kin would be favored. We can also see how the system of the moral feelings might evolve as inclinations supporting the natural duties and as stabilizing mechanisms for just schemes. If this is correct, then once again the principles of justice are more securely based.
>
> These remarks are not intended as justifying reasons for the contract view. (Rawls 1971, 503–4)

Surely, in a way, Rawls is trying to do precisely what Frank needs. He is trying to show, from an evolutionary perspective, why morality would pay. He is just not primarily interested in how morality is put into play. What he is certainly not doing is denying that the sentiments are needed.

The point to be concluded thus far is that the third of the earlier-sketched ways of getting biological altruism (through morality) is not identical to the second (through reason), but that their aims are basically the same. Even Rawlsian justice fits in here. Life is enough of a crapshoot that we can never be entirely certain where we might end up—even in the same family people are born with different talents (sexes for a start), and we are all likely to be young or old or sick or otherwise in need of attention. So a Rawlsian system is justified for us all in an overall, selfish-gene sort of way. The problem now is to get it to work in practice, and here is where a sentiment-based morality comes in. The work of Frank and others of the same ilk is crucial here. With justice, Frank and those similarly inclined can rightfully argue that without moral sentiments the system, however rational, just could not get off the ground. So pure rationality, however powerful, could not achieve its own ends. This is what the commitment problem is all about.

Finally, do pure rationality and an emotion-based morality always agree in basic principles? This question recently has been answered negatively, with some reason and some authority, by the philosopher and game theorist Brian Skyrms (1998). He argues that in real-life, evolution-driven situations, pure rationality often gives way before biological forces and the contingencies of the situation—how things start off, for instance. Certainly we should not think that a problem will have one unique solution, and that different end results might obtain. For instance, take a population with both those who work together (cooperators) and those who do not (defectors), and let us suppose a certain, limited choosiness. On a first encounter cooperators recognize each other and interact (to their mutual benefit) but other pairings lead to naught. Then on subsequent meetings everyone interacts with what or whom they encounter. Here cooperators do well together, defectors do badly together, but defectors and cooperators do terrifically for defectors and not so well for cooperators.

Then, if defectors are initially common, by and large cooperation will not pay. Defectors will wipe them out. There are not enough cooperators to make a difference. Most will meet defectors and lose out. If cooperators are initially common, then defectors can never really get a toehold. Here then we will get a result that a theory of rational choice would altogether bar, for defecting would seem to be the only possible sensible (rational) approach. Yet in this model, "As the population approaches 100 percent cooperators, cooperators almost always pair with cooperators at the first stage. Defectors get to random pair with those left at the second stage, but there aren't many cooperators left. The result is that the expected fitness of cooperation exceeds that of defection" (Skyrms 1998, 57).

Skyrms argues that, in real life, cooperators will tend to cluster together and recognize each other—perhaps through kinship relations—and that this will mean that ultimately helping others will pay.

Positive correlation of strategies with themselves is favorable to the development of cooperation and efficiency. In the limiting model of per-

fect self-correlation, evolutionary dynamics enforces a Darwinian version of Kant's categorical imperative: *Act only so that if others act likewise
fitness is maximized.* Strategies that violate this imperative are driven to
extinction. If there is a unique strategy that obeys it, a strictly efficient
strategy, then that strategy goes to fixation. In the real world correlation
is never perfect, but positive correlation is not uncommon. The categorical imperative is weakened to a tendency, a very interesting tendency,
for the evolution of strategies that violate principles of individual rational choice in pursuit of the common good. We can thus understand
how Kropotkin was right. ". . . [B]esides the *law of Mutual Struggle* there
is in nature *the law of Mutual Aid*." (Skyrms 1998, 61–62)

As Skyrms (1998, 106) concludes, "In this setting, rational choice
theory completely parts ways with evolutionary theory. Strategies
that are ruled out by every theory of rational choice can flourish under favorable conditions of correlation. Perfect correlation enforces a
Darwinian version of Kant's categorical imperative."

The basic conclusion is that the thinking of people such as Frank
and Skyrms does force on my evolutionary ethicist some revisions in
the position held hitherto. Yet even given the points made earlier at
the end of the last section, these are not genuinely unfriendly revisions. Rather, they help the would-be naturalist in ethics to be truer to
his or her beliefs than before. After all, the naturalist welcomes new
empirically based arguments, even if these require the jettisoning of
earlier-held views. The evolutionary ethicist must recognize that all
sorts of matters such as contingency can be important, and that pure
rationality can be but an imperfect guide.

Other issues might be raised, particularly concerning the empirical
adequacy of the claims of people such as Frank and Skyrms, or indeed about the whole Darwinian adaptationist framework within
which they work. Recently the philosopher Elliott Sober and the biologist David S. Wilson (1997) have mounted a defense of group selection and an attack on individual selection, arguing that one need not
apply a selfish-gene perspective on human sociality. Frank is critically
referred to as one of those psychological egoists for whom altruistic
behavior is "a kind of self-interest that is only apparently altruistic."
Yet quite apart from questions we might have about the validity of
any argument for group selection over individual selection, we have
seen no reason at all for (and much to counter) the belief that Frank
(or the evolutionary ethicist here described) in any sense thinks that
altruistic behavior is only "apparently altruistic." The whole point
about sentiments and emotions is that they give you genuine feelings.
Selfish genes may tend to human selfishness, but they do not neces-

sarily produce selfish people. The Darwinian argues that this is one such place where one has an exception.

Another vein of criticism comes from the philosopher Paul Griffiths (1997). In major respects he is respectful and praising of Frank. Griffiths is particularly appreciative of the fact that, when faced with hypothetical claims, Frank tries to back up his position with reference to experiments, performed by him or others. Yet good intentions do not always yield confirming conclusions.

> Unfortunately, not all of Frank's explanations of emotions are backed up by experimental results. He suggests that love is designed to ensure commitment to the pair bond after a partner has lost the qualities for which they were initially valued. Despite some admirable efforts to find objective evidence of selflessness in relationships, Frank is open to the charge that he has constructed a "just-so story" for something that is a normative ideal rather than a description of actual human behavior. Melvin Konner . . . argues that societies have only rarely established pair bonds on the basis of romantic love and suggests that if this emotion had a biological function it would be to facilitate adultery and abandonment rather than continuation of the pair bond. (Griffiths 1997, 119)

This criticism may not be entirely fair. Frank does offer some support for the idea that love can be a powerful emotion, driving people beyond their direct material payoff and on to a commitment situation where they can benefit in a broader, more long-run sense. Even if he fails to convince at this particular point, any interesting hypothesis or theory surely will push out beyond the known and make claims that (at the time of making) are not yet fully supported. Indeed we do now have a broad base from which to make claims about social behavior, and specifically about the social behavior and thinking of humans. Frank (as Griffiths acknowledges) tries to base his claims on empirical findings and experiments.

So let us leave things here. This is an ongoing area of research and, as is well shown by the work of Frank and Skyrms, a good theory or paradigm throws up more interesting questions every time it makes an advance. We have only just begun to develop and exploit the evolutionary approach to ethics. Much remains to be done.

References

Alexander, Richard D. 1987. *The Biology of Moral Systems.* New York: Aldine de Gruyter.

Axelrod, Robert. 1984. *The Evolution of Cooperation.* New York: Basic Books.

Dawkins, Richard. 1976. *The Selfish Gene.* Oxford: Oxford University Press.

Ferguson, Niall. 1998. *The Pity of War*. London: Allen Lane.

Frank, Robert. 1988. *Passions Within Reason: The Strategic Role of the Emotions*. New York: Norton.

———. 1999. "Cooperation Through Emotional Commitment." Ithaca, N.Y.: Cornell University, typescript.

Griffiths, Paul E. 1997. *What Emotions Really Are: The Problem of Psychological Categories*. Chicago: University of Chicago Press.

Hirshleifer, John. 1987. "On the Emotions as Guarantors of Threats and Promises." In *The Latest on the Best: Essays in Evolution and Optimality*, edited by John Dupré (307–26). Cambridge, Mass.: MIT Press.

Mackie, John. 1978. "The Law of the Jungle." *Philosophy* 53: 553–73.

Murphy, Jeffrey. 1982. *Evolution, Morality, and the Meaning of Life*. Totowa, N.J.: Rowman and Littlefield.

Rawls, John. 1971. *A Theory of Justice*. Cambridge, Mass.: Harvard University Press.

———. 1980. "Kantian Constructivism in Moral Theory." *Journal of Philosophy* 77: 515–72.

Ruse, Michael. 1986. "Evolutionary Ethics: A Phoenix Arisen." *Zygon* 21: 95–112.

———. 1989. *The Darwinian Paradigm: Essays on Its History, Philosophy and Religious Implications*. London: Routledge.

———. 1995. *Evolutionary Naturalism: Selected Essays*. London: Routledge.

Schelling, Thomas 1960. *The Strategy of Conflict*. Cambridge, Mass.: Harvard University Press.

Skyrms, Brian 1998. *Evolution of the Social Contract*. Cambridge: Cambridge University Press.

Smith, Adam 1976 [1759]. *The Theory of Moral Sentiments*, Editors. Raphael, D. D., and A. L. Macfie. Oxford: Oxford University Press.

Sober, Elliott, and David S. Wilson. 1997. *Unto Others: The Evolution of Altruism*. Cambridge, Mass.: Harvard University Press.

Wilson, Edward O. 1978. *On Human Nature*. Cambridge: Cambridge University Press.

PART IV

COMMITMENT IN
HUMAN SOCIAL GROUPS

T HE PREVIOUS chapters build to the general conclusion that humans are intrinsically social animals whose psychology cannot
be understood without a solid foundation of knowledge about
the benefits and costs of social life, the social strategies we use, and
how our emotional capacities make these strategies possible. Many of
our relationships and memberships in groups clearly are based on
commitment. Now we can finally consider several examples of social
institutions to see if they offer evidence on the importance of commitment, and if ideas about commitment can help us to better understand social life. Our examples come from medicine, law, and religion.

Individuals who work in these areas are all professionals: doctors,
psychologists, lawyers, and ministers. The authors of all three chapters note the special obligations of such professional practitioners.
Psychotherapists are obligated not to exploit patients for sex or
money. Goodenough explores in some detail not only the ethical expectations of the legal profession, but examples in which lawyers are
expected to—and do—act in the best interests of their clients when
they easily could use their position to profit from deception. Ministers, by the very nature of their role, are expected to behave according
to principles, and to abjure worldly benefits at the expense of their
parishioners. The very idea of a profession is based on situations in
which the client is vulnerable because he or she lacks the knowledge
needed to determine whether the quality of service is good or not.
Furthermore, the intimacy of each of these situations opens people to

exploitation. Examples abound, of course, of rapacious psychiatrists, sleazy lawyers, and sinful ministers. Yet as Goodenough points out, the remarkable thing is that such a large part of professional practice proceeds ethically, despite manifest opportunities for cheating. Training in ethical standards is central to all professions, and this certainly is a factor. The importance of reputation is, however, perhaps underemphasized in these chapters. Professionals who stray from high standards are liable to be the subject of gossip that can ruin them, even if no official sanction is entertained. Like Caesar's wife, most professionals strive to avoid even the appearance of behavior that would deserve reproach. The enormous costs of deviation may help to explain why behavior in these situations so often is genuinely moral behavior.

The utility of an evolutionary perspective on commitment is especially evident in the treatment of mental disorders. Since we lack a comprehensive theory about how relationships work, much psychotherapy remains a matter of intuition and experience. Recognizing the role of commitment in marriages and work relationships is no panacea, but it does help to make sense of some otherwise apparently irrational actions, such as vengeful pursuit of a wayward spouse, or staying with an employer who is loyal but stingy. A perspective on commitment also illuminates the therapeutic relationship itself, and why psychotherapy is "the impossible profession." Patients seek commitment from their therapists, but most are acutely aware that they are paying for every minute. Consider also the disorders related to attachment. Some people remain attached too closely for too long to their parents or lovers, while others, especially those who never experienced unconditional love, cannot believe that people are capable of genuine commitment.

Each chapter finds evidence for the role of natural selection in shaping capacities that make commitment possible. In the clinic, attachment and a series of pathological syndromes testify to the central role of commitment in human psychology. People who lack a capacity for commitment are as impaired as those who have only one leg. The law offers equally vivid evidence. Goodenough emphasizes that commitment does not seem to come from the law, but much of law seems to reflect a deep natural human capacity for commitment. He applies systematic tests, looking at how widespread the trait is, whether it is seen in animals, and whether it would likely be selected for in the course of evolution, and concludes that evidence exists for commitment on all three criteria.

Religion is perhaps the crowning example. As Irons notes, people crave membership in a group with transcendent values. They monitor others in the group to ensure that their behavior is determined by principles, not calculation. Such a social setting makes all of life seem more meaningful and safe—and for good reason. People in such religious groups can engage safely in trusting, committed relationships that would be foolhardy elsewhere. Irons sees religion as "made possible by commitment." Many of the rituals and membership costs he describes as precisely what one would expect of a group that exists in large part to make commitments possible. Other authors have speculated about whether natural selection has shaped a religious tendency. The approach advocated here provides a plausible answer. People have a built-in capacity for commitment, and they seek out social groups that facilitate such relationships and ideologies that advocate acting according to principle instead of calculation. By no means does Irons suggest that religion is only this and nothing more, and he is careful to note the difficulties involved in taking a scientific look at something so personal and meaningful. Nonetheless, the opportunity exists, as he says, to use commitment to build a small but secure bridge between science and religion. Given that religion is perhaps the most potent personal and social force in the world, and often is excluded from attempts to understand human behavior, any progress in this direction will be welcome indeed.

Chapter 11

Commitment in the Clinic

RANDOLPH M. NESSE

H UMAN BEINGS are difficult to understand in large part because they are so irrational. If they would simply maximize
their inclusive fitness in a straightforward way, their actions—
and their difficulties—would be far easier to understand and treat;
but they don't. Their behavior (our behavior!) often arises from passions that induce actions that seem to have nothing to do with a sensible reproductive strategy.

- A woman comes to the clinic depressed because her life is constrict-
  ing as she cares for her demanding husband, who is being progressively impaired by multiple sclerosis. Attractive, wealthy men encourage her to leave, but she stays.

- A couple is in the midst of a divorce. One day both call their mutual friends to reveal damaging secrets about one another. The next
  day they make up and vow to love each other forever.

- A middle manager in a large corporation impulsively quits after
  having been insulted by his supervisor. He has no other job prospects.

- An attractive and intelligent young woman is brought to a clinic by
  her parents after she tells them about her religious cult's plans for a
  mass suicide.

- A single middle-aged woman gives up her lucrative career and
  spends most of her time teaching piano to friends who pay her a
  pittance.

- Teenagers drive wildly on manicured lawns, wrecking them for no apparent reason, despite the risks of being caught.

- A man who gets into college and the priesthood chooses the priesthood.

- A father drives for hours every night, looking for the men who raped his daughter a year ago, even though he has no way to recognize them.

- An attractive young man is so shy that he cannot even talk to the many women who want to date him.

- A woman reports that she wants to have a family but cannot because she has been unable to consummate her marriage after three years.

The psychiatric clinic is the birthplace and graveyard of theories of human nature. Clinicians are desperate to find ways to explain what they see. They winnow and stack the rich data from clinical observations into diverse theories, many of which do well in describing the phenomena and sometimes even predicting how people will act. Personality theories, psychodynamics, theories based on attachment and self, family dynamics, behaviorism, and cognitive theories all flourish. The thoughtful clinician is overwhelmed. None of the theories start from first principles, and criteria for choosing among them are not clear-cut. Most clinicians, however, do choose. Many remain loyal to Freud's perspective, while others denigrate it. Some cling to learning theory and try to recondition their patients. Some blame societal conditions. Others emphasize the roles of family and marital conflicts, or emphasize faulty patterns of thinking. Still others focus on individual differences in genes and brain structures to seek the causes of mental disorders.

Each of these perspectives contains some truth. Yet eclecticism is a swamp in which both patients and clinicians quickly become mired. Successful treatment requires a framework that makes sense of problems. A narrative with a villain provides a target to attack. This may be why most clinicians hold fast to one or another school of thought that blames one or another causal factor (Frank 1975). Yet the same rich data that gives rise to theories also challenges them. When they tackle the complexities and apparent unpredictability of individual human passions, theories crash and burn.

What we lack is a solid theory that explains how relationships work. Medicine has physiology; psychology needs a comparable understanding of relationships and motivation. When we have it, we will do much better at understanding why people are so often in conflicts that give rise to hate, love, anxiety, guilt, and depression. An evolutionary approach to relationships grounded in biology would seem to offer just what the doctor ordered; indeed its arrival has occasioned much excitement and some real progress (McGuire and Fairbanks 1977; Wenegrat 1984; Glantz 1987; Slavin and Kriegman 1992; Gilbert, Price, and Allen 1995; McGuire and Troisi 1998). In particular some clinicians now attend far more than previously to the significance of genetic kinship (Essock-Vitale and Fairbanks 1979), and some have begun analyzing how resources are exchanged in reciprocity and hierarchical relationships, and how emotions mediate the negotiation of these exchanges (Sloman et al. 1994; Gilbert, Price, and Allen 1995; Sloman and Gilbert 2000). For those who are not already familiar with these ideas, they will be reviewed briefly prior to illustrating their value in the clinic, how they quickly meet their limits, and what an understanding of commitment can add.

The basic principles of kin selection are just now beginning to transform how clinicians understand relationships. For instance, many advocates for abused children remain unaware of the powerful role of biological kinship in protecting against child abuse (Daly and Wilson 1981; Gelles and Lancaster 1987). In the clinic the influence of kinship is illustrated vividly by a case in which the family had split into two warring camps, the woman and her children from a previous marriage versus the man and his daughters from a previous marriage. In another case, when a ten-year-old boy was evaluated for depression, he said his father cared only about the other two children, not him. The mother denied it and tried to end the treatment, but after long patient inquiry, the father finally admitted that he had never believed that the boy was his own son.

The nature of cooperation and competition between siblings also is illuminated by an inclusive fitness perspective. Siblings have good genetic reasons to help each other outside the family, but within the family they compete for resources. Cultural traditions that gave priority to one child, usually the eldest son, now have been replaced by an expectation that all children will be treated equally. Often children recognize that this is not the case, despite their parents' protestations. These insights gradually are making their way into family therapy circles where sibling conflict more often is seen as expected now— something to be managed, not cured.

Relationships between mothers and infants also appear dramatically different from an evolutionary perspective (Hrdy 1999; Low 2000). Wildly speculative theories about infant psychology and the trauma of weaning (Klein 1988) now can be replaced by knowledge about the intrinsic conflicts of interest between mothers and infants (Trivers 1974). We now know that, as suggested by many previous theories, a time does exist early in life when the interests of the mother and her child are nearly, but not quite, in complete synchrony. We also know that mothers tend to allocate resources according to what best will enhance their inclusive fitness. In wealthy societies these choices can be avoided or concealed, but in our ancestral environment mothers had to make choices that today seem impossibly difficult (Shostak 1983; Hrdy 1999). Even in utero, conflicts between mothers and fetuses can result in serious problems such as diabetes and hypertension of pregnancy (Haig 1993). Later in life, weaning conflicts, struggles with a "willful child," and conflicts in adolescence (Weisfeld 1977) all make far more sense when viewed in light of evolutionary principles. Much remains to be done to better understand the role of kinship in human relationships, how it is mediated, and how it goes wrong and causes conflict and suffering (Davis and Daly 1997). Such work eventually will improve treatment, as principles of kin selection are incorporated as a foundation for understanding family relationships and conflicts.

Increasing understanding about the workings of reciprocity relationships also is starting to influence clinical practice. Trading favors judiciously gives a selective advantage that has almost certainly shaped special capacities to accomplish this (Trivers 1971; Axelrod 1984; Glantz 1987). Usually modeled using game theory and the prisoner's dilemma, the benefits of repeated cooperation are substantial but unstable, because of the temptation to defect and the risk that the other will defect. Following the lead of Trivers and others (Trivers 1971; Tooby and Cosmides 1990), I have argued elsewhere that the four boxes defined by the prisoner's dilemma define situations that have arisen so frequently in the course of our evolution, and with such a profound influence on fitness, that each has shaped distinct emotions that increase the ability to cope with them (Nesse 1990). Repeated cooperation leads to friendship and trust. An intuition that the other will defect leads to suspicion. Recognition that the other already has defected leads to anger. A temptation to defect leads to anxiety, and betrayal of a social obligation arouses guilt. Such exchanges, and the emotions that mediate them, are the bedrock of social life; covering it is a rich organic soil of culture and traditions that give rise to luxuriant vegetation that varies wildly in different locations, and involves much pathology.

Clinicians, even those who know and appreciate the power of kin selection and reciprocity, find that these principles do scant justice to the tangled webs of relationships that give rise to individual psychopathology. For instance, when someone fails to follow through on a commitment, say to get married, the result is not "Oh well, I will find someone else"—blind rage is more likely. Yes, one person has defected and anger is the emotion expected in an evolutionary view of reciprocity. Yet clinicians who spend dozens of hours over a period of weeks talking to the participants in such a debacle are swept up in a conflict whose escalation quickly leads them to consider higher levels of complexity.

For instance, the therapist gradually begins to understand that the jilted bride had not told her fiancé that she might not be able to have children. He had not told her that he was planning to drop out of law school. Their parents' consent was privately grudging owing to religious differences. Then there was that phone call from his high school girlfriend. She thought she had found a man who would provide the secure kind of environment that her father had not been able to, but then her fiancé insisted on leaving her on her own while he went hunting. He thought he was treating her as an adult, but she felt abandoned and began acting more dependent on him, and asking for more reassurance. She began demanding that he make public declarations of his commitment; this made him more fearful and more insistent that she participate eagerly in new kinds of sex, just when she only wanted to be cuddled. No theory will ever be able to embrace all the factors that shape such a situation. This is why providing psychological treatment always will be an art form as well as a science. To incorporate as much information as possible, a clinical narrative is the most comprehensive and efficient framework, but the scientific value of such ideographic approaches is severely limited.

This chapter considers the role of subjective commitment in complex human relationships and psychopathology and argues that: much of the complexity in human sociality arises because many relationships are based on subjective commitment; natural selection may have shaped specific emotional capacities to mediate such commitments; much psychopathology arises from the exigencies of those commitments; and understanding the mechanisms that mediate subjective commitment will lead to more effective treatments. More broadly, understanding commitment strategies may offer a link between the vast complexity of human lives and the forces of natural selection that have shaped their minds. We humans think and talk and make complex multistep plans to prepare for situations years ahead of time. Our actions depend not just on stimuli we respond to, but also on what we believe about human nature in general, and about the future actions of specific individuals. If natural selection has shaped mechanisms to allow us to cope with complex and competing commitments, this knowledge should yield a deeper understanding of psychopathology, and should also give us new powers to make life more bearable.

Overview of Subjective Commitment

Commitments influence others by signaling an individual's future intentions. A commitment is more than a mere prediction, plan, or wish. A commitment implies that an individual will keep trying to reach a self-imposed goal or expectation, even if that becomes difficult or disadvantageous (Klinger 2000). Saying you will eat dinner tonight is not a commitment. Saying you will fast for three days is far more difficult, and thus a commitment. Promising to meet someone for lunch is a small commitment. Promising to stay with and help one partner for the rest of your life—now *that* is a serious commitment. Plans become commitments only when they are likely to require sacrifice (Hirshleifer 1987). This is very different from a model of an animal acting straightforwardly to maximize inclusive fitness. The whole idea of a commitment is that, in some specified future circumstance, an individual will act in ways that are the opposite of those that would increase fitness (Frank 1988).

Many people are put off by attempts to interpret personal relationships in terms of simple reciprocity (Kohn 1990). They insist, often vehemently, that their relationships are not merely to exploit others in order to benefit their genes. While it must be true that genes that influence behavior can become more common only if they result in behaviors that tend to advance a person's genetic interests must be true, these indignant objections are, nonetheless, understandable. The advantage does not go to those who take advantage of others, it goes to those who can convince others that they will behave in ways that are not necessarily in their best interests—that is, that they will fulfill their commitments. As in defecting in a prisoner's dilemma game, the maximum short-term advantage may come from not following through on a commitment, but often—in fact usually—people must do what they say they will do, or suffer the terrible consequences of exclusion. Even more than satisfying our desires, we seem to be designed to want to please others. Anxiety and guilt may have special utility in a species that relies on subjective commitments (Brickman 1987; Gilbert 1989; O'Connor and Berry 1999).

Most commitments are contingent: a person commits to doing X if the other does Y. While some commitments are to personal goals, most are promises to help someone or threats to harm someone. If two people both believe that the other will help them, even when that would offer no advantage at all, they can form an alliance far stronger and more valuable than any that could be created by calculated self-interest. Social institutions facilitate such agreements by creating new incentives enforced by third parties (contract law is the exemplar).

Personal relationships such as marriage or friendship, however, even when socially defined, depend primarily on *subjective* commitment. Internal states and their attendant feelings mediate actions in personal relationships. The link between subjective and externally enforced commitments is complex. Social constructions such as marriage that change the external contingencies also change the subjective emotional response to a situation. If escape from the commitment is impossible, the mind runs far less to the alternatives with all the attendant desire, guilt, and ambivalence.

A capacity for commitment generally is valued. We associate making and keeping commitments with character, and we admire (or fear) people who do this. Sometimes we describe such people as noble or having character. Reputation is so important because it makes our commitments potent influences. One of the most crucial facts about a person is whether she or he has a reputation for following through on commitments. People who lack or lose such a reputation are consigned to the social periphery.

Attachment

That human relationships are based on something more than learning and optimal exchange has long been obvious. Our deepest relationships and feelings arise from emotional commitments to other people. This is often called *attachment*, following the work of John Bowlby (Bowlby 1969). Harlow's studies put to rest the notion that infant monkeys behaved mainly to get food (Harlow and Harlow 1962). They preferred foodless terry cloth surrogate mothers to wire forms supplied with a milk bottle. Even geese, in Lorenz's studies, followed not the source of food, but whatever they saw moving during a critical period early in life (Alcock 1997). This imprinting object was not only a safety signal early in life, but also later served as a model for finding appropriate mates. Bowlby put these findings together with his clinical experience as a psychoanalyst and concluded that human infants got a selective advantage by their motivation to stay close to their mothers. He called this tendency attachment. Even though Bowlby did not know about kin selection and the difficulties with group selection, he recognized that natural selection likely had shaped specific motivational mechanisms to ensure the proximity of mothers and infants.

This insight provided the impetus for an enormous amount of research, much of it focused on variations in attachment (Ainsworth et al. 1978). We now know that an infant's pattern of attachment to its mother is remarkably consistent across months and even years. Infants who are securely attached tend to stay that way unless they experience trauma, while avoidant or anxiously attached infants tend to stay that way. The theory assumes that these patterns of attachment are determined primarily by how the mother treats the infant. Typically, "normal" attachment is seen as desirable, while any other pattern is thought to be pathological. The possibility that genetic differences may account for individual differences in attachment style, and that genes shared by the mother and child may account for the similarities of their attachment patterns, has been met with considerable resistance (Goldsmith and Carman 1994). In a similar vein, only recently has any interest been shown in considering the possibility that differences of attachment style are facultative adaptations that may improve a baby's chances in certain kinds of situations (Chisholm 1996). Bowlby relied heavily on developmental explanations for adult patterns of relationships. This has spilled over into a strong tendency to describe adult attachments in terms of the utility of attachment for infants, when very good and very different reasons exist for adults to have emotional attachments.

Hazen and Shaver have found ways to categorize people in terms of their attachment style (Hazen and Shaver 1994). The consistency of attachment styles across time seems to depend on the "internal working model" a person has of how others will act toward them and how they should act in return (Berscheid 1994). Adults who are "secure" see others favorably, and tend to trust people and be capable of close relationships. "Ambivalent" individuals want relationships but are untrusting and believe others are likely to disappoint them. "Avoidant" individuals have a negative view of human nature and tend to assume that others are untrustworthy (Reis and Patrick 1996). Bartholomew and Horowitz offer a four-category scheme that includes secure, dismissing, preoccupied, and fearful attachment styles (Bartholomew and Horowitz 1991). The distinctive characteristics of attachment styles may make sense as strategies for managing committed relationships. Their consistency over time may arise not only from genes, but also from the self-perpetuating nature of beliefs about others. People who can trust others often find trustworthy partners. Those who cannot trust others have their negative beliefs repeatedly confirmed.

We may assume that early experiences set a developmental trajectory that settles into self-perpetuating expectations about relationships with good reason. Also, our adult attachments may well utilize the same brain and mental mechanisms as those that make infantile attachment possible. Nonetheless, the functions of attachment in adult life may be quite different and important in their own right. Subjective commitment may be the engine generating the strong feelings that bind us to others in adulthood. People who lack these capacities suffer serious disadvantages.

Syndromes Related to Subjective Commitment

One of the best ways to identify the functions of a trait is to observe what happens when it is absent or malfunctioning. Several syndromes of absent or otherwise defective commitment are especially constructive in this regard.

Obsessive-compulsive personality (OCP) is a syndrome very different from obsessive-compulsive disorder (OCD) (Diaferia et al. 1997). People with OCD are preoccupied with the fear that some small oversight will lead to catastrophe that will harm others. They perform apparently bizarre rituals—repeatedly washing, organizing, or checking things to prevent the danger, or at least to try to relieve their pervasive anxiety (Goodman et al. 1989). All kinds of people get OCD. In some cases it seems to result from streptococcal-induced autoimmune damage to a part of the brain called the caudate nucleus (Goodman et al. 1989). Our focus here is a different disorder, obsessive-compulsive personality disorder.

People with OCP tend to have an analytical, intellectualized, cold view of life. They are preoccupied with duty and often outraged by other people who are not so constrained. They are very concerned with their obligations and those of others. They try to control everything and everyone in their vicinity. They often cannot understand why others become frustrated with them. Many of them do not experience passions in the same way that other people do, and they cannot understand other people's emotional outbursts. Predictably, people with OCP can be extremely difficult to live with. While most people make romantic commitments in a state of passion, the person with obsessive-compulsive personality is more prone to negotiate a contract. While others express rage at some betrayal, the person with OCP is liable to harbor silent, steady, simmering fantasies of revenge.

Obsessive-compulsive personality disorder can be interpreted as a deficiency in the emotions that make subjective commitment possible. The person with OCP simply cannot understand it when others act on passions. Such people have trouble believing that others are sincere in their fervent promises. They experience invitations to emotional commitment as attempts at manipulation. Since they tend to do their duty exactly and with great scrupulousness, and expect the same of others, they are often disappointed in this regard. People with OCP have a huge capacity for moral commitment but a deficient capacity for emotional commitment.

Other disorders are characterized by nearly the opposite condition: a proneness to make quick, profound emotional attachments, but to be lackadaisical about moral commitments. In previous times this often was called hysteria. In both sexes, however, some individuals are prone to make rash, passionate commitments. The person who cannot understand falling in love has one kind of problem; the person who falls in love head over heels in a moment, but for only a few days, has a different kind of problem.

The term *borderline personality* refers to a condition that once was thought to be in between neurosis and psychosis, but now is recognized as a distinct syndrome characterized by extraordinarily quick development of intimacy, followed by profound insecurity and demanding behavior that frighten others away (Swartz et al. 1990; Gunderson and Phillips 1991). People tend to develop deep relationships over a period of months and years. During this time they test each other's reliability and personal characteristics. Some desperate individuals, however, want to bypass all that and make lifelong promises quickly. They often idealize potential partners. Other people naturally are intrigued but wary. They soon find that they fail to live up to the exaggerated expectations. People lured into the emotional orbit of such a desperate person often become frightened and withdraw. This creates, in the life of someone with a borderline personality disorder, a long history of quick intimacies followed by rejection. The expectation that this will be the pattern for future relationships sets up a positive-feedback spiral leading to profound and sometimes intractable pathology. Patients with borderline personality disorder also tend to use certain interpersonal strategies excessively and rigidly (Paris 1994). In particular they use a strategy called *splitting*, in which they idealize and offer to help one person, while denigrating that person's friends. The strategy can work, and appears frequently in everyday life, especially in politics. Patients with borderline personality disorder, however, use the strategy so crudely and consistently that it dominates their lives. In essence splitting is a desperate attempt to establish committed relationships by promising more than can be delivered, and by undermining other competing relationships.

Thus far the discussion has focused mainly on commitments to help others, but threats are equally effective commitments, and they too are associated with specific kinds of pathology. Some individuals learn early on that threats are effective social manipulators and may use them as a rigid and nearly exclusive strategy. If such people can attain a position of power, they sometimes can succeed with this limited repertoire. If not, they alienate people and enter a downward spiral. Conversely, those who cannot use threats at all are likely to be vulnerable to manipulation unless they live in a very well-ordered social group. People who repeatedly make threats they don't follow through on soon find their threats ignored.

Sociopathy can be viewed as a defect in the capacity for commitment. Many sociopaths who lack a capacity for guilt can, nonetheless, imitate commitment exceedingly well. Sociopathy in fact can be interpreted as a strategy that exploits people's wishes for committed relationships (Cleckley 1964; Mealey 1995). The sociopath often is expert in knowing what others want and how to get their trust. He does not, however, keep his commitments. Often he has been raised in a home where the expectation of others to keep their commitments simply doesn't exist (Rutter, Giller, and Hagell 1998). While many phenomena associated with sociopathy can be interpreted in reciprocity terms, the manipulative sociopath gets people to believe his promises. In short, he pretends to make emotional commitments, and then exploits those who believe him. Here the concept of commitment helps to bridge the gap between attachment pathology and the origins of sociopathy.

In the clinic suicide threats are of particular significance. Some simply reflect the hopelessness that attends interminable pain, physical or psychic. Frequently, however, a suicide threat is a communication that reminds others of what they might lose. All too often, though, such threats do not reunite the social network. They can become chronic as others vacillate between attempts to help and wishes to criticize or avoid the person making the threat. The relationship between depressive disorder and its associated suicidal wishes thoroughly complicates this matter to the point where even experienced clinicians have great difficulty. Suicide threats tragically illustrate the paradox of commitment strategies when a person who has threatened suicide feels compelled to take action in order to maintain his or her reputation for following through on commitments. This may help to explain why it is so difficult and dangerous for relatives and friends to challenge the seriousness of the suicidal threats.

Origins of Psychopathology

Psychopathology often arises, as we all know, from relationship difficulties. On one hand, this is not surprising. After all, the main determinants of reproductive success for humans are relationships and social success, and groups are the main venue of competition (Humphrey 1992; Buss 1984; Tooby and Cosmides 1989; Cosmides and Tooby 1989). On the other hand, why must life be so difficult? Why can't people simply make and keep stable relationships? Life would be so much easier and happier. The reciprocity model only begins to explain the difficulty. From its perspective, we are all trying to find generous cooperators, and yet we are on the lookout for cheats and we attempt to deceive others to gain an advantage when we can. Some evolutionists see social systems as providing rewards to those who can cheat in the subtlest ways (Trivers 1976; Alexander 1987). The prisoner's dilemma provides a good model for business, but it is very limited when it comes to intimate relationships and even politics, where influence is exercised by promises and threats backed up by reputation.

Extraordinary complexities arise from the apparent intrinsic contradictions of commitment strategies. The goal in making a commitment is to convince others that you will follow through on behavior that will not be in your interests in some future situation. How can you convince them of this? You can tell them in ever more fervent and sincere tones but it is usually more effective to put your reputation on the line by making public proclamations of your commitment or to engage a third party to enforce the contract. The most convincing evidence, however, is beginning to carry out the commitment. Thus when potential mates become ill, they watch to see if their partner becomes more or less helpful. Zahavi has argued that individuals often "test the bond" by acting uncooperative to see if the partner's commitment will persevere despite difficulties and lack of rewards (Zahavi 1976). He cites the example of courting birds—cardinals—in which the male must provide food to and accept days of abuse from the female before she will agree to mate. An alternative explanation is that she is testing his abilities more than his commitment, and is comparing his prowess to those of other males. Her actions also constrain him from pursuing other mates, thus perhaps decreasing the risk that he will desert the nest after mating.

Something very similar seems to go on in human relationships, most notably in so-called lovers' spats. In the early phases of courtship partners sometimes withdraw from one another, perhaps to see if the other will tolerate this; but acting cold, hostile, or stingy in order to see how the other reacts is a risky strategy that is notoriously prone to misfiring. Both partners are, after all, trying to discern the other's commitment. What is testing of the bond from one perspective simply may be abandonment and demonstration of unfaithfulness from the other's perspective. That relationships develop slowly with gradually increasing exchanges of resources and obligations is interesting in and of itself. Our best friends are old friends, and to begin to trust others takes a long time. This time can be cut considerably, and the risks of commitments reduced dramatically, if both partners are members of a group that provides both increased information about a person's character and increased punishments for defection.

The presence of third parties inserts complications into committed relationships. Clinicians who study families and groups repeatedly note that the primary structure of social life is the triad (Zuk 1981). The purity of any relationship is shaken by compromises required when a third person is involved. One in fact could generalize this to multiperson political interactions. Individuals attempt to create alliances with third parties, but every such commitment is likely to conflict with some other commitment. Thus the great difficulties faced by politicians who must try to ingratiate themselves with members of different groups. People are listening to see if these politicians will say one thing to one group and one thing to another. To succeed, they must. Unfortunately straightforwardness seems not to work very well, except when an advantage can be gained by getting strong support from one group at the expense of another. In short, conflict between competing commitments is a fact—perhaps the most basic fact—of everyday social life.

Our psychodynamics seem to be designed to protect us from excessive cognizance of these difficulties (Nesse and Lloyd 1992; Slavin and Kriegman 1992). Some people are, however, all too aware of them, and suffer greatly in trying to please everyone all the time. A comment on neurosis is germane here. The essence of neurosis is a deep fear that others will abandon you or attack in response to any apparent misdeed (Shapiro 1965). Neurotic people feel that they have no alternatives in situations when others become angry or threaten to leave. Neurotics try to understand what they might have done differently and how better to please the other (Horney 1937). One cannot, of course, please everyone all the time. Worse still, exploiters are attracted to such people and take advantage of them until they reach a breaking point. One wonders whether the prevalence of neurosis in modern societies, and the proliferation of treatments to ameliorate the symptoms, may be related to the contrast between our mass society and the small groups from which we evolved. In ancestral societies people had only a few social roles and obligations and did not have to juggle many roles, and they may often have had alternatives if the current situation became intolerable. By contrast, in modern societies most of us juggle multiple conflicting commitments in social groups from which there is no escape. We can't please all of the people all of the time, and the pressure on our identities is substantial.

This leads naturally to a brief consideration of guilt, a common psychiatric symptom. While sometimes interpreted by evolutionists as a manipulation, I suspect guilt is better interpreted as an internal motivator to maintain commitments (Gilbert 1997; Keltner and Buss-well 1996). The fear of experiencing anxiety before a violation of com-mitment, and of experiencing guilt after a violation, provide strong motivators to maintain subjective commitments even in situations where doing so is obviously not in the person's interests (O'Connor and Berry 1999). This provides powerful motivation for moral behav-ior. The fact of guilt, and the human capacity for moral behavior, pro-vides some of the most powerful evidence that natural selection has shaped the human capacity for subjective commitment.

As noted earlier in the section on attachment, what people believe about their own capacity for commitments and other people's capac-ity for commitments has a profound effect on how they live their lives. Someone who never has had experience with others fulfilling their promises will be unwilling to trust others and unwilling to enter into commitments. Such a person's social world is fundamentally dif-ferent from that of someone who believes that subjective commit-ments are possible. An extensive psychiatric literature describes the importance of a capacity for "basic trust," and the pathology that characterizes its absence (Balint 1979). People who believe that com-mitted relationships are possible are capable of such relationships and they thus gain advantages, even though they are vulnerable to exploi-tation. People who believe that others are incapable of making com-mitments will be unable to do so themselves; this belief is thus self-perpetuating. Those who hold it, and who are held by it, live in a world that is genuinely more ruthless than the parallel social world occupied by others.

The preoccupation of many social scientists with social construc-tions and their effects on social and individual life is germane here. What people believe about others and their relationships certainly is influenced by what they learn in childhood. Later in life, learning to view others as, for instance, *Homo economicus*, has tangible effects on behavior. Economists, for example, are less prone to public contribu-tions, most likely a result of being exposed to the field, not because of preexisting personality traits (Frank 1992). With good reason we may expect that similar effects result from exposure to views that humans are just fitness maximizers.

Psychotherapy

Psychotherapy is a solution with a problem. Hundreds of different brands each claim to be effective. As noted earlier, it appears that many are helpful, especially those that can recruit the confidence of both therapist and patient (Frank 1975). Interestingly, most all of them are based to one extent or another on creating a relationship. Absolutely crucial, and at the heart of every therapeutic relationship, is trust. Trust first that the treatment will work, but equally important is trust in the therapist's ability and willingness to fulfill commitments. One of my teachers once said, "Lie to your mother, lie to your lover, lie to your boss, but never never give any patient the least reason to mistrust anything you say or do." If one of the mechanisms of change in psychotherapy is learning how to create and manage committed relationships, then one easily can see why trust is so central.

The therapeutic relationship is, however, inherently paradoxical. Psychotherapy is, as Malcolm has said, "the impossible profession" (Malcolm 1982). It is not exactly an exchange of friendship for money, but often it seems that way to patients, especially in the early stages of therapy. They suspect that a therapist who demands payment cannot have a genuine emotional commitment. Patients keep trying to figure out whether this is a reciprocity relationship or a committed relationship. They provoke confrontations to test the therapist's commitment. Beginning therapists are likely to suspect their own motives; and some therapists lack a real commitment to the other person's welfare. In many cases, though, a therapist can offer a novel experience of a committed relationship that can literally change a person's social reality. Some people can use this experience to escape from their prior assumptions, habits of behavior, and misconceptions about others in order to create kinds of relationships of which they previously were incapable. If all goes well, at a certain point this capacity becomes self-generating and the person is off into a new social world with a new set of skills and capacities. This is not easy, however, and the outcome is by no means assured.

The other bedrock of psychotherapy is empathy. In evolutionary writings empathy has been seen as a mind-reading skill that gives advantages not only by allowing one to sense what others need in order to provide it, but also to use this knowledge to better manipulate others (Krebs and Dawkins 1984). In the psychotherapeutic literature empathy generally refers to deeply intuitive understanding of what life is like for the other. The essence of empathy is understanding a person's goals, how they are pursuing those goals, what resources they have, what resources they need, the obstacles that limit their ability to achieve their goals, the threats to the resources they have, the dilemmas they face in making decisions about how to pursue goals, and the complex trade-offs involved in pursuing conflicting goals. This is too much to process logically; instead the mind seems to have a special capacity to allow us to experience life from the point of view of another. Good therapists start with a native capacity for empathy and hone it by long experience. As a result, they really are sometimes aware of situations and feelings that their patients are not.

As I write this, I am struck by how old fashioned some of these concepts seem. Instead of a review of the data on the efficacy of behavioral versus cognitive behavioral versus interpersonal therapy, the discussion here is about commitment, empathy, guilt, trust, identity, and the delicacy of dealing with the unconscious. That the quality of the relationship is crucial to the success of the treatment is certain; why then do newer therapies tend so consistently to objectify syndromes and emphasize cognitions over emotions and standardization over individualized interventions? Perhaps this tendency arises from the same cultural factors that have given us *Homo economicus* as a model for ourselves. Perhaps understanding the biology of commitment can offer a route to the scientific study of phenomena that have faded from sight as measurements and money have ascended.

Commitment to Goals

Commitment to reaching a goal is substantially different from the kinds of commitment discussed so far. Commitments to threats and promises influence others by letting them know you will not behave according to short-term self-interest. A commitment to a goal also involves an intent to persist despite difficulty, but its influence is not on the other so much as on the self (Klinger 1975). The extent to which human action is organized in terms of goal pursuit, and its strong influence on mood, is striking once you begin to look for it (Gollwitzer and Moskowitz 1996). We can be conditioned to respond to cues, but more often we try to achieve a goal we have in mind. Our behavior, like that of all organisms, is not fragmented into bouts of only a few minutes for obvious reasons—the main one being the start-up costs involved in any activity, whether eating, hunting, or helping a child. Stopping a task before some natural end point is wasteful. Humans differ from most other organisms, however, in that our actions are structured around goals that persist across days and months. We see an end in mind and strategize the best way to reach it. When one tactic does not work, we try another. Whether the goal is moving a rock, planting a field, catching a tiger, winning an election, or publishing a paper does not matter—action is organized in pursuit of the goal (Martin and Tesser 1996).

One difficulty with this kind of behavioral organization is the possibility that much effort may be wasted in pursuit of an unreachable goal. At some point, when apparently efforts will not succeed, to give up and do something else is best (Carver and Scheier 1990). Note that the decision depends on a belief about the future—whether efforts eventually will or will not succeed. A large literature in psychology documents the tendency for unproductive efforts to arouse low mood that disengages effort from an unreachable goal (Brickman 1987; Diener and Fujita 1995; Emmons and King 1988; Klinger 1975). When a person is unable to give up trying to attain an unreachable goal, because the goal is crucial to the person's overall life strategy or because so much has been invested in getting this enterprise started, then low mood escalates into depression in which all motivation is turned off. The obvious question is why people don't behave rationally. If one potential spouse repeatedly rejects you, why waste the effort? Why not turn to someone else? If you can't get a promotion at one job, why not quit and take another? The answers to such questions help to explain why people stick with commitments to difficult goals, and thus the origins of many depressions (Nesse 2000).

The mechanisms that regulate goal pursuit seem irrational. People don't just give up their dreams the way a foraging animal would give up on one patch and move to another (Charnov 1976). Our commitment to a goal often seems senseless. As Buddhists have long noted, desires that persist even when unfulfilled are the cause of much suffering (Miller 1995). There are several possible evolutionary answers to this conundrum. The first and most obvious is that precisely when a goal is unreachable is hard to determine. If considerable effort has been put into reaching a goal, and alternative enterprises are not available, then the slightest possibility of success may be enough to justify persistence. This may help to explain the Concorde effect—the psychological tendency for people to continue investing in a project even when no net payoff is forthcoming. The big goals for humans, of course, are social. Here prediction is tricky at best. Perhaps the heir to the crown will marry you after all if you persist in your courtship! Perhaps your efforts to lead a group will suddenly be welcomed if the leader falls ill.

The advantages of persisting are of particular interest. Just as a capacity for subjective commitment can induce costly behavior that gives an advantage only in the long run and on the average, a tendency to persist in the pursuit of a goal can maintain effort and planning through dry spells when an enterprise gives no benefits. In both cases the capacity for commitment provides a long-term advantage that carries strategies over periods where efforts apparently are being wasted.

Goals do not, of course, exist in isolation; effort toward each one is a trade-off. Time spent in the gym takes time away from working. Deciding to have a family dramatically decreases the resources available for everything else in life. Major conflicts between strategies create a life crisis. When one of two physician spouses gets a good job offer in a small town, the crisis is obvious. When a woman wants to have children and her husband thinks they cannot afford them, the problem is more subtle, but equally serious. Such situations pit commitments to goals against commitments to people. People are extremely reluctant to give up either kind of commitment. Emotionally they are torn by such situations with a power that testifies to the depth of commitments. A game theory optimal solution may be an alternative, but that is not what people seek. They want to proceed with their commitments intact. Often, this is not possible. The conflict arouses depression until something gives.

This outline touches on only a few of the aspects of psychopathology and treatment that can be illuminated by subjective commitment. Much more can be said, especially about the role of commitment in relationships and difficulties therein. The goal here is only to illustrate some of the ways the theory of subjective commitment can assist in understanding psychopathology. My hope is that this theory will provide a bridge between the basic biology of relationships and the complex phenomena seen in the clinic.

References

Ainsworth, M., M. Blehar, E. Waters et al. 1978. *Patterns of Attachment: A Psychological Study of the Strange Situation*. Hillsdale, N.J.: Lawrence Erlbaum.

Alcock, John. 1997. *Animal Behavior: An Evolutionary Approach*. 6th ed. Sunderland, Mass.: Sinauer.

Alexander, Richard D. 1987. *The Biology of Moral Systems*. New York: Aldine de Gruyter.

Axelrod, Robert. 1984. *The Evolution of Cooperation*. New York: Basic Books.

Balint, M. 1979. *The Basic Fault*. New York: Brunner/Mazel.

Bartholomew, H., and L. M. Horowitz. 1991. "Attachment Styles Among Young Adults: A Test of a Four Category Model." *Journal of Personality and Social Psychology* 61: 226–44.

Berscheid, Ellen. 1994. "Interpersonal Relationships." *Annual Review of Psychology* 45: 79–129.

Bowlby, J. 1969. "Attachment Theory, Separation Anxiety, and Mourning." In *American Handbook of Psychiatry*. Vol. 6. *New Psychiatric Frontiers*, edited by David A. Hamburg and H. Keith Brodie. New York: Basic Books.

Brickman, Philip. 1987. *Commitment, Conflict, and Caring*, edited by C. B. Wortman and R. Sorrentino. Englewood Cliffs, N.J.: Prentice-Hall.

Buss, D. M. 1984. "Evolutionary Biology and Personality Psychology: Toward a Conception of Human Nature and Individual Differences." *American Psychologist* 39: 1135–47.

Carver, Charles S., and Michael F. Scheier. 1990. "Origins and Functions of Positive and Negative Affect: A Control-Process View." *Psychological Review* 97(1): 19–35.

Charnov, E. L. 1976. "Optimal Foraging: The Marginal Value Theorem." *Theoretical and Population Biology* 9: 129–36.

Chisholm, James. 1996. "The Evolutionary Ecology of Human Attachment Organization." *Human Nature* 7(1): 1–38.

Cleckley, Hervey M. 1964. *The Mask of Sanity: An Attempt to Clarify Some Issues About the So-Called Psychopathic Personality.* 4th ed. St. Louis: C. V. Mosby.

Cosmides, Leda, and John Tooby. 1989. "Evolutionary Psychology and the Generation of Culture, Part II. Case Study: A Computational Theory of Social Exchange." *Ethology and Sociobiology* 10(1–3): 51–98.

Daly, M., and M. I. Wilson. 1981. "Abuse and Neglect of Children in Evolutionary Perspective." In *Natural Selection and Social Behavior: Recent Research and Theory,* edited by R. D. Alexander and D. W. Tinkle. New York: Chiron Press.

Davis, J. N., and M. Daly. 1997. "Evolutionary Theory and the Human Family." *Quarterly Review of Biology* 72(4): 407–35.

Diaferia, G., I. Bianchi, M. L. Bianchi, P. Cavedini, S. Erzegovesi, and L. Bellodi. 1997. "Relationship Between Obsessive-Compulsive Personality Disorder and Obsessive-Compulsive Disorder." *Comprehensive Psychiatry* 38(1): 38–42.

Diener, Ed, and Frank Fujita. 1995. "Resources, Personal Strivings, and Subjective Well-Being: A Nomothetic Ideographic Approach." *Journal of Personality and Social Psychology* 68(5): 926–35.

Emmons, Robert A., and Laura A. King. 1988. "Conflict Among Personal Strivings: Immediate and Long-Term Implications for Psychological and Physical Well-Being." *Journal of Personality and Social Psychology* 54(6): 1040–48.

Essock-Vitale, S. M., and L. A. Fairbanks. 1979. "Sociobiological Theories of Kin Selection and Reciprocal Altruism and Their Relevance for Psychiatry." *Journal of Nervous and Mental Disease* 167(1): 23–28.

Frank, Jerome D. 1975. *Persuasion and Healing.* New York: Schocken Books.

Frank, Robert H. 1988. *Passions Within Reason: The Strategic Role of the Emotions.* New York: Norton.

———. 1992. "The Role of Moral Sentiments in the Theory of Intertemporal Choice." In *Choice Over Time,* edited by G. Loewenstein. New York: Russell Sage Foundation.

Gelles, Richard J., and Jane Beckman Lancaster. 1987. *Child Abuse and Neglect: Biosocial Dimensions, Foundations of Human Behavior.* New York: Aldine de Gruyter.

Gilbert, Paul. 1989. *Human Nature and Suffering.* Hove, UK: Lawrence Erlbaum.

———. 1997. "The Evolution of Social Attractiveness and Its Role in Shame, Humiliation, Guilt and Therapy." *British Journal of Medical Psychology* 70: 112–47.

Gilbert, Paul, John Price, and Steven Allen. 1995. "Social Comparison, Social Attractiveness and Evolution: How Might They Be Related?" *New Ideas in Psychology* 13(2): 149–65.

Glantz, K. 1987. "Reciprocity: A Possible New Focus for Psychotherapy." *Psychotherapy* 24: 20–24.

Goldsmith, H. H., and C. Carman. 1994. "Temperament and Attachment: Individuals and Relationships." *Current Directions in Psychological Science* 3: 53–57.

Gollwitzer, Peter M., and Gordon B. Moskowitz. 1996. "Goal Effects on Action and Cognition." In *Social Psychology: Handbook of Basic Principles*, edited by E. T. Higgins and A. W. Kruglanski. New York: Guilford Press.

Goodman, Wayne K., Lawrence H. Price, Steven A. Rasmussen, Carolyn Mazure, Pedro Delgado, George R. Heninger, and Dennis S. Charney. 1989. "The Yale-Brown Obsessive Compulsive Scale, II. Validity." *Archives of Psychiatry* 46: 1012–16.

Gunderson, J. G., and K. A. Phillips. 1991. "A Current View of the Interface Between Borderline Personality Disorder and Depression." *American Journal of Psychiatry* 148(8): 967–75.

Haig, David. 1993. "Genetic Conflicts in Human Pregnancy." *Quarterly Review of Biology* 68: 495–532.

Harlow, H. F., and M. K. Harlow. 1962. "Social Deprivation in Monkeys." *Scientific American* 207: 136–46.

Hazen, C., and P. R. Shaver. 1994. "Attachment as an Organizational Framework for Research on Close Relationships." *Psychological Inquiry* 5: 1–22.

Hirshleifer, Jack. 1987. "On the Emotions as Guarantors of Threats and Promises." In *The Latest on the Best: Essays on Evolution and Optimality*, edited by J. Dupré. Cambridge, Mass.: MIT Press.

Horney, Karen. 1937. *The Neurotic Personality in Our Time*. New York: Norton.

Hrdy, Sarah Blaffer. 1999. *Mother Nature: A History of Mothers, Infants, and Natural Selection*. New York: Pantheon Books.

Humphrey, Nicholas. 1992. *A History of the Mind*. New York: Simon & Schuster.

Keltner, D., and B. Busswell. 1996. "Evidence for the Distinctness of Embarrassment, Shame, and Guilt: A Study of Recalled Antecedents and Facial Expressions of Emotion." *Cognition and Emotion* 10(2): 155–72.

Klein, Melanie. 1988. *Love, Guilt and Reparation*. London: Virago.

Klinger, Eric. 1975. "Consequences of Commitment to and Disengagement from Incentives." *Psychological Review* 82: 1–25.

———. 2000. "Commitment." In *Encyclopedia of Psychology*. New York: American Psychological Association and Oxford University Press.

Kohn, Alfie. 1990. *The Brighter Side of Human Nature: Altruism and Empathy in Everyday Life*. New York: Basic Books.

Krebs, John, and Richard Dawkins. 1984. "Animal Signals: Mind-Reading and Manipulation." In *Behavioral Ecology: An Evolutionary Approach*, edited by J. R. Krebs and N. B. Davies. Sunderland, Mass.: Sinauer.

Low, Bobbi S. 2000. *Why Sex Matters*. Princeton, N.J.: Princeton University Press.

Malcolm, Janet. 1982. *Psychoanalysis, the Impossible Profession*. New York: Vintage Books.

Martin, Leonard L., and Abraham Tesser. 1996. *Striving and Feeling: Interactions Among Goals, Affect, and Self-Regulation*. Hillsdale, N.J.: Lawrence Erlbaum.

McGuire, Michael T., and L. A. Fairbanks. 1977. *Ethological Psychiatry: Psycho-*

pathology in the Context of Evolutionary Biology. New York: Grune and Stratton.

McGuire, Michael T., and Alfonso Troisi. 1998. *Darwinian Psychiatry*. Cambridge, Mass.: Harvard University Press.

Mealey, Linda. 1995. "Sociopathy." *Behavioral and Brain Sciences* 18(3): 523–99.

Miller, Timothy. 1995. *How to Want What You Have: Discovering the Magic and Grandeur of Ordinary Existence*. New York: Henry Holt.

Nesse, Randolph M. 1990. "Evolutionary Explanations of Emotions." *Human Nature* 1(3): 261–89.

———. 2000. "Is Depression an Adaptation?" *Archives of General Psychiatry* 57: 14–20.

Nesse, Randolph M., and Allen T. Lloyd. 1992. "The Evolution of Psychodynamic Mechanisms." In *The Adapted Mind: Evolutionary Psychology and the Generation of Culture*, edited by J. H. Barkow, L. Cosmides, and J. Tooby. New York: Oxford University Press.

O'Connor, Lynn E., and Jack W. Berry. 1999. "Interpersonal Guilt, Shame, and Psychological Problems." *Journal of Social and Clinical Psychology* 18(2): 181–203.

Paris, Joel. 1994. *Borderline Personality Disorder: A Multidimensional Approach*. Washington, D.C.: American Psychiatric Press.

Reis, Harry T., and Brian C. Patrick. 1996. "Attachment and Intimacy: Component Processes." In *Social Psychology: Handbook of Basic Principles*, edited by E. T. Higgins and A. W. Kruglanski. New York: Guilford Press.

Rutter, Michael, Henri Giller, and Ann Hagell. 1998. *Antisocial Behavior by Young People*. Cambridge, UK/New York: Cambridge University Press.

Shapiro, David. 1965. *Neurotic Styles*. New York: Basic Books.

Shostak, M. 1983. *Nisa: The Life and Words of a !Kung Woman*. New York: Vintage Books.

Slavin, Malcolm, and Daniel Kriegman. 1992. *The Adaptive Design of the Human Psyche: Psychoanalysis, Evolutionary Biology, and the Therapeutic Process*. New York: Guilford Press.

Sloman, Leon, and Paul Gilbert, eds. 2000. *Subordination and Defeat: An Evolutionary Approach to Mood Disorders*. Mahwah, N.J.: Lawrence Erlbaum.

Sloman, Leon, John Price, Paul Gilbert, and Russell Gardner. 1994. "Adaptive Function of Depression: Psychotherapeutic Implications." *American Journal of Psychotherapy* 48: 1–16.

Swartz, M., D. Blazer, L. George et al. 1990. "Estimating the Prevalence of Borderline Personality Disorder in the Community." *Journal of Personality Disorders* 4: 257–72.

Tooby, John, and Leda Cosmides. 1989. "Evolutionary Psychology and the Generation of Culture, Part I: Theoretical Considerations." *Ethology and Sociobiology* 10(1–3): 29–50.

———. 1990. "The Past Explains the Present: Emotional Adaptations and the Structure of Ancestral Environments." *Ethology and Sociobiology* 11(4–5): 375–424.

Trivers, Robert L. 1971. "The Evolution of Reciprocal Altruism." *Quarterly Review of Biology* 46: 35–57.

———. 1974. "Parent-Offspring Conflict." *American Zoologist* 14: 249–64.

————. 1976. Foreword. In *The Selfish Gene*, by Richard Dawkins. New York: Oxford University Press.

Weisfeld, Glenn E. 1977. "A Sociobiological Basis for Psychotherapy." In *Ethological Psychiatry: Psychopathology in the Context of Evolutionary Biology*, edited by M. T. McGuire and L. A. Fairbanks. New York: Grune and Stratton.

Wenegrat, B. 1984. *Sociobiology and Mental Disorder: A New View*. Menlo Park, Calif.: Addison-Wesley.

Zahavi, Amotz. 1976. "The Testing of a Bond." *Animal Behaviour* 25(1): 246–47.

Zuk, Gerald H. 1981. *Family Therapy: A Triadic-Based Approach*. Rev. ed. New York: Human Sciences Press.

Chapter 12

Law and the Biology of Commitment

Oliver R. Goodenough

H AS NATURAL selection shaped a human capacity for subjective commitment? This is really not a single question, but many. This chapter will explore a number of these embedded issues, looking to the law as a source of evidence on human psychology. To begin with, what do we mean by commitment? In the evolutionary context the idea grows out of problems in the interaction of separate biological entities. There are often benefits to be gained by all participants from a coordinated action, but achieving coordination presents problems (for example, Dugatkin 1997). A basic difficulty is often illustrated by the game theory example of the prisoner's dilemma (Maynard Smith 1982; Axelrod 1984; Badcock 1997; Dugatkin 1997; Johnstone 1998). To achieve a common good, a risk of sacrifice must be undertaken by one of the players. The other player can choose to achieve a short-term benefit by taking the sacrifice without reciprocating—the all too tempting free rider approach. Solutions to this basic stumbling block have been at the heart of a number of major transitions in evolution (Maynard Smith and Szathmáry 1995) and have occupied a number of evolutionary theorists in biology and their counterparts in economics (for example, Vega-Redondo 1996).

It is becoming clear that cooperative action is not a problem with a single solution, either in theory or in nature itself. The list of established possibilities in animal behavior includes *kin selection*, where the likelihood of genetic identity skews the payoffs to encourage cooperation and "altruism" (Hamilton 1963, 1964; Trivers 1971; Axelrod 1984); *reciprocal altruism*, where players in a repeat game, by establishing reciprocated habits of nondefecting behavior, can produce a relatively stable pattern of cooperation (Trivers 1971; Axelrod 1984; Badcock 1997); *communication and signaling*, where a promise about performance is made to induce the other player to take the step of risk (Zahavi 1975, 1977; Maynard Smith 1991; Johnstone 1997); *hierarchy*, provided that the "skew" in benefit distribution is not too great (Kokko and Johnstone, 1999); and *culturally transmitted expectations and constraints*, which can both reinforce existing mechanisms and establish new cooperative pathways (Boyd and Richerson 1990; Goodenough 1995; Sober and Wilson 1998).

One of the significant problems in signaling—giving a promise of performance to solicit a performance in return—is deceit (for example, Dawkins and Krebs 1978; Rue 1994; Johnstone 1998). The fraudulent inducement of a performance is the free rider's response to a system of signaling. One apparently stable solution to this problem is the use of costly signals. This *handicap principle*, first suggested in the biological context by Zahavi (1975, 1977) and provided with a firm formal grounding by Grafen (1990), has been applied beyond its original context of sexual selection (for example, Møller 1994) into other contexts where signaling can play a role in supporting some form of coordinated activity (for example, Maynard Smith 1991; Zahavi and Zahavi 1997; Johnstone 1997, 1998).

Sometimes the cost of the signal is irretrievable (such as the construction of a peacock's tail) and must simply be put in the balance against the hoped-for gains from the induced behavior. Alternatively, the cost may be partially or fully contingent, only actually expended in the case of a defection. A contingent cost has the decided advantage of allowing the honest signaler to have its cake and eat it too. In either case a costly signal can be seen as a form of commitment—a hard to reverse undertaking to incur a cost or pass up a benefit, which will ensure a benefit for the other party in the interaction if it in turn takes its necessary step. As Hirshleifer (ch. 4 herein) points out, the commitment may promise a benefit, as in the effort of a male bird building a nest to attract a mate (Brooke and Birkhead 1991, 1228), or threaten a harm (Adams, ch. 5 herein), as in avian agonistic displays (Deag and Scott 1999; generally Dawkins and Krebs 1978). In summary, under this kind of approach, a commitment can be seen as a way to support the honesty of a communication of some kind, whether about a current state or future action, and the expectation of result that this engenders can lead to cooperative behavior.

Commitment in Humans

In most animals the potential for commitment as a support for cooperation appears limited to particular behavioral contexts. In humans its scope is greatly enlarged. Humans can make deals about lots and lots of things. The *generalized* ability for commitment to support cooperative interaction is an important aspect of plasticity in human behavior. And just as there are many contexts in which human commitments can be made, humans can support their deal making in lots of ways. People use many techniques of commitment to establish the honesty of a promise. Swearing—that is, invoking Divine punishment if falsity is occurring—may not be common in our contemporary, secular business culture, but taking the name of the Lord in vain was a serious enough concern to rate inclusion in the Mosaic Ten Commandments. Oaths were also an important factor in Roman courts: "The procedure [of relying on oaths] may seem irrational but the taking of a formal oath to the gods was a matter of the utmost solemnity for most Romans. Even the worst rogue would hesitate to perjure himself in such circumstances" (Borkowski 1997, 76). Oath taking is still a primary safeguard of the truthfulness of court testimony in the United States. As a general matter, swearing has the advantage of being wholly contingent in its costs, but it has the downside of being open to the parasitism of nonbelief.

Another formerly honored technique for demonstrating and eliciting commitment in the diplomatic sphere was the exchange of hostages, sometimes used to seal bargains between political leaders in the ancient world (for example, Appian 1912 [c. A.D. 160]; Kelley 1988; see also Schelling, ch. 2 herein). Here too the cost is at least partially contingent. The exchanged relative would live on—sometimes in comfort—provided that the undertaking for peace, support in war, or whatever, was honored. The term *hostage* now generally applies to a compelled taking of captives, a practice illegal under U.S. law (18 U.S.C. 1203). The modern use of certain kinds of security interests and credit instruments (at its most extreme, the "suicide credit") can substitute property and monetary "hostages" as a guaranty of good behavior (generally Steiner 1999).

Even architecture can signal commitment. The cost of the marble palaces built by banks on the most prominent corner in towns around the world constitutes a highly visible pledge of the reliability of the institutions that inhabit them. Consumerism has been linked to costly signaling (Miller 1999). Modern advertising sometimes presents a blank newspaper page with only a tiny corner of text—extravagant "waste" to show quality (Ambler 2000). It will be interesting to see what emerges in the virtual world of electronic commerce as the equivalents of these tokens of tangible security.

Law is another context in which human commitment is manifest. In the Anglo-American legal tradition, for instance, contracts and fiduciary duties reflect somewhat different capacities for commitment. These laws expect that people will make and keep commitments to other people, even at considerable cost to themselves. It seems unlikely, however, that these laws are the original source of this capacity. The law provides a supporting framework for expectations of commitment, but does not create them: law follows the existing promptings of human behavior more often than it leads them. Nonetheless, legal examples demonstrate the benefits that can be gained from subjective commitment and support the arguments that the capacity has been shaped by evolutionary forces. Such examples also suggest that commitment may be particularly useful as a means of supporting cooperation in circumstances where the sharing of the mutualist benefits of coordinated action are sufficiently skewed in their distribution among the players so as to stymie tit-for-tat-style reciprocity.

The discussions of law in this chapter will largely take the legal "data" at face value, providing an introduction to the relevant doctrines on their own terms, as lawyers report and argue them. Although I will not undertake any kind of quantitative survey or other formal analysis of results, I will only use generally recognized legal authority. Such data are not "scientifically" controlled in any traditional sense, but they do represent widely held and cited approaches, which reflect a broadly shared understanding of the psychology and mechanisms depicted. An additional characteristic of legal data is its often anecdotal quality. Although anecdote is proverbially suspect as proof, it can often be legitimately helpful as a tool of explanation and argument (Goodenough 1999). And in the Anglo-American legal system, the cited anecdote of case law is constantly compared back against reality. Those cases that stand the test of time and use in the law become prose formulas, specific abstractions, with probative value that goes beyond their own single example.

Contract Law

The law is full of instances of people using techniques of commitment to establish the honesty of their intentions. The Anglo-American law of contracts is all about this. Contract law institutionalizes reciprocal commitments, providing an outside force to keep the commitment honest. One widely used definition of a contract is: ". . . a promise or set of promises for breach of which the law gives a remedy, or the performance of which the law in some way recognizes as a duty"

(Williston and Lord 1991, 2). The prevailing theory on what should make a contract binding focuses on the importance of holding people to their promises, particularly those promises that elicit some kind of detrimental reliance from the other party. In a classic statement of this idea Fried develops the reliance argument into one of commitment:

> Perhaps the statement of intention in promising is binding because we not only foresee reliance, we invite it: We intend the promisee to rely on the promise. . . . A promise invokes trust in my further actions, not merely in my present sincerity. We need to isolate an additional element, over and above benefit, reliance and the communication of intention. That additional element must *commit* me, and commit me to more than the truth of the statement. (Fried 1981, 11)

An institution affirming such commitment, Fried continues, allows humans to pursue mutual benefit in a cooperative manner:

> More central to our concern is the situation where we facilitate each other's projects, where the gain is reciprocal. Schematically the situation looks like this:
>
>> You want to accomplish purpose A and I want to accomplish purpose B. Neither of us can succeed without the cooperation of the other. Thus I want to be able to commit myself to help you to achieve A so that you will commit yourself to help me achieve B.
>
> Now if A and B are objects or actions that can be transferred simultaneously there is no need for commitment. As I hand over A you hand over B, and we are both satisfied. But very few things are like that. We need a device to permit a trade over time: to allow me to do A for you when you need it, in the confident belief that you will do B for me when I need it. Your commitment puts your further performance into my hands in the present just as my commitment puts my future performance into your hands. A future exchange is transformed into a present exchange. And in order to accomplish this all we need is a conventional device which we both invoke, which you know I am invoking when I invoke it, which I know that you know I am invoking, and so on. (Fried 1981, 13–14)

With its emphasis on commitment as a means for allowing cooperative interchanges to go forward, this approach closely resembles signaling and commitment theory in biology.

Nor is it just contract *theory* that seems to reflect principles of commitment and handicap. The often lengthy process of formal contracting involves costly signaling as well. Negotiating and drafting contracts can be exacting and expensive. The documents for major commercial transactions can run to hundreds of heavily argued pages, and the bill to hundreds of thousands, if not millions, of dollars. On one level, all of this legal care can be seen as a prudent defensive measure, designed to help in litigation if things go astray. Certainly lawyers argue this to their clients. Nonetheless, these very same clients, when facing the legal bill, can condemn the process as a kind of licensed parasitism, with lawyers making the system unduly complicated to divert resources to themselves.

The handicap principle offers yet another explanation. Formal contracting may be a commitment signal, convincing both by its sheer cost and by demonstrating that the client is taking the law—the mechanism for commitment—seriously. To be effective commitment must be recognizable, and in the communication modes of contemporary American business culture there is something just as reassuring in the *fact* of a hard-negotiated, hundred-page agreement as in its *contents*. This signal of commitment can replace the extensive gift giving that is the basis for building trust through reciprocity in some other business cultures. Equally, there can be something very unsettling in trying to do a deal with someone who says, "Oh, I don't worry about the language of the formal agreement. Just have your lawyers type something up and I'll sign it." Lawyers, like many luxury goods, may be conferring their chief benefit by their very cost (for example, Frank 1999; Miller 1999).

In my selection of evidence I have so far confined myself to the Anglo-American tradition, often referred to as the "common law" approach. By training and experience I am not familiar enough with other legal taxa to comment as confidently about them. Evidence in the literature, however, clearly documents contractual systems in the European (Marsh 1994), Chinese (Jones 1994; Brown 1997; Zhao 1997; Zhong and Williams 1998), Japanese (Kawashima 1974) and Islamic (Amin 1986; Comair-Obeid 1996; Pearl 1987) legal traditions, although there is also evidence of variation in just how these conventions play out (for example, Kawashima 1974; Jones 1994). Even if this were not the case, examples from a single legal tradition, like results from studies on a single animal species or from a single ethnography in anthropology, can still be helpful to this part of our question. If one tradition shows these properties, then clearly they are within the *capacity* of humans. A single bird species can demonstrate the possibility of animal flight, even though other species, such as the ostrich, may show that flight is not universal to all birds.

Distinguishing *Subjective* Commitment

The Anglo-American law of contract illustrates at least one context in which humans use a kind of commitment to signal the honesty of their promises. Contractual commitments have an objective, transactional nature, however, that distinguishes them from the kind of commitments we are searching for in this volume: the question posed is whether humans have a capacity for *subjective* commitment. Most of the forms of commitment discussed so far, whether within or outside the law, are matters of objective fact and calculation, set in contexts of reciprocity—what Frank (ch. 3 herein) calls *contractual commitments*. If you have clear legal recourse for a debt, or my brother as a hostage for my good behavior, my subjective mental state about what you are asking me to do is relatively unimportant, beyond the question of whether or not I would view the loss of my brother or the invocation of the law as a significant cost. As the saying went during the Vietnam war, overtly calling on the male calculus of reproductive success, "if you have them by the balls, their hearts and minds will follow" (variously attributed, for example, *Forbes* 1995; Ibison 1996; Dynes 1997; McPhedran 1997).

But will they? One of the paradoxes of humans is that they appear to have "hearts and minds" that will commit emotionally—to people, to places, to faiths, to abstract ideals—in ways that confound this cost-and-benefit-ensured realism. As Luther's great hymn has been translated into English:

> Let goods and kindred go, this mortal life also.
> The body they may kill. God's truth abideth still.
> His kingdom is forever. (Luther 1529)

Stirring words—but do we really have a capacity for such selflessness in the cause of a subjective commitment? Is Luther's commitment only a discounting of heavenly bliss against short-term worldly sacrifice, or does it reflect a more complex human trait? Can such a commitment operate outside of the contexts of classical reciprocity? And can the step be an internal one, where the only cost put at risk is in the subjective coin of personal honor, self-image, and character? In light of these questions two linked factors can differentiate a subjective commitment from the workaday world of the objective pledge.

The first embodies notions of duration and true immutability of purpose. The commitment is not just transactional, tied to a particular cost-benefit calculation. The law of fiduciary duties, in its relatively mundane way, suggests that such a higher standard of commitment can be expected and supported in human interactions. The second, perhaps harder, element is the internal nature of the promise. Although cost-benefit concerns about reputation may play a part, and such cultural props as legal penalties may help support the decision, in a truly subjective commitment the holder of the pledge will be the psychology of the pledge giver. Paradoxically, the possibility of an evolutionary reward for such a capacity of self-policing honesty may well depend on the ability of its possessor to send a hard-to-cheat signal of its existence. Law—particularly in its practice—may offer insights on this point as well.

Fiduciary Duties

Fiduciary duties is a label applied in the law to a cluster of requirements for selfless behavior. The unifying theme is that someone must put his or her selfish goals aside and work instead for the benefit of another person or institution. The classic example of someone owing fiduciary duties is the trustee of a trust. Among these duties is the requirement for loyalty by the trustee. As one treatise puts it, "The trustee owes a duty to the beneficiaries to administer the affairs of the trust solely in the interests of the beneficiaries, and to exclude from consideration his own advantages and the welfare of third persons. This is called the duty of loyalty" (Bogert 1987, 341). In such a circumstance all of the trustee's conduct

> . . . which has any bearing on the affairs of the trust must be actuated by consideration of the welfare of the beneficiaries and them alone. He is in a position of such intimacy with those he is representing and has such great control over their property that a higher standard is established by the court of equity than would prevail in the case of an ordinary business relation. (341–42)

One result of this rule is to disallow transactions between the trustee and the trust itself, such as buying or selling real estate, or investing the trust's assets in the trustee's enterprises. Here the law steps in to help prevent selfishness.

> It is a well-known quality of human nature that it is extremely difficult, or perhaps impossible, for an individual to act fairly in the interests of others whom he represents and at the same time to consider his own financial advantage. In most cases, consciously or unconsciously, he will tend to make a choice which is favorable to himself, regardless of its effect on those for whom he is supposed to be acting. (342)

Fiduciary duties arise elsewhere in society. The old saying that "a public office is a public trust" reflects expectations that our elected officials are supposed to meet (for example, Coffee 1998, n188 and related text). Fiduciary duties are also recognized in business. Partners in a business partnership or in a joint venture, for instance, have been held to owe each other a particularly demanding loyalty. The classic, often cited formulation of this duty was propounded in the case of *Meinhard v. Salmon*, a tale worth telling in some detail.

Walter J. Salmon was in the real estate business in New York City. In 1902 he leased the northwest corner of Forty-second Street and Fifth Avenue from Louisa M. Gerry for a term of twenty years. The corner was occupied then by the Hotel Bristol. Salmon undertook to convert the hotel into shops and offices. He needed cash—$200,000— to make the conversion, and either by choice or necessity sought half the required amount from Morton H. Meinhard. Meinhard was not himself in real estate—he made his money as a woolen merchant. In return for his investment Meinhard was to receive 40 percent of the net profits from the project for the first five years of the lease and 50 percent thereafter. Salmon, as the real estate specialist, would provide all the management for the property (*Meinhard v. Salmon* 1928, 461–62).

During the early years, the building was operated at a loss. By the end of the lease, as New York boomed, this had completely turned around: "[T]he profits became large, with the result that for each of the investors there came a rich return. For each, the venture had its phases of fair weather and of foul. The two were in it jointly, for better or for worse" (*Meinhard v. Salmon* 1928, 462). The court characterized the two as "coadventurers," and held that they owed each other "fiduciary duties akin to those of partners" (462). There was no question that Salmon treated Meinhard fairly during these years.

In 1921 the lease was nearing its end, and the property was due to revert to Elbridge T. Gerry, presumably a relative of Louisa Gerry, who was now its owner. Gerry also owned neighboring properties along Fifth Avenue and Forty-second Street and thought that he could arrange better terms if he packaged the holdings together into a single lease of greater size. The existing buildings could be torn down, and something bigger and better built in their place. After negotiating unsuccessfully with a number of possible developers, in January 1922 Gerry approached Salmon with the deal. They quickly came to an agreement, and Salmon set up Midpoint Realty Company to carry out the project. A new multiyear lease was signed on January 25, 1922. It included a commitment to build a new building, costing at least $3 million, no later than seven years into the lease term. During the negotiation of this new agreement, no one said anything about it to Meinhard. Only in February did the news reach him, and then he demanded to be included in the new project. When Salmon refused, Meinhard sued, asking to take over a 50 percent share of the deal.

The question was whether Salmon owed Meinhard, by the nature of the commitment between them, not only the fair share of the existing project, but also the right to share in any new opportunity that might arise for the property as well. The case was heard on appeal by a panel lead by Benjamin N. Cardozo, one of the most famous—and eloquent—American jurists of his time. To him, Salmon's commitment was enduring and demanding:

> Joint adventurers, like copartners, owe to one another, while the enterprise continues, the duty of finest loyalty. Many forms of conduct permissible in a workaday world for those acting at arm's length, are forbidden to those bound by fiduciary ties. A trustee is held to something stricter than the morals of the marketplace. Not honesty alone, but the punctilio of an honor the most sensitive, is then the standard of behavior. As to this there has developed a tradition that is unbending and inveterate. (*Meinhard v. Salmon* 1928, 458)

Held to this standard, Salmon's failure to disclose the possibility of the new project, and to give Meinhard a chance to come in on it, breached the duty to Meinhard, and the majority of the court directed Salmon to cut Meinhard in on half the deal.

There was a minority view. Judge Andrews, joined by two others, felt that Salmon had lived up to his duties. Meinhard had received the benefit of his bargain with Salmon: fair treatment and a good profit during the term of the original lease. The promise made by Salmon to Meinhard was transactional, not open-ended. The offer of the new lease—which Salmon had not solicited and which covered a much larger property—was not sufficiently connected with this existing deal to give Meinhard a stake in it (*Meinhard v. Salmon* 1928, 550–52). The dissent did not question that duties were owed; rather it saw them as having been satisfied by the fair treatment in the expected context.

Cardozo's approach illustrates the understanding in the common law that partners have made a special kind of commitment to each other. It requires not just living up to a specific deal, but also an open-ended putting forward of the interests of another. Whether in the context of trusts or business ventures, fiduciary duties describe a requirement for self-denial that goes beyond the "workaday" calculus of expected reciprocity. This looks like a version of the expanded selflessness that makes up the first element of subjective commitment suggested here.

Law as Evidence for Natural Selection

The law contains evidence of the presence of both objective and subjective commitment in human affairs. Even if we take the capacities as established, however, the ultimate question posed in this book remains to be answered: Is the capacity for subjective commitment in humans shaped by natural selection? Using such a culturally grounded system as law to support conclusions about the biological foundations of human behavior presents challenges. More typically, legal scholars have used behavioral traits with an established evolutionary basis to help understand law (for example, Gruter 1991; Fikentscher 1992; Elliott 1997; Jones 1997; Goodenough 1997b; Hanna 1999). Such scholarship has sought insights about the biological underpinnings of our behavior to help inform the cultural construct of the law. At its best this work uses animal comparison and evolutionary reasoning to provide working hypotheses, supporting evidence, and an intellectual framework for investigation into the species-typical characteristics of humans. Less helpfully, comparison and theory can be offered by themselves as "proof" that some postulated trait must exist in humans (sometimes without much concern about whether or not the trait is actually observed), and that the trait has immutable roots in our evolved, genetic nature (for a discussion of this problem, see Emlen 1995). The significant behavioral differences between our two closest primate relatives, chimps and bonobos (for example, de Waal 1997), and the astonishing variability of evolutionary solutions generally, remind us of the dangers of offering any particular example of animal behavior as proof for some aspect of human nature. The proper challenge is to develop and use a solid, biologically grounded model of the conduct of our own species, a true *human* zoology. The investigation into a capacity for subjective commitment undertaken in this volume is part of just such an undertaking.

In this endeavor we are using a different kind of reasoning. We are looking at specifically human data, in this case legal, to help understand the existence and source of certain kinds of specifically human behavior. Does the capacity for subjective commitment exist in people and, if so, is it rooted in the biological end of our motivational spectrum? This chapter will suggest two paths to such inferences. The first approach relies on somewhat speculative, commonsense starting points; the second proposes a more objective set of criteria—including comparison and theory as part of the mix—for evaluating the role of natural selection in human legal behavior. Neither of these approaches is as rigorous as hypothesis testing under controlled conditions—other chapters in this book explore the possibilities of that kind of work (for example, Cohen and Vandello, ch. 8 herein). Nonetheless, in the study of animal behavior there is always a role for both fieldwork and lab experimentation, and in human zoology the law represents a rich, if somewhat idiosyncratic, pool of data on the wild behavior of Homo sapiens.

What Legal Facts Tell Us About Natural Selection: Two Propositions

The first approach to using law to explore our questions about the source of human commitment rests on a pair of propositions about the relationship of legal rules and institutions to the cultural and biological basis for human action. These propositions, while by no means proved, draw on appealing notions of parsimony and common sense. To get to biological evolution, we must first ask whether law itself has created the commitment expectations found in contracts and fiduciary duties. Purely legal structures could follow excellent evolutionary logic—indeed it would be surprising if they did not. The first proposition, however, opposes this view.

Proposition One. Law—and particularly the common law—follows the preexistent promptings of human expectation more often than it leads them. Although this proposition has long antecedents (for example, Maine 1861; Holmes 1991 [1881]; Goodenough 1995, 1996, 1997a; see also Gewirtz 1996), it is by no means uncontroversial (see, for example, Madow 1993).

Whatever the value of the opposing view on some issues, however, a leading role for law seems unlikely for these propensities of commitment. In the Anglo-American tradition the place of commitment in the common law reflects a historical process of discovery and development rather than a legislative initiative. Indeed when legislators and academic drafting committees get hold of these doctrines, they seem more interested in containing and diluting the standard of commitment than in inventing and expanding it. The most recent version of the Uniform Partnership Act (1997), for instance, starts its discussion of fiduciary duties in §404(a) with the language of limitation: "The only fiduciary duties a partner owes to the partnership and the other partners are the duty of loyalty and the duty of care set forth in subsections (b) and (c)." This pattern continues in the specifics: "(b) A partner's duty of loyalty to the partnership and the other partners is limited to the following. . . ." Although the content of the subsequent rules in this formulation still resembles Cardozo's, the spirit of enthusiastic leadership on the issue seems decidedly lacking.

If law is not the original source for human commitment rules, where do they come from? Cultural inheritance could still be the source of the observed capacity for commitment. One of the imperative roles of culture—whether formalized in law or felt in our prelegal behavioral intuitions (Goodenough 1997a)—is to provide us with buffers against and patches around some of our less happy biological inheritance. Culture may well be the source of much of our cooperative ability (for example, Boyd and Richerson 1990; Goodenough 1995; Wright 2000). Culture certainly *manifests* systems for making and recognizing commitments; still, is it the root of these systems? Here we are finally at the nub: Has our capacity for commitment been shaped by natural selection on the biological level? The fact that we see it in culture is hardly dispositive; in dealing with our evolved, precultural nature, culture can be indifferent to its predilections and promptings, it can seek to suppress them, or it can seek to work with and support them. What is the case with commitment?

I do not advocate that the law is or should be some kind of reflection of the current state of our biological predilections on social matters. Law and culture can help to suppress "natural" predilections that may be thought destructive, cruel, or otherwise undesirable. Even when doing so, however, they may well be building on *other* predilections to achieve the result. The fact that contracting and fiduciary behavior stand in opposition to some of our more "antisocial" tendencies toward greed, acquisitiveness, and deception does not mean that they are not in their turn evolutionarily grounded. Indeed the selfish tendencies find expression in the law as well. Property, for instance, helps support the egocentric exclusion of others from a particular resource. But one of the most important advances of modern evolutionary thinking is the understanding that evolution is as much about finding solutions to cooperative opportunities as it is about red-in-tooth-and-claw competition. As the theoretical work cited at the beginning of this chapter demonstrates, the tension between the prosocial and the pro-individual is played out across biological evolution. There are plenty of evolved psychological propensities for culture and the law to recruit on both sides of the problem. Biology is as likely to be the cooperative hero (if your thinking goes that way on the social-individual tension) as the antisocial villain.

Based in considerations of parsimony and the talent of both evolution and the law for recycling and reinforcing existing mechanisms for new uses (for example, Holmes 1881; Elliott 1986; see generally Richerson and Boyd 1989), I suggest the following.

Proposition Two. When shaping prosocial rules, culture and its legal expression are likely to recruit and amplify existing human prosocial capabilities. For instance, kin selection is recruited in the military to create fictive family bonds inside a unit (Goodenough 1995, 309; Badcock 1986, 139). While culture may be able to construct entirely new motivational mechanisms in the human brain, the deeply felt emotional underpinning we find in commitment seems a matter of recruitment. A good reading of Rawls (1972) may stir our intellect, but it is unlikely to drive us into a motivational frenzy of prosocial enthusiasm.

A system of considered ethics is not where most legal structures are grounded at a behaviorally effective level.

These two propositions, taken together, suggest that the objective commitment of contract law and the more subjective commitment of fiduciary duties both have their roots in our evolved nature. This conclusion, however, like its premises, depends on relatively common-sensical propositions about how law and culture work. This kind of approach needs further evidentiary support before it can be firmly asserted.

What Legal Facts Can Tell Us About Natural Selection: Three Criteria

A second possible program for assessing the precultural origins of human behavior rests on three relatively objective criteria. While none of the following considerations are in themselves probative, taken together they can be persuasive.

Is the Trait Observed Broadly in Humans?

It is reasonable to expect that widely practiced human behaviors are more likely to be rooted in our evolved past than are rare behaviors (for example, Singer 2000). Similarly, locally idiosyncratic traits are more likely to come from the promptings of that culture than are widely shared practices. Cross-cultural comparison, however, is not a complete answer to our question: cultures can both widely suppress evolved traits and widely create similar, evolutionarily stable behavioral answers to opportunities or problems. Furthermore, the evolved tool kit can contain a broad range of possible conduct, the expression of which may be environmentally triggered. The presence of a trait in only a few cultures might simply reflect the rarity of the necessary environmental cues rather than the cultural source of the behavior. As a matter of probability, however, broadly observed behavior is more likely to be part of a biologically based, species-typical repertoire than is rarely observed activity.

Is the Trait Observed in Other Animals?

Again, this is suggestive but not dispositive. On the side of caution, different animals can separately evolve similar responses to similar problems, and what animals have evolved biologically, humans can have arrived at through mechanisms of culture. Nonetheless, the presence of a trait in other, presumably noncultural, species confirms that a path through biological evolution is possible. In this comparative exercise looking at our closer animal kin can be particularly interesting. Harvey and Pagel (1991, 38) suggest that phylogenetically related species are more likely—although by no means guaranteed—to be similar in their responses to similar environmental situations. Applied to our problem, this suggests that if we find the trait in near relatives as a result of biological evolution, then we are more likely also to have come to it in the same way. Looking farther afield, however, also has its advantages: if we see cooperative behavior supported by commitment in species at some evolutionary distance from our own, it can help as an antidote to the anthropomorphizing that can afflict comparisons with our primate kin. Furthermore, assumptions that primate social behavior is not also culturally grounded are more and more open to question (for example, Whiten et al. 1999; de Waal 1999).

Is Selection for the Trait Supported in Evolutionary Theory?

This is to some degree a matter of avoiding the impossible. It is difficult to posit an evolutionary origin for a trait that seems to fly in the face of evolutionary theory. On the other hand, the stretching of evolutionary logic to cover almost any possible scenario occurs with some regularity in behavioral zoology. For instance, the handicap principle has been invoked to explain how both emphasizing and minimizing size and ability can be adaptive (Zahavi and Zahavi 1997); this may be justified, but it smacks of having it both ways. The widely used metaphor of the "just-so story" has its basis in reality. But evolutionary theory, applied with some rigor, restraint, and parsimony, is capable of making useful—if still weak—predictions about people. Productive traits that can evolve often seem to do so, and the repeated evolution of cooperative solutions has been charted (Maynard Smith and Szathmáry 1995). And even more important, the logic of a hypothesis like subjective commitment can be tested through such tools as game theory. The work of Grafen (1990) on the handicap principle demonstrates the utility of rigorously testing the theoretical basis of an evolutionary proposition.

Of course, the predictions of evolutionary theory are only as useful as the premises for applying the theory were accurate. If the process involves harking back to some kind of posited ancient environment, whose details are provided by reasoning backward from current observation, the possibility for putting a gloss of natural selection on our current cultural presumptions is particularly strong.

In seeking for evolutionarily predicted solutions to the problems of human sociality we must recall that evolutionary logic can apply to the development of cultural systems and traits as well. The ability to create and transmit culture can itself be seen as an evolved, biological response to selective pressures (for example, Laland et al., forthcoming). At this level even wholly cultural practices have a basis in natural selection. Indeed one could question the entire culture versus evolution distinction underlying the discussions of natural selection and the capacity for commitment in this book. The simple answer for any believer in both evolutionary theory and a capacity for subjective commitment is that the latter *must* be based in the former.

Applying the Three Criteria to the Law of Commitment

The objective, transactional commitment of contract law looks a strong candidate for natural selection under the three-part approach. Contracting is observed widely across a variety of cultures and back into history. Commitment-based signaling following a contractual logic has been described in a variety of other species (Johnstone 1998). The theoretical discussions of contract law and evolutionary science are highly congruent, indeed so closely related that the possible infection of evolutionary theory by legal ideas seems a caution worth remembering. But what about the more subjective, open-ended commitment that appears to inform fiduciary duties? Here the answers are less clear-cut, and further work could profitably be done on each of the three tests.

Cross-Cultural Comparison

Fiduciary duties, or their equivalent, are less easily identified cross-culturally than are contractual ones. The Anglo-American concept of a trust has been seen as idiosyncratic and hard for lawyers outside the common-law tradition to grasp (Sonneveldt 1992). Other scholars, however, have pointed to widespread equivalents to the trust in other systems, and to the use of fiduciary concepts in these equivalents (for example, Lupoi 1999). Interesting parallels exist in Islamic law. At a general level the Qur'an states: "God doth command you to render back your Trusts to those to whom they are due" (S.iv.58). The waqf may provide a parallel to holding property in trust (Gerholm 1985, 131–33; Pearl 1987, 194ff., Schoenblum 1999, passim), and evidence exists for the presence of fiduciary duty in Islamic family law (Pearl and Menski 1998, 425–26), although this may also reflect the preconceptions of the British reporters of the phenomenon. On the basis of this brief survey, some positive evidence shows that this kind of trait exists in different cultures. Further comparative work would clarify the picture.

Comparison with Other Species

In the second test, looking at other species, there is an abundant literature on at least one kind of long-term commitment: the pair-bonding of reproductive couples. Reproductive pair-bonding is widespread in birds (Lack 1968); it is also found in a variety of other animals, including mammals (Kleiman 1977; Goosens et al. 1998) and, in a fashion, fish (for example, Reavis and Barlow 1998). Evidence has even been found for multiseasonal polygynous fidelity in grey seals (Amos et al. 1995). This picture of widespread commitment is clouded by the relative frequency of extra-pair breeding (for example, Goosens et al. 1998; Johnson et al. 1998; Otter et al. 1998) and by the compulsory element of mate guarding in many pairings (for example, Johnson et al. 1998; Watts 1998; Feh 1999). In some ways the persistence of long-lasting social monogamy in the face of these failures is more surprising than the failures themselves, and is suggestive of a kind of commitment mechanism that transcends a short-term strategy of tit-for-tat-style benefit.

A growing literature describes relatively long-lasting coalitions in other zoological contexts. Cooperative bonds have been reported in female primates (Chapais 1992; Datta 1992); female bonobos (de Waal 1997); male baboons (Noë 1992); male chimps (de Waal 1992; Nishida and Hosaka 1996; Watts 1998); dolphins (Conner et al. 1992); and hyaenas (Zabel et al. 1992). Partnering for mate guarding and dominance among males has been observed in chimps (de Waal 1992; Watts 1998). An example in horses has been recently reported in *Animal Behaviour* (Feh 1999); the story it tells stands as a complement to the history of Meinhard and Salmon.

Since 1974 a herd of horses has ranged relatively wildly over a 740-acre pasture in the marshes of the Camargue, a coastal region of southern France. Starting with fourteen horses, the herd peaked at ninety-four in 1981. Since 1980 horses have been removed from time to time to prevent overgrazing, and they have received no supplemental feeding or veterinary care. Over the years the horses have been intensively observed. Careful behavioral records have been kept; the horses have been weighed twice a week since 1979; blood tests have established reliable paternity records. Within the herd, most horses live in smaller family groups, made up of one or two adult males and a variable number of females and their colts. A "bachelor" group of unattached males is part of the herd as well.

Feh's report focuses on the reproductive strategies of thirteen stallions from the herd. They were tracked from birth to ages ranging from eleven to fourteen years. Thanks to the blood tests, exact results of the varying strategies could be determined. As the stallions came to breeding age at about four years old, they would first try to monopolize a group of mares on their own, although few succeeded in the first try at this approach. At this stage two options were available: they could join the bachelor group and hope to mate with otherwise attached mares in "sneaks," or they could form a two-male group with another stallion—a kind of equine partnership—with enough combined authority to prevent incursions by other stallions and to keep the mares in the group. A total of ten of the thirteen started such partnerships. For six of them, it was a temporary measure, lasting only a few years until the individual path was tried again. For the other four, the bond was more permanent; one pairing lasted sixteen years and ended only with the death of one of the stallions. Stallions showed no significant tendency to pair up with near relations, although, given the makeup of the herd, most horses were related to some degree.

Each pair had a dominant and subordinate partner. Typically the subordinate did the greater share of the defensive fighting and also sired a smaller share of the foals. Nonetheless, for both horses in a permanent partnership, the reproductive payoff of teaming up as opposed to a life of sneaks was clear. Although each member of a pair had fewer foals, on average, than a single stallion leading a family group, their reproductive rate was considerably higher than that of the bachelors depending on sneak copulations for their chance to sire offspring. Moreover, while the dominant did rather better than twice as well as the subordinate in siring foals, the subordinate still did rather better than three times as well as the bachelors (Feh 1999, 710 and fig. 2). In addition, foals raised in groups with paired stallions in alliances proved more successful in survival after birth (711).

The stability of one of these long-term partner bonds was tested by the researchers when they arranged a new breeding opportunity. Four thirteen-year-old stallions were removed from the herd and introduced to six new mares, previously unknown to them. After twenty-one minutes of relative mayhem, the situation settled down. One of the stallions, the most dominant in the prior group, had set up with three mares on his own. The second most dominant ended up a bachelor—his same status as before. The two least dominant, partners in the prior herd, had teamed up again in a group with the other three mares. There was an interesting wrinkle on this renewed partnership, however, fully captured in the filming of the release done by the experimenters. As Feh (1999) relates:

For the first 15 min., the subordinate alliance stallion tried to monopolize a mare on his own without participating in the defense of the dominant's mares against the other stallions. In the 16th minute, the dominant attacked the subordinate repeatedly, tearing out part of his lip.
From this moment on, the subordinate cooperated in the defense of the
mares.

Feh suggests that this represents coercion by the dominant in the
alliance, forcing the subordinate into cooperation, and in a sense it
must. But perhaps there is evidence of something more. The apparent
ferocity of the response, and the fact that it was directed at a defecting
partner, suggest something akin to the fury of Meinhard when Salmon cut him out of the new deal at Forty-second Street and Fifth. At
the risk of anthropomorphizing, was there some kind of generalized
expectation of cooperation between these two horses, something that
went beyond a particular set of transactions and represented a kind of
subjective commitment, enforced with savage indignation when the
junior partner tried to quit and set up on his own? Whatever the case,
the reestablished partnership persisted both during the three months
spent in the new small group and after reintegration of the stallions
into the herd together with their old mares. It is only one story, but an
intriguing one.

Evolutionary Theory

Can this idea of subjective commitment find support in evolutionary
theory? Cooper and Wallace (1998) demonstrate that forming fixed
partnerships in a repeat game yields a significant advantage. It is a
plausible next step, and the job both of this volume and future research, to explore and map the evolutionary pathways to a generalized, psychologically subjective commitment. The psychological
agents that could support this strategy in humans are well worth
tracking down as well. Presumably the committed state needs both to
exist and be recognized to reap its full benefits (for example, Irons, ch.
13 herein). Perhaps the ability for subjective commitment is linked to
a particular kind of niche—such as the two-stallion breeding group or
other mate-guarding alliance—that needs a long-term mechanism of
cooperation that will outlast the day-to-day computations of flawed,
disproportionate reciprocity. Cases have shown—the stallions among
them—that cooperation can remain mutually advantageous, even
though the increased benefits are skewed enough that tit-for-tat-style
reciprocity becomes a hard pathway to its success (for example, Noë
1992; Kokko and Johnstone 1999). Human societies, which often contain significant stratification, may reflect this pattern, relying on
methods in addition to reciprocity and coercion for maintaining order

and coordinated action. It may not be so much a social contract as a social commitment that binds us together in our cooperative tasks.

Whether observed across whole societies or in more specialized roles requiring and requiting trust, human examples can demonstrate the utility of something akin to subjective commitment as a means to gaining access to a small but still attractive piece of a greatly expanded, cooperative pie. One such instance may be the role of lawyers themselves, an example that also provides hints about the final step in our examination of subjective commitment: the possibility of a purely internal mechanism for committed action.

The Attorney Niche: Profiting from the Internal Bargain of Subjective Commitment

The specialized role of lawyers in society suggests that there can be profitable niches, at least among humans, for those with a generalized, internal commitment to a role of self-restraint. Of course, the role of the attorney is not just a matter of personal integrity. The law strongly supports the lawyer's commitment to selflessness. To begin with, attorneys under the U.S. legal system owe fiduciary duties to their clients. Other than the significant exception of the fee they are to earn (for example, New York State Bar Association (1999), DR 2–106), the Lawyer's Code of Professional Responsibility has a number of provisions requiring attorneys to put their clients' interests before their own (for example, New York State Bar Association, EC 5-1 to 5-24, DR 5-101 to 5-109). A general statement of this requirement is set forth in Ethical Consideration 5-1:

> EC 5-1. The professional judgment of a lawyer should be exercised, within the bounds of the law, solely for the benefit of the client and free of compromising influences and loyalties. Neither the lawyer's personal interests, the interests of other clients, nor the desires of third persons should be permitted to dilute the lawyer's loyalty to the client.

This role is further supported by the law of agency, which provides that agents (in this case attorneys) generally owe fiduciary duties to their principals (in this case clients) (Restatement [Second] of Agency §§13, 387–98). Noncompliance with these stated rules may result in severe penalties; but penalty is not the only mechanism supporting the behavior of lawyers. Commitment also plays a part.

The American legal profession sends costly, hard-to-counterfeit signals of objective commitment, starting with the process of becoming a lawyer. Law school, a prerequisite for admission in most states, takes three years and costs nearly $100,000 for many students. Loans are available, meaning that many graduate with the equivalent of a home mortgage to support. For those who end up in debt, the cost is a direct personal sacrifice, borne for years, and not some kind of parental indulgence. Next is the hurdle of the bar exam, a demanding test that comes at the end of ten weeks of nonstop cramming (Grant 1998). The barriers to entry into the profession are sometimes vilified as a way to restrict the market, particularly daunting to those traditionally oppressed in American society (for example, Johnson 1997). While such criticisms have merit, these kinds of hurdles can also provide a context in which reasonably honest signaling is possible. The high price and restrictions on entry, like the bank's marble building, represent significant sunk costs that stand to be lost if there is defection and deceit (see Spence 1974).

So far, however, the argument goes more to objective commitment—the kind that a particular costly external handicap can support. But this calculus of handicap versus defection is not the only bulwark that professionalism provides against attorney cheating. There is substantial evidence that the legal system has energetically sought to create and recruit forms of subjective commitment as part of a creed of "altruistic" professionalism (for example, Abel 1990; Shepard 1997). There is also good evidence that the success of this effort is mixed at best, and that the whole approach has been open to question and attack in recent years (for example, Pearce 1996; Wendel 1999). Nonetheless, the public affirmation of an ethic of subjective commitment may be an important element, working with other mechanisms, in establishing and maintaining the perception of trustworthiness that transactional lawyers, despite all the jokes, must sustain if they are to play their role in the business of society.

Although purely a personal observation, based on more than twenty years in the law, I am convinced that many, many lawyers hold a real, deeply felt dedication to client service. For every crooked lawyer who loots the client funds entrusted to him, there are hundreds who live up to the expectation of honest dealing. To dismiss the subjective understanding of this ideal shared by so many lawyers as mere self-deception seems needlessly cynical and motivationally selective. It would also be too idealistic to deny that the capacity for such commitment can be beneficial in the long run to those who possess and demonstrate it. Finding the middle ground between these two errors is necessary in all of our attempts to place "altruistic" human behavior into the context of evolutionary analysis. On the one hand, the proximate psychological mechanisms for prosocial activity should not be sneeringly dismissed by evolutionary science as delusional or impossible. On the other, such mechanisms should not be romantically detached from our evolved nature or from the underlying requirements of replication and selection that must be solved over and over again by all living things. The challenge is to find the dynamics that make such positions reconcilable.

By publicly requiring a commitment to trustworthiness, and activating through education and other means the subjective mechanisms of most lawyers to adhere to this commitment, the profession has helped to maintain a status in society that so far has withstood the buffets of the all-too-inevitable defectors. Let me illustrate this with a *completely* subjective example. Some years ago, as a very junior attorney I was once personally responsible for routing approximately $200 million in loan proceeds from one bank account to another. The months of negotiation were over; the hundreds of pages of documentation signed and sealed in at least two languages. Very senior and experienced attorneys had worked on the deal through these stages. All that remained was a final set of notices to come to the clients of the firm for which I worked and for instructions to be sent about where and when to transmit the money through an interbank transfer. Seeing to these final steps fell to me. The upshot was that all the money would go where I directed it, when I directed it. My job required little skill—comparing a few pieces of paper to the required model, getting a few banking details right, and sending the right messages to the right people. What was required was trust, both in this little skill and in the fact that I would exercise it selflessly. At the time this seemed perfectly ordinary—who else would they trust to handle it? I do not relate this story to impress anyone with my probity: in Wall Street practice this kind of attorney role is not at all unusual. The obstacles to any attempt to abscond with the money were significant, of course, and penalties for failure severe; nonetheless, they were not the active impediment. As my employers confidently expected, defection wasn't psychologically possible.

This perceived and practiced subjective commitment to trustworthiness is one of the things that allow lawyers to occupy profitable niches in the commitment strategies of others. This benefit to the lawyers is recognized in the Preamble to the Lawyer's Code of Professional Responsibility:

> But in the last analysis it is the desire for the respect and confidence of the members of the profession and of the society which the lawyer serves that should provide to a lawyer the incentive for the highest possible degree of ethical conduct. The possible loss of that respect and confidence is the ultimate sanction. So long as its practitioners are

guided by these principles, the law will continue to be a noble profession. This is its greatness and its strength, which permit of no compromise. (New York State Bar Association 1999)

The role, whatever its nobility, is not self-sacrificial. Whatever its psychological basis, the long-term benefits of the attorney niche can be significant. Like the subordinate horse in a Camargue pairing, the share from the cooperative benefit may be smaller than that accruing to the dominant/client, but it is more than the attorney would earn without playing a role. And unlike the subordinate stallion, a successful attorney can take a piece of many, many opportunities. Indeed the greater the attorney's fidelity to one client, the more she or he can likely earn from providing this service to others. Whether through commitment, reputation, or a combination of the two, one good job invites the next. Even so, defection is probably "rational" at many points in a legal career. In retrospect, giving me at age twenty-six even relatively brief control over $200 million looks pretty remarkable. The payoff from a successful defection would have been hugely more than the sum benefit that I could ever achieve as a lawyer, even had I stayed a relatively prosperous Wall Street attorney. My probity, however, was taken for granted by everyone—including myself. Had I successfully signaled subjective commitment to my employers, and they to their clients? It takes the kind of "hands off no matter what" commitment of the attorneys, bankers, and others involved, a commitment both held and communicated, to keep the wheels of a sophisticated system of finance turning (for example, Black 1997). The lack of a body of intermediaries with such a dependable ethic is one of the stumbling blocks, along with a lack of contract enforcement, to faster economic development in emerging economies such as Russia (for example, Fox and Heller 1999). On the other hand, the fee to my then firm from the overall transaction in which I transferred the $200 million was in all probability well into the six figures, and my own salary was more than generous.

In humans at least, the niche for truly committed, reliable players in repeat cooperative games can be very comfortable. Is this something more generally applicable across evolution? Where there is a large potential benefit from cooperative activity, and yet a sizable skew in the distribution of that benefit, a mechanism for a tit-for-tat kind of reciprocity may actually destroy long-range cooperation. It would not be surprising to find that evolution had constructed stable pathways to such a niche in the psyches of humans and other animals, pathways that in humans may well include the kind of commitment we call fiduciary duties. So far, however, I can bring from the law only the beginnings of the evidence that must be offered in the argument that our psychological pathways include a capacity for making, keeping, and communicating a fully internal bargain, and that such a capacity is rooted in our evolved nature. Indeed the existence of the external, coercive structure of the law, fully engaged on these matters, suggests that any such internal pathways will at best be subject to periodic failure and parasitism. Nonetheless, examples of a dynamic balance between internal and external mechanisms of human commitment are not evidence that one or the other domain does not exist.

The phrase *the selfish gene* is a brilliant shorthand for *one* of the postulates of modern Darwinism, but it is *not* a statement of unavoidable destiny for evolutionary systems. Contemporary science understands that the history of evolution is as much about finding solutions to cooperative opportunities as it is about red-in-tooth-and-claw competition. Science has identified a number of mechanisms through which such solutions can occur, among them techniques of commitment and handicap. Evidence from the law supports the idea that at least one element of what we might call subjective commitment—an extended, open-ended selflessness—can be distinguished as its own part of the solution in humans. This evidence is consistent with the further idea that this capacity has a basis in natural selection, although arguments drawn from legal data about evolutionary processes must be carefully made and evaluated. The law also helps to illustrate the benefits that such a commitment can bring, and suggests that it can help to support forms of mutualism and cooperation where the distribution of benefits is sufficiently skewed that they could not be supported by the more evenhanded requirements of traditional reciprocity.

As to the last step in the chain of a truly subjective commitment, examples drawn from the law in this chapter are suggestive about the existence of an evolved mechanism in humans for making, keeping, and communicating wholly internal commitment steps. Further study in the law may yet supply more compelling evidence on this element of the problem.

I am particularly grateful for the support and intellectual nurturing of the Gruter Institute for Law and Behavioral Research, for the generous sabbatical policies of Vermont Law School, and for the hospitality and resources of the Department of Zoology and the Faculty of Law at the University of Cambridge, all important factors in allowing this piece to be written. The insightful comments of Kevin Laland, Randolph Nesse, and Jack Hirshleifer on earlier drafts of this chapter are also gratefully acknowledged.

References

Abel, Richard L. 1990. "Taking Professionalism Seriously." *1989 Annual Survey of American Law*: 41–63.

Ambler, Tim. 2000. "Advertisers Should Seek to Increase Wastage." *Admap* (February): 14–17.

Amin, Sayed Hassan. 1986. *Commercial Law of Iran*. Tehran: Vahid Publications.

Amos, Bill, Sean Twiss, Paddy Pomeroy, and Sheila Anderson. 1995. "Evidence for Mate Fidelity in the Grey Seal." *Science* 268: 1897–98.

Appian. 1912 [*c*. A.D. 160]. "The Mithridatic Wars." In *Roman History*, translated by Horace White. Vol. 2, bk. 12. Cambridge, Mass.: Harvard University Press.

Axelrod, Robert. 1984. *The Evolution of Cooperation*. New York: Basic Books.

Badcock, Christopher. 1986. *The Problem of Altruism, Freudian-Darwinian Solutions*. Oxford: Basil Blackwell.

———. 1997. "Reciprocity and the Law." *Vermont Law Review* 22(2): 295–303.

Barnett, Randy E. 1992. "Some Problems with Contract as Promise." *Cornell Law Review* 77: 1022–33.

Black, Julia. 1997. *Rules and Regulators*. Oxford: Clarendon Press.

Bogert, George T. 1987. *Trusts*. 6th ed. St. Paul, Minn.: West Publishing.

Bogus, Carl T. 1996. "The Death of an Honorable Profession." *Indiana Law Journal* 71: 911–47.

Borkowski, Andrew. 1997. *Textbook on Roman Law*. 2d ed. London: Blackstone Press.

Boyd, Robert, and Peter J. Richerson. 1990. "Culture and Cooperation." In *Beyond Self-Interest*, edited by J. J. Mansbridge. Chicago: University of Chicago Press.

Brooke, Michael, and Tim Birkhead. 1991. *The Cambridge Encyclopedia of Ornithology*. Cambridge: Cambridge University Press.

Brown, Ronald C. 1997. *Understanding Chinese Courts and Legal Process: Law with Chinese Characteristics*. The Hague: Kluwer Law International.

Chapais, Bernard. 1992. "The Role of Alliances in Social Inheritance of Rank Among Female Primates." In *Coalitions and Alliances in Humans and Other Animals*, edited by Frans B. de Waal and Alexander Harcourt. Oxford: Oxford University Press.

Coffee, John C., Jr. 1998. "Modern Mail Fraud: The Restoration of the Public/Private Distinction." *American Criminal Law Review* 35: 427–65.

Comair-Obeid, Nayla. 1996. *The Law of Business Contracts in the Arab Middle East*. London: Kluwer Law International.

Conner, Richard C., Rachel A. Smolker, and Andrew F. Richards. 1992. "Dolphin Alliances and Coalitions." In *Coalitions and Alliances in Humans and Other Animals*, edited by Frans B. de Waal and Alexander Harcourt. Oxford: Oxford University Press.

Cooper, Ben, and Chris Wallace. 1998. "Evolution, Partnerships and Cooperation." *Journal of Theoretical Biology* 195: 315–28.

Craswell, Richard, and Alan Schwartz, eds. 1994. *Foundations of Contract Law*. Oxford: Oxford University Press.

Datta, S. B. 1992. "Effects of Availability of Allies on Female Dominance Structure." In *Coalitions and Alliances in Humans and Other Animals*, edited by Frans B. de Waal and Alexander Harcourt. Oxford: Oxford University Press.

Dawkins, Richard, and John R. Krebs. 1978. "Animal Signals: Information or Manipulation?" In *Behavioral Ecology: An Evolutionary Approach*, edited by John R. Krebs and Nicholas B. Davies (282–309). Oxford: Blackwell Scientific Publications.

Deag, John M., and Graham W. Scott. 1999. "Conventional Signals in Avian Agonistic Displays: Integrating Theory, Data and Different Levels of Analysis." *Journal of Theoretical Biology* 196: 155–62.

de Waal, Frans B. 1992. "Coalitions as Part of Reciprocal Relations in the Arnheim Chimpanzee Colony." In *Coalitions and Alliances in Humans and Other Animals*, edited by Frans B. de Waal and Alexander Harcourt. Oxford: Oxford University Press.

———. 1997. *Bonobo: The Forgotten Ape*. Berkeley: University of California Press.

———. 1999. "Cultural Primatology Comes of Age." *Nature* 399: 635–36.

de Waal, Frans B., and Alexander H. Harcourt. 1992. "Coalitions and Alliances: A History of Ethological Research." In *Coalitions and Alliances in Humans and Other Animals*, edited by Frans B. de Waal and Alexander Harcourt. Oxford: Oxford University Press.

Dugatkin, Lee Alan. 1997. *Cooperation Among Animals: An Evolutionary Perspective*. New York: Oxford University Press.

Dynes, Michael. 1997. "Afghan Allies Prepare to Take Kabul." *The London Times*, August 13, 1997, Overseas news.

Elliott, E. Donald. 1986. "Managerial Judging and the Evolution of Procedure." *University of Chicago Law Review* 53: 306–36.

———. 1997. "Law and Biology: The New Synthesis?" *St. Louis University Law Review* 41: 595–624.

Emlen, Stephen T. 1995. "Can Avian Biology Be Useful to the Social Sciences?" *Journal of Avian Biology* 26(4): 273–76.

Feh, Claudia. 1999. "Alliances and Reproductive Success in Camargue Stallions." *Animal Behaviour* 57: 705–13.

Fikentscher, Wolfgang. 1992. "The Sense of Justice and the Concept of Cultural Justice." In *The Sense of Justice*, edited by Roger D. Masters and Margaret Gruter. Newbury Park, Calif.: Sage.

Forbes, 1995. "Forbes FYI." October 23, 1995, 198.

Fox, Merritt B., and Michael A. Heller. 1999. "Lessons from Fiascos in Russian Corporate Governance." University of Michigan Law School, Law and Economics working paper no. 99–012. Available at *papers.ssrn.com/paper. taf?abstract—id = 203368*.

Frank, Robert H. 1999. *Luxury Fever: Why Money Fails to Satisfy in an Era of Success*. New York: Free Press.

Fried, Charles. 1981. *Contract as Promise: A Theory of Contractual Obligation*. Cambridge, Mass.: Harvard University Press.

Gerholm, Thomas. 1985. "Aspects of Inheritance and Marriage Payment in North Yemen." In *Property, Social Structure and Law in the Modern Middle East*, edited by Ann Elizabeth Mayer. Albany: State University of New York Press.

Gewirtz, Paul. 1996. "I Know It When I See It." *Yale Law Journal* 105: 1023–47.

Goodenough, Oliver R. 1995. "Mind Viruses: Culture, Evolution and the Puzzle of Altruism." *Social Science Information* 34(2): 287–320.

———. 1996. "Go Fish: Evaluating the Restatement's Formulation of the Law of Privacy." *South Carolina Law Review* 47(4): 709–82.

———. 1997a. "Retheorizing Privacy and Publicity." *Intellectual Property Quarterly* 1: 37–70.

———. 1997b. "Biology, Behavior and Criminal Law: Seeking a Responsible Approach to an Inevitable Interchange." *Vermont Law Review* 22: 263–94.

———. 1999. "Information Replication in Culture: Three Modes for the Transmission of Culture Elements Through Observed Action." *Proceedings of the AISB '99 Symposium on Imitation in Animals and Artifacts.* Sussex: The Society for the Study of Artificial Intelligence and the Simulation of Behavior.

Goosens, Benoît, Lautent Graziani, Lisette P. Waits, Etienne Farand, Séverine Magnolon, Jacques Coulon, Marie-Blaude Bel, Pierre Taberlet, and Dominique Allainé. 1998. "Extra-pair Paternity in the Monogamous Alpine Marmot Revealed by Nuclear DNA Microsatellite Analysis." *Behavioral Ecology and Sociobiology* 43: 281–88.

Grafen, Alan. 1990. "Biological Signals as Handicaps." *Journal of Theoretical Biology* 144: 517–46.

Grant, J. Kirkland. 1998. "The Bar Examination: Anachronism or Gate Keeper to the Profession?" *New York State Bar Journal* 70 (May–June): 12–18.

Gruter, Margaret. 1991. *Law and the Mind: Biological Origins of Human Behavior.* Newbury Park, Calif.: Sage.

Hamilton, William D. 1963. "The Evolution of Altruistic Behavior." *American Naturalist* 97: 354–56.

———. 1964. "The Genetical Evolution of Social Behavior." *Journal of Theoretical Biology* 7: 1–52.

Hanna, Cheryl. 1999. "Sometimes Sex Matters: Reflections on Biology, Sexual Aggression, and Its Implications for the Law." *Jurimetrics* 39: 261–69.

Harvey, Paul H., and Mark D. Pagel. 1991. *The Comparative Method in Evolutionary Biology.* Oxford: Oxford University Press.

Henderson, James A., Jr. 1991. "Judicial Reliance on Public Policy: An Empirical Analysis of Products Liability Decisions." *George Washington Law Review* 59: 1570–1613.

Holmes, Oliver W., Jr. 1881. *The Common Law.* Boston: Little, Brown. Reprint, New York: Dover, 1991.

The Holy Qur'an. Translated by Abdullah Yusuf Ali. Birmingham: Islamic Propagation Centre.

Ibison, David. 1996. "Business Sees Resurgence of Islamic Values." *South China Morning Post,* May 2, 1996, Business 5.

Johnson, Alex M., Jr. 1997. "The Underrepresentation of Minorities in the Legal Profession: A Critical Race Theorist's Perspective." *Michigan Law Review* 95: 1005–62.

Johnson, Arild, Jan T. Lifjeld, Percy A. Rohde, Craig R. Primmer, and Hans Ellegren. 1998. "Sexual Conflict over Fertilizations: Female Bluethroats Escape Male Paternity Guards." *Behavioral Ecology and Sociobiology* 43: 401–8.

Johnstone, Rufus A. 1997. "The Evolution of Animal Signals." In *Behavioural*

Ecology: An Evolutionary Approach, edited by John R. Krebs and Nicholas B. Davies. 4th ed. Oxford: Blackwell Science.

———. 1998. "Game Theory and Communication." In *Game Theory and Animal Behavior*, edited by Lee Alan Dugatkin and Hudson Kern Reeve. Oxford: Oxford University Press.

Jones, Owen D. 1997. "Evolutionary Analysis in Law: An Introduction and Application to Child Abuse." *North Carolina Law Review* 75: 1117–1242.

Jones, William C. 1994. *The Great Qing Code*. Oxford: Clarendon Press.

Kawashima, Takeyoshi. 1974. "The Legal Consciousness of Contract in Japan." *Japanese Law and Legal Theory* 7: 1–21. Reprinted in *Japanese Law and Legal Theory*, edited by Koichiro Fujikura. Aldershot, UK: Dartmouth, 1996.

Kelley, Furgus. 1988. *A Guide to Early Irish Law*. School of Celtic Studies, Dublin Institute for Advanced Studies, Dublin.

Kleiman, Devra G. 1977. "Monogamy in Mammals." *Quarterly Review of Biology* 52: 39–69.

Kokko, Hanna, and Rufus A. Johnstone. 1999. "Social Queuing in Animal Societies: A Dynamic Model of Reproductive Skew." *Proceedings of the Royal Society of London, Biology* 266: 571–78.

Lack, David. 1968. *Ecological Adaptations for Breeding in Birds*. London: Methuen.

Laland, Kevin N., John Odling-Smee, and Marcus W. Feldman. Forthcoming. "Niche Construction, Biological Evolution, and Cultural Change." *Behavioral and Brain Sciences* 23(1). Current version available at *www.cogsci.soton.ac.uk/bbs/Archive/bbs.laland.html*.

Lupoi, Maurizio. 1999. "The Civil Law Trust." *Vanderbilt Journal of Transnational Law* 32: 967–88.

Luther, Martin. 1529. "Ein' feste Burg ist unser Gott." Translated 1853 as "A Mighty Fortress Is Our God" by Frederick Henry Hodge. Text available at *tch.simplenet.com/htm/m/mightyfo.htm*.

Madow, Michael. 1993. "Private Ownership of Public Image: Popular Culture and Publicity Rights." *California Law Review* 81: 127–240.

Maine, Henry Sumner. 1861. *Ancient Law*. Text available at *www.socsci.mcmaster.ca/~econ/ugcm/3113/maine/anclaw/*.

Marsh, Peter D. V. 1994. *Comparative Contract Law: England, France, Germany*. Aldershot, UK: Gower.

Maynard Smith, John. 1982. *Evolution and the Theory of Games*. Cambridge: Cambridge University Press.

———. 1991. "Honest Signaling: The Philip Sidney Game." *Animal Behaviour* 42: 1034–35.

Maynard Smith, John, and Eörs Szathmáry. 1995. *The Major Transitions in Evolution*. Oxford: Oxford University Press.

McPhedran, Ian. 1997. "Stray Words Shoot Us in the Foot." *The Canberra Times*, July 29, 1997, A2.

Meinhard v. Salmon. 1928. *New York Reports* 249: 458–553.

Miller, Geoffrey. 1999. "Waste Is Good." *Prospect* (February): 18–23.

Møller, Andes Pape. 1994. *Sexual Selection and the Barn Swallow*. Oxford: Oxford University Press.

New York State Bar Association. 1999. *The Lawyer's Code of Professional Responsibility*. Available at *www.nysba.org/opinions/codes/code.html*.

Nishida, Toshisada, and Kazuhiko Hosaka. 1996. "Coalition Strategies Among Adult Male Chimpanzees of the Mahale Mountains, Tanzania." In *Great Ape Societies*, edited by William C. McGrew, Linda F. Marehat, and Toshisada Nishida. Cambridge: Cambridge University Press.

Noë, Ronald. 1992. "Alliance Formation Among Male Baboons: Shopping for Preferable Partners." In *Coalitions and Alliances in Humans and Other Animals*, edited by Frans B. de Waal and Alexander Harcourt. Oxford: Oxford University Press.

Otter, K., L. Ratcliffe, D. Michaud, and P. T. Boag. 1998. "Do Female Black-Capped Chickadees Prefer High Ranking Males as Extra-Pair Partners?" *Behavioral Ecology and Sociobiology* 43: 25–36.

Pearce, Russell G. 1996. "The Professionalism Paradigm Shift: Why Discarding Professional Ideology Will Improve the Conduct and Reputation of the Bar." *New York University Law Review* 70: 1229–76.

Pearl, David. 1987. *A Textbook on Muslim Personal Law*. 2d. ed. London: Croom Helm.

Pearl, David, and Werner Menski. 1998. *Muslim Family Law*. 3d. ed. London: Sweet and Maxwell.

Rawls, John. 1972. *A Theory of Justice*. Cambridge, Mass.: Harvard University Press.

Reavis, Robert H., and George W. Barlow. 1998. "Why is Coral-Reef Fish *Valenciennea strigata* (Gobiidae) Monogamous?" *Behavioral Ecology and Sociobiology* 43: 229–37.

Richerson, Peter J., and Robert Boyd. 1989. "The Role of Evolved Predisposition in Cultural Evolution, or Sociobiology Meets Pascal's Wager." *Ethology and Sociobiology* 1–3: 195–219.

Rue, Loyal D. 1994. *By the Grace of Guile: The Role of Deception in Natural History and Human Affairs*. Oxford: Oxford University Press.

Schoenblum, Jeffrey A. 1999. "The Role of Legal Doctrine in the Decline of the Islamic Waqf: A Comparison with the Trust." *Vanderbilt Journal of Transnational Law* 32: 1191–1230.

Shepard, Randall T. 1997. "What Judges Can Do About Legal Professionalism." *Wake Forest Law Review* 32: 621–33.

Singer, Peter. 2000. *A Darwinian Left*. New Haven: Yale University Press.

Slawson, W. David. 1996. *Binding Promises: The Late 20th-Century Reformation of Contract Law*. Princeton, N.J.: Princeton University Press.

Sober, Elliott, and David Sloan Wilson. 1998. *Unto Others: The Evolution and Psychology of Unselfish Behavior*. Cambridge, Mass.: Harvard University Press.

Sonneveldt, Frans. 1992. "The Trust—An Introduction." In *The Trust: Bridge or Abyss Between Common and Civil Law Jurisdictions*, edited by Frans Sonneveldt and Harrie L. van Mens. Deventer, The Netherlands: Kluwer Law and Taxation.

Spence, Andrew Michael. 1974. *Market Signaling: Information Transfer in Hiring and Related Screening Processes*. Cambridge, Mass.: Harvard University Press.

Steiner, Beat U. 1999. "An Updated Primer on Letters of Credit." *Colorado Lawyer* (April): 5.

Trivers, Robert. 1971. "The Evolution of Reciprocal Altruism." *Quarterly Review of Biology* 46: 35–57.

———. 1972. "Parental Investment and Sexual Selection." In *Sexual Selection and the Descent of Man*, edited by B. Campbell. Chicago: Aldine de Gruyter.

Vega-Redondo, Fernando. 1996. *Evolution, Games and Economic Behavior*. Oxford: Oxford University Press.

Watts, David P. 1998. "Coalitionary Mate Guarding by Male Chimpanzees at Ngogo, Kibale National Park, Uganda." *Behavioral Ecology and Sociobiology* 44: 43–55.

Wendel, W. Bradley. 1999. "Public Values and Professional Responsibility." *Notre Dame Law Review* 75: 1–123.

Whiten, Andrew, Jane Goodall, W. C. McGrew, T. Nishida, V. Reynolds, Y. Sugiyama, C. E. G. Tutin, Robert W. Wrangham, and C. Boesch. 1999. "Culture in Chimpanzees." *Nature* 399: 682–85.

Williston, Samuel, and Richard A. Lord. 1991. *A Treatise on the Law of Contracts*, 4th ed. Vol. 1. Rochester, N.Y.: Lawyers Cooperative Publishing.

Wright, Robert. 2000. *Nonzero: The Logic of Human Destiny*. New York: Pantheon.

Zabel, Cynthia J., Stephen E. Glickman, Laurence G. Frank, Kaya B. Woodmansee, and Geoffrey Keppel. 1992. "Coalition Formation in a Colony of Prepubertal Spotted Hyaenas." In *Coalitions and Alliances in Humans and Other Animals*, edited by Frans B. de Waal and Alexander Harcourt. Oxford: Oxford University Press.

Zahavi, Amotz. 1975. "Mate selection—A Selection for a Handicap." *Journal of Theoretical Biology* 53: 205–14.

———. 1977. "The Cost of Honesty (Further Remarks on the Handicap Principle)." *Journal of Theoretical Biology* 67: 603–5.

Zahavi, Amotz, and Avishag Zahavi. 1997. *The Handicap Principle: A Missing Piece of Darwin's Puzzle*. New York: Oxford University Press.

Zhao, Yohong. 1997. "Contract Law." In *Introduction to Chinese Law*, edited by Wang Chenguang and Zhang Xianchu. Hong Kong: Sweet and Maxwell Asia.

Zhong, Jianhua and Mark Williams. 1998. *Foreign Trade Contract Law in China*. Hong Kong: Sweet and Maxwell Asia.

Chapter 13

Religion as a Hard-to-Fake Sign of Commitment

WILLIAM IRONS

T HIS CHAPTER presents a theory of religion derived from thinking in game theory about the strategic value of commitments and hard-to-fake signals of commitment (Schelling 1960; Hirshleifer 1987; Frank 1988). An inflexible commitment to behave in a particular way can serve one's interests in the majority of cases even if in particular situations the behavior is contrary to self-interest. Such a commitment does this by changing what others expect from us and thereby changing the way they behave toward us. For example, a commitment to be scrupulously honest in dealing with others can cause them to trust us in situations where they cannot monitor our behavior closely to be sure we are treating them fairly or keeping promises made to them. This trust can form the basis for mutually supportive relationships that would not be possible without such trust. Such a commitment among members of a group can create a social compact in which group and individual interests are not in conflict as long as all members of the group adhere to the compact (compare Alexander 1987; Ridley 1996). To be effective, however, commitments must be real. A real commitment to behave in a particular way even if it is contrary to self-interest is by definition irrational, in the sense that it is not subject to revision in light of future cost-benefit analyses. Owing to the advantage of such commitments, natural selection has favored in human beings the psychological propensity to form and communicate such commitments. These commitments come in many forms.

Human emotions are examples of such commitments and their detectable signs serve as credible signals of these commitments (Hirshleifer 1987; Frank 1988). Human emotions and their external signs are relatively uniform from one society to another, with the result that people who lack a language or culture in common usually can read each other's signals of emotion accurately (Ekman 1973). Human beings, however, also have developed the ability to create and elaborate cultural commitments and signals of commitment and to tie these to an emotional substrate so that a culturally specific credible signal of commitment can be sent within a particular society (Irons 1991, 1996a, 1996b, 1996c). The most elaborate and effective of these cultural signals are religions (Irons 1996a, 1996b, 1996c). Religion basically is a commitment to behave in certain ways without regard to self-interest. Most frequently religion entails a commitment to become a supportive member of a particular religious community and to adhere to its code of ethics. Most religions are expressed in elaborate rituals that are costly in time and sometimes in other ways. These rituals also provide extensive opportunities for members of a community to monitor one another's commitments to the community and its moral code, thereby facilitating the formation of larger and better-united groups. This has been especially important because human evolution has been driven in large part by group-group competition and by an accompanying expansion of within-group cooperation (Alexander 1987). The result is a strong propensity built into human psychology to learn culturally specific signals of commitment and to use these to create and maintain within-group cooperation. The most powerful cultural signals of commitment are religious ones, and thus evolution has built into human beings a strong propensity to seek a religious orientation toward life and to hold this orientation to be of the highest value.

The theory presented here assumes there are features of the human brain that underlie the nearly universal tendency of human beings to absorb a religion while growing up, and to take this religion seriously (in at least some contexts). This is not, however, a theory specifically about how the neural networks and hormonal underpinnings of the human mind produce this tendency; for a discussion of this issue see Ashbrook and Albright (1997). Rather, what is presented here is a theory about how religion has helped human beings to survive and reproduce in past human populations. In the terminology of the ethologist Niko Tinbergen (1963) it is a theory about the function of the human propensity to be religious—that is, a theory about the adaptive value of this propensity. For a complementary scientific discussion of religion with a broader perspective see Hinde's (1999) *Why Gods Persist.*

In addition to explaining a theory of religion as commitment, this chapter discusses ways in which the theory can be evaluated empirically, and some of the implications for the significance of religion in human affairs.

What Is Religion?

Religion is not easy to define to everyone's satisfaction. Religious traditions vary a great deal, and trying to find a common thread that runs through them all is challenging. The following two definitions are useful, and I will try to combine them to come up with a suitable working definition. The first comes from William James (1982 [1902], 53):

> [R]eligion, in the broadest and most general terms possible, . . . consists of the belief that there is an unseen order, and that our supreme good lies in harmoniously adjusting ourselves thereto.

The second comes from Clifford Geertz (1966, 4):

> [A] system of symbols which act to establish powerful, pervasive and long-lasting moods and motivations in men [and women] by formulating conceptions of a general order of existence and clothing these conceptions with an aura of factuality such that the moods and motivations seem uniquely realistic.

James's definition emphasizes the idea of an unseen order and the closely related idea that we will find the greatest good in "harmoniously adjusting" to this order. The idea of the unseen as the source of the greatest good seems to me to be central to religion cross-culturally. Geertz's definition, however, emphasizes the importance of a system of symbols that create long-lasting moods and motivations and make them seem realistic.

I suggest that both of these definitions capture elements that are central to religion. These can be combined by defining religion as follows. *The common element of religion cross-culturally is a belief that the highest good is defined by an unseen order combined with an array of symbols that assist individuals and groups in ordering their lives in harmony with this order and an emotional commitment to achieving that harmony.* The specific symbols vary widely from one tradition to another, but the most common elements are rituals and sacred stories that are used to communicate the basic emotional commitment that forms the core of the religion.

In formulating this definition I am assuming that Geertz's "long-lasting moods and motivations" that seem "realistic" can be equated with an emotion-based commitment. The emphasis placed on belief in James's definition also needs to be balanced with other elements of religion besides belief. The rituals, sacred stories, and other symbols of a religion are expressions of emotions that are, in my opinion, more central to the religion than beliefs. These are the signals of commitment that are crucial to making religion work as a basis for within-group cooperation. Evidence in fact shows that ritual mildly alters the state of one's mind and has the consequence of causing us to concentrate on certain emotions and to plant those emotions firmly in our memories (D'Aquili 1983; D'Aquili, Laughlin, and McManus 1979). Both participation in rituals and the recitation of sacred stories produce in the practitioners of religion a sense of the sacred or the numinous that is central to religion (compare Rappaport 1999).

Philip Hefner (1993), a contemporary Christian theologian, offers the criterion of ultimacy as part of the definition of religion, and one might want to add this criterion to the aforementioned definition. I am convinced, however, that James's "supreme good" already contains this criterion.·

Certain secular ideologies, such as Marxism, notably share some of the characteristics of religions: they have rituals and symbols and they can inspire strong commitments. Some would argue, however, that Marxism lacks the idea of an unseen order and therefore is not quite the same thing. Some might argue that the utopia promised by Marxism is unseen; yet it is not part of an unseen order. Rather, like many other expectations about the future of the secular world, Marx's utopia is a particular, possible (some believe) future development within the visible order of historic events. I prefer to call ideologies such as Marxism secular analogs of religion and recognize that they share some of the characteristics of religion, but not all by the working definition used here. Any cross-culturally valid definition of religion has to be fuzzy. The way to handle a fuzzy category is to recognize the core elements of the category, and to not get too exercised about the fact that we cannot draw a clear boundary between things falling inside and outside the category.

A tendency to appeal to an unseen order is indeed something that human beings can easily invent and learn when they are seeking to form a community on the basis of commitment. This causes people to add elements to secular philosophies and secular political commitments that appeal to an unseen order. When I once suggested to post-Soviet friends that Marxism is not quite a religion, they pointed out that when they were in school in the Soviet Union, they were taught that everything that Marx and Lenin had predicted for the next hundred years was absolutely correct. This they quite reasonably pointed out is impossible for any human being and is implicitly an appeal to an unseen order. One can find other such tendencies for secular philosophies to move toward an appeal to an unseen order. The Manifest

Destiny in the history of the United States is another example. Religion is a fuzzy category, and some arrays of symbols that assist individuals and groups in ordering their lives make a stronger appeal to an unseen order than others. Whether any particular set of symbols is a religion or not depends on the extent to which it appeals to an unseen order. Some arrays of symbols fall at the center of our definition of religion and others fall on the fuzzy boundaries. Nevertheless, this definition can serve as a working definition for inquiries into the evolutionary origin and function of religion. Also, this definition comes as close as any definition can to capturing the essence of something that occurs in all human societies, albeit in dizzyingly varied forms.

Indirect Reciprocity

The significance of commitments in human social life can be seen more clearly if we understand the role of indirect reciprocity in establishing cooperation. In his 1987 book *The Biology of Moral Systems* Alexander suggested that much of human evolution was a response to group-group competition and runaway selection for larger and better-united groups. He also suggested indirect reciprocity as a strategy that assisted human beings in forming larger and better-united groups. Indirect reciprocity is an extension of Trivers's (1971) idea of reciprocal altruism: that natural selection can favor altruistic acts if they increase the probability that the altruist will receive reciprocal aid in the future. Indirect reciprocity is based on the notion that reciprocal aid can flow back to the altruist by an indirect route. More specifically the idea is that human beings observe others when they are interacting with third parties, and use this information to decide whether to behave altruistically toward the person observed. Individual A observes individual B being altruistic to individual C, and A responds by being altruistic to B. Indirect reciprocity can be summarized as being nice to nice people. Both logic and experience suggest that human beings also expand this strategy to include being nasty to nasty people—that is, to strategies of reciprocal selfishness or reciprocal spitefulness. Strategies of this sort have the advantage of making it possible to gather a larger amount of information about the members of one's community than would be possible if one relied entirely on sizing people up while interacting with them directly. Our sensitivity to what others think of us and our great interest in observing others all suggest that this is indeed an important strategy in human social life. Our vast interest in gossip further reinforces the impression that human beings are adapted to strategies of indirect reciprocity (compare Dunbar 1996).

A recent simulation of strategies of indirect reciprocity by Nowak and Sigmund (1998) suggests that indirect reciprocity can be a successful strategy under the right conditions. Conditions are right when the benefit-to-cost ratio for altruistic aid to others is high enough to compensate for occasional misdirection of aid to individuals who are inaccurately identified as altruists. Nowak and Sigmund suggest that these conditions may well have been met in the evolution of human societies, and that such strategies played an important role in human history.

Boyd and Richerson (1992) have expanded our theoretical understanding of indirect reciprocity by defining and exploring what they call *moralistic strategies*. Moralistic strategies are strategies of observing others and punishing those who break some rule, combined with punishing those who fail to punish rule breakers. They have run computer simulations that suggest this type of strategy can easily create strong pressure on people to conform to rules even when the rules are costly to follow. In effect moralistic strategies consist of policing others combined with an expectation that others will play the police role too and punishing them when they fail to do so. Logically this kind of strategy also can consist of rewarding those who obey the rules or rewarding those who perform acts of exemplary altruism. Further, this strategy can consist of punishing those who fail to reward good behavior and rewarding those who reward good behavior. The permutations are numerous. The logic of these complex strategies of policing others seems intuitively to be what human beings do. Their intuitive familiarity supports, to a degree, the theory that human beings are finely adapted to indirect reciprocity.

Commitments and Signals of Commitment

In a social environment in which indirect reciprocity is a crucial strategy, commitments and credible signals of commitment are extremely effective strategies. If we are being continually observed and sized up and rewarded and punished for our behavior, what would make more sense than to send credible signals of commitments that will encourage others to act in our interests? Earlier chapters in this volume explain how signals of an inflexible commitment can cause others to behave in our interest, and how the signals of such commitments are more valuable if they are hard to fake. As noted earlier, human emotions and their detectable symptoms are examples of such signals. In addition to these relatively universal and developmentally inflexible signals of commitment we also have evolved the capacity to use cultural signals of commitment. Cultural signals have the advantage of being flexible. As circumstances change people can modify the signals they send and even invent new ones. This allows people great flexibility in the use of cultural signals of loyalty to particular groups or to particular codes of behavior. All of these can be changed and changed again to adjust to new circumstances relatively rapidly, compared to the speed of biological evolution.

For such signals of commitment to be successful they must be hard to fake. Other things being equal, the costlier the signal the less likely it is to be false. One can point to numerous cultural practices that are not only costly but also difficult to fake for other reasons as well. College degrees, for example, are reliable signs that the individuals who have earned them are intelligent and are willing to pursue a difficult task over a long time (Frank 1988). Employers looking for people with these qualities to hire can take a college degree as a reliable sign that prospective hires have these qualities. Yanomamo men who frequently challenge other men to club fights and in the process acquire numerous scars on their heads can display these scars as reliable signals that they are not inclined to back down from a fight. Their habit of displaying these scars by shaving the central portion of their scalp makes the signal conspicuous.

Military basic training can serve a similar function. An enlistee shows his or her loyalty to the military organization and willingness to obey orders without question by enduring the difficult, exhausting, and risky experience of basic training. Conscripts may not seem to fit this model, since they have no choice as to whether or not to endure military basic training. Yet the fact that those placed in command over such conscripts insist on strict obedience to many onerous orders and severely punish disobedience is a hard-to-fake signal that they are serious about making any subordinate regret any form of disobedience. A wide range of onerous initiation rituals has a similar effect of displaying, in a very credible sign, obedience and loyalty in new initiates. These rituals also serve as signals of their superiors' insistence on obedience and respect for tradition.

Religions also appear to fit this model of being hard-to-fake signals of commitment. Religions ordinarily are learned over a long span of time while an individual is growing up. Religious traditions are sufficiently complex to be difficult for an outsider—one who has not spent years learning the tradition—to imitate. Faking membership in a religious community to which one does not belong would be very difficult for most people. Further, the elaborateness of religious rituals allows individuals numerous opportunities to monitor one another for signs of sincerity. Most of all the process of learning and practicing a religion is time consuming and often costly in other ways.

The fact that the practice of some religions is more costly than others does not present a theoretical difficulty. That some cultural strategies will be more effective than others is to be expected. Other things being equal, we should expect that more costly religions are more effective at creating intragroup cooperation. We also might predict that the greater the need for cooperation, or the greater the difficulty of creating cooperation, the more costly will be the religious institutions supporting it.

Religion as a Signal of Commitment

One way to clarify how religion works as a commitment and as a signal of commitment is to explore briefly an ethnographic example. I shall use my own experience with the Yomut Turkmen of northern Iran as such an example (compare Irons 1975). During the thirty months I spent living with that group, I was impressed with the extent to which their version of Islam played a central role in their lives. Many years later when I encountered the theory of commitment, it occurred to me that their religious practices serve them well as signals of commitment. The following discussion of Yomut religious practices is offered as a way of illustrating and clarifying the theory, not as empirical support of the theory. The question of empirical testing is discussed later in this chapter.

Among the Yomut, all adults were required to pray five times a day. The prescribed prayers had to be preceded with a ritual washing and had to be performed in a clean place while facing "the house of God" in Mecca. While traveling with Turkmen, it was a regular occurrence that one of my traveling companions would announce that the time for prayer had arrived. Everyone would dismount from his horse, or the bus would stop, and everyone would get off and begin to look for water for the required ablutions and would inquire as to the direction of Mecca. When necessary, the requirement of a clean place to pray could be met by unrolling a prayer rug and using it as the place for prayer. Then the faithful would perform the ritual of prayer, which involved assuming a number of postures and reciting a fixed set of prayers in Arabic. While not traveling, the five-times-a-day ritual still played an important role as prayer rugs were rolled out, ritual washings were performed, and different individuals carried out the ritual prayers. Nevertheless, the ritual seemed most conspicuous when traveling because it always required more effort. One had to interrupt travel, had to find water and a clean place for prayer, and usually had to make inquiries about the direction of Mecca. Much more recently it occurred to me that one encounters strangers more frequently while traveling and that this is an ideal time to signal a commitment one shares with these strangers. I even have the impression that some Turkmen were a little more regular in their prayers when traveling and encountering strangers than when at home. Watching people perform such rituals always instilled in me (an outsider) a sense of the sacred, a sense that these people were striving for a harmony with a higher good defined by an unseen order. Perhaps more important, it clearly instilled such a sense in the believers themselves. The fact that the time of prayer was prescribed meant that all believers (in the same time zone) were saying their prayers at approximately the same time. This communicated a sense of unity among all believers wherever they were. Many of the other rituals also carried this sense of unity among the worldwide community of Islam.

Although the five-times-a-day prayer was the most conspicuous signal of one's commitment to Islam and to the worldwide community of believers, there were numerous others. One consisted of the month of fasting, when all adults (except pregnant or lactating women or those who were ill) fasted from sunrise to sunset. The fast itself qualifies, to some degree, as a costly and therefore hard-to-fake signal of commitment. The fast, however, usually was accompanied by feasting and visiting after sunset, as well as rising early to partake of a large meal before sunrise. The routine of feasting before sunrise and after sunset combined with the fast dominated the day's routine and focused everyone's attention on religion. The evening feast was accompanied by much visiting between different families in the same community and frequent group prayers. All this further enhanced consciousness of religion.

On the Day of Sacrifice everyone who could afford it was to sacrifice some animal and use it to prepare a feast to which all in the vicinity were invited. All were aware that this was the day when the pilgrims to Mecca were making a similar sacrifice near the "house of God." In addition, life cycle events were celebrated, such as the birth of a son, circumcisions, weddings, funerals, and the annual keeping of death days. Keeping death days consists of putting on feasts in honor of deceased parents or other close relatives on the anniversaries of their death. Something was always going on that reminded people of their commitment to harmony with the unseen order revealed by their religion.

One conspicuous message about social behavior conveyed by these numerous signals was a division of the human world into an in-group and an out-group, and a message of commitment to cooperation to the in-group. Most world religions send a message of the sort. During my time with the Turkmen, as a member of the out-group I struggled with the fact that cooperation with outsiders was basically less desirable than cooperation with insiders and did my best to look as Muslim as I could. I learned a few of their prayers, fasted during the Month of Fasting, and listened carefully as religious teachers tried to convert me. All ethnographers who are immersed for an extended time in a community very different from that of their origin eventually ask themselves, What if I were to spend the rest of my life here? When these thoughts occurred to me, it always seemed obvious that, were I to stay, conversion to and conspicuous practice of Islam would be the best route to acceptance by the local community.

The rituals of Islam also communicated commitment to a set of rules concerning appropriate moral behavior. They reinforced basic moral rules of not lying, not stealing, not killing, and not committing adultery. The obligatory giving of alms to the poor or religious students also communicated an important message. All Muslims are required annually to give a defined portion of their wealth to the poor or to those who devoted themselves full time to the study or teaching of religion. After the agricultural harvest in the late spring, the Yomut would calculate 10 percent of their crop yield as the obligatory donation that was then given to either poor families or to individuals devoted full time to religion. In the fall a similar reckoning of what each individual owned in livestock was tallied and donations were made to the poor or to religious students and teachers. These practices communicated by example the obligation of all who are sufficiently prosperous to take care of the less fortunate (the poor) and the obligation of all who have the means to support the moral foundation of the community (full-time students and teachers of religion).

I believe that recognizing the signals of commitment contained in religious rituals is a fundamental part of being human. Most of us send and receive such signals at least some of the time. Many are so routine as to not attract much attention. Yet when we reside in a community different from that in which we were reared, we are especially conscious of what for us are exotic signals of commitment. During my thirty months of residence with the Yomut, they definitely communicated some commitments to me. They communicated a commitment to the worldwide community of Muslims, a commitment to basic morality, and a commitment to care for the most unfortunate members of their society. This is how I would describe their religious commitments. If I were to try to phrase these commitments in terms familiar to the Yomut, I would summarize them as a commitment to obey the will of God as revealed by the prophet Muhammad. For the Yomut, it is God's will that they should be committed to the worldwide community of believers, should adhere to basic rules of morality, and should aid the least fortunate members of their communities.

Empirical Evaluation

The foregoing discussion of my own experience as an ethnographer clarifies how religion serves as both a commitment and a set of hard-to-fake signals of commitment. Such experience cannot, however, be seen as a test of this theory; its role is descriptive and suggestive. Testing of theory is another matter.

Fortunately recent research by Sosis (2000) has begun the task of testing this theory of religion as commitment. Sosis used a database on nineteenth- and early twentieth-century communes (Oved 1988) to compare religious with secular communes. He predicted that religious communes would be better at facilitating collective action than would secular ones, and hence that religious communes would be less likely to dissolve. He used this prediction to test the theory that religion facilitates intragroup cooperation by serving as a hard-to-fake signal of commitment.

The database he used contains data on 277 communes founded between 1663 and 1937. Sosis limited his analysis to communes founded in the nineteenth and early twentieth centuries because no secular communes existed before the nineteenth century. He also eliminated communes for which information was not sufficient to classify them as religious or secular, and he eliminated all Hutterite colonies as well. The latter groups, the Hutterite colonies, which are religious communes, were eliminated because he felt their presence in his sample would bias the outcome too heavily in favor of the hypothesis being tested. Hutterite colonies are extremely successful compared to other communes, as revealed by the fact that the twenty Hutterite colonies in Oved's sample have not only survived (unlike all the others in the sample save one, a secular colony), but have grown to include approximately four hundred colonies today. By the measure of current survival, Hutterite colonies are overwhelmingly the most successful communes in Oved's database. Eliminating these groups left a sample of 88 religious communes and 112 secular ones.

All of these communes except one eventually disbanded or died out, but the religious communes had markedly greater powers of survival. Sosis did an analysis of the rates of survival of communes and discovered that secular communes were four times as likely as religious ones to dissolve in any year of their existence. The difference was highly significant, with a p-value of .00001. This means that the chances of his result being an artifact of sampling error are 1 in 100,000. Oved's study of the history of communes in America convinced him that the dissolution of a commune always is preceded by a loss of faith in the ideology on which the group is based, although often other causes are involved such as natural disasters, suppression by outsiders, or the death of a charismatic leader. Sosis is convinced that all communes must survive these other types of threats to their existence and can do so if they maintain faith in their ideology. The real cause of failure, according to Sosis, is loss of faith in their ideology, which then renders these communes unable to survive other threats to their existence.

Sosis is rightly cautious in interpreting his results, claiming that much more research is needed. Yet as far as his results go, they suggest that religious ideologies are more effective than secular ones at the difficult task of persuading human beings to live in a community where property is held in common and where the risk of being exploited by free riders is great.

Sosis currently is extending his research on communes by studying kibbutzim in Israel. The majority of kibbutzim are secular, but a small minority of them are religious. The data Sosis has gathered so far indicate that the religious kibbutzim are economically more successful. The secular kibbutzim have had economic problems since the 1970s and have survived only as a result of a combination of government subsidy, Jewish philanthropy, and debt forgiveness from Israeli banks. The religious kibbutzim have not had similar economic difficulties; in fact they have been more successful economically than the secular kibbutzim in every year of their existence. This is especially interesting in light of the fact that the rituals of the religious kibbutzim impose a definite economic cost. For example, the members of the religious kibbutzim, in contrast to members of secular kibbutzim, abstain completely from all forms of labor one day a week.

Future Testing

Sosis's (2000) research shows that the ideas presented in this chapter are testable. Many more tests will be necessary, however, before we can be confident that religions serve effectively as hard-to-fake signals of commitment that enhance intragroup cooperation. At this point some logical predictions can be made that may serve as the basis for future testing.

It should be possible to extend Sosis's prediction of enhanced community survival to groups other than communes. In societies that prefer extended families, those with greater signs of religious participation should hold together longer. The same should be true of village-level communities where village fissioning is frequent. For example, Chagnon's classic study of the Yanomamo (1975, 1997) has shown that Yanomamo villages go through a continual process of growth and fissioning. He has shown that the average genetic relatedness of village members is a strong predictor of fissioning with splitting becoming more likely as relatedness declines (Chagnon 1975). Religious practice might also be a predictor. One may expect that as villages grow and become more prone to internal conflict, the frequency of shamanic rituals will increase. In this case such activity in effect would be an attempt to hold the village together despite internal conflict. One also might predict that those with more frequent rituals and greater participation in them would hold together longer. One might extend this prediction further to large social units as well: for example, chiefdoms with more elaborate religious rituals and more elaborate religious justification for their existence would hold together longer.

Not all individuals are religious and, among those who are, some are more religious than others. If one of the central functions of religion is to communicate commitments, then one would expect *those who have the greatest need to communicate a commitment would be those who are most religious*. This idea could be used to make cross-cultural predictions about the comparative religiosity of men and women. Among the Yomut of northern Iran, men are markedly more religious than women. They are more regular in their prayers and more prone to offer religious justifications for their actions. This makes sense when one reflects that men travel widely seeking pasture for livestock, for trade, or for other reasons. While traveling they encounter strangers and also a wide range of people who, while not strangers, know them only superficially. Religious practices (especially the five-times-a-day prayers) are for them a useful way of advertising good character. Yomut women, in contrast, rarely encounter individuals who are not close kin of some sort. They travel primarily to visit kin, and do so only under the guardianship of close male relatives. For them, the need to display good character is less pressing, since most of those whom they encounter already know them well.

Initial impressions from interviewing on the island of Utila in the Bay Islands of Honduras suggest that, in contrast to the Yomut, among this group women are more religious on average. This is a group I studied in 1996 along with Lee Cronk and Shannon Steadman (both then associated with Texas A&M University). The analysis of the tape-recorded interviews is not yet complete, but as far as the analysis has gone the following description seems to be accurate. While interviewing men and women about their mate preferences, men frequently stated that they sought women who attended church as wives because such women would be "true"—that is, faithful to their husbands (Cronk, personal communication). Women expressed no such preference for men who attend church. This signal of fidelity is especially important because Utilian men are away from home frequently for long periods of time on labor migration. For many Utilian men, labor migration is their primary source of income. During their most productive years, many of them are away from the island nine or ten months out of every year working in the merchant marines, on oil rigs, or other work that allows them to utilize their extensive maritime skills (Lord 1975). Among Utilians, women are much more religious than men, and the majority of those who attend religious services are women.

Notably, infidelity presents a different problem for males than for females (Daly and Wilson 1983). For males, their mates' infidelity entails the risk of investing extensively in the rearing of children who are not genetically their own. For women, infidelity threatens to divert their husband's resources away from their children. For a female Bay Islander, loss of a husband's resources is not greatly threatened as long as the husband continues to send home money and to return periodically. Yet for the absent husband, detecting a wife's infidelity is more difficult. Thus hard-to-fake signals of fidelity are of greater importance to men than to women in the Bay Islands.

One might also inquire whether or not *variation in religiosity over the life cycle does not also reflect changes in the need to signal some commitment.* In my own middle-class, suburban environment, individuals who have not been associated with a religious congregation for many years commonly seek out and join a congregation once they have children, and explain their action as a response to the need to provide children with a religious education. Why do people who for years felt no need for religion think their children need religion? Could it be that at some level the signals sent by religion are seen as necessary for the moral education of children? Of course, religion also plays a role in allaying anxiety (Malinowski 1954). The tendency of older people or the terminally ill to become more religious may relate to this alternate function of religion. For young healthy parents, however, death anxiety does not seem the main motivation for religion and their own statements in fact point to the role of religion in child rearing.

That religions support the social status quo is a common textbook idea in anthropology. Actually this is only a part of the picture. I suggest that *people tend to use religion to express commitments that are advantageous for themselves.* The more powerful members of society are likely to express religious commitments that support the status quo. For these individuals, the status quo is to their advantage. Individuals of lesser power and status, however, are likely to express commitment to changes in the status quo whether expressed subtly or more openly. After all, religion in many cases has been a vehicle for social change and even social revolution. Thus the signal may differ with gender, with social class, and with other social variables reflecting differences in interests. This idea might be tested by having readers study ethnographies to determine what commitments are expressed by local religious practices and a separate set of readers examine the same sources to see how the interests of one class, gender, or other social category differ. Both sets of readers would have to be unaware of the research project's goals so as not to be biased by them. The results then could be compared to see whether people use religion to express commitments advantageous to themselves, or to the social categories to which they belong.

As societies change, or more precisely, as people try to change societies, they will change the commitments they signal with their religious practice. Current efforts to formulate feminist theologies in our own society may reflect this. This also may be reflected in current interest in new religions (or newly discovered old religions) such as Wicca, which is a very women-centered religion. This prediction is a logical corollary of the aforementioned statement that people tend to use religion to express commitments that are advantageous to themselves. As people set new goals for social change they are likely to devise new forms of religious expression (or revive long-forgotten old ones) to signal commitment to these changes.

War should enhance religiosity. The imminent threat of the strongest form of group-group competition should activate our propensity to use the strongest possible signals of group loyalty. This prediction may be hard to test because war threatens death and destruction, and religion also functions to allay anxiety in the face of such threats. The best way to test it would be to identify those for whom war is not a direct threat to themselves or their kin. Members of a nation or other group at war who are residing away from the war zone may provide such a test. The theory predicts that diaspora communities that include people whose families are not in the homeland would become more religious in response to an attack on the homeland that does not threaten the diaspora community itself. Perhaps the support of Greeks for their Serbian coreligionists during the recent NATO bombing of Serbia may provide a valid example of the phenomenon predicted here.

The commitments expressed by a religion will be those that are most important to its practitioners. Relevant examples can be found in Weber's ideas about the relationship of capitalism to Protestantism, or in the use of shamanism among the Yanomamo to express a commitment to aggressive defense of kin. (See the film *Magical Death*, produced by Chagnon and Asch 1973.)

These predictions are offered to make the case that the theory presented here is testable. Whether testing will lead to confirmation or disconfirmation remains to be seen. In my opinion, however, testing these predictions will enhance our understanding of religion.

The Role and Importance of Religion in Human Affairs

Does the theory suggested here give us a new perspective on religion? The theory of religion as it applies to commitment emphasizes the vital importance of religion to most human communities and the fundamental importance that religion plays in the lives of most human beings. The theory also suggests that the core of religion is not belief (which scientists and intellectuals are prone to criticize), but rather, for the most part, commitment to socially constructive behavior. As such, most religions deserve great respect.

One can point out, of course, that the influence of religion is not always constructive. Throughout history, for some groups and individuals religion has provided the motivation for ethnic cleansing or for terrorism. Religion, like all human social institutions, can be a force for good or evil. What we need to recognize is that religion is usually a powerful force and very often a force for basic morality and concern for the well-being of others. The fact that it can be a destructive force suggests that it is the job of religious leaders and all religious persons to distinguish the constructive from the destructive potential of religion and to channel their religious energies in constructive directions. The alternative of attempting to banish religion from human life is, in my opinion, not a viable one. The propensity to be religious is too deeply ingrained in human nature. The more useful course of action is to encourage the best forms of religion, those which will do the most to create such fundamental goals as peace and justice.

I also have become convinced that religion is a fundamentally different kind of thinking and feeling and behaving than is science. Evolutionary psychologists might say that religion and science are expressions of different psychological modules, or perhaps expressions of distinct learning rules activated by different situations (compare Barkow, Cosmides, and Tooby 1992). Science and technology must always be accompanied by the assumption that all ideas, beliefs, theories, or whatever, are provisional. The good scientist should strive for the obsolescence of his or her current idea. Being provisional, however, does not go with commitment. Commitments need to be inflexible. Thus religion is, in my view, more a moral stance and an orientation to the universe based on faith. Religion answers basic questions that science cannot answer. The most fundamental of these questions is the question of how we should live, what life goals we should set, and what life goals we should urge our children and our neighbors to adopt (Gilbert 2000). Finding a truly satisfying answer to these questions requires commitment (leaps of faith, some might say), not provisional thinking and continual testing. Religion and science are both necessary. We are better off if we accept each as having its own sphere and to try to find constructive ways to relate one to the other.

In developing and presenting the theory in this chapter I have tried to think as a scientist and at the same time be as respectful of religion as I can. I have discovered this is not an easy task. One anonymous referee for this chapter said that it "denigrates scientists who have an absolute commitment to the search for the truth, and who have a community of such people whose respect for one another is determined by such commitments." None of the referees offered similar condemnations from the point of view of religious people, but in other contexts I have been told that my ideas, as seen by religious people, are both naive and patronizing. The comments from both the scientific and religious points of view remind me of the Islamic metaphor to the effect that the path leading to paradise is as thin as the edge of a razor. If one deviates to either side of this narrow path one falls into an abyss. The path of full respect for both science and religion, if it exists, is very narrow indeed. It may even be vanishingly small. Nevertheless I have tried to follow it in this chapter, and will continue to attempt to find and follow this path in the future. I am sure that many will claim I have fallen into an abyss. Yet I may, if I'm very lucky, contribute to increased harmony between two powerful forces in human affairs.

References

Alexander, Richard D. 1987. *The Biology of Moral Systems*. New York: Aldine de Gruyter.

Ashbrook, James B., and Carol Rausch Albright. 1997. *The Humanizing Brain: Where Religion and Neuroscience Meet*. Cleveland, Ohio: Pilgrim Press.

Barkow, Jerome H., Leda Cosmides, and John Tooby, eds. 1992. *The Adapted Mind: Evolutionary Psychology and the Generation of Culture*. Oxford: Oxford University Press.

Boyd, Robert, and Peter J. Richerson. 1992. "Punishment Allows the Evolution of Cooperation (or Anything Else) in Sizable Groups." *Ethology and Sociobiology* 13(3): 171–95.

Chagnon, Napoleon A. 1975. "Genealogy, Solidarity, and Relatedness: Limits to Local Group Size and Patterns of Fissioning in an Expanding Population." *Yearbook of Physical Anthropology* 19: 95–110.

———. 1997. *Yanomamo*. 5th ed. New York: Harcourt Brace.

Chagnon, Napoleon A., and Timothy Asch. 1973. *Magical Death*. Watertown, Mass.: Documentary Educational Resources. Film.

Daly, Martin, and Margo Wilson. 1983. *Sex, Evolution, and Behavior*. 2d ed. Boston: Willard Grant Press.

D'Aquili, Eugene G. 1983. "The Myth-Ritual Complex: A Biogenetic Structural Analysis." *Zygon: Journal of Religion and Science* 18(3): 247–69.

D'Aquili, Eugene G., Charles D. Laughlin, Jr., and John McManus. 1979. *The Spectrum of Ritual*. New York: Columbia University Press.

Dunbar, Robin. 1996. *Grooming, Gossip, and the Evolution of Language*. Cambridge, Mass.: Harvard University Press.

Ekman, Paul, ed. 1973. *Darwin and Facial Expressions*. New York/London: Academic Press.

Frank, Robert H. 1988. *Passions Within Reason: The Strategic Role of the Emotions*. New York: Norton.

Geertz, Clifford. 1966. "Religion as a Cultural System." In *Anthropological Ap-

proaches to the Study of Religion, edited by Michael Banton. London: Tavistock Press.

Gilbert, Thomas L. 2000. "A Scientist's Perspective." Paper presented in the Epic of Creation course at the Zygon Center for Religion and Science. Chicago (January 3).

Hefner, Philip. 1993. *The Human Factor: Evolution, Culture, and Religion*. Minneapolis: Fortress Press.

Hinde, Robert A. 1999. *Why Gods Persist: A Scientific Approach to Religion*. London and New York: Routledge.

Hirshleifer, Jack. 1987. "The Emotions as Guarantors of Threats and Promises." In *The Latest on the Best: Essays on Evolution and Optimality*, edited by John Dupre. Cambridge, Mass.: MIT Press.

Irons, William. 1975. *The Yomut Turkmen: A Study of Social Organization Among a Central Asian Turkic Speaking Population*. Anthropological paper no. 58. University of Michigan, Museum of Anthropology.

———. 1991. "How Did Morality Evolve?" *Zygon: Journal of Religion and Science* 26(1): 49–89.

———. 1996a. "Morality as an Evolved Adaptation." In *Investigating the Biological Foundations of Human Morality*, edited by James P. Hurd. Lewiston, New York: Edwin Mellen Press.

———. 1996b. "Morality, Religion and Human Evolution." In *Religion and Science: History, Methods, Dialogue*, edited by W. Mark Richardson and Wesley J. Wildman. New York: Routledge.

———. 1996c. "In Our Own Self Image: The Evolution of Morality, Deception, and Religion." *Skeptic* 4(2): 50–61.

James, William. 1902. *The Varieties of Religious Experience: A Study in Human Nature*. Reprint, New York: Penguin Books, 1982.

Lord, David G. 1975. "Money Order Economy: Remittances in the Island of Utila." Ph.D. diss., University of California at Riverside.

Malinowski, Bronislaw. 1954. *Magic, Science and Religion and Other Essays*. Garden City, New York: Doubleday.

Nowak, Martin A., and Karl Sigmund. 1998. "Evolution of Indirect Reciprocity by Imaging Scoring." *Nature* 394(6685): 573–77.

Oved, Yaacov. 1988. *Two Hundred Years of American Communes*. New Brunswick, N.J.: Transaction Books.

Rappaport, Roy. 1999. *Ritual and Religion in the Making of Humanity*. Cambridge: Cambridge University Press.

Ridley, Matt. 1996. *The Origins of Virtue*. London: Viking.

Schelling, Thomas C. 1960. *The Strategy of Conflict*. Cambridge, Mass.: Harvard University Press.

Sosis, Richard. 2000. "Religion and Intragroup Cooperation: Preliminary Results of a Comparative Analysis of Utopian Communities." *Cross-Cultural Research* 34(1): 71–88.

Tinbergen, Niko. 1963. "On Aims and Methods of Ethology." *Zeitschrift fur Tierpsychologie* 20: 410–33.

Trivers, Robert L. 1971. "The Evolution of Reciprocal Altruism." *Quarterly Review of Biology* 46(4): 35–57.

Weber, Max. 1976 [1905]. *The Protestant Ethic and the Spirit of Capitalism*. London: George Allen and Unwin.

Chapter 14

The Future of Commitment

Randolph M. Nesse

I N 1883 Lord Kelvin mounted a major challenge to Darwin's theory. He claimed that the time required for evolution was inconsistent with the laws of physics. "Essential principles of thermodynamics have been overlooked. . . . It is quite certain that the solar system cannot have gone on, even as present, for a few hundred thousand or a few million years, without an irrevocable loss . . . of a very considerable proportion of the entire energy initially in store" (Kelvin, Tait, and Darwin 1888, 468–69). He reasoned that the sun's heat must come mainly from the friction of meteors, because "No other action, except by chemical action can be conceived . . . [and this] would only generate about 3,000 years of heat" (493). He concluded, "The inhabitants of the earth cannot continue to enjoy the light and heat essential to their life for many million years longer, unless sources now unknown to us are prepared in the great storehouse of creation" (494). Many found his argument convincing. He was, after all, Britain's preeminent scientist, famous for engineering the first successful transatlantic cable. Furthermore, his conclusion was based on the established, rigorous science of physics.

In just a few years, however, it became clear that he was wrong. Fossil and astronomical evidence showed that the earth was far older than 100,000 years. By the end of the nineteenth century Curie and others had discovered radioactivity. By 1934 it was apparent that nuclear reactions fuel the sun and keep the earth's core molten. We now know that the sun and the earth were formed about 5,000 million years ago and that the universe is about 13,000 million years old. Kelvin's logic was fine, but because he assumed that all energy was mechanical or chemical, his result was off—by a factor of 120,000.

In recent decades two principles—kin selection and reciprocity—have come to dominate explanations for cooperation. The advance they represent cannot be overestimated. They are as central for understanding social behavior as the laws of thermodynamics are for understanding physics. Together with a gene-centered view of evolution, they provide a new, solid foundation for understanding relationships and social behavior. They have revolutionized the study of animal behavior. While political and emotional objections have slowed their application to human behavior, their utility is enormous. They are providing new insights into the workings of relationships, families, and social groups.

It is increasingly clear, however, that kin selection and reciprocity are not sufficient to explain all social phenomena. The oldest and most significant evidence is the very existence of mental mechanisms for guilt and sympathy (O'Connor 2000). While they can be interpreted as manipulations or devices for managing exchange relationships, they often give rise to actions far different from those predicted by rational choice theory (RCT). More recently, hundreds of studies in behavioral economics find that nonrational decisions are ubiquitous (Fehr and Falk 1999). While some of these deviations from RCT merely reflect the limitations of generally effective mental mechanisms (Gigerenzer, Todd, and ABC Research Group 1999), others are better explained by evolved social predispositions that likely give superior outcomes. Further evidence comes from psychological studies showing that close relationships are harmed if attention is called to the favors exchanged. This book offers many more examples, especially in parts III and IV.

The basic principle of sociobiology remains clear and incontrovertible: behavior regulation mechanisms for all species are shaped, inevitably and necessarily, to induce actions that tend (in the long run, on the average, in the natural environment) to increase the frequency of that individual's genes in future generations. It is increasingly obvious, however, that maximizing reproductive success often requires keeping promises and fulfilling threats even when that requires profound sacrifices of personal short-term interests. That natural selection has shaped special mental capacities to make this possible, including a capacity for commitment, seems likely.

What We Have Learned

The chapters in this book offer an overview of commitment from the perspectives of several different disciplines. A single-authored volume could be more consistent, but would fail to capture the diverse points of view that are brought together here. Early on in this project,

I found this diversity dizzying and spent weeks trying to reconcile different positions. While that effort was worthwhile, premature attempts to resolve all the apparent contradictions are unjustified. This is a new area of work and it needs to avoid premature closure that glosses over important differences. While much effort remains to further unpack the idea of commitment and to understand how it works, we are far ahead of where we started. Like natural selection, commitment is a simple idea whose elaborations are subtle and complex. The level of complexity is not overwhelming, though; it is just about right for a core concept with wide explanatory power.

The chapters in part I describe and define commitment in wonderful depth and detail. I will not summarize them here, but instead will draw a few crucial distinctions from those chapters that begin the process of unpacking the concept of commitment. Nine questions can help to classify a commitment:

- Whom is the commitment intended to influence: the self, other individuals, a group, or a spiritual being?
- Is the commitment a preemptive action that leaves the next move to the other, or is it a statement of intent regarding some future action?
- Does the commitment represent a threat to harm, or a promise to help?
- Does the commitment bring benefits now with costs later, or costs now with benefits later?
- Are the effects of the commitment probabilistic, or is the outcome highly predictable?
- Does the commitment make options impossible, or only more costly?
- Is fulfilling the commitment contingent on some event or some action by others, or is it noncontingent?
- What controls incentives after the commitment is made: the situation itself, a third party, a group, or does the individual who made the commitment continue to control incentives?
- Why would others believe the commitment: incentives in the situation itself, incentives controlled by a third party, the benefits of reputation, or internal motives?

A full exposition on each of these questions would (and no doubt eventually will) fill other books. Here I will only briefly comment on some of them. The first question identifies whom the commitment is intended to influence. Most commitments are intended to influence others, but people make some commitments to influence themselves.

They anticipate that they will not be able to restrain their impulses in a future situation, so they take action now to make certain options are either impossible or too costly (Elster 1979; Burnham and Phelan 2000). If you ask your friends to bind you to the mast, or you sign yourself into a locked drug rehabilitation ward, some options are eliminated outright (question 6). If you tell your friends about your commitment to lose twenty pounds, your option to give up your diet is not impossible, but it does become embarrassing. People often voluntarily take actions to influence their own behavior by eliminating options that are tempting in the short term but undesirable in the long term.

The second distinction is between preemptive actions that leave the next move to the other, versus commitments that refer to future behavior, a difference emphasized by Hirshleifer (ch. 4, this volume). This is important because the former is relatively simple and is tractable in game theory. The latter kind of commitment—to future actions—is the main focus of this book.

Another major difference is between threats and promises. The idea of commitment highlights their deep similarities, and the correspondingly profound possibility that our capacities for good and evil have parallel origins. Yet many of the phenomena involved are distinct. Promises usually obtain benefits now based on a commitment to provide costly help later, and they tend to be contingent on the other person fulfilling a corresponding promise. In contrast, threats are not mutually agreed on, and they tend to be contingent on another person's lack of compliance. To consider promises and threats together in this book has been essential, but their many important differences suggest that separate treatments often will be preferable.

The fourth distinction is whether the commitment requires costs now for benefits later or vice versa. When a small person stands up to a bully, the costs come quickly while the benefits, if any, are only in the long run. Conversely, when you promise to stay with someone in sickness and in health, some benefits to the relationship come soon but the costs are later and uncertain, as are the benefits if you are the one who gets sick. When benefits come first, the problem is why someone will follow through and pay the costs later. When the costs come first, the problem is how to motivate accepting costs now, especially if the benefits are by no means certain but only possible.

The final two distinctions are the basis for the categories provided in the introductory chapter. They call attention to the core problem of commitment: Why would others believe that someone would do something that is not in his or her self-interest? The global distinction here is between commitments that are secured and those that are not. A secured commitment is like a loan secured by collateral; tangible costs and benefits make it worthwhile for the person to fulfill his or her commitment. When a commitment is unsecured, however, no tangible incentives enforce fulfillment. Such subjective commitments are at center stage here.

The chapters in part II consider the role of subjective commitment in animal behavior. They find related phenomena, especially of preemptive actions, but no compelling examples of subjective commitment. As all three authors note, however, we have not yet looked hard. Having commitment in mind may allow us to see phenomena we have missed, especially those mediated by reputation. It may well turn out that commitment strategies are possible only for species that can accurately signal their future intent. The vigorous claw snapping of vulnerable molting shrimp, described by Adams, seems to represent a mere bluff. The chimpanzee "quiet signals" described by Silk may well qualify as commitments. The guppies described by Dugatkin certainly recognize and influence each other, but this seems to reflect reciprocity at most. Overall, the exercise of looking for commitment strategies in animals motivates useful attempts to operationalize the concept in behavioral terms, but the task remains difficult. The fact that three distinguished ethologists do not find definitive evidence for clear-cut subjective commitments in animals is valuable information. Each of the authors describes strategies for going about looking more carefully for commitment and related phenomena. Perhaps their suggestions eventually will allow us to see phenomena we have not looked for previously.

Part III, in contrast, provides abundant examples of commitment and subjective commitment in humans. Much of what goes on in honor societies seems to illustrate commitment strategies. Similarly, many phenomena involved in group enforcement of norms seem to fit into a commitment framework, and the selection forces that emerge from such groups offer a powerful route by which natural selection could shape capacities for commitment. The existence of the moral passions offer the strongest evidence we have for such a possibility. These chapters provide a rich starting point for anyone who wants to find detailed examples of the role of commitment in human life.

Part IV further documents the importance of commitment in social groups, including law, psychotherapy, and religion. Aspects of law that are otherwise difficult to explain look to be based on commitments. Psychotherapy can be understood in part as an investigation of how people's beliefs about commitments influence their relationships. Those who have experienced inconsistent or exploitative relationships have an opportunity to find new ways to relate to others. The consternation patients experience in a relationship that is committed but based on monetary payment is explained by a commitment framework. This framework goes further yet, and suggests that some aspects of human groups seem to be shaped by the effects of commitments, including defined group boundaries, initiation rituals, ideologies, and costly signals of loyalty to the group. Conversely, many aspects of groups seem to exist largely to facilitate commitments to cooperate and to limit the utility of coercive threats.

Some economists challenge the very existence of subjective commitments on the straightforward grounds that they are effective only if people believe that others will do things that are not in their interests (Field 2001). If people are assumed to act in their own self-interest, then beliefs in such commitments usually will be false and therefore tendencies to believe such commitments should be eliminated by natural selection. Emotions should do nothing to change this assessment. In short, subjective commitments require actions that decrease fitness, so people should not believe them. Commitments not believed cannot influence people and therefore should not exist. This critique calls attention to the need for explicit accounts of why subjective commitments are not made useless by deception. The general theoretical answer, as outlined in the first three chapters and throughout the book, is that individual decisions that seem inconsistent with RCT can nonetheless give a long-term advantage via reputation, and via the sum payoffs from many commitments with probabilistic payoffs. A more specific answer comes from observation: subjective commitments are ubiquitous, they are believed, and they do influence people. If you know that a person has taken spiteful revenge in the past, you anticipate this and adjust your behavior irrespective of what RCT says about the payoffs in the current situation. Whether by reputation or other means, anything that convinces people that a commitment likely will be kept will influence behavior. Emotional displays and unreasonable behavior may not be reliable signals, and they certainly can be deceptive, but they do establish that the actor's behavior cannot be readily predicted on the basis of simple self-interest.

Many subjective commitments are enforced by pledges of reputation that make the cost of reneging very costly indeed—assuming, of course, that the person has a reputation to begin with. We distrust strangers partly because we know nothing about their reputation. Yet if we know a person's character has integrity, then we are influenced by his or her threats or promises. This makes reputation a valuable resource; people who lack it are socially feeble. Fear of losing reputation thus can motivate fulfilling even costly commitments. This is the simplest explanation as to why people believe subjective commitments—it also is a potent explanation for how natural selection could have shaped tendencies to fulfill commitments, even when doing so requires actions that considered alone directly decrease fitness. This can explain how natural selection could have shaped moral faculties for fulfilling commitments and following rules even when that is very costly. In the social life of humans, the power of reputation is profound.

Some subjective commitments are maintained even when that would not be justified by costs to reputation. I remain unsure whether these reflect a whole additional route to commitment, or whether they are better studied as phenomena made possible by commitment mechanisms shaped by natural selection. Certainly many of us rely on such commitments for most of our important relationships. When you promise to stay married to someone, the commitment is largely emotional. If you defend a friend who has been unfairly treated by your company, your loyalty is likely to be costly. We care deeply about subjective commitments; they are a central theme in religion and great literature. Finally, what we believe about commitments shapes the social realities of our lives (Miller 1999). In short, commitments are extremely important to human social life.

What Commitment Needs Now

Work of several kinds is needed to develop and study commitment: scholarship, modeling, measurement, and experimental and field studies. This book starts with the seminal work of Schelling, Frank, and Hirshleifer, and ranges extraordinarily widely, but it has hardly begun to incorporate relevant work from many important areas. Social psychology, for instance, has developed a body of relevant research on trust. Personality researchers have studied individual differences related to commitments. Also in psychology, the concept of emotional commitments to goals and close relationships have been explored in depth (Klinger 2000). These concepts are somewhat different than the notion of commitment described here, but the interface has much to offer. In economics and political science a growing literature investigates trust and social capital, as well as the influence of loyalty (see other volumes in this series). Behavioral economics is such a huge field now that considerable work will be needed to determine which results can be interpreted sensibly in terms of commitment (Fehr and Schmidt 2000). Anthropology and sociology also must involve similar lines of thinking and research. Certainly commitment is a major theme in centuries of work by moral philosophers. To try to bring these different lines of thought together to see what they have already said about phenomena related to commitment is terribly important. I hope that the scholars in these other fields will understand that a book such as this cannot hope to cover all the relevant contributions; it is just a beginning.

Studies of commitment would benefit greatly from a rigorous model. Verbal descriptions simply won't do. We need defined variables and postulated relationships among them that will allow us to determine how commitment strategies can work and under what circumstances. Why this has not been accomplished more than it has already (see Hirshleifer, ch. 4 herein, and Frank 1988, appendix) may be all too apparent. One reason is the need for many variables. Another is the need to accommodate not only general reputation, but also individualized relationships (Axelrod 1997). A model based on observed patterns of human relationships might have the following characteristics. Imagine a multiplayer game in which each agent can, on each move, invest any proportion of his or her reserves in a joint venture with any other individual or group. Each player privately seals cash in an envelope and gives it to a central authority, who sums the amounts contributed to each venture and then adds interest of perhaps 10 percent before distributing the sweetened pot equally among the investors. To include randomness, the payoff would vary, perhaps with a standard deviation of 15 percent of the total, with occasional larger deviations. Posting of outcomes offers a translucent indication of others' cooperativeness, but owing to the random variation, players can never be sure if the results from a given investment resulted from partners being generous or stingy or from the random variations. On some rare moves the blind would be unexpectedly broken and all investments would be revealed. Some cost would be needed for getting information about others' actions and reputations. To do well in such a game an agent must invest in mutual ventures. Yet this exposes the investor to the risk that others will cheat slyly, by putting in less than an equal share, or that they will defect by investing nothing. Another problem is how to get others to be willing to invest with you. This game combines characteristics of a public goods game with aspects of individual and generalized reciprocity models. I would be pleased and not at all surprised to learn that someone has tried already to operationalize something along these lines. Many game theorists have addressed issues and models close to these (Axelrod 1986; Skyrms 1996; Gintis 2000; Nowak et al. 2000).

What strategies would work best in such a game? Would steady intermittent slight cheating yield a superior return, or would others notice the inferior rate of return, and act on that information and on information from the occasions that reveal the actual investments? It might well work better to invest more than one promises in order to avoid suspicion and preserve relationships with good partners. Just as in human society and many economic models, no one strategy is likely to dominate. I think it is likely, however, that what many people do in actual life would probably work in the game: increase investments slowly in ventures with a few people and with groups who appear generous and trustworthy and whose actions and reputations can be monitored closely. If many individuals play this strategy, those who make investments on the basis of RCT would be isolated. Those who are caught cheating are likely to be excluded from the game, or at least forced to play with others who have equally bad reputations.

Economics and sociobiology often have been criticized for promoting simplistic models of human behavior. This criticism is justified. Like other organisms, we humans are designed to maximize reproductive success, but how we do so may be too complicated to incorporate into a tractable model. Adding other crucial factors that strongly influence people's cooperation behaviors, such as kinship, ethnicity, social groups, ideologies, and other factors, would complicate matters further. Real social life is so complex that it may have been a potent force shaping human intellect (Alexander 1974; Humphrey 1976) and, perhaps, capacities for making and assessing commitments.

This brings us to the general issue of measurement. If you were going to describe and measure commitments, how would you do it? The nine distinctions at the beginning of this chapter are only a start. Specific examples are everywhere waiting for careful observation and description: spouses caring for their sick partners, jealous lovers threatening murder, disgruntled employees seeking revenge, and employees who stay in a low-paying job out of loyalty to a committed employer. Identifying and measuring commitment is awkward in that it is only one factor in a relationship that also may well include reciprocity, kinship, mutualisms, and other influences. Nonetheless, analysis of the role of commitment in actual relationships is certainly a good starting point.

Such detailed observations and descriptions of commitment in natural settings will provide a foundation for measurements that make possible studies of variations between subjects, within subjects, and across cultures. The study of personality variations in tendencies to commitment is primary, even though it is no substitute for the study of how situations influence commitments. Even a moment's attention reveals the vast diversity of human capacities for commitment. A certain percentage of people are sociopaths who have no feelings to motivate loyalty or principled behavior. Having no personal experience of such feelings, they are likely to interpret other people's commitments as manipulations: sociopaths cannot benefit from commitments except by using con strategies to gain the confidence of those they fleece. On the other extreme are those socially sensitive souls who spend every conscious minute (and many others also) worrying about

whether they have done their duty, whether they have offended anyone, and what people will think of them. The simple fact of this wide
variation is remarkable. Individuals in other species also have personalities that persist across the lifespan, but to observe such a huge
range of variation in such a core trait is remarkable. Also important is
the genetic contribution to these traits. Behavioral genetic studies of
twins show that 40 percent or more of the tendency to social sensitivity and sociopathy arises from genetic differences (Bouchard 1994).
It is important to try to discover whether this variation is the result of
random genetic drift, whether it reflects frequency-dependent selection for different strategies that offer the greatest benefits when rare
(Mealey 1995), or whether we are in the midst of a transition in which
genetic tendencies to capacities for commitment-based cooperation
are spreading but not yet completely dominant.

Studies are needed to find out how a person's commitments vary
depending on the situation and the actions of others. Our major life
commitments are too stable to be readily studied, yet most of us have
a relationship with say, our grocer, based on some combination of
mutualism and reciprocity, although even here are hints of commitment. Your grocer may try to instill feelings of loyalty by occasional
free offers, and by generously replacing anything you feel is defective, whether it is or not. Retail corporations seem generally to have
settled on quite lenient return policies that give the consumer the benefit of the doubt. They have learned that trying to argue over a dollar
here and there will lose them customers in the long run. In fact one
angry customer may cost them ten other customers. Generous return
policies may be an example of principled moral behavior that requires
accepting many short-term losses. Some unscrupulous consumers exploit these policies, but corporations must accept this cost in order to
maintain a good reputation. In the world of work, employers always
are trying to get their employees to believe that the company is committed to them. Sometimes this is true, as when the employees of
Malden Mills were kept on after the factory burned. When employees
are deceived, however, the repercussions are dramatic. Some say this
accounts for a period of low employee morale at Northwest Airlines,
where employees apparently perceived that their sacrifices in bad
times would make them partners in good times. No such luck. When
the economy revived, only the bosses and shareholders reaped big
rewards. The sense of betrayal of an apparent commitment seems to
have aroused persisting anger that is turned readily into job actions.
Even beyond such examples, an evolutionary perspective has much
to offer business management (Nicholson 2000).

Variations in commitment also could be addressed using experimental methods. Some of this already has been done, for instance in

the experiments by Clark and Mills showing that people become more distant, not closer, when a friend suggests an explicitly reciprocal exchange (Mills and Clark 1994; Clark and Mills 1993). Similar methods could manipulate the circumstances in groups, so as to foster or inhibit the use of commitment strategies. Probably much along these lines has been done, and is ready to be brought into the commitment framework.

Finally there is the urgent need to look at commitment across cultures, and in different subcultures. My anthropologist colleagues tell me that the very idea of guilt is hard for people in some cultures to comprehend. Today's newspaper has a story about how politicians in certain countries tend to expect other nations to act ruthlessly in their self-interest, and how befuddled they are when they encounter anything else. If these cross-cultural differences prove as substantial as they seem, this makes it seem that the capacity for commitment is more a creation of particular cultures than a universal human capacity shaped by natural selection. Of course, the mental and emotional predispositions that make commitment possible may be shaped by natural selection for other purposes, perhaps limited to a few close relationships. Some cultures may use these capacities to create larger-scale commitments that give big advantages to their members. Also, the capacity for commitment possibly has been shaped for large-scale social situations and lies in wait, ready to be expressed when doing so is likely to be worthwhile.

Did Natural Selection Shape a Capacity for Commitment?

Our core question is whether natural selection shaped mental mechanisms that facilitate making and assessing commitments. While the evidence is not yet ironclad, there are good reasons to think the answer is yes. Commitments are central and ubiquitous in social life. We are preoccupied with our reputation and the knowledge about the reputations of others. Our reputations determine whether others believe our commitments, and we need to know if we should trust commitments made by others. We have emotions and moral capacities that are otherwise hard to explain. Our close relationships explicitly avoid the appearance of reciprocal exchange. Social institutions, especially religions, seem to be designed to foster commitments; and our distinctive human capacities for empathy, foresight, intelligence, and love and hate appear to be just what is needed to make and assess commitments. These general factors, combined with the detailed explications throughout the book, offer convincing evidence that we have mental capacities for commitment. This does not necessarily mean that natural selection shaped our capacities for commitment specifically due to the direct benefits of making commitments. Indeed quite possibly these capacities were shaped somewhat indirectly by social selection. While the capacity for commitments gives benefits, strong selection is likely against people who lack such a capacity, because they will have fewer allies and will be vulnerable to exclusion from the group.

Threats may prove easier to study both in the field and in the lab. Also, the reasons why people respond to threats may be different from why they respond to promises. Imagine walking down a dark street at night, and suddenly someone pokes something in your back and says, "Give me your wallet or I will shoot you." Your wallet, like that of most people, has only $50 in it, and the prison term for armed robbery is twenty years, so you could quickly calculate that the thief must be bluffing. Even if the chance of being caught is small, the benefits to the thief just aren't worth it. It especially is not worthwhile to kill you, since that would set off a manhunt that most likely would lead to capture and years spent in prison. So if you were like some economists, you might conclude that the threat must be a bluff since the cost-benefit ratio is so wildly irrational. Yet most of us, less rational but perhaps longer-lived, would freeze and give up our money. Perhaps we are calculating that the value of the wallet is nothing compared to even a small chance of being killed. This is a reflection of the smoke detector principle—that is, the tendency of normal systems to express inexpensive protective defenses, such as cough or anxiety, whenever there is even a small chance that danger is actually present (Nesse, forthcoming). These systems normally give many false alarms, but a net advantage in the long run. Such exigencies well might make threats work successfully, even thoroughly irrational threats such as murder or suicide.

A parallel question that requires further study is why people believe that others will keep commitments. Parts III and IV offer substantial evidence that people do make and keep and believe commitments to cooperate; but what are the advantages? Several have not been fully explored. First, while reciprocity provides benefits only when you have other rewards to offer in turn, commitment provides help when you need it most—when you are sick or excluded from the group or when you are simply down and out. A person who can call on help in such critical times has a huge advantage over those who can get help only when they have something to offer in return. Such help, of course, usually depends on the other person's expectation that you would do the same for him or her. This requires careful attention to that person's needs, ensuring that the relationship does not appear to be based merely on reciprocal exchange. Those who can believe in others' commitments are more likely to be able to make credible commitments of their own.

A closely related benefit is having allies who can give political support. Reciprocity envisions two actors with individual and differentiated interests. When two people become partners, however, their interests merge. They try to help and protect each other in every circumstance. Studies of primates offer many hints. Chimpanzees spend much of their time making and preserving alliances that they use to challenge the status hierarchy above and to defend attacks from below (de Waal 1982). An individual without allies is hopelessly weak. Such alliances can be interpreted as trading favors, but observation shows that the unity of interests is much more general; and so it is with humans and their friends. We expect friends to take our side in conflicts. Friends do not carefully and objectively consider all the aspects of the situation before deciding if they will offer support, they just automatically offer it. Indeed, if reproductive success depends on social success, and social success depends on political alliances, then these alliances well might shape social tendencies different from those expected to arise from reciprocity, an idea worth looking into. Notably such alliances can be characterized by mutualisms: neither party has a chance to succeed without the continuing efforts of the other. Moreover, in the case of chimpanzees or, for that matter, that of humans as depicted in Shakespeare's Henry VI trilogy, as soon as the alliance reaches its goal it dissolves and the erstwhile partners now fight as their interests diverge. This is discouraging to a point of view that would like to see commitments as enduring beyond those situations in which they offer benefits.

Another more mundane advantage of basing cooperation on commitment is reduced monitoring and bookkeeping costs. Even when trading baby-sitting, tallying and recording every minute is a drain and a source of potential conflict. A more relaxed attitude invites exploitation, but reaps major efficiency benefits. If each partner strives to offer a little more than expected instead of a little less, this offers manifold advantages. Such agreements of course could be interpreted as a metareciprocity game in which the players commit to repeated cycles of cooperation that eventually become habitual. Yet the emotional predispositions for friendship are powerful, and quite different from those that would be shaped by mere reciprocity. Nonetheless, when a relationship becomes too unbalanced, related emotions usually motivate actions to reestablish fairness or else end the relationship. If the relationship has been based on commitments, the sense of betrayal is likely to be intense.

Social groups give rise to perhaps the most important and intriguing advantage of a tendency to commitment-based cooperation. The benefits of cooperation between individuals have been emphasized here, as elsewhere, because analyses of individual relationships are more tractable. Yet as Boyd and Richerson and others going back at least to Hobbes have suggested, groups manage to enforce tight norms of behavior by punishing deviants (Boyd and Richerson 1985; Gintis 2000). This raises the question of why being one of those who imposes punishments is advantageous. In many groups, however, you don't have to be a whistleblower to punish deviants. All you need to do is support those who support you and the group, and to turn away when others want your help. By making alliances with those who help you and ignoring others, individuals acting strictly in their own interests create powerful forces of selection. This is a bit different from cultural group selection increasing the frequency of traits that benefit groups—it is better described as social selection (West-Eberhard 1987; Jason, Brodie, and Moore 1999). When individuals pursue their own interests in social groups, this may create emergent forces of selection that pose serious fitness costs to those who show no capacity for commitment. Social selection works in the short term to shape individual behavior to conform to group norms as well as tendencies to learn the benefits of following social customs and to try to please others in the group. This is what Simon meant by *docility* (Simon 1990). In the long term such forces of social selection also can be forces for natural selection. Individuals who exclusively pursued their own interests, even by subtle reciprocity strategies, may have done poorly indeed, both because they had few allies in the group and because they were at constant risk of being "cast out of Society" where they likely "perishith" (Hobbes 1996 [1651]).

Even though it is a likely engine of social complexity, commitment can be very simple. All it takes is one person with a modicum of three core human capacities: foresight, language, and moral passions. If that person uses foresight to anticipate how others will respond to changed expectations, language to communicate a commitment, and moral passions to inhibit tendencies that might prevent fulfillment, then others will be influenced and social life is changed. The benefits of thus influencing people could well motivate keeping commitments that seem senseless when considered in isolation. Once many people start using such strategies, a tangled bank of social complexity is born, with personalities of many kinds communicating with escalating subtlety in the elaborately constructed groups and rituals that are the framework of human society.

References

Alexander, Richard D. 1974. "The Evolution of Social Behavior." *Annual Review of Systematics* 5: 325–83.

Axelrod, Robert. 1986. "An Evolutionary Approach to Norms." *American Political Science Review* 80(December): 1095–1111.

———. 1997. *The Complexity of Cooperation: Agent-Based Models of Competition and Collaboration. Princeton Studies in Complexity.* Princeton, N.J.: Princeton University Press.

Bouchard, Thomas J. 1994. "Genes, Environment, and Personality." *Science* 264 (5166): 1700–1701.

Boyd, Robert, and Peter J. Richerson. 1985. *Culture and the Evolutionary Process.* Chicago: University of Chicago Press.

Burnham, Terry, and Jay Phelan. 2000. *Mean Genes: From Sex to Money to Food, Taming Our Primal Instincts.* Cambridge, Mass.: Perseus Publishing.

Clark, Margaret S., and Judson Mills. 1993. "The Difference Between Communal and Exchange Relationships: What It Is and Is Not." *Personality and Social Psychology Bulletin* 19(6): 684–91.

de Waal, Frans B. M. 1982. *Chimpanzee Politics: Power and Sex Among Apes.* New York: Harper and Row.

Elster, Jon. 1979. *Ulysses and the Sirens: Studies in Rationality and Irrationality.* London: Cambridge University Press.

Fehr, Ernst, and Armin Falk. 1999. *Homo Reciprocans and Homo Cooperation.* Zurich: University of Zurich Press.

Fehr, Ernst, and Klaus M. Schmidt. 2000. "Theories of Fairness and Reciprocity—Evidence and Economic Applications." Paper read at 8th World Congress of the Economic Society. Seattle.

Field, Alexander. 2001. *Altruistically Inclined? The Behavioral Sciences, Evolutionary Theory, and the Origins of Reciprocity.* Ann Arbor: University of Michigan Press.

Frank, Robert H. 1988. *Passions within Reason: The Stragic Role of the Emotions.* New York: W. W. Norton.

Gigerenzer, Gerd, Peter M. Todd, and ABC Research Group. 1999. *Simple Heuristics That Make Us Smart: Evolution and Cognition.* New York: Oxford University Press.

Gintis, Herbert. 2000. *Game Theory Evolving.* Princeton, N.J.: Princeton University Press.

———. 2000. "Strong Reciprocity and Human Sociality." *Journal of Theoretical Biology* 206: 169–79.

Hobbes, Thomas. 1996 [1651]. *Leviathan.* Cambridge: Cambridge University Press.

Humphrey, Nicholas K. 1976. "The Social Function of Intellect." In *Growing Points in Ethology*, edited by P. G. Bateson and R. A. Hinde. London: Cambridge University Press.

Kelvin, William Thomson, Peter Guthrie Tait, and George Howard Darwin. 1888. "Appendix D: On the Secular Cooling of the Earth. Appendix E: On the Age of the Sun's Heat." In *Treatise on Natural Philosophy.* Cambridge: Cambridge University Press.

Klinger, Eric. 2000. "Commitment." In *Encyclopedia of Psychology.* New York: American Psychological Association and Oxford University Press.

Mealey, Linda. 1995. "Sociopathy." *Behavioral and Brain Sciences* 18(3): 523–99.

Miller, Dale T. 1999. "The Norm of Self-Interest." *American Psychologist* 54(12): 1053–60.

Mills, Judson, and Margaret S. Clark. 1994. "Communal and Exchange Relationships: Controversies and Research." In *Theoretical Frameworks for Personal Relationships*. Hillsdale, N.J.: Lawrence Erlbaum.

Nesse, Randolph M. Forthcoming. "The Smoke Detector Principle: Natural Selection and the Regulation of Defensive Responses." In *The Unity of Knowledge*. New York: New York Academy of Sciences.

Nicholson, Nigel. 2000. *Executive Instinct: Managing the Human Animal in the Information Age*. New York: Crown Business.

Nowak, Martin A., Kaven M. Page, and Karl Sigmund. 2000. "Fairness versus Reason in the Ultimatum Game." *Science* 289(5485): 1773–75.

O'Connor, Lynn E. 2000. "Pathogenic Beliefs and Guilt in Human Evolution." In *Genes on the Couch: Explorations in Evolutionary Psychotherapy*, edited by P. Gilbert and K. G. Bailey. East Sussex/Philadelphia: Brunner-Routledge/Taylor & Francis.

Simon, H. A. 1990. "A Mechanism for Social Selection and Successful Altruism." *Science* 250: 1665–68.

Skyrms, Brian. 1996. *Evolution of the Social Contract*. New York: Cambridge University Press.

West-Eberhard, Mary Jane. 1987. "Sexual Selection, Social Competition, and Speculation." *Quarterly Review of Biology* 58: 155–83.

Wolf, Jason B., Edmund D. Brodie III, and Allen J. Moore. 1999. "Interacting Phenotypes and the Evolutionary Process II: Selection Resulting from Social Interactions." *American Naturalist* 153: 254–66.

Index